Challenging the Chip

Challenging
the Chip

*Labor Rights and
Environmental Justice in the
Global Electronics Industry*

Edited by

TED SMITH, DAVID A. SONNENFELD,
AND DAVID NAGUIB PELLOW

with LESLIE A. BYSTER, SHENGLIN CHANG,
AMANDA HAWES, WEN-LING TU,
AND ANDREW WATTERSON

Foreword by
JIM HIGHTOWER

TEMPLE UNIVERSITY PRESS
Philadelphia

*This volume is dedicated to the memory of
Helen Clark (National Semiconductor, Scotland) and
Jim Moore (IBM, USA), who, even while battling terminal
cancers, gave their utmost to improve the electronics industry's
labor, health, and environmental practices for the benefit of
electronics workers and nearby communities around the world.*

Temple University Press
1601 North Broad Street
Philadelphia PA 19122
www.temple.edu/tempress

⊗ The paper used in this publication meets the requirements of the American
National Standard for Information Sciences—Permanence of Paper for Printed
Library Materials, ANSI Z39.48-1992

Library of Congress Cataloging-in-Publication Data

Challenging the chip : labor rights and environmental justice in the global electronics
    industry / edited by Ted Smith, David A. Sonnenfeld, and David Naguib Pellow ; with
    Leslie A. Byster, Shenglin Chang, Amanda Hawes, Wen-Ling Tu, Andrew Watterson ;
    foreword by Jim Hightower.
        p.   cm.
    Includes bibliographical references and index.
    ISBN 1-59213-329-0 (cloth : alk. paper)—ISBN 1-59213-330-4 (pbk. : alk. paper)
    1. Electronic industries.   2. Employee rights.   3. Environmental justice.
    4. Globalization.   I. Smith, Ted, 1945–   II. Sonnenfeld, David Allan, 1953–.
    III. Pellow, David Naquib, 1969–

HD9696.A2C425 2006
331.7′621381—dc22

                                                                    2005058007

2   4   6   8   9   7   5   3   1

Contents

Foreword

Technology Happens

TAKE CARS. After Henry Ford began mass production, it took only a flash in time for these four-wheeled chunks of technology to wholly transform our landscape, environment, economy, culture, psychology, and ... well, pretty much our whole world. For better or worse, cars created freeways, shopping malls, McDonald's, drive-in banking—even the Beach Boys!

The true story of the automobile, however, is not about the immutable march of technology, but about the ordinary folks who have battled the barons of industry over the years to humanize and democratize the tramp-tramp-tramp of technological forces. I think of the bloodied but unbowed workers in Flint, Michigan, for example. They launched a heroic sit-down strike in 1937 for better pay and fair treatment, leading not only to the creation of the United Auto Workers, but also to a new power relationship between bosses and workers, advancing middle-class possibilities for all Americans. I think, too, of the scientists, environmentalists, and other grassroots activists who fought—and are still fighting—for cleaner, safer, and more fuel-efficient automobiles (including pushing for advanced auto technology that requires no gasoline, no oil subsidies, and no more oil wars).

Such grassroots rebels, willing to confront authority and challenge the status quo, are the essence of America's democratic spirit—and we need that rebellious spirit more than ever. A new wave of technology is sweeping the land. It is embodied in the tiny chips (and the computers they power) that are radically and rapidly transforming our world—and, like the automobile, not always for the better.

I must admit that I'm just as hooked as the next person on the plethora of high-tech doo-dads. While I'm personally a bit of a techno-phobe (I don't even have a doorbell at home, for example), my little business is totally wired. I'm a Luddite with a Web Site (www.jimhightower.com), and there is no doubt in my mind about the value of technology.

I do have serious doubts, however, about the *values* of many of the top executives who are profiting so enormously from this high-tech explosion. Over the years I have repeatedly been left whopper-jawed by the self-serving short-sightedness of the high-tech barons who have managed to inflict the staggering amounts of pollution, worker health problems, and overall worker abuse so well chronicled in *Challenging the Chip*. It seems to me that the idealistic techno-nerds who provided so much of the inspiration for this industry have been pushed aside by the bottom-liners and greed mongers who are riding the revolution into the billionaires club, while production workers are forced to work two or three jobs to put food on the table for their families, all the while risking debilitating illness as the long-term price for being a part of the technology's advance.

The story of the "dark side of the chip" needs to be told and retold, and it needs to be understood throughout our "global village" before it is too late to do anything about it—although for some of the unfortunate ones it is already too late. This book provides a long-overdue reality check on the happy talk that saturates our airwaves, courtesy of the billions of advertising dollars spent to persuade us all that we need to buy the latest gadgets. And what better way to cut through the B.S. than by hearing from the pioneering, frontline rebels who are daring to challenge the chip.

Read about them and rejoice in their successes—they are the unsung heroines and heroes of our time. As much as we can be dazzled by the electronic wizardry around us, this book shines a much-needed light on the human cost of the high-tech revolution: the impact on the workers who make our fancy toys, as well as the impacts on their children.

Challenging the Chip explains how the high-tech industry first blossomed in what was then called the "Valley of Heart's Delight," but was soon transformed into Silicon Valley. It documents how such Santa Clara Valley fruit-processing workers as Alida Hernandez got reinvented as "clean room" workers in a deplorable pattern that is still being replicated around the world.

To these agricultural workers with limited education and few options, the shift from hard, hot, seasonal work in the packing sheds to "clean industry" jobs seemed a dream come true, but ended up proving the old adage, "Be careful what you wish for." Jim Moore grew up in California's Central Valley, but left his home for one of those "dream jobs"—it ultimately took his life because of his exposure to trichloroethylene (TCE), a cleaning solvent that the industry kept using for years. For close to three decades, production workers and their advocates in the high-tech industry have tried to call attention to such toxic hazards in "clean room" manufacturing and to get health-protective changes for workers and their families. Like the Flint workers in 1937, they have been battling bosses for humane and safe working conditions.

The book recounts how the Santa Clara Center for Occupational Safety and Health (SCCOSH) was the first group in the United States to take on high-tech health hazards. Learning that TCE had been shown to cause cancer, these feisty folks began back in 1978 to get the chemical banned from California's workplaces. Then, in the 1980s, SCCOSH spun off Silicon Valley Toxics Coalition (SVTC), and together they called for the removal of the reproductively toxic glycol ethers from semiconductor manufacturing through their "Campaign to End the Miscarriage of Justice."

One of the most poignant battles chronicled in *Challenging the Chip* was waged by Helen Clark, a semiconductor worker and brave leader of a group called PHASE Two in Scotland. She challenged the industry to stop using the poisons that were hurting so many workers—the same poisons that ultimately took her life. Her tireless efforts with her grassroots group were able to get the Scottish occupational health authorities to conduct one of the world's first health studies of semiconductor workers.

There are stories in *Challenging the Chip* about electronics workers who have suffered from toxic exposures and banded together, from the Southwestern United States and the Maquiladora region on the U.S.-Mexico border, to Malaysia, Taiwan, Thailand, China, and India. I am moved by the story of Wen-Shen Liu, the child of a mother who was exposed to toxic chemicals while working for an RCA factory in Taiwan. She died of hepatoblastoma at age three. Her mother later died of breast cancer, one of hundreds of victims that worked for RCA. I'm inspired to learn that the families of these workers have banded together to form the RCA Workers' Self-Help Group to fight for justice, even after the company packed up and left Taiwan.

I remember meeting some of the authors of this book in the late 1980s when they came to Texas to challenge SEMATECH, the Austin-based semiconductor research consortium, forcing it to face unpleasant realities and eventually become a premier environmental health and safety leader for the electronics industry. I liked their kick-ass style and was impressed when the authors and their activist groups finally got Congress to earmark millions of dollars so that SEMATECH could develop cleaner production technologies.

I also remember the day I saw the report, "Exporting Harm," which brought home to us Americans some chilling photos of the impacts of our toxic electronics industry on villagers in rural China. I was appalled to learn that our e-waste, generated in such huge quantities by our throw-away culture, is being shipped to China, where it is being "recycled" in backyard processing shops. Unprotected and uninformed workers there strip our discarded computers by hand, not only poisoning themselves but also letting the toxins leach into the water supply, causing severe environmental and health problems. This report put a human face on the dark side of globalization and proved beyond a doubt that toxic wastes run downhill in a global economy. And, as a chapter in this book points out, this is all happening because the U.S. government is the only industrial nation in the world that has refused to ratify the Basel Convention, the international treaty that explicitly bans the export of hazardous waste from rich to poor countries.

Another example in the book that hits home to me is the Dell campaign, showing that a determined local group can have a dramatic global impact. While many people are familiar with the meteoric rise of gabillionaire Michael Dell and the company he founded in Austin, few are aware that Dell Inc. was a ticking environmental time bomb, carelessly loading its computers with deadly toxins and not taking responsibility for the poisonous impact of throwing used computers in the dump. But the in-your-face organizing tactics of the Computer Take Back Campaign and their Austin-based ally, Texas Campaign for the Environment, branded the company and Michael himself as being literally filthy rich, embarrassing them into coming to the table to develop a responsible recycling program for their products.

We need a lot more "people's histories" like those in this book—the stories of brave and creative women and men who fight back when their lives and their children's lives are threatened. These are the stories of people challenging the corporate elite and speaking truth to power—whether the power be the corporations or the governments that allow these practices to continue. Such stories teach us that when people come together across traditional boundaries—geographic, political, racial, etc.—they actually can change the world.

Acknowledgments

SCORES OF PEOPLE around the world have been involved over the course of several years in the conceptualization, development, editing, and production of this volume. The "Global Symposium on Strategies for a Sustainable High-Tech Industry," held November 2002 in San Jose, California, in which this volume has its origins, was sponsored by the International Campaign for Responsible Technology (ICRT), and hosted by the Silicon Valley Toxics Coalition (SVTC). That symposium could not have taken place without financial support from the University of California's Institute for Labor and Employment (ILE), the University of California at Berkeley's Institute for International Studies (IIS), and others. To the participants and supporters of that conference, the editors of this volume would like to express their enduring thanks.

Subsequently, the ILE, through a Collaboration and Dissemination Grant, supported a series of editorial workshops in San Diego, California; Wageningen, the Netherlands; and Chiang Mai, Thailand, involving contributors to this volume and others. Other organizations supported those workshops, as well, including California Cultures in Comparative Perspective, University of California, San Diego; the Environmental Policy Group, Wageningen University, the Netherlands; Washington State University Tri-Cities; and the SVTC. Those workshops were critical in further developing the chapters in this book, as well as developing connections between contributors and others worldwide. The editors acknowledge and thank all participants in and supporters of those far-flung workshops.

Thirty-two contributors worked very hard with few complaints and much dedication to develop their chapters for this volume. They put up with gentle and not-so-gentle reminders and prodding to complete their manuscripts, add references, and strengthen arguments, even while continuing their intensive, day-to-day involvements addressing many of the problems and issues they were writing about. Thirteen individuals contributed to this volume not only as writers but also as manuscript reviewers: Leslie Byster, Shenglin Chang, Anibel Ferus-Comelo, Ken Geiser, Amanda Hawes, Boy Lüthje, Glenna Matthews, Jim Puckett, Wen-ling Tu, Kishore Wankhade, Andrew Watterson, David Wood, and Fumikazu Yoshida. Byster, Chang, Hawes, Tu, and Watterson went even further, contributing also as section and/or manuscript editors. Leslie Byster played a key role in making this book possible in other ways as well, from organizing the conference that brought contributors together in 2002, to the non-trivial task of coordinating permissions and source material for the photographs in this volume. Regrettably, we were too late in formally recognizing Leslie's contributions to include her as a co-editor; had we been able to do so without delaying production of the book, we would have done so. The editors would like to express their deep appreciation and heartfelt thanks to all; this book would not be without you.

Others, too, played a critical role in the development and quality production of this volume. More than a dozen distinguished colleagues from around the world generously donated their time and expertise as peer reviewers on draft chapters. Their thoughtful and constructive comments were important in pointing out weak spots and suggesting ways the authors might further develop their arguments and presentation, resulting in much-strengthened contributions. External reviewers included: Tamara Barber, Sander van den Berg, Garrett Brown, Angana Chatterji, Kyle Eischen, Koichi Hasegawa, Karen Hossfeld, Hsin-Huang Michael Hsiao, Kris van Koppen, Ching Kwan Lee, Kate O'Neill, Dara O'Rourke, Ruth Pearson, Alvin So, and Ryoichi Terada. At the request of Temple University Press, J. Timmons Roberts, Director of the Program in Environmental Science and Policy at the College of William and Mary, Virginia, and an additional, anonymous, peer reviewer took hours from full lives and busy schedules to read the entire book manuscript, make extensive notes, and communicate helpful suggestions that improved the quality and clarity of the volume. Colleagues in our "home" institutions also put up with and supported our obsessive, long-term involvement with this book project, and will be greatly relieved, and we hope appreciative, to see the final product.

Among the many who have supported this collaborative, action research writing effort, a few merit special mention and appreciation: Peter Olney, former Associate Director of the University of California, Institute for Labor and Employment; Rajah Rasiah, Professor of Technology and Innovation Policy, University of Malaya, Malaysia; and Voravidh Charoenloet, former Director of the Center for Political Economy, Chulalongkorn University, Thailand. Peter Wissoker, former Senior Editor with Temple University Press, was a strong and effective advocate of this volume from the beginning; his efforts and support were greatly appreciated. Coming on well along in the process, William Hammell did a remarkable job of taking over editing of this volume at Temple, and effectively shepherded it into print. Donna Maurer, a professional editor, did a splendid job of helping to make the text more readable and consistent throughout the volume. Heather Dubnik contributed her considerable skills and experience in constructing the index. Tamara Barber graciously assisted with translation of Raquel Partida's chapter; Kenji Liu and Henry Norr made insightful and caring editorial suggestions. The cover design benefited from the creative inputs of Innosanto Nagara of Design Action, Gopal Dayaneni, Alfie Ebojo, and others. Our apologies to anyone overlooked.

Lastly, it should be noted that the views reflected in this work are those of the individual authors, not necessarily of the editors, nor of our home institutions. We do, nevertheless, take full responsibility for the final form in which the various parts of this work are presented.

THE EDITORS
San Jose, California; Richland, Washington;
and San Diego, California, USA
April, 2006

TED SMITH, DAVID A. SONNENFELD, AND DAVID N. PELLOW

1 The Quest for Sustainability and Justice in a High-Tech World

OF THE MILLIONS of words written over the past several decades about the electronics industry's incredible transformation of our world, far too few have addressed the downsides of this revolution. Many are surprised to learn that environmental degradation and occupational health hazards are as much a part of high-tech manufacturing as miniaturization and other such marvels. Although most consumers are eager to enjoy their latest computers, televisions, cellular phones, iPods, and electronic games, few relate the declining prices of these and other electronic technologies to the labor of Third World women, who are paid pennies a day. Fewer still realize that the amazingly powerful microprocessors and superminiaturized, high-capacity memory devices harm the workers who produce them and pollute the surrounding communities' air and water. Consumers who are inundated with well-financed marketing hyperbole rush out to buy the newest electronic gadgets and components, unaware that their old, obsolete goods add to the mountains of toxic electronic junk piling up around the world. They are likewise clueless about the fact that most electronics gadgets are assembled under working conditions as dangerous as those in the early industrial era in Europe and the United States.

The reason for this widespread ignorance is that the health and ecological footprints of the global electronics industry remain largely hidden from most consumers' view. High-tech manufacturing has contaminated its workers, as well as the air, land, and water of communities wherever these firms are located and wherever their wastes accumulate—from Silicon Valley (United States) to Silicon Glen (Scotland), from Silicon Island (Taiwan) to Silicon Paddy (China). Just as harmful are the endemic social inequalities and economic stratification that these firms promote. Although CEOs and upper management enjoy multimillion dollar salaries and "golden parachutes," many production workers live in large, densely packed dormitories and other substandard, crowded forms of housing, as they face wage stagnation and job insecurity. Not surprisingly, the production workers, who often labor under sweatshop conditions, are mostly women, immigrants, and people of color in the United States, Latin America, and Western Europe, as well as recently urbanized women in Asia. Similarly, the wage gap between men and women in the industry continues to loom large.

This book embodies the vision of many of the inspirational leaders around the world who are challenging the patterns of health, environmental, and social injustice that have arisen as a hidden aspect of the high-tech revolution. All of us share the perspective popularly attributed to anthropologist Margaret

Mead, "Never doubt that a small group of thoughtful, committed people can change the world. Indeed, it is the only thing that ever has." Although we acknowledge the accomplishments of the high-tech revolution's pioneers— Gordon Moore, Bill Gates, Bill Hewlett and David Packard, Michael Dell, and many others—we also want to highlight and amplify the incredible accomplishments of the unsung heroines and heroes of this revolution's "other side," who have been fighting to transform the electronics industry to better address the needs of its workers and affected communities around the world. Women like:

- Amanda Hawes, founder of the Santa Clara Center for Occupational Safety and Health, and an attorney who, for more than 30 years, has been fighting to improve working conditions and advocating for chemically exposed electronics workers with cancer as well as the children of exposed workers born with severe birth defects;
- Lorraine Ross, a San Jose, California, housewife whose daughter's serious birth defects gave her the strength to mount a remarkable challenge to Fairchild Semiconductor Corporation's polluting practices in Silicon Valley, which led to the formation of the Silicon Valley Toxics Coalition;
- Dr. Orapan Metadilogkul, an occupational health physician in Thailand who confronted the Seagate Corporation when it was compromising its workers' health in the 1990s and who faced severe retaliation for her efforts; and
- Helen Clark, a Scottish semiconductor worker who gave her life fighting to provide a voice for poisoned workers at National Semiconductor's plant in Silicon Glen and who spurred the formation of PHASE Two in Scotland.

These and many other courageous individuals who have suffered the industry's "unintended consequences" have been among the key leaders responsible for the metamorphosis from discouragement to hope for a more sustainable future in Silicon Valley, as well as in many other high-tech centers around the world.

This volume is the product of a movement that began at the grassroots level, with ordinary people facing injustice on their jobs and in their communities: women who were exposed to toxic chemicals in semiconductor plants and denied protection or compensation; people who were harassed and fired for trying to organize labor unions; female community residents who gave birth to children with serious birth defects after drinking water tainted with toxic solvents that had leaked from semiconductor plants; desperately poor, rural peasants forced to move into cities throughout Asia who are being poisoned by the tons of electronic waste (e-waste) dumped on their communities every day.

These stories have striking similarities, whether they occur in Silicon Valley, Asia, or Latin America, and whether the company is named IBM, Fairchild, National Semiconductor, Dell, RCA, Sony, Lenovo, or United Microelectronics Corporation. By linking workers, residents, toxic exposure survivors, labor activists, environmentalists, consumers, and academics in the North with those in the South, our goal is to inform and connect people in each phase of the electronics life cycle. From the extraction of raw materials; to the manufacture and testing of components; to the assembly of final products; to their shipping, marketing, and use; to their ultimate disassembly and disposal, we are following the products, documenting their impacts, and joining together to prevent and reverse the harm they have caused.

This book profiles workers, environmentalists, and their advocates across national borders who are highlighting injustices, as well as signs of hope, in both the private and the public sectors. This effort is not about attributing blame; rather, its aim is to *re-articulate responsibility and provide a vision of what a sustainable electronics industry can look like.* Activists from Europe, Asia, and the United States, for example, have concluded that electronics producers must take greater responsibility for problems associated with the global export of e-waste. The Computer TakeBack Campaign (CTBC) in the United States and similar efforts elsewhere in the world are making significant progress in transforming the public debate in support of *extended producer responsibility* and product take-back (see Byster and Smith, "Electronics Production Life Cycle"; Raphael and Smith; Tojo; Wood and Schneider, this volume). Electronics products are being designed with increasingly short life spans—"Happy Meal" electronic games are disposed of with the rest of the trash, cell phones are discarded in a matter of months, computers become obsolete in a few short years. Consumers have the power and responsibility to stop such environmentally unsound practices. For instance, when confronted about their wasteful practices, Dell and Hewlett-Packard responded with innovations in product design and end-of-life disposal (see Raphael and Smith; Wood and Schneider, this volume). But although activists have succeeded in having a number of firms sign agreements and endorse principles of sustainability (see Appendices D and E), most electronics firms have yet to embrace sustainable product design, manufacturing, and disposal.

The contributors to this volume include many of the world's most articulate, passionate, and progressive visionaries, scholars, and advocates involved in documenting and challenging the global electronics industry's social and environmental impacts. From Asia, North America, and Europe, the authors are renowned for their contributions to the science and politics of labor rights and environmental and social justice and bring this perspective to the high-tech sector through this book. One irony is that, in order to connect with each other and the rest of the world, activists have become some of the most dedicated and savvy consumers and users of the very technology tools developed by the industry that we challenge. Clearly, we are not antitechnology. Our goal is to find creative ways to successfully encourage the industry to live up to its promise and become a leading force for sustainability.

One critical challenge of contemporary democracy is to help ordinary people knowledgeably participate in governing complex technological systems and industries (cf. Habermas 1976; Feenberg 1991, 1999). This book aims to contribute to discussions and campaigns by concerned community members, electronics workers, health professionals, academics, labor leaders, environmental activists, and others who are developing alternative visions for the regulation and sustainable development of electronics design and manufacturing, assembly/disassembly, and waste disposal around the world. As editors and contributors, we are attempting to do something rather challenging: to bridge the divide between technical specialists and the broader population in analyzing and organizing citizen initiatives with respect to a critical global industry. Thus, this book aims not only to examine the electronics industry's global impacts on production workers and the environment, but also to contribute to existing efforts by workers, advocates, and policymakers to ensure a greater commitment to sustainability in the global electronics sector.

Throughout this book, we address the fundamental questions that lie just beneath the surface of the electronics industry's public relations juggernaut:

- What are the industry's impacts on its own workers, surrounding communities, and natural environments around the world?
- What role has inequality by race/ethnicity, class, gender, and geography played in the industry's evolution?
- How can the global electronics industry be transformed into more sustainable systems of production, use, and disposal?
- Can high-tech development sustain comprehensive and equitable growth, or will it continue to result in growing economic polarization?

The Political Context

This volume has strong roots in the political activism and policy interventions initiated over the last several decades by the Santa Clara Center for Occupational Safety and Health (SCCOSH), the Silicon Valley Toxics Coalition (SVTC), the Campaign for Responsible Technology (CRT), and the International Campaign for Responsible Technology (ICRT), all based in San Jose, California. Formed in 1976, SCCOSH was the first nongovernmental organization (NGO) in the world to research, document, and call attention to the occupational health impacts of the many toxic chemicals used in electronics manufacturing. It developed the baseline information on high-tech hazards that has informed the work of many other NGOs over the years (see Hawes and Pellow, this volume). When reports began appearing in local news media about toxic chemicals leaking out of electronics workplaces and into the groundwater in Santa Clara Valley, SCCOSH spun off SVTC to open up a new environmental front. Since 1982, SVTC has focused on the ecological and community health impacts of the electronics boom.

For several decades, SCCOSH and SVTC have served as the environmental conscience of the electronics industry. Both organizations have been responsible for significant changes in how the industry is regulated by government, as well as for important environmental and occupational health transformations within the industry. In response to the rapid expansion of electronics manufacturing outside of Silicon Valley, in 1992 they initiated the U.S.-based CRT to unite diverse organizations and communities; to promote broader participation in the design and development of sustainable technologies; to strengthen locally based organizing by sharing experiences, information, resources, and strategies; and to provide a larger context for advocacy groups dealing with technology-related concerns. The CRT tracked the global expansion of electronics manufacturing and built a network of grassroots organizations and individuals. Participants were united by the recognition that their diverse, but related problems—all associated with the rapid development of electronics manufacturing—could be overcome only by extending democracy into the technological decision-making process.

In several states (California, Texas, Arizona, New Mexico, Oregon, and Massachusetts) and locations around the world (Scotland, Japan, Malaysia, Taiwan, the Philippines, and Mexico) where electronics development was booming, the CRT built relationships with community, environmental justice, environmental, and labor organizations. In its collaboration with the Southwest Network for Environmental and Economic Justice (SNEEJ), CRT formed the Electronics Industry Good Neighbor Campaign to organize good neighbor agreements designed to protect environmental, occupational, and public health. This network succeeded in changing relationships between electronics firms and impacted local communities. In other cases, this work impacted environmental regulation of the industry by government. In still other cases, the work led to industry improvements, such as when the CRT prevailed on the U.S. Congress to direct SEMATECH, the semiconductor research consortium, to develop more environmentally sustainable technologies.

In 1997, CRT's vision took a dramatic leap forward at the European Work Hazards Conference in the Netherlands, when participants concluded that responsible technology had become a *global* issue and needed to be tackled as such. The participants recognized that developing and sharing knowledge across borders that linked occupational and environmental health with workers' rights was a critical, unmet need, and they resolved to establish the *International* Campaign for Responsible Technology (ICRT) to "ensure that the high-tech industry and governments become accountable to their host communities and people, and that the industry use the best practices to improve health and safety and reduce environmental impacts" (see Byster and Smith, "From Grassroots to Global," this volume).

ORIGINS OF THIS VOLUME

In November 2002, ICRT organized the "Global Symposium on Strategies for a Sustainable High-Tech Industry," its first international gathering. The symposium provided an exciting venue for leading activists and academics from around the world to share their diverse, yet similar efforts in addressing the many challenges of high-tech development. Participants from more than a dozen countries developed creative strategies for addressing the myriad problems associated with electronics manufacturing, assembly, disassembly, and disposal. During the meeting, delegates visited the Semiconductor Industry Association's headquarters to present their stories and concerns about occupational and environmental health to the head of the chip industry trade

PHOTO 1.1. Family members and supporters of former RCA (Taiwan) workers who died of cancer are joined by Ted Smith, then Executive Director of the Silicon Valley Toxics Coalition (SVTC) at a March 2001 rally in Taiwan. Participants called on the company to pay benefits and medical costs, and to clean up contamination from more than fifteen years of high-tech manufacturing. Courtesy of Hsen Chung Lin, TAVOI.

association. At the conclusion of the symposium, participants adopted the following mission statement:

> We are an international solidarity network that promotes corporate and government accountability in the global electronics industry. We are united by our concern for the lifecycle impacts of this industry on health, the environment, and workers' rights.

One of the major activities emphasized during the symposium was the need for research and publication on such topics as environmental protection, labor rights, and globalization. Participants also committed to further develop strategies for organizing and empowering workers and communities and to identify opportunities for approaching regulatory institutions. At the same time, participants recognized the need to continue efforts that would compel firms to reduce their toxic impacts and promote sustainable solutions. This book is a direct outgrowth of those gatherings and discussions.

GEOGRAPHICAL AND SECTORAL SCOPE

This volume has two geographical frames of reference. The first is in the vicinity of San Jose, California, otherwise known as "Silicon Valley," where the U.S. electronics industry has its roots (see Pellow and Matthews, this volume) and continues to have a very important presence. There is a 30-year history of community and worker dialog and struggle with the electronics industry in Silicon Valley. The story only *begins* there, however, as the region has been viewed as *the* model for electronics and "clean" economic development throughout the world. Unfortunately, this misconception persists, as the Silicon Valley "miracle" has been exported or mimicked in Europe, Asia, and the Americas, with serious social and environmental consequences.

Though "the Silicon Valley story" has been widely told, important new chapters still are being written. The environmental consequences of electronics manufacturing in Silicon Valley are making more headlines today than ever before. Numerous campaigns have focused on electronic waste, the toxic poisoning of workers, and other issues (see the unprecedented series of articles by *New York Times* columnist, Bob Herbert [2003a, 2003b, 2003c, 2003d]; as well as related coverage in the *San Francisco Chronicle*, *Washington Post*, *San Jose Mercury News*, and the *Guardian* [UK], and on many Internet sites). The court battles between IBM and its former employees over the impact of toxics on their health, and the dramatic confrontations and negotiations between environmentalists and high-tech industries (e.g., Dell, and most recently, Apple) over electronic waste disposal, are just two of the many stories that have appeared regularly in the news.

Global citizen action focused on the electronics industry has strong links with Silicon Valley, as well. The lessons and possibilities for community governance, environmental health, and social justice after companies moved to "greener pastures" in other nations are inextricably linked. For example, when electronics firms, toxics, and waste moved to lower-cost areas of the world, workers and activists were able to mobilize more effectively there because they had learned from Silicon Valley's tragedies, as well as the U.S. activists' successes in their efforts to expose these problems. NGO efforts to publicize the inequities of globalization brought the struggles of workers and residents from around the world to electronics consumers in North America and Europe. Likewise, socially responsible investment firms' emerging focus on inequality and governance brought many of these issues into the boardrooms of global electronics companies.

The volume's second geographical frame of reference encompasses parts of the world increasingly integrated into global networks of electronics production, consumption, and disposal, with their own rich and important histories of engagement with the industry (cf. Castells 1996, 2000). Recent international conferences and informational tours in China, Thailand, Japan, Taiwan, Mexico, Sweden, the Netherlands, Scotland, and elsewhere have brought this "global village" much closer together, convening activists from Asia, Europe, and their counterparts in the United States (cf. Photos 1.1, 1.2, 6.1, and 7.1).

It is critical for civic actors everywhere that these geographically dispersed and disparate experiences are documented, made more visible, and are well analyzed. Likewise, leading advocates and analysts must do more to come together with progressive leaders within the industry. Together, they can improve the sustainability not only of the industry, the communities where the factories are located, and the workers who provide their labor, but also of the planet itself.

PHOTO 1.2. Participants at the Beijing conference on e-waste and clean production in the electronics industry, April 2004. Courtesy of Silicon Valley Toxics Coalition.

Contributors to this volume write about multiple sectors within the global electronics industry, including semiconductors (Lüthje; LaDou; Watterson; Hawes and Pellow; McCourt; Yoshida); electronic components (Foran and Sonnenfeld; Partida; Tojo); office equipment (Yoshida); personal computers (Lüthje; Wood and Schneider); consumer electronics (Ferus-Comelo; Leong and Pandita; Pandita; Garcia and Simpson; Chang, Chiu, and Tu; Ku; Tojo); and electronic waste (Puckett; Agarwal and Wankhade). As electronics manufacturing covers a vast array of production processes (see Lüthje, this volume, for a further discussion of the structure of the global electronics industry), this is not all inclusive. Taken together, however, the industry sectors addressed in this book represent the many challenges and opportunities that workers, communities, firms, and governments around the world face when dealing with the social and environmental impacts of a dynamic, important, and powerful industry.

ORGANIZATION OF THIS VOLUME

Although an understanding of geographical and sectoral characteristics is important for mapping the electronics industry's development and growth, we organized this book around three broad, integrative themes: the globalization of electronics manufacturing, labor rights and environmental justice, and product end-of-life-cycle issues (i.e., e-waste and extended producer responsibility).

Global Electronics

As a major driver of corporate-led globalization, the high-tech industry has rapidly diversified its operations from Silicon Valley to all corners of the world, motivated by the drive to find lower costs, a docile and capable workforce, and reduced regulation. Throughout this book, we explore the globalization of the electronics supply chain (from components to subassembly, to final assembly and testing, etc.) and product life cycle (from manufacturing, to sales and marketing, to consumption, to obsolescence and waste recycling/disposal/processing). This book takes a holistic, sectoral approach, which conveys the electronics industry's overall footprint, rather than any one particular point in the supply chain or product life cycle.

The volume begins with the historical and global questions most important to the study of the industry. It then considers the social and environmental impacts of production and assembly practices, and concludes with an examination of the problem of electronic waste and end-of-life policy dilemmas affecting all nations. The supply-chain and life-cycle approaches demonstrate electronics' effect on both human beings and the natural environment from production to consumption, through disposal. Some call this a "cradle to grave" approach, whereas others refer to it as a "cradle to cradle" approach. Several chapters in Part I take a global view of key dynamics in the sector, including its structural characteristics and health impacts, and the important role of women and migrant workers. Other chapters in Part I present a bird's-eye view of working and environmental conditions and practices of electronics manufacturing in China, India, Thailand, and Central and Eastern Europe.

Labor Rights and Environmental Justice

People of color, immigrants, and women often work in the most dangerous and lowest-paying jobs in this industry around the globe (Pellow and Park 2002; see also Ong 1987; AMRC 1998). Their level of employee power and union representation is universally very low, and many industry leaders continue to insist that electronics remain virtually union-free in order to thrive (Eisenscher 1993; Robinson and McIlwee 1989).

Part II of this book presents the stories of workers and environmentalists confronting dangerous work hazards, antiunion hostility, and environmental health perils in the United States, Mexico, Scotland, Taiwan, and elsewhere. These chapters make it clear that workers are struggling to document and overcome the health problems they face, building international unions, and collaborating with environmentalists to bring about local and global policy changes. Although the most vulnerable populations are on the front lines of environmental and economic injustice, and daily threats continue as a result of poor occupational health and labor conditions, nearly all workers in the industry are subjected to these problems. Although electronics manufacturing workers, assemblers and "disassemblers"[1] face hazards and injustice, engineers, chemists, technicians, and other highly paid, white-collar workers also are routinely exposed to toxic chemicals on the job and have no union representation. It is significant that the first workers to bring the issue of workplace cancer to IBM management were chemists in San Jose whose voices were ignored. Part II concludes with an essay on the future of international labor organizing in electronics.

Electronic Waste and Extended Producer Responsibility

Environmentalists working to reign in the international trade in hazardous wastes since the 1980s (Greenpeace, Basel Action Network) recently identified the next generation of this problem: the trade in electronic waste. E-waste is typically traded or dumped from North to South, but as nations like India and China increasingly modernize, their own industries and consumers are contributing to the problems as well. Contributors to this section are important leaders of the global movement to expose and monitor e-waste exporters and reform the practices of firms and governments that allow it. Extended producer responsibility (EPR)—extending companies' traditional responsibility to include products' impacts throughout their life cycles, including end-of-life responsibility—has become the broad, unifying goal, and activists around the world are succeeding in their efforts to institutionalize these policies in legislation and company practices. Part III of this volume reveals the power of local and international grassroots movements to shape corporate practices, government legislation, and transnational agreements. The stories told are global in scope, but focus especially on Japan, India, China, Europe, and the United States. The section concludes with an inspiring account of the successful U.S. campaign to compel the country's number one computer retailer, Dell Computer, to accept greater responsibility for taking back and safely disposing of its obsolete products.

Additional Resources

Following the main sections of the book, several significant historical documents are appended for readers' reference and use. These include the text of the "Principles of Environmental Justice" from the First National People of Color Leadership Summit in Washington, DC, in 1991; the SVTC's and CRT's "Silicon Principles of Socially and Environmentally Responsible Electronics Manufacturing" from 1996; sample shareholder resolutions; the "Computer Take-Back Campaign Statement of Principles" from 2004; and the "Electronics Recycler's Pledge of True Stewardship" from 2003, respectively. Final pages of the volume include a list of acronyms used throughout the book; a complete, integrated bibliography to facilitate research on the global electronics industry; and a directory of key organizations around the world engaged in ongoing advocacy related to the industry.

The global electronics industry is ever evolving and changing, as are the advocates working for its greater sustainability. Thus, having up-to-date online information is an important part of staying informed, making effective policies, and achieving greater sustainable practices in the global electronics industry. For links to updated and supplemental information for this book, please see this volume's Web page on our publisher's Web site (www.temple.edu/tempress) as well as Web sites of the organizations listed in the "Resources" section at the end of this volume.

VISION FOR THE FUTURE

Electronics industry leaders have produced enormous technical innovations over the years, but have not kept sufficient pace with the socially and environmentally oriented advances that are available to them. Changes in the industry too often have come about only after tragedies, negative media exposure, the publication of research documenting systematic environmental and labor abuses, or considerable pressure from activists and government agencies (cf. Mazurek 1999, Pellow and Park 2002). Electronics industry leaders and employees have essential roles to play in incorporating more socially and environmentally oriented technology designs and industrial practices in operations around the world. There are signs this is happening, as high-tech employees empower themselves to work for change from within and as physicians, attorneys, community activists, and policymakers apply pressure from without. There is a great abundance of creative genius and brainpower within the electronics industry. Although a few industry leaders have stepped forward, many more need to dedicate their creativity and energy toward creating a sane and sustainable production, consumption, and waste management system.

All of the contributors to this book believe it is imperative that scholars, activists, practitioners, workers, industry leaders, and policymakers explore the consequences—both negative and positive—of the continuing electronics boom and the related high-technology revolution. It is critical that we better understand the relationship between the economic globalization and the globalization of social and environmental ills. Finally, after documenting these concerns and relationships, we also must develop strategies to regulate, harness, and document the power of electronics and the global economy for the greater good of humanity and the natural world. There are many examples of how this industry can provide important leadership on the issues of concern—such as resource conservation, energy efficiency, and phasing out toxic and ozone depleting chemicals.

Our view is that the future of sustainability, environmental justice, and labor rights cannot lie solely in the hands of either the social movements or the captains of industry and representatives of the state. All citizens and stakeholders must help determine the future of this industry, its employees, and the environment of impacted communities around the world. We are united in the vision expressed at a gathering of the Trans-Atlantic Network for Clean Production in Soesterberg, Netherlands, May 1999:

ELECTRONICS SUSTAINABILITY COMMITMENT

Each new generation of technical improvements in electronic products should include parallel and proportional improvements in environmental, health and safety, as well as social justice attributes.

NOTE

1. Disassemblers break down electronic equipment and components for salvageable materials.

I. GLOBAL ELECTRONICS

DAVID A. SONNENFELD

HIGH-TECH ELECTRONICS manufacturing commenced in Silicon Valley, California, and select locations in Europe and Japan in the mid-twentieth century, and has since established operations around the world, including locations in Scotland, Taiwan, South Korea, and Malaysia, among others. The industry has shifted its global geography almost as rapidly as its product life cycles, investing billions of dollars in new manufacturing facilities, including in such unlikely places as Borneo. Early in the twenty-first century, new locations for electronics hardware manufacturing include Central and Eastern Europe (CEE) and mainland China, with new centers of engineering design and software development developing rapidly in India, Vietnam, and elsewhere.

The first three chapters of Part I of this volume provide readers overviews of several important aspects of the global electronics industry: composition of and structural dynamics within the sector (Lüthje); occupational health in semiconductor manufacturing—arguably the most important as well as toxic segment of the industry (LaDou); and the critical role of women and migrant workers in the global electronics labor force (Ferus-Comelo). These chapters draw on the experiences of both older electronics manufacturing sites, especially Silicon Valley, California, and newer locations of globally oriented electronics production, including China, India, Malaysia, and Thailand. Other chapters in Part I present bird's-eye views of three of today's most rapidly developing electronics manufacturing venues: China (Leong and Pandita), India (Pandita), and Central and Eastern Europe (Watterson); and of a key link in the global electronics supply chain, Thailand (Foran and Sonnenfeld).

Hierarchies of power, profitability, and control are embedded within the structure of global electronics. Key firms such as Intel and Hewlett-Packard remain headquartered in Silicon Valley, even while their manufacturing operations are distributed around the world. Some of the most well-known brand owners manufacture none of their own products, rather sourcing everything from contract manufacturers (Lüthje; see also Partida, this volume). Other firms with operations in countries with low-wage labor markets and modest high-tech capabilities specialize in the lower end of the global electronics supply chain: labor-intensive manufacturing; assembly and testing of electronic components, subassemblies, and parts[1] (Foran and Sonnenfeld; see also García and Simpson, this volume). The global division of labor among firms and sites of electronics manufacturing continues to shift, depending not only on organizational, but also political-economic factors such as the willingness and ability of host governments to subsidize firms and facilities, give tax credits or holidays, provide an educated but docile workforce (Ferus-Comelo), prevent trade unionism (Lüthje), and otherwise provide conditions conducive to profit maximization, operational flexibility, and labor control.

A number of important insights regarding the dynamics and characteristics of globalization in electronics manufacturing in the early twenty-first century can be gleaned from the chapters in Part I and elsewhere in this volume: First, *for much of its life, the global electronics industry has operated beyond the control of national governments*. Countries and communities often have been placed in the position of suitors or competitors, offering the best incentive package to prospective firms or investors, rather than being able to demand improved workplace and environmental conditions (Byster and Smith, "Electronics Production Life Cycle," this volume). Until recently, and in most places, regulation of electronics manufacturing has been piecemeal and disjointed—if it existed at all. Stepping tentatively into the void, local communities occasionally have taken the lead (cf. the Hazardous Materials Model Ordinance and the Toxic Gas Model Ordinance in Silicon Valley, as discussed in Byster and Smith, "Grassroots to Global," this volume).

Second, *financial stakes are high for electronics firms and host countries*, with new wafer fabrication facilities ("fabs") requiring investments of over a billion U.S. dollars and research and development efforts carried out by multinational consortia rather than by individual firms or countries. Entire national and regional economies rise and fall on the *cyclicality* of global electronics manufacturing. In the late 1990s, Thailand's single largest private employer was Seagate Technologies, with headquarters in Scott's Valley, California, a manufacturer of hard-disk drives and components. In Malaysia during the same period, a large percentage of the country's foreign exchange earnings were based on shipments of electronic hardware and components. A regional economic crisis combined with a global economic slowdown and an overproduction of semiconductors at the end of the twentieth century had devastating consequences in a whole series of electronics-led developmental states including Thailand, Malaysia, South Korea, and Taiwan.

Third, although the electronics industry continues to enjoy substantial economic power and the admiration of many government officials, its success has brought *devastating impacts to the health, well-being, and in some cases, lives of young women and (im)migrant laborers*—those least prepared to understand, let alone engage with, the conditions of their labor (Ferus-Comelo). The industry's ecological footprint has been considerable, with groundwater pollution and resource depletion an important part of its widespread legacy. The industry has aggressively resisted not only government regulation, but also formal, organized representation of workers' rights, and compensation to individuals and communities affected by the toxic substances that have been integral to electronics manufacturing and disassembly (Ferus-Comelo; Foran and Sonnenfeld; see also Steiert; Hawes and Pellow; Puckett; Agarwal and Wankhade, this volume).

Fourth, although the industry has globalized, *popular responses also have globalized,* though more slowly and considerably less well financed. Public health advocates such as LaDou, Watterson, and others, for example, not only have been personally involved and engaged in documenting health impacts of the industry around the world, but also have called for the establishment of new, international protective regimes for worker and community health and safety in the face of a highly mobile and toxic global industry (see also Steiert; Byster and Smith, "Electronics Production Life Cycle," this volume). Labor advocates, too, continue to seek new, creative transnational linkages in support of the thousands of workers employed and at risk in the sector (Ferus-Comelo; see also McCourt; Ku; Steiert, this volume).

Fifth, despite continuing industry resistance to regulation, *new supranational institutions and grassroots initiatives show promising signs of influencing industry environmental practices.* The European Union's Waste Electrical and Electronic Equipment (WEEE) and Reduction of Hazardous Substances (RoHS) directives have had a major impact on the "greening" of global electronics supply chains (see Geiser and Tickner; Tojo, this volume). Many firms have implemented voluntary environmental, and even occupational health management systems, such as the International Organization for Standardization's Environmental Management Systems framework, known as ISO 14000, and the British Standards on Occupational Health and Safety Management Systems (BS 8800) (Foran and Sonnenfeld). Citizens groups have been remarkably effective in applying consumer and media pressure on leading firms to adopt such measures as the Electronic Recycler's Pledge (see Raphael and Smith; Wood and Schneider; Appendix A, this volume).

Finally, *cultural* dimensions of the globalization of electronics have become important, as well: As electronic components become more universal and embedded in a multitude of manufactured goods from electronic games to mobile phones, pacemakers to automobiles, so too do the emergent global *values* of *extended producer responsibility* (see Raphael and Smith; Tojo; Wood and Schneider; Byster and Smith, "Electronics Production Life Cycle," this volume), *corporate responsibility* (Foran and Sonnenfeld; see also Hawes and Pellow; Garcia and Simpson; and Ku, this volume), and *social and environmental justice* (see Pellow and Matthews; Partida; Chang, Chiu, and Tu; Steiert; and Byster and Smith, "Electronics Production Life Cycle," this volume).

Few things characterize both the hope and desperation of social relations in the present era more than the two-headed hydra of *globalization* and *electronics*: Most major sociotechnological influences on our lives—from high-tech warfare to television, terrorism to air travel, and laptops to mobile phones—can be derived or constructed from the two. The chapters in this and other parts of the book demonstrate convincingly how the global electronics industry has come to have such a determinative influence not only on *our* lives, but also and especially on the lives of those who produce (and disassemble) such terrible and wonderful things for us. Further, they document the critical efforts of citizens, and public and private institutions to counter that influence and encourage the industry and its constituent firms to move rapidly and responsibly towards greater social and environmental sustainability.

NOTE

1. Examples include an integrated circuit (component), read-write arm (disk drive subassembly), and disk drive (part).

2 The Changing Map of Global Electronics

Networks of Mass Production in the New Economy

ELECTRONICS IS one of the largest manufacturing sectors in the global economy. However, this characteristic is often obscured by the prevailing view of "high-tech" as a science—and service-based industry—an image that has been cautiously cultivated since grassroots environmental and labor activists began to expose the "dark side of the chip" (Siegel and Markoff 1985). Since then, a myriad of academic and media writers and researchers have been dealing with the postindustrial economy in high-tech centers throughout the world (e.g., Castells 1996; Gilder 1989; Negri and Hardt 2000)—mostly neglecting more problematic impacts of electronics production for the environment, workers, and working-class communities. In particular, the focus on science, service, and software distracts the public's view from the social and political situation in the often-huge production complexes in newly industrializing countries in Asia, Latin America, and Central and Eastern Europe.

For an adequate understanding of the "high cost of high-tech" (Siegel and Markoff 1985), we must consider the enormous complexity of the global electronics industry and its production systems, as they have unfolded during the past two or three decades. The economics of the electronics industry is characterized by permanent and very rapid changes in technologies and industry structure, driven by an emergence of industry segments led by highly specialized newcomer firms, by a global reconcentration of technology and production resources in new markets, and by increasing separation of manufacturing from brand-name firms focusing on product development, design, and marketing. As a brief introduction into this industry structure and its economic logic, this chapter will provide some basic definitions and statistics, examine the fundamental transformation from old-style electronics manufacturing to new network-based industry models, discuss the trend toward large-scale outsourcing in electronics manufacturing, and describe some implications for the shape of the industry's global production networks.

WHAT IS HIGH-TECH?

The term *high-technology* is widely used in publications on electronics and information technology (IT); however, it is not scientific. Created by business media writers during the 1970s, high-tech usually refers to modern information technologies based on microelectronics, not only to a wide range of applications in consumer goods, automobiles, and aircrafts but also to non-electronics fields, such as biotechnology. With regard to electronics, recurring shifts in market-defining technologies such as the personal computer (PC) "revolution" of the 1980s, or the emergence of the Internet in the 1990s, have shaped the public's understanding of high technology. Similarly, various concepts of integration and convergence of information technologies such as "multimedia," "telematics," and "mechatronics" created by technologists, the media, and social scientists during recent decades have produced changing connotations of the nature of high-tech (see Lüthje 2004b).

For economists, defining high-tech electronics and information technology as an industry is difficult for three major reasons: (1) there have been constant and highly unpredictable shifts in technologies, demand patterns, and corresponding strategies of market segmentation and control in major industry segments; (2) many key products are services or "immaterial" in nature, such as software, data services, and key system architectures (even when they appear on a piece of hardware like a computer game on a CD); and (3) most products are manufactured through complex chains of suppliers, which contribute certain components or key products only, but at the same time form large industries in their own right (like the chip and disk-drive industries, which are suppliers to PC manufacturers). Hence, a definition of the electronics industry cannot be based on certain hardware products with relatively stable physical and value characteristics (like automobiles, steel tubes, or T-shirts). At the same time, the generation of value has shifted fundamentally away from hardware and component technology toward architectural design standards, software, and knowledge-intensive services (Ernst 2002, 319).

Such dynamics reflect changing social divisions of labor within electronics, between electronics and related industries (e.g., aerospace, automobile, engineering, or biotechnology); between intellectual and manual labor (i.e., "design and development" vs. manufacturing); as well as changing geographical patterns of location and concentration, as symbolized by the emergence of new, high-tech districts such as Silicon Valley (Sayer and Walker 1992; Storper and Walker 1989). Definitions of industry segments must include constantly evolving products and markets, as in the case of the PC industry of the 1980s (led by Intel and Microsoft); and the networking industry under the guidance of a new brand of equipment suppliers, such as Cisco, and software firms, such as Netscape, in the 1990s. As the creation of new industrial sectors always implies new forms of market segmentation (Ernst and O'Connor 1992), a model of profit maximization governs each sector, defining a specific sphere of capital accumulation (for an extensive discussion, see Aglietta 1979; Esser, Lüthje, and Noppe, 1997).

The chip industry, for example, did not exist statistically until the early 1970s, since integrated electronics firms, such as IBM, Philips, and Siemens, produced chips for their own internal use in other products. It was not until the emergence of independent chip producers from Silicon Valley and the subsequent shift of older integrated producers to mass production for the open market that chip manufacturing became a viable industry to be counted as a statistical category of its own. By the same token, many industry definitions insufficiently reflect the value created by suppliers and subassemblers. Most of a PC's economic value is in the microchip and other components, like disk drives or graphics cards, and also in the manufacturing services performed by major contract manufacturers and subassemblers. However, some of these industry segments (like contract assembly) are not even listed in standard industry statistics (Lüthje 2001a; Sturgeon 1999).

From this perspective, only broad categories can be employed to define and measure high-tech, and it always makes sense to look at electronics and IT as an integrated complex of several subsegments with rapidly changing boundaries. One of the most precise industry statistics reflective of these trends is provided by the American Electronics Association (AEA), the representative organization of electronics manufacturing companies in the United States. Based on the relatively new U.S. North American Industrial Classification System (NAICS), the AEA defines the high-tech industry along three major general production-related groupings—manufacturing, communications services, and software and tech services—altogether comprising 49 product groups (AEA 2003a; see Table 2.1).

A closer look at the categories listed in Table 2.1 reveals that the sectoral division of labor cannot be analyzed along the lines of clearly defined different processes of production, as, for instance, in the relationship between automobile manufacturers and their suppliers in various industries such as steel, sheet metal, and plastics manufacturing or automotive electronics. One general distinction can be made between the production of microchips and electronics systems manufacturing. The chip industry ("Semiconductors and Related Devices," NAICS 334413) is the core of the electronics industry's production system, with highly specialized know-how in manufacturing processes and notoriously high cost of investment.

However, within this category there are at least three types of companies with very different models of production. Integrated device manufacturers (IDMs), such as Intel, AMD, Renesas, or Infineon, integrate product development and massive manufacturing operations, employing both manufacturing workers and engineers in large numbers. In contrast to the IDM firms, so-called "fabless" chip producers are mere design houses with no manufacturing at all (e.g., Qualcomm and Broadcomm in communications chips, or Nvidia and ATI in graphic chips). A third group is the "foundries," contract manufacturers for chips that are mostly working for the aforementioned fabless chip makers. Foundries typically are not directly engaged in product development; rather, they are expert in highly sophisticated manufacturing know-how, including substantial capabilities in the engineering of manufacturing processes and manufacturing-related elements of product development.

In most segments of electronics systems manufacturing, such as "Computer & Peripheral Equipment," "Communications Equipment," "Consumer Electronics," and in most "Electronic Components," manufacturing processes are generic and well known throughout the industry. Core processes in these fields include the assembly of printed circuit boards ("Printed Circuit Assembly," NAICS 334418), currently mostly performed on highly automated machinery based on Surface Mount Technology (SMT); and the assembly of hardware systems (often called "box-build"; included in "Electronic

TABLE 2.1. Statistical Definition of the High-Tech Industry

MANUFACTURING

Computers & Peripheral Equipment: Electronic Computers (334111)[a]; Computer Storage Devices (334112); Computer Terminals (334113); Other Computer Peripheral Equipment (334119)

Communications Equipment: Telephone Apparatus (334210); Radio and TV Broadcasting & Wireless Communications Equipment (334220); Other Communications Equipment (334290); Fiber Optic Cables (335921)

Consumer Electronics: Audio & Video Equipment (334310)

Electronic Components: Electron Tubes (334411); Bare Printed Circuit Boards (334412); Electronic Capacitors (334414); Electronic Resistors (334415); Electronic Coils, Transformers, & Other Inductors (334416); Electronic Connectors (334417); Printed Circuit Assembly (334418); Other Electronic Components (334419)

Semiconductors: Semiconductors and Related Devices (334413); Semiconductor Machinery (333295)

Defense Electronics: Search, Detection, Navigation, Guidance, Aeronautical, and Nautical Systems and Instruments (334511)

Measuring & Control Instruments: Automated Environmental Controls (334512); Industrial Process Control Instruments (334513); Totalizing Fluid Meter and Counting Devices (334514); Electricity Measuring & Testing Equipment (334515); Analytical Laboratory Instruments (334516); Other Measuring & Controlling Devices (334519)

Electromedical Equipment: Electromedical and Electrotherapeutic Apparatus (334510); Irradiation Apparatus (334517)

Photonics: Optical Instrument and Lenses (333314); Photographic & Photocopying Equipment (333315)

COMMUNICATIONS SERVICES

Communications Services: Wired Telecommunications Carriers (517110); Paging Services (517211); Cellular & Other Wireless Telecommunications (517212); Telecommunications Resellers (517310); Satellite Telecommunications (517410); Cable and Other Program Distribution (517510); Other Telecommunications (517910)

SOFTWARE AND TECH SERVICES

Software Publishers: Software Publishers (511210)

Computer Systems Design & Related Services: Custom Computer Programming (541511); Computer Systems Design (541512); Computer Facilities Management (541513); Other Computer Related Services (541519)

Internet Services: Internet Service Providers (518111); Web Search Portals (518112); Data Processing, Hosting, & Related Services (518210)

Engineering Services: Engineering Services (541330)

R&D & Testing Labs: Research & Development in the Physical, Engineering, & Life Sciences (541710); Testing Laboratories (541380)

Computer Training: Computer Training (611420)

---

[a]Numbers are the North American Industrial Classification System (NAICS) codes for the respective category.

Source: Adapted from AEA (2003a).

Computers," NAICS 334111), still mostly done by manual labor on assembly lines or in smaller workgroups, depending on the nature and the volume of the product. The fact that most technologies and processes in electronics systems manufacturing are standardized makes them easily transferable, the basis for the emergence of large-scale contract manufacturing companies. Few pockets in systems manufacturing require highly specialized know-how, especially assembly of disk drives ("Computer Storage Devices," NAICS 334112), manufacturing of raw printed circuits boards ("Bare Printed Circuit

Boards," NAICS 334412), and the assembly of precision machinery in fields such as industrial electronics (e.g., the category, "Measuring & Control Instruments"; see Table 2.1).

However, even in a detailed statistical system such as NAICS, it is difficult to trace the changing industry structure and its impact on workers and communities in high-tech centers. This is particularly true with regard to the labor market. Most NAICS-based industry statistics make it very difficult to differentiate between blue-collar and white-collar segments of the industry, because high-tech manufacturing includes a number of industry segments that have outsourced most manufacturing and thus employ mostly white-collar workers, such as engineers and sales managers (e.g., in "Communications Equipment," or "Consumer Electronics"). Also, industry statistics based on NAICS exclude most temporary workers, who are employed extensively throughout the high-tech industry (see AEA 2003a).

FROM FORDISM TO WINTELISM

Since the 1980s, electronics and IT have undergone massive restructuring; this is at the heart of the sector's accelerated ups and downs, as well as its occasional massive recessions. The industry has been reshaped by new types of companies specializing in hardware and software products for the PC industry, computer servers, Internet equipment, and all kinds of mobile computing devices, like laptops and handheld digital assistants. Such specialized companies were initially created during the 1970s in Silicon Valley in California, particularly among the newly emerging chip companies, such as Intel, National Semiconductor, and AMD, and later in the PC industry, led initially by Apple and later by Microsoft and Compaq. Other than the first generation of computer and electronics companies, such as IBM and Digital Equipment in the United States, Fujitsu in Japan, and Siemens in Germany, many Silicon Valley companies did not produce entire computer systems, but only some key components, such as microprocessors or software operating systems (Ferguson and Morris 1993).

With the PC revolution since the latter half of the 1980s, some of these companies, like Intel, Microsoft, Sun, and Cisco, acquired global dominance. This engendered a massive shift in industry structure, accompanied by a crisis in many older computer companies (most visibly IBM and Digital Equipment) around 1990. Most of the older computer companies designed and produced the key components of their computer systems, including computer chips, operating software, and hardware. With the emergence of specialized technology, in companies like Intel and Microsoft, the computer's production system, and later the telecommunications industry, became increasingly "modular": computers, servers, and Internet routers began to be assembled from standard components like chips, operating software, disk drives, modems, and displays, which can be bought on the open market and assembled and configured in various ways for products of different competitors (Lüthje 2001a). The trend toward modularization mirrors similar developments in other basic manufacturing industries, such as automobile production (Moody

1997). However, in electronics, ultralean production through outsourcing and segmentation of the value chain is much more protracted: electronics and IT are in pioneering positions in relation to most technology-intensive manufacturing.

The electronics industry of the 1990s has been characterized as the "Silicon Valley system" and the "horizontal computer industry" (Grove 1996). Referring to the brand names of Microsoft and Intel, some economists also use the term "Wintelism" (Borrus and Zysman 1997). This concept refers to the strategies of market control developed by the key players of the vertically disintegrated computer industry during the late-1980s and the 1990s. Market control is based on the ability of these companies to define new products by breakthrough technologies or product designs and to secure profits by creating a quasi-monopoly position for a certain period of time (as in the cases of Intel's microprocessor, Microsoft's PC-operating system, and Cisco's Internet router). In addition to older models of monopolistic market control, the proliferation of the respective products is reinforced by technical standardization, which allows a maximum number of downstream developers and manufacturers to cooperate on follow-up and auxiliary products, thereby creating a ripple effect for disseminating the market leaders' "open-but-owned" product architectures (Borrus and Zysman 1997). Manufacturing is no longer considered a core competency for market control. Most of the key companies in the "Wintelist" segments of the industry do not have their own manufacturing; only the very top monopolists like Intel can afford enormous investments in new plants and processes.

Pointing to the combination of networks of specialized companies on the one hand and highly concentrated, large-scale manufacturing complexes on the other, contemporary electronics can be characterized as being based on network-based mass production (Lüthje 2001b; Lüthje, Schumm, and Sproll 2002). The changes in the industry's division of labor under this new regime can be described with four basic facts:

- Most electronics and IT products have become complex commodities, assembled from traded parts and components supplied by various industry segments. The control of the time cycle of new technologies and products has become the industry's chief problem of manufacturing organization.
- As market control has shifted from assemblers to "product definition companies," product innovation is increasingly separated from manufacturing. This also implies that brand-name companies have been losing interest in keeping manufacturing close to their headquarters in industrialized countries.
- In contrast to older industries, like automobile manufacturing, the current electronics industry has no "focal corporations" that coordinate the value chain through their own manufacturing operations. The "supplier pyramid" governed by large-scale, final assemblers is replaced by networks of interacting industry segments. Hierarchy is defined by the flagships' ability to control technological development in key market segments (Borrus, Dieter, and Haggard 2000; Ernst 2002).

- The acceleration of technology and product development has produced enormous instability across the value chain. Rapid expansion through the creation of new product markets is accompanied by old-style cycles of overproduction and surplus capacities—a situation that was at the core of the high-tech industry's massive slump in 2001 and 2002.

FABLESS MANUFACTURING

The growth of the Wintelist industry model has engendered a rapid expansion of subcontracting networks in manufacturing. Traditionally, subcontractors were relatively small firms in high-tech centers like Silicon Valley that assembled printed circuit boards and standard electronic components like resistors, coils, or cables. During the 1990s, a new type of subassembly firm emerged: contract manufacturers (CMs). These companies, which tend to be very large and global in scope, provide integrated manufacturing services for brand-name companies, known in the industry as electronics manufacturing services (EMS). In contrast to traditional subassemblers, CMs provide every element of systems manufacturing, including product engineering, highly automated assembly of printed circuit boards, final assembly and configuration of computers and other electronics devices (box-build), as well as components purchasing, distribution logistics, and repair services (Sturgeon 1997, 1999).

Contract manufacturers have become important players in the production chain, currently accounting for about 15 to 20 percent of global value added in electronics manufacturing. As listed in Table 2.2, these companies have multibillion-dollar revenues. Their toughest competitors are found among another brand of subcontractors called original design manufacturers (ODMs), most of them based in Taiwan, which assemble products for brand-name companies but still own the product design. (These companies, for example, manufacture most of the world's notebook computers sold under brand names like Dell and Compaq/Hewlett-Packard [HP].) The small-scale subcontractor has

TABLE 2.2. Top Ten Electronics Contract Manufacturers, 2003

Company	Country	Revenue (bn[a]US$)	Type of Business
Flextronics	US	13,822	EMS
Solectron	US	11,144	EMS
Foxconn (Hon Hai)	TW	10,899	EMS/OEM
Sanmina-SCI	US	10,795	EMS
Quanta	TW	8,576	ODM
Celestica	CDN	6,735	EMS
Asustek	TW	5,747	ODM/OBM
Jabil Circuit	US	5,170	EMS
Compal	TW	4,760	ODM
Mitac	TW	4,564	ODM

[a]bn, billion.
Source: Adapted from "EB 300: The Rankings," *Electronic Business*, August 1, 2004.

not disappeared, however. Currently, most companies of this kind are concentrated in low-wage manufacturing areas, where they supply cheap, standard components assembled at low wages for CMs and brand-name companies. China's Guangdong province is said to have the largest concentration of such low-end suppliers in the world (Shameen 2003).

The birth of contract manufacturing was marked by IBM's entry into the PC market in 1981. At that time, "Big Blue" (IBM's nickname) contracted the assembly of the motherboards to a no-name manufacturing company, SCI, of Huntsville, Alabama. Since the mid-1980s, some newcomer companies in the computer and network equipment industries in Silicon Valley—Sun and Cisco in particular—have teamed up with specialized contractors like Solectron (a former solar energy company) and Flextronics, who subsequently became leading players in the new industry. Companies like Sun and Cisco are essentially fabless. In other words, they have minimal or no manufacturing capacities of their own, just like brand-name firms in the garment and shoe industries, such as Nike (Sturgeon 1999).

The relationships of contract manufacturers with older brand-name firms in the United States and Europe rapidly developed during the second half of the 1990s. This happened mainly by acquiring entire plants through contract manufacturers from established companies like IBM, Texas Instruments, and Lucent. In 1997, the Swedish telecommunications manufacturer, Ericsson, was the first European, brand-name firm to sell off entire production units, followed by Europe's largest electronics producer, Siemens, which sold an important server manufacturing facility in Germany in 1999 and several other PC and mobile-phone plants in 2000. The slump in the early 2000s in electronics manufacturing because of oversupply of high-volume, low-cost production resulted in a new round of outsourcing deals, led by Ericsson and Alcatel of France in Europe, and Compaq/HP, IBM, and Lucent in the United States.

The rapid expansion has brought about a diverse spectrum of outsourcing relationships. For fabless technology definition companies, such as Cisco, 3Com, and Microsoft (for its X-Box game console), contract manufacturers perform full-scale system manufacturing. Older brand-name companies maintain similar production relationships through their outsourced plants, often competing with their own remaining facilities. Specialized mass-producers in the computer industry like Dell, Compaq, and HP's Computer Systems Division, which still consider final assembly to be an important interface with the customer, use CMs for the large-scale manufacturing of printed circuit boards or preassembled product kits. In addition, such companies outsource systems assembly in key foreign markets, mostly to medium-size local contract manufacturers. The only major brand-name firms that have been cautious about using contract manufacturers have been Japanese and Korean electronics firms, which prefer to rely on subcontractors within their own corporate "families" (Lüthje, Schumm, and Sproll 2002). However, recent trends also indicate a growing trend of contract manufacturing for major Japanese electronics companies, such as Sony's shift in 2003 of its "PlayStation" game console to the Chinese plants of two major Taiwanese assemblers, HonHai (also known under the brand name Foxconn) and Asustek (*South China Morning Post*, March 13, 2003).

The global recession of the early 2000s accelerated the trend toward large-scale outsourcing. In 2001 and 2002, EMS industry's former growth rates of 25 percent or more per year declined to zero, and it even experienced a modest contraction. Since then, however, the business media have been full of news on outsourcing deals between well-known multinational brand-name firms, such as IBM, Ericsson, Lucent, Philips, and Siemens, with major contract manufacturers, indicating that EMS will remain a growth business. In some cases, contract manufacturers have taken on the task of restructuring the supply chains of several major original equipment manufacturers (OEMs) at a time, as in the case of Sanmina-SCI, which took over most PC manufacturing for IBM and also added plants from HP in Europe (*Financial Times*, March 28, 2003). The fastest growing players since have been the CMs from Taiwan, which are said to be most efficient in exploiting the economies of low-cost manufacturing in China. The largest Taiwanese player, Foxconn, has seen revenues grow by up to 60 percent in recent years. According to figures from the government of the People's Republic of China (*People's Daily*, June 16, 2003), the company has become the mainland's second largest exporter; its campus in the southern high-tech metropolis of Shenzhen houses tens of thousands of workers.

It should be noted, however, that outsourcing is not only becoming dominant at the lower and mid-tiers of the electronics food chain but also in the technological core of the electronics industry, chip making. In this industry segment, a new generation of chip companies emerged during the 1980s—mostly in Silicon Valley and other U.S. high-tech centers—which focused exclusively on the design of specialized chips, mostly Application Specific Integrated Circuits (ASICs). In the face of the explosion of investment costs for new automated chip plants during this period, these companies were established and grew without owning any fabrication facilities (Angel 1994). The fabless chip companies became one of the largest success stories in the electronics industry since the late 1980s and an important factor for the resurgence of the U.S. chip industry *vis-à-vis* the massive competition from Japanese and Korean chip firms. Fabless chip makers farmed out manufacturing to foundries.

The contract manufacturers include some of the established "fab-owning" chip producers selling excess capacities and companies, mostly based in Taiwan or Singapore, which exclusively manufacture chips by contract (Mazurek 1999). The chip foundry phenomenon is behind Taiwan's rise to become a global powerhouse in chip manufacturing during the second half of the 1990s. The lead companies of this industry, such as Taiwan Semiconductor Manufacturing Co. (TSMC) and United Microelectronics Corp. (UMC), are among the world's foremost chip makers, with a reputation for having the most advanced and efficient manufacturing processes.

GLOBAL FLAGSHIP NETWORKS

The developments described here also have caused massive changes in the global division of labor in the electronics industry. Historically, the electronics industry had been on the forefront of shifting labor-intensive assembly work to low-cost locations in Third World countries. Starting in the 1960s and 1970s, the growth of offshore assembly shaped what then was called the "New International Division of Labor" (cf. Fröbel, Heinrichs, and Kreye, 1977). U.S. merchant chip makers from Silicon Valley were among the first to build global manufacturing organizations with relatively large chip assembly plants in Asian locations, especially in Hong Kong, Singapore, the Philippines, and Malaysia (Ernst 1983). These plants often employed thousands of workers—most of them women—who were considered best suited for the tedious work of wiring tiny microchips (see Photo 2.1). The workplace in these plants in many ways resembled the assembly lines of early twentieth-century capitalism; they mostly consisted of manual labor with very segmented tasks and supervisors' and managers' strict control over the workers. In the chip industry, those plants mostly performed the back-end work of packaging chip wafers into little plastic cases, including wiring, soldering, and testing. The more sophisticated elements of chip making, design, prototyping, and wafer fabrication were located close to the headquarters of major chip makers in regions like Silicon Valley and other emerging chip-production centers in the western United States, such as Austin, Texas; Portland, Oregon; and Phoenix, Arizona (Henderson 1989).

With the massive further globalization of production throughout the 1980s and 1990s, the international division of labor has changed significantly. The

PHOTO 2.1. Women assembly workers in an electronics factory, China. Courtesy of Apo Leong, Asia Monitor Resource Centre.

"global assembly line" has been superseded by complex "systemic" (Ernst 1997) forms of international production that link local and regional industry clusters with global strategies of product development and marketing. Most high-tech districts in industrialized and newly industrializing countries develop certain competitive advantages with regard to the manufacturing and the design of specific products or components, like Silicon Valley in chip development and semiconductor machinery, Singapore in hard-disk drives (HDDs), and Taiwan in motherboards and notebook computers (Lüthje, Schumm, and Sproll 2002). These regions combine their strengths in a specific segment of electronics with cost- and logistics-related advantages, like low wages, proximity to certain key markets, and well-developed infrastructure in air, sea, or road transport, offering a global infrastructure for brand-name companies to locate and optimize production along a complex set of parameters, including wages, transportation and communication costs, taxes, tax benefits and government subsidies, tariffs, and political stability.

This shift in the international division of labor has been closely related to the overall trend of vertical specialization in the electronics industry. As Borrus, Ernst, and others have explained in detail, the vertically specialized industry model of the 1990s was essentially based on global or cross-national production networks (Borrus, Dieter, and Haggard 2000). The developments of the last five to ten years have been characterized by the demise of the traditional type of integrated, multinational manufacturing companies, like IBM, General Electric, and Philips as the driving force behind the internationalization of production. As these companies have lost important terrain to specialized newcomers from Silicon Valley and other high-tech regions, global production increasingly has become based on networks of interacting companies and suppliers, controlled by certain "flagship" companies (Ernst 2002). A typical example of such a flagship company is Cisco, the world-market leader in Internet-switching equipment. This company commands a vast network of suppliers in product development, software design, and even basic research. At the same time, it is almost entirely fabless; more than 95 percent of the manufacturing of Cisco routers, switches, and peripherals is performed by a network of contract and ODMs in about 15 locations worldwide.

In this context, specific forms of global production are emerging in various segments of the electronics industry. The "international division of labor" established during the 1970s still prevails among chip makers with fabrication facilities of their own (IDMs). Companies such as Intel and AMD still maintain a very strong concentration of core technological processes like design, prototyping, and wafer manufacturing in the United States and, in European locations, like the new microelectronics complex in Dresden, East Germany. The massive plants of these players in Asia and some places in Latin America (e.g., Costa Rica) mostly perform assembly functions; however, the current highly automated environment is very different from that of the 1970s and 1980s (Lüthje 2001b).

As opposed to the fab-owning segment of the chip industry, the contract foundry industry has engaged in a full-scale shift of wafer fabrication, the core manufacturing process of chip making, to newly industrializing countries.

The wafer fabs maintained by companies like TSMC and UMC in Taiwan, Chartered Semiconductor in Singapore, and Silterra in Malaysia feature fully integrated manufacturing and development capabilities at the highest technological standards. In this industry segment, the trend toward full-scale outsourcing induced by the rapidly rising investment costs has driven technology transfer to newly industrializing countries at a pace and scope that seemed unthinkable a decade ago (Ernst 2002). This trend was accelerated by the recession of the early 2000s. As investment costs for new chip plants easily can reach US$3 billion each and more, even the most cash-rich, integrated manufacturers are increasing their outsourcing rapidly. The German chip maker Infineon, for instance, plans to triple its outsourcing volume to at least 30 percent of its total production, to reduce future losses from overcapacities, as experienced during the downturn of 2001 (*Business Week*, November 3, 2003).

The relationship between the large-scale outsourcing on the part of global brand-name leaders and the transfer of integrated manufacturing capabilities to low-cost countries is equally visible in the EMS industry. At an even larger geographical scope, contract manufacturing companies offer "one-stop shopping" for production, design, and logistics services to multinational OEM customers. This has resulted in a massive buildup of integrated manufacturing capacities in low-cost countries in every major region of the world market, particularly in Malaysia, China, Mexico, and Hungary. Most of these plants—many of them full-scale industrial parks—offer a wide spectrum of manufacturing and support functions, such as printed circuit-board assembly, final assembly (box-build), metal stamping, plastic injection molding, and manufacturing of raw printed circuit boards, including the related functions of process, component, and software engineering. Propelled by the recent recession, there is also an increasing array of higher end production, including prototyping and product introduction, moving to these regions. As we can generalize, at the manufacturing end of global production networks, there is a massive vertical reintegration of work processes, bringing back integrated mass production as we know it from the age of "Fordism," albeit in new fashion, in a number of manufacturing centers in low-wage countries (Lüthje 2002a; Sproll 2003).

One important trend in this field is the massive shifting of engineering work to developing countries. Here, manufacturing-related segments of the electronics industry are now following the software industry, which since the 1990s has seen a large-scale shift of low- and mid-end engineering work to developing countries, particularly to India with its "software capital" of Bangalore. Similar trends are currently underway in the engineering of electronics hardware and components, most prominently in chip design, resulting in an ongoing shift of relatively well-paying engineering and design jobs away from industrialized countries. The increased fears of a "great tech job exodus" (Beckman 2003; Müller 2003) among the higher skilled "knowledge workers" in electronics centers in the United States, Europe, and Japan is a direct result of outsourcing strategies based on the ongoing fragmentation and global relocation of the production systems described here.

THE CHALLENGE: CONTROLLING NETWORKS
OF MASS PRODUCTION

The high-tech industry of the twenty-first century has developed into a global system of network-based mass production that combines decentralized and highly flexible forms of industry organization with traditional economies of manufacturing in large-scale plants and corporations. The most striking feature of this development is that modern mass production is increasingly concentrated in a number of high-tech regions in low-cost countries (China, Malaysia, Mexico, and Hungary, in particular), where highly integrated plants with state-of-the-art manufacturing technology are employing thousands of workers. In the industrialized countries, the large-scale shift of manufacturing resources creates the impression that high-tech is becoming a "postindustrial" service industry based on networks of specialized, fabless, and science-based companies. A global perspective, however, reveals that the specialization at the top of global production systems is matched by an increasing vertical integration at the bottom (i.e., in mass-manufacturing plants in low-cost regions). At the same time, an increasing amount of engineering work has shifted to low-cost countries, creating hierarchies in the division of labor usually found in manufacturing industries.

The simultaneous process of specialization and global reintegration has not only reshaped the electronics industry's model of production significantly but also reinforced the chronic economic instability of high-tech. The bursting of the high-tech "bubble" during the first few years of the twenty-first century was not only a result of unprecedented speculation and overblown profit expectations, caused by largely uncontrolled financial markets (Brenner 2002) but also was related to the production system's profound transformation during the 1990s. On the one hand, the increasing separation of technological design and development, marketing, and market control from manufacturing has enabled brand-name companies to play a game of "breakthrough innovations" and extra profits at an ever faster pace. On the other hand, the massive movement of manufacturing to global networks toward subcontracting has shifted the risk of the Wintelist industry system to no-name contract manufacturers and the workers and communities in their major manufacturing locations. Set against this background, the big divide in the era of Wintelism is the increasing separation of brand-name control from the social and ecological impact of high-tech manufacturing.

For environmental and labor activists in the high-tech industry, this creates a whole set of new challenges. The following chapters of this book discuss the changing conditions from a variety of perspectives. The common problem encapsulated in the question of how to establish or reestablish social and political control over a global production system that is becoming both more concentrated and more fragmented at the same time. One key question—well known by other industries based on global networks of subcontracting like garment, toys, and sports shoes—is how to hold brand-name producers responsible for the labor, safety, and environmental conditions in and around their subcontractors' plants. However, the complexity of the high-tech industry makes this task much more difficult than in the aforementioned industries.

One example of this phenomenon is the plant closures and relocations of work in the first few years of the twenty-first century in U.S. and European high-tech manufacturing centers. In the United States, not one contract manufacturing plant is represented by a union. Although contract manufacturing became an important production infrastructure for all kinds of electronics-related manufacturing (besides computers, telecommunications, industrial, and automotive electronics), U.S. unions never considered organizing drives in this new industry—even as AFL–CIO President Sweeney and major unions were talking frequently about organizing the new U.S. low-wage force during the late 1990s. When Lucent sold a former key plant in North Andover, Massachusetts, to Solectron in 2002, unionized workers responded with broad community-based action but never saw any serious effort by their international union (the Communications Workers of America [CWA]) to raise the question of electronics manufacturing outsourcing as a strategic problem for major U.S. unions in key manufacturing industries. In Europe, even well-established unions like IG Metall in Germany lost its presence in plants that were sold from multinationals, such as Siemens, to contract manufacturers. In spring 2004, Siemens threatened to close its last remaining phone manufacturing factory in Germany by shifting the work to low-cost locations in Hungary, mostly to contract manufacturer Flextronics. In a highly politicized conflict, Siemens wrenched massive concessions from its workers, including wage cuts and a drastic increase in weekly working hours. Now, after such devastating experiences affecting their core membership, IG Metall and the International Metal Workers Federation are beginning to discuss organizing strategies in the contract-manufacturing sector (see Steiert, this volume).

Reestablishing social and ecological control over current global production systems of high-tech is linked to the massive challenge of organizing and reorganizing union representation and a viable workers' movement in the electronics industry's centers of production. At the same time, the size and key position of electronics and IT for technological, industrial, and social development call for a new set of national and international industrial policies that link control over technological development and markets with establishing and reinforcing social standards of work in the industry. Such challenges have existed in many advanced manufacturing industries in the more developed countries for some time. Today, the global scope of production networks in high-tech calls for genuine, global strategies of advocacy, policymaking, and control.

NOTE

This chapter emerged from work of the Institute of Social Research project on electronics contract manufacturing, sponsored by the German research foundation DFG. My thanks for continued cooperation, discussions, and comments to the members of this group, Wilhelm Schumm, Martina Sproll, Stefanie Hürtgen, and Peter Pawlicki.

3   Occupational Health in the Semiconductor Industry

HUNDREDS OF CHEMICALS, metals, and toxic gases are used in the semiconductor industry, which also subjects workers to radiation exposures, as well as ergonomic and other occupational stressors. However, because of its rapid development, and its obsession with secrecy, the internal workings of the industry are poorly understood. Only a few articles on industrial hygiene and occupational and environmental health and safety in this industry have been published, and these have been mostly limited to the United States. With rare exceptions, Asia and Europe have neither reported accurate rates of illness and injury nor published the results of industry or academic institutional research on health and safety issues (see Watterson; Ferus-Comelo; Foran and Sonnenfeld; Leong and Pandita, this volume). This chapter reviews the industry's occupational health issues, summarizes findings from the few existing studies that have failed to look specifically at clean room workers' health, and documents disclosures from IBM's recent widely publicized trial (see also Hawes and Pellow, this volume).

OCCUPATIONAL HEALTH: AN OVERVIEW

Semiconductor-chip making is a light manufacturing operation. Workers incur fewer severe work-related injuries than do workers in heavier manufacturing. Nonetheless, they are at high risk for musculoskeletal pain and injuries. Upper-extremity symptoms are common among fabrication workers, and have a dose–response relationship with hours of work per day (Pocekay et al. 1995). In a study in Malaysia, musculoskeletal pain and injuries occurred in the majority of semiconductor workers (Chee, Rampal, and Chandrasakaran 2004). Significant associations were found between prolonged standing and leg pain, between prolonged sitting and neck and shoulder pain, and between prolonged bending and shoulder, arm, back, and leg pain (Chee and Rampal 2004).

Occupational illnesses are common among electronics workers, particularly semiconductor workers. The U.S. Bureau of Labor Statistics (BLS) reported that, averaged across all manufacturing industries, occupational illnesses accounted for 6.3 percent of all work-loss cases in 2001. The rate in the electronics industry was higher, 9.5 percent, and the rate in the semiconductor component was higher yet, 15.4 percent (see Table 3.1). Moreover, a study of the reporting of occupational illnesses in California found that semiconductor companies properly reported less than half of all cases that

TABLE 3.1. Work-loss Occupational Illnesses as Percentages of All Reported Injuries and Illnesses

	1997	1998	1999	2000	2001
All Manufacturing Industries	6.1	5.9	6.1	6.1	6.3
Electronic Components and Accessories (367)	8.4	7.5	10.0	8.3	9.5
Semiconductor and Related Devices (3674)	12.3	9.2	14.9	9.9	15.4

Source: Bureau of Labor Statistics, U.S. Department of Labor, 2003.

should have been reported by Occupational Safety and Health Administration (OSHA) criteria (McCurdy, Schenker, and Samuels 1991). In a similar study in California, work-related carpal tunnel syndrome cases were found to be underreported by a factor of 6:1. Employer health insurance, rather than workers' compensation, was the source of payment for most medical bills (Maizlish et al. 1995). Such underreporting is likely to underlie the pattern of employers' reluctance to institute preventive measures, because the true impact of the workplace on worker health is not disclosed to regulatory agencies empowered to require such measures.

BLS data for 2001 showed that 2.4 percent of work-loss cases for workers in all manufacturing industries were the result of "exposure to caustic, noxious, or allergenic substances." The corresponding rate for the electronics industry was much higher, 6.2 percent, and for semiconductor workers it was 8.5 percent (Table 3.2). These occupational illness data reflect the widespread use of toxic materials in the semiconductor industry. The manufacture of integrated circuits requires the use of many metals, chemicals, and toxic gases in a wide variety of combinations and plant settings.

It has not been possible to learn what happens to health and safety safeguards when industries in developed countries transfer their manufacturing operations to developing countries, but it is clear that occupational injuries and diseases are grossly underreported in most developing countries. Workers in all countries should be entitled to the basic benefits of health and safety laws, including workers' compensation. At present, very few workers in developing countries have such protections.

TABLE 3.2. Percentages of Work-loss Injuries and Illnesses Involving Exposures to Caustic, Noxious, or Allergenic Substances

	1997	1998	1999	2000	2001
All Manufacturing Industries	2.6	2.5	2.4	2.2	2.4
Electronic Components and Accessories (367)	5.1	7.3	6.0	7.6	6.2
Semiconductor and Related Devices (3674)	8.4	8.6	9.7	7.7	8.5

Source: Bureau of Labor Statistics, U.S. Department of Labor, 2003.

THE EARLY YEARS

During the early years of the semiconductor industry, it was the general policy of the companies to keep secret the chemicals and processes they used. A company seldom had more than a nurse to provide medical care on site, and practicing physicians who were referred cases of illness or injury were told little or nothing about the nature of the work environment. By the mid-1970s, reports of chemical exposures among production workers had begun to surface. In 1979, four workers repeatedly exposed to chemical fumes and vapors at the Signetics plant in Sunnyvale, California, were required to spend a full year sitting in the company cafeteria, drawing full pay but doing no work. Signetics' rationale for this personnel decision to limit workers' compensation benefits may seem obscure, but it should be noted that the company avoided not only paying workers' compensation benefits but also having to report to the State of California some 1,000 lost days of work due to chemical exposures in a single year. The National Institute for Occupational Safety and Health (NIOSH) health hazard evaluation was begun at the request of the Electronics Committee on Safety and Health (ECOSH). This first ever investigation of an electronics manufacturer, however, received only limited cooperation from the company. The NIOSH medical investigators observed that "because of the restrictions placed on the investigation [by Signetics] the true population at risk and the true population affected could not be satisfactorily identified." The investigation concluded that "a significant occupationally-related health problem" existed at the Signetics facility and recommended further study which was never done (NIOSH 1980).

The first publication addressing occupational health in the semiconductor industry was a report based on a survey conducted by the California Department of Industrial Relations in 1981 (Wade et al. 1981). Participating companies carefully limited their cooperation, but the survey nonetheless brought to light a number of high-risk chemical exposures, as well as a list of carcinogens and reproductive toxicants used in semiconductor-chip manufacture. The list included arsenic, asbestos, beryllium, chromium, nickel, carbon tetrachloride, glycol ethers, and many other chemicals and gases. There was no discussion of the nature or extent of worker exposures to these chemicals, metals, and gases, and this very limited survey provided neither industrial hygiene exposure data nor worker health data.

The first report of potential health problems appeared in the medical literature in 1983. It described a study of the workers' compensation experience of the semiconductor industry in California and included a partial description of workplace exposure hazards (LaDou 1983). At that time, the incidence rates of occupational illnesses in semiconductor workers were three times higher than the average for other manufacturing industries in California, and their incidence rates of "systemic poisoning" from chemical exposures were six times higher. Indeed, the semiconductor industry's rate of chemical-related illness was higher than that of any other single industry. It was then apparent that semiconductor manufacturing was not the "clean" industry the public had been led to believe it was. In fact, it is one of the most chemical-intensive industries ever developed.

A later publication extended the list of chemicals of concern as carcinogens and reproductive toxicants to include benzene, chloroform, dichloromethane (methylene chloride), 1,4-dioxane, tetrachloroethylene, trichloroethylene, epichlorohydrin, formaldehyde, and cadmium compounds. Epoxy resin systems widely used in the encapsulation of chips added more chemicals to the list, including glycidyl ethers, ethylene oxide, propylene oxide, 3,4-epoxy-1-butene, 2,3-epoxyhexadecane, m-phenylenediamine (MPDA), 4,4' methylenedianiline (MDA), diaminodiphenylsulfone (DADDPS, DDS, dapsone), o-toluidine, 2,4-toluene diamine, methylenebis-o-chloroaniline (MOCA), benzidine, urea-formaldehyde, and quinones (Garabrant and Olin 1986).

REPRODUCTIVE STUDIES

Because many semiconductor workers are women of childbearing age, the risk of adverse reproductive outcomes was examined among workers at Digital Equipment Corporation (DEC) in Massachusetts. Personal interviews were conducted with manufacturing workers, spouses of male workers, and an internal comparison group of nonmanufacturing workers (Pastides et al. 1988). Elevated rates of spontaneous abortion were observed for women working in clean rooms (31.3 abortions per 100 pregnancies for photolithographic workers; 38.9, for diffusion workers; and 17.8, for unexposed women). No other significant difference in reproductive outcomes was identified. The authors stressed the tentative nature of their findings and called for more definitive studies. National publicity spurred the major semiconductor companies to respond with further studies of their own.

IBM, then and now one of the largest semiconductor manufacturers in the world, engaged the School of Hygiene and Public Health at Johns Hopkins University to study reproductive problems among IBM employees. The retrospective portion of the study, conducted at facilities in New York and Vermont, was reported in 1992 (Gray 1993). It showed an increased rate of spontaneous abortion among women who worked in two specific clean-room areas (see also Corn and Cohen 1993; Correa et al. 1996). For reasons that remain unclear, birth defects, cancer, and other health measures were not studied. The small prospective reproductive study included few spontaneous abortions, giving an equivocal result.

The Semiconductor Industry Association (SIA) sponsored researchers at the University of California, Davis, to conduct a retrospective cohort study of 6,088 women in some of the SIA member companies (Schenker 1992). In this group, there had been 904 eligible pregnancies, and 113 of these pregnancies had resulted in spontaneous abortions eligible for inclusion in the analysis. The crude risk ratio (RR) for women working in fabrication versus nonfabrication areas was 1.43 (95 percent confidence interval [CI] $= 0.95$–2.09). This study provided the most compelling demonstration to date that semiconductor manufacturing work is associated with a reproductive risk (see also Schenker et al. 1995). The excess occurred in settings where industrial hygiene air measurements were in compliance with current occupational standards. This suggests several possibilities, none of them welcome: that present standards are inadequately protective, that routes of exposure not included in the standards are important, that the relevant agents were not measured, and that agents are acting with an unexpected synergy.

The SIA would not support research activity by the UC Davis team beyond that of a reproductive study. During the planning phase of the SIA study, it was agreed that the study would be a comprehensive assessment of all health parameters. Years later, it was learned that the SIA had controlled the allocation of research funds, limiting the funding to no more than 20 percent for studies of health issues other than spontaneous abortion (LaDou 2000). The use of this stratagem to limit the scope of the study was strongly criticized by health and safety experts, but their concerns fell on deaf ears.

IBM and the SIA attribute the reproductive findings to previous exposures of the workers to ethylene glycol ethers, and by the mid-1990s could state that these solvents were no longer used by their member companies in the United States. Yet in Taiwan and other Asian countries, glycol ethers are still used as the major solvents in the electronics industry. More than 3,000 tons of the most toxic of the glycol ethers are used annually in Taiwan. Large quantities of hazardous chemicals such as glycol ethers, acetone, and dimethyl formamide are used in Asia as raw materials. The Taiwanese electronics industry accounts for more than 90 percent of the total use of glycol ethers in that highly industrialized country (Loh et al. 2004). Many of the outdated technologies are exported to newly industrialized countries as newer technologies are installed in the more highly developed industries of Japan, the United States, and Europe. Thus there is particular concern about the many workers, mostly in countries that do not enforce occupational health and safety regulations, who have inherited jobs that use chemicals, technologies, and equipment that are no longer acceptable in developed countries. Equally disturbing are reports that several of the so-called safe substitute propylene glycol ethers have carcinogenic or developmental toxicity. For example, in June 2004, California's Proposition 65 listed propylene glycol mono-t-butyl ether as a chemical known to the State to cause cancer; as of mid-2005 the National Library of Science's Haz-Map database listed propylene glycol monomethyl ether as a reproductive toxicant (see www.hazmap.com; accessed October 12, 2005).

For more than a decade, the semiconductor industry has refused to conduct follow-up studies that would reassure the public health community that the reproductive problem reported by both the SIA study and the IBM study was corrected by removing the ethylene glycol ether solvents from their manufacturing processes in favor of other solvents including propylene glycol ethers. Since its inception, the industry also has failed to conduct any studies of birth defects, despite the fact that most production workers are women of childbearing age. This failure to conduct studies also extends to the industry's refusal to assess the incidence rates of birth defects among workers' offspring through the use of birth defects registries in states where large numbers of workers live. The U.S. Environmental Protection Agency (EPA) sponsored a program known as the Common Sense Initiative that sought to involve various industries in planning and implementing health research projects. The EPA, working with California's Department of Health Services, developed a broad-based community consensus proposal to utilize California's Health Registries to study the rates at which disease occurs among electronics workers and their families. The purpose of the study was to develop a record-keeping system with which the computer and electronics industries could monitor incidence rates for cancers, birth defects, and other health parameters. Before the study could move forward, however, an industry group defeated the proposal in 1998 and gave the EPA little hope of further cooperation (LaDou 1998).

CANCER STUDIES

Semiconductor workers may be subject to risks of occupational cancers in parallel with the risks of occupational reproductive effects. In one early study, Vågerö and Olin (1983) evaluated the general cancer incidence pattern in the electronics industry. They used the Swedish Cancer Environmental Registry, which was created by linking the 1960 census to the Swedish Cancer Registry of 1961 to 1973. All subjects who were classified in the census as working in the electronics or electrical manufacturing industry in 1960 were compared with the general population ages 15 to 64. The study population included 54,624 men and 18,478 women, for whom 1,855 and 1,009 reports of cancers were identified, respectively. The control population contained more than three million individuals. The total risk estimates were 1.15 for men and 1.08 for women, but the relative risk estimates for lung cancer, bladder cancer, and malignant melanoma were significantly increased to 1.52, 1.22, and 1.35, respectively. A subpopulation of workers was further examined with regard to cancers of the mouth, pharynx, and respiratory system. Among males, the incidence of lung tumors was moderately but significantly elevated (RR = 1.36). There were 13 cases of pharyngeal cancers, yielding a risk estimate of 3.0. In a subgroup composed of workers who largely held assembly jobs, there were five nasal cancers, representing more than a fourfold risk increase.

IBM Cancer Studies

In 1985, a chemist working in the Material Analysis Department at the IBM research facility in San Jose, California, wrote a memo to IBM Corporate Headquarters (Adams 1996), alerting IBM officials to a cluster of cancers that his colleagues had experienced. Among the group of 12 workers in a research and development laboratory, two had died of brain cancer, two had died of lymphatic cancer, and two had died of gastrointestinal cancers. When two more developed bone tumors and the group's leader later died of brain cancer, the survivors pressed hard to bring IBM's attention to the issue. Although such clusters are notoriously difficult to evaluate, this set of events was particularly striking. IBM researchers and consultants have known about the cluster for many years.

IBM also commissioned a study of brain cancer mortality among electronics workers (Beall et al. 1996). The IBM Corporate Mortality File cited in the study report recorded deaths for virtually all U.S. IBM employees, from outside sales agents never exposed to chemicals to the bunny-suited workers in the clean rooms. The study had severe limitations. Information about specific agents the workers had been exposed to in their work environments, such as electromagnetic fields (EMF), ionizing radiation, or chemical agents, was not available. The IBM study did find that mortality from brain cancer among male electronics workers increased as the duration of employment in "technical jobs" lengthened. This is consistent with trends previously reported by Thomas et al. (1987): namely, that the risk of dying from brain cancer is highest among electrical and electronics workers with long-term work histories—specifically, those of ten years or more—and with probable exposures to solders and organic solvents. The Thomas et al. study found that the risk of astrocytic tumors among electronics manufacture and repair workers was increased tenfold among those employed for 20 years or more.

THE HSE STUDY

In late 2001, the Health and Safety Executive (HSE) of the United Kingdom announced the results of its study of cancer rates in a small sample of workers at the National Semiconductor (NSUK) plant at Greenock in Scotland (HSE 2001). That study found that the overall mortality rate from all causes of death was lower among semiconductor workers than it was for Scotland as a whole, though the total incidence of cancer was about the same. However, HSE identified higher than expected incidences of three particular types of cancers among women workers and one type in men. There were 11 cases of lung cancer in women—two to three times as many as expected; three cases of stomach cancer—four or five times as many as expected; and 20 cases of breast cancer—five more than expected; as well as three deaths from brain cancer among men—about four times as many as expected. No important excess of any other type of cancer was identified.

A very small group of employees was used in the HSE study, and a substantial fraction of them had little or no exposure to the chemicals of concern. The HSE investigators simply defined all NSUK Greenock employees as subjects, thereby seriously limiting the opportunities to demonstrate increased cancer risks in the workers who were most heavily exposed.

The small sample size and weak study design concerned many of us who had reviewed the HSE study proposal (see Bailar et al. 2000). Still, the results substantially reinforce the concerns that prompted the investigation and suggest work-related causes for several kinds of cancer. It is remarkable that four apparent excesses in cancer were found in a study with a weak design and a total of only 71 deaths. However, the relative risks are still subject to very wide uncertainty, and the range of effects (including other cancers and other causes of death) may be substantially larger or smaller than the present data indicate. Cancers are fairly common (except for brain cancer) at three of the sites reported, and important, but small increases in less common sites could have been missed simply because the study was too small to detect them. The somewhat low total mortality rate (presumably a healthy-worker effect), with a near-average cancer registration rate, suggests the possibility of some real elevation in the cancer risks over what these specific workers might otherwise have experienced.

For cancers, as for reproductive toxicity, the very limited research is a reason for concern. Though the findings are not conclusive, it is clear that more detailed studies are urgently needed to determine whether there is a workplace risk, and if so, to determine its specific nature and size. In a news release dated 11 December 2001, NSUK stated, "there was no scientific evidence of increased cancer risk for employees working at our facility" [available on the company's Web site]. This is the very outcome that Bailar and his colleagues (2000) warned against when the study was proposed—that a small, poorly designed study with little chance of netting definitive findings would be used to argue against doing it right. Fisher (2002) emphasized,

> It is too early for the HSE investigators to characterize a 4-fold excess of brain cancer deaths as "probably not work-related." It is critical that future cancer studies of the semiconductor industry investigate possible associations between solvent exposure and brain cancer. (p. 96)

When the HSE published the results of its cancer study at NSUK, it announced that it would inspect all UK semiconductor plants over the course of the following year. The HSE inspected 25 plants operated by 22 different companies. Twenty-two percent of the plants failed to meet minimum legal requirements for provision of health care, ventilation, and health surveillance. Only five plants complied with minimum legal requirements for every issue inspected. As a result, the HSE issued 13 improvement notices and one prohibition notice to five of the companies. HSE inspectors were critical of the standard of occupational health services. Many of the plant physicians and nurses used by the companies were part-time and were employed by outside entities, not by the companies themselves. Most of the doctors were general practitioners, some of whom had never even visited the plants. Exposures to dangerous substances in the plants were not adequately monitored. In the case of arsenic, a carcinogen widely used by British semiconductor companies, "there was virtually no keeping of health records. This is particularly worrying given that the industry has consistently disputed that the cancers suffered by its workers are work-related" (Watterson, LaDou, and PHASE Two 2003, 393).

IBM ON TRIAL

In 2003, a suit against IBM involving two plaintiffs with cancer, James Moore (with non-Hodgkin's lymphoma) and Alida Hernandez (with breast cancer), came before a jury in San Jose, California. In the course of legal discovery, attorneys for the plaintiffs asked for employee records, and the court granted access to the same Corporate Mortality File on IBM employees in the United States, dating back more than 30 years that Beall and Delzell had relied on for their study (Beall et al. 1996). IBM had attempted to block plaintiff attorneys' access to the file, maintaining that it contained no helpful data, but was overruled. The case was widely reported in the news media as were many of the findings of the Clapp and Johnson study, leading IBM officials to respond that, "In a workforce as large as IBM's, many workers will, by simple chance, contract unusual diseases" (McKie 2004). "There's no evidence that any workers' illnesses were caused by their work at IBM" (McCook 2004).

Once access was granted, attorneys for the plaintiffs asked epidemiologists Clapp and Johnson to study IBM's Corporate Mortality File. In two declarations submitted to the Court and now part of the public record, Dr. Clapp presented findings from this research (Clapp 2003a, 2003b). He and Johnson found patterns of mortality in the IBM workforce consistent with occupational exposures to solvents and other carcinogenic materials used in IBM manufacturing processes. The files contained data on decedents between 1969 and early 2001. The final number of records used for analysis was 31,961, and comprised 27,288 males and 4,673 females. There had been 7,703 cancer deaths in men, where 7,208 would have been expected (proportionate mortality ratio [PMR] = 106.9; 95 percent CI = 104.9–108.9; 99 percent CI = 104.2–109.6). Among the females there were 1,668 cancer deaths compared to 1,455 expected (PMR = 114.6; 95 percent CI = 110.3–119.2; 99 percent CI = 108.9–120.6). PMRs for all sites were found to be significantly elevated when the IBM workers were compared with the U.S. population.

There was excess mortality in IBM males due to cancers of the large intestine, pancreas, kidney, testis, thyroid, central nervous system, and all lymphatic and hematopoietic tissues, and melanoma. In females, there was excess mortality due to cancers of the lungs and bronchus, breast, other female organs, and central nervous system, and all lymphatic and hematopoietic tissues. The types of cancers that increased the most were consistent with the findings of other studies of semiconductor workers and studies of workers in other industries exposed to the same chemicals. Key findings were the excess deaths due to brain, kidney, lymphatic, and hematopoietic cancers and melanoma. Another stunning finding was a significant excess of breast cancer deaths in female manufacturing workers at the San Jose plant, where plaintiff Alida Hernandez worked for 15 years prior to her breast cancer diagnosis (Clapp 2003a, 2003b).

After pretrial hearings, and a review of Clapp's declarations, Judge Robert A. Baines ruled that the analysis of IBM's Corporate Mortality File data contained in Dr. Clapp's public Court declarations was inadmissible as evidence in the trial:

> This same study, again, assuming that it is a valid study, could be used to show any number of things, such as if . . . everyone in manufacturing drank coffee in the company cafeteria . . . coffee served in the company lunch-room causes cancer. (Regalado and Bulkeley 2004)

In an editorial in *Science*, Donald Kennedy stated that, "The judge refused to admit these findings, calling them irrelevant and prejudicial, thus combining a scientific judgment with a legal one" (Kennedy 2004). Clapp and Johnson's analyses were relevant both to the cause of plaintiffs' cancers and to IBM's capacity to track disease patterns in its workers without disclosing to those workers even the existence of its Corporate Mortality File let alone patterns shown by its data. Given that the premise of the claim was corporate fraud and concealment (one of the few bases for workers to sue their employer rather than be limited to no-fault workers' compensation as a remedy), exclusion of these data from the jury's deliberations was of critical importance. After losing the case, a plaintiffs' attorney said that the prohibition of using Clapp's analysis of IBM's Corporate Mortality File data in the trial had meant that, "I fought the case with one hand tied behind my back" (Regalado and Bulkeley 2004). Soon thereafter, IBM announced that it had settled all the outstanding lawsuits with over 50 current and former California workers (Bulkeley 2004).

In a move that upset IBM, Clapp subsequently submitted his analysis for inclusion in a special issue of the scholarly journal, *Clinics in Occupational and Environmental Medicine* devoted to the electronics industry. IBM lawyers sent a letter cautioning Clapp not to publish the details of his analysis, stating that it was protected by a court order guaranteeing its confidentiality (Ferber 2004a; see also Ferber 2004b)—despite the public availability of Clapp and Johnson's overall findings in court records.

In normal circumstances, the matter would have ended there, but Clapp was not finished. He called me in my role as Guest Editor of the *Clinics* special issue to report that he had engaged a private attorney, who had advised him that he could proceed with the planned publication. According to his lawyer, Indira Talwani, of Segal, Roitman & Coleman, in Boston, Clapp had the legal right to publish his research findings. One basis for her conclusion was that, for all their sword-rattling after the fact, IBM's lawyers had failed to seal a lengthy deposition taken in the San Jose case that contained his analyses as marked exhibits (Clapp 2003a, 2003b). Furthermore, the controversial paper was in the public domain, with some of its findings being cited in the *New York Times* in columns by Bob Herbert (2003a, 2003b, 2003c, 2003d). Boston University General Counsel's Office agreed to represent Clapp in any further legal developments regarding publication of the paper in question. As of March 2006, the paper had yet to be published.

While successfully delaying the publication of the Clapp study, IBM retained the epidemiologists at the University of Alabama who had conducted the firm's prior cancer studies (Beall et al. 1996) to do a further study of cancer risk among workers at two semiconductor plants. Workers were evaluated for cause-specific mortality rates compared with general population rates (Beall et al. 2005). The healthy-worker effect was noted in lower-than-expected mortality overall, but brain cancer was again associated with semiconductor exposures despite the fact that the workforce was divided into many subgroups that made it difficult to analyze individual cancer risks (Herrick et al. 2005). This technique was successfully used by HSE in a UK reproductive study allowing that agency to assert that no reproductive harm occurred at NSUK (Elliott et al. 1999). Nonetheless, despite a journal paper written to dispel concerns, length of employment was associated positively with brain cancer among IBM workers. Other cancers with increased relative risks were leukemia, non-Hodgkin's lymphoma, ovarian, and prostate.

No apparent effort was made to utilize the company industrial hygiene records of worker exposures to a number of carcinogens. In discussing possible improvements of their study, the authors stated that,

> Another improvement would be the use of more quantitative exposure rankings based upon actual measurements of exposure, which could be accomplished by historical records of industrial hygiene measurements of airborne contaminants, as well as the archived records of chemical use for the three facilities. As IBM has maintained these records, a quantitative reconstruction of historical exposures to agents known or suspected as carcinogens may be possible. Although this reconstruction was outside the scope of the current project, it could be incorporated in a future investigation. (Herrick et al. 2005, 995)

Cancer Study Proposals

The HSE has announced proposals for following up its investigation of cancer risks at NSUK's Greenock facility. After five years of deliberations, HSE now recommends that all four of the cancers highlighted in its initial investigation be studied further. The study they propose "will therefore collect some information on stomach and brain cancer but it will focus in detail on lung and breast cancer" (HSE 2005). The failure to expand the cancer study to include a larger population of semiconductor workers and the award of the research contract to an organization that has done commercial consultancy work for NSUK in the past are serious disappointments.

In March 2004, the SIA announced that it will proceed with a retrospective epidemiologic study to investigate whether or not wafer fabrication workers in the U.S. chip industry have experienced higher rates of cancer than non-fabrication workers. The decision follows the completion by a team from Johns Hopkins University Bloomberg School of Public Health of a study to determine whether it is scientifically feasible to conduct a retrospective cancer study among U.S. employees. "Planning for the study will begin immediately" (SIA 2004). In July 2005, Vanderbilt University's Cancer Center was disclosed as the contractor to perform the SIA cancer study on U.S. electronics workers. Given the SIA's history, it is likely that some time may pass before a study is authorized and funded and its results are submitted to a peer-reviewed journal; and given the level of intrusion by the SIA in its former research activities, the results may not be trustworthy.

CONCLUSION

Many U.S. semiconductor companies are large enough and have the technological capacity to track a wide range of health outcomes and to conduct cancer epidemiology studies of their own workers. For example, Hillman in 1982 detailed IBM's sophisticated electronic medical and environmental monitoring system, replete with the capacity to track chemical exposures against acute and chronic illness and ultimately cause of death. Despite the capacity to conduct research, few studies have been undertaken by companies or have been published to date. It may well be that studies are conducted internally, but the results are not shared with the public unless they are favorable to the industry. For many years, the SIA has been "considering" a cancer study, but this consideration has yet to produce tangible results. In short, more than 50 years after its inception, there has been no definitive study of cancer and reproductive hazards in the semiconductor industry *anywhere* in the world.

The semiconductor industry should have begun monitoring the health of its employees relative to their work environments from the time the companies were formed—taking coordinated, proactive steps to reduce exposures and prevent chronic disease. Given their superior technological capabilities, such an effort would have been entirely feasible and realistic, and had they implemented such programs, the health problems that are now surfacing might well have been averted. The semiconductor industry's failure to do so from the outset, compounded by its continued resistance to serious scrutiny, makes it imperative that public health and safety agencies in all locations where this industry operates become and remain engaged at this critical time.

4   Double Jeopardy

Gender and Migration in Electronics Manufacturing

ON NOVEMBER 19, 1998, more than 6,300 workers from fourteen production units of a US$1 billion Indian multinational company went on an indefinite strike in Bangalore, the "Silicon Valley of India."[1] About 80 percent of these striking workers were women between the ages of 18 and 25. This was the bitterest high-profile labor dispute that Bangalore had experienced in decades. At the heart of the dispute was an apprenticeship program that the company had abused to retain shop-floor workers in tenuous employment on subminimum wages for many years. Besides a lack of job security, the women had to stand all day with no fans or chairs for relief from the heat and fatigue. They had no breaks, needed permission to use the toilet, and were forced to work overtime without extra pay.

Both the conditions that these workers faced and their courage to change them are part of a prevailing reality at the bottom of the labor market in the global electronics industry. Many production workers in key industrial clusters throughout the world are women and either internal or transnational migrants. Yet, with the exception of a brief burst of studies during the 1980s, the electronics industry has been conspicuously absent in discussions related to the politics of race, gender, migration, and employment. In contrast, there has been a steady growth in efforts to analyze the participation of migrant women and the nature of employment in the global garments industry. This disparity is all the more remarkable given the striking similarities between the two industries—their growth as a pillar of national development in many countries; the staggering power, wealth, and influence of the leading multinationals; the pyramid-shaped corporate structure; the use of subcontracting; and the intolerable exploitation of workers. The antisweatshop movement that has taken root in North America and Western Europe now presents an opportunity to draw attention to the proletarians of the "IT [information technology] revolution" and to demand corporate responsibility on a global scale.

This chapter has three parts. The first explores reasons for the apparent preferential employment of young, migrant women in electronics manufacturing, arguing that this is mainly due to the corporate search for ever-greater flexibility and productivity. The second section shows that this emphasis on flexible production, which has proven to be an effective corporate strategy, in practice frequently violates workers' fundamental rights. The third section presents some examples of the response from workers and labor organizations. This paper draws from reports of management practices and working conditions in the electronics industry throughout the world, supplemented by primary research in two important nodes of the electronics industry—Silicon Valley, California; and Bangalore, India.

FEMINIZATION AND MIGRATION FOR FLEXIBLE PRODUCTION

Between 1985 and 2000, women represented more than half of the electronics production workforce in Hong Kong, Macau, Singapore, Taiwan, the Czech Republic, Malaysia, Indonesia, Puerto Rico, Slovenia, Cuba, the Philippines, Thailand, and Sri Lanka. The latest figures available show that the proportion of female employment in this industry was highest in Hong Kong (79 percent), Macau (69 percent), and Malaysia (68 percent; see Table 4.1).

Women's employment in the electronics industry broadly reflects the geographical specialization in industrial segments. A survey of forty-four countries between 1990 and 2000 showed that women formed the majority of the workforce in a variety of countries: in Slovakia, Bulgaria, and the Czech Republic in office and computer equipment manufacturing; in Bulgaria, the Czech Republic, Latvia, Mexico, Portugal, and Slovakia in radio, television, and telecommunications equipment production; in Cyprus, the Czech Republic, Portugal, Slovakia, and Slovenia in electronic components production; and in Argentina, Bermuda, the Czech Republic, Ireland, the Philippines, Portugal, and Slovenia in medical, precision, and optical equipment manufacturing (ILO 2002).

Since the 1960s, the global labor market in electronics manufacturing also has drawn workers across national borders. Immigrant workers in electronics production tend to be women, and there is a growing trend toward the "feminization of migration," as women migrate from such countries as the Philippines, Bangladesh, and Sri Lanka to high-tech hot spots in Singapore, Hong Kong, Malaysia, and Taiwan (David 1996, 39). In some countries, electronics manufacturing draws internally displaced workers. The industry predominates in Export Processing Zones (EPZs), Free Trade Zones (FTZs),

TABLE 4.1. Percentage of Female Employment in the Electronics Industry in Select Countries

Country	1985	1990	1995	1999
Hungary	47.4	45.0	n/a	n/a
Japan	45.6	n/a	39.1	37.0
Korea	50.9	49.1	45.6	41.2
Macedonia	30.0	27.3	22.2	n/a
Malaysia	73.7	75.4	66.5	67.8
Manaus, Brazil	n/a	54.3	49.5	42.3
Portugal	46.7	33.7	45.5	n/a
Puerto Rico	n/a	61.0	53.4	52.8
Taiwan	58.8	54.5	52.7	n/a
USA	41.9	42.7	41.8	n/a

Source: Elaborated from the United Nations Development Organization (UNIDO 2003); Departamento Intersindical de Estatística e Estudos Sócio-Econômicos (DIEESE 2001), for Brazil; and ILO (1998), for Macedonia.

and other specially designated industrial zones, which have mushroomed throughout the world as a result of export-oriented development policies. Nearly all of the workers in these zones, such as the Batamindo Industrial estate in Indonesia, are migrant women from other, poorer regions of the country (David 1996; Holdcroft 2003; Kelly 2002; Rosa 1994).

Some commentators have suggested that women workers are typically young and single (Fuentes and Ehrenreich 1983). However, other studies have shown some geographical variation in the age, marital status, and level of formal education of the women employed in electronics manufacturing, especially in comparison to garment workers (Chhachhi 1997a, 1999; Fernández-Kelly 1983; Goldstein 1989; Rosa 1994). Generally, women and migrants work in machine operation, assembly, packaging, and quality control in a variety of workplaces, from the sprawling factories that employ thousands of production workers, as in Mexico, Thailand, and China (see Leong and Pandita, this volume) to units of 10 to 15 employees, or even in their own homes, as uncovered in Silicon Valley, California. As the following sections show, electronics firms achieve flexible and efficient production by employing women and migrants.

Labor Control and Productivity

Several studies on electronics employers' recruitment practices have attributed an apparent preference for women workers, particularly in Asia, to gendered cultural and biological stereotypes. The "nimble fingers" thesis argues that managers perceive women as more suitable than men for assembly work because they are seen to have "natural" traits, such as manual dexterity ("fast-fingered women"), patience, and a tendency to be meticulous (Elson and Pearson 1980; Lim 1978). These allegedly innate feminine characteristics are required to manipulate intricate wires and repeat the same finite number of tasks all day. Managers tend to undervalue the mental concentration and "aptitude and alertness" that an assembler in fact applies to ensure high product quality.[2] Chhachhi's (1999) study of the electronics industry in Delhi, India, found that women's jobs are often downgraded as "unskilled" and casualized, regardless of the actual skills the job entails (see also Standing 1999). Such an appraisal of who is capable of boring, monotonous, manual work also has racial dimensions in Silicon Valley (Hossfeld 1990).

Youth implies that workers have little or no experience with waged employment; thus they have more modest expectations than do older women workers, especially those who were formerly employed in unionized workplaces (Chhachhi 1999; Rosa 1994). Companies also deliberately recruit young women because they are in better physical health than older women, with sharper eyesight and quicker reflexes (Elson and Pearson 1989; Hossfeld 1991a). Women in Thailand's EPZs typically work for a couple of years before returning to their places of origin to set up their own small businesses or to start families (Theobald 1996). In some segments of the industry that require a trained, skilled workforce and in places where there is a relative shortage of qualified workers, retaining workers is a high priority. However, in parts of such countries as China and Malaysia, where the labor market is fairly loose for jobs in which little training is involved, labor turnover is not a serious concern, because the workers' physical productivity declines over time, mainly due to occupational health hazards and injuries (see CAFOD 2004; Standing 1999). Sometimes management actively promotes a high labor turnover so that they can minimize the nonwage costs that accrue over time.

At a domestic firm in Bangalore, managers exert great pressure on workers to force them to resign voluntarily (Ferus-Comelo 2005). For example, once women workers get married, line supervisors aggravate their working conditions by assigning them compulsory overtime without extra pay, so that family members will pressure them to quit their jobs. If they become pregnant, they are assigned to the most arduous tasks. They are forced to stand all day, to work in heated areas of the shop floor with no breaks, or to load and unload heavy consignment, to make their jobs as unbearable as possible. Only a few manage to endure this treatment and are retained, whereas most are replaced by a fresh group of women.

Labor control is further extended to the workers' reproductive roles. In many countries, such as Costa Rica, Honduras, Mexico, Thailand, and China, women are subjected to pregnancy tests as a routine part of the job screening process and sometimes even throughout their job tenure (CAFOD 2004; David 1996; Wong 2002). Women who are pregnant are either denied jobs or fired. If a migrant worker in Taiwan gets pregnant, not only can her contract be terminated, but also, despite a change in the law that allows pregnant workers to stay, she faces the choice of abortion or deportation (Stein 2003). To avoid losing their jobs, women in India and Thailand have frequent, unsafe abortions (CLIST 2003; Rajalakshmi 1999). By monitoring women's bodies this way, companies try to avoid any legally mandated social costs of reproduction, such as higher health care bills, maternity leave, and child care.

Numerical Flexibility

Although workforce characteristics and related social attributes consolidate labor control, the nature of electronics production and the industry's structure equally create a niche for migrant women workers in precarious employment (Hossfeld 1991a). To achieve flexibility in order to respond to fluctuating market demands, managers give priority to the unencumbered expansion and contraction of the labor force. They increasingly rely on contract labor, that is, workers who are recruited on a casual basis through temporary hiring agencies for short-term "on-call" assembly jobs. These workers, who are frequently foreign or internal migrants, are not considered direct employees of the companies for whom they work.

Such two-tiered systems are practiced in mature high-tech sites like Silicon Valley, as well as in new industrial nodes, such as Bangalore (Ferus-Comelo 2005). According to an executive manager of the largest employment agency in Silicon Valley, 10 to 35 percent of a workforce of 6,000 placed in jobs weekly where "you might find the United Nations, at least 20 to 30 different countries represented," are in electronics firms and a majority do assembly work. Contract workers in Bangalore are hired at two levels—"skilled" and "unskilled"—regardless of their technical training and other qualifications. Casual workers are forced to take a day off each month so that they do not have continuous, six-month employment, which would legally qualify them for permanent status.

In Penang, Malaysia, overseas contract workers are recruited by agencies in Indonesia and Bangladesh to provide managers numerical flexibility during production slowdowns when their contracts are not renewed. At the same time, however, such workers are a source of labor-market stability, as their visas are conditional on employment in a specific company, which prevents them from job hopping (Kelly 2002). At MMI Precision, a factory producing electronic parts and components in Thailand, 700 of the 2,500 workers are casual employees recruited by 11 different agencies (Wong 2002). Similarly, of the 7,000 workers at an IBM plant in Guadalajara, Mexico, only 500 were hired directly by IBM or its contract manufacturer, Sanmina SCI. The remaining 6,500 were hired through different recruitment agencies (CAFOD 2004).

Differences in workers' employment status can be traced along gender lines, as women are often overrepresented among the workers in part-time casual employment (ILO 1998). A study of Nokia's employment practices at its plant in Manaus, Brazil, showed that of the 265 workers hired indirectly through labor agencies, 212 (80 percent) were women and 53 (20 percent) were men. An additional four women were designated as "trainees," thus raising the total number of women working in the plant to 750 in comparison to 606 men (SO 2002).

Insecure employment for women workers extends to home working, as home assembly is one way that electronics manufacturers can attain the speed of delivery required by their customers. Numerous reports have documented the employment of immigrant women in home-based electronics assembly in such places as New York, Madrid, and Silicon Valley (Dangler 1989; Ewell and Ha 1999a; Portes, Castells, and Benton 1989). However, Chhachhi (1999, 20) argued that, despite the few cases of home-based work in Delhi, India, there is "no trend toward home-based work" because of the pressure for quality control and the financial risk of releasing expensive imported components outside the factory and strict oversight. This was confirmed in an analysis of the supply chain strategy of electronics production implemented in Bangalore (Ferus-Comelo 2005), suggesting that there are spatial variations in the industry's reliance on home-based work.

THE HUMAN TOLL OF HIGH-TECH

Women and migrants' working conditions in the electronics industry need to be understood within the broader context of economic necessity and their limited opportunities for safe, secure, well-paying jobs (Dangler 1989; Kabeer 2000). Migrant workers tend to compare the conditions of employment in the electronics industry to former employment or to the bleak economic and political situations they have left behind in their places of origin (Beech 2003; Hossfeld 1991b). Women workers, particularly in countries with strict gender-based cultural restrictions, also rate highly the noneconomic benefits of their jobs, such as personal independence, the importance of which cannot be underestimated (Balakrishnan 2002; Ong 1987). This does not, however, mean that working conditions in the electronics industry are ideal. Due to the nature of electronics manufacturing and the organizational structure adopted by corporate management, young, migrant women face a number of labor rights violations.

The most common problem is compulsory overtime with no extra pay. A survey conducted among 200 workers in 20 electronics companies in Penang, Malaysia, found that 60 percent of workers had to do overtime, and half did at least five hours of overtime per day (Wangel 2001). In China, very long, compulsory overtime is the norm, and workers typically clock an average of 100 to 120 hours of overtime per month, with a seven-day work week (CAFOD 2004; see also Leong and Pandita, this volume). They often must put in off-the-record, illegal overtime to achieve the minimum hourly wage. In some places, such as Malaysia and Indonesia, and in Sri Lanka's EPZs, migrant women lead highly regimented lives in hostels, which allows plant managers to control and monitor workers' availability for overtime and leaves workers no other viable alternative (Kelly 2002; Rosa 1994). Migrant workers in South Korea, who are limited to a single three-year stay, are considered trainees their first two years and are thereby exempt from most of the country's labor laws, especially those related to minimum wage and overtime (Stein 2003).

An ILO survey of wages in electronics production showed that women throughout the global industry typically earned less than men. The wage

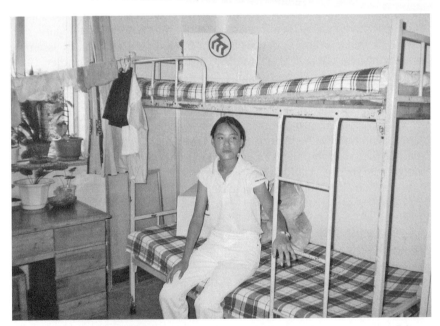

PHOTO 4.1. Chinese electronics worker in her dormitory room. Courtesy of Apo Leong, Asia Monitor Resource Centre.

differential between men and women was greatest in Japan and Malaysia, worsening over time in Japan and improving in Malaysia. Women's earnings were less than 70 percent of men's Thailand, Singapore, Cyprus, and Korea (ILO 1998). Lower wages often are justified by the inaccurate perception that women workers are secondary (to male) wage earners in their households and therefore can afford to work for less (Hossfeld 1990; Mitter 1986). A gender difference in wages also may be due to the occupational segregation that characterizes this industry and the higher proportion of women working part time or on a temporary basis (ILO 1998).

The management practice of outsourcing production to contract manufacturers and a wide, global network of suppliers increases the pressure on firms at the lower end of the chain to deliver cost savings (see Lüthje, this volume). Consequently, the subcontractors seek ways to minimize their labor costs and thereby gain or retain production orders. This form of restructuring has serious negative implications for workers at the tail end of subcontracting chains, which is where most migrant women work.

An expansion of jobs in small units or the informal economy, including home-based work, allows women the flexibility to combine employment with domestic commitments (Balakrishnan 2002; Dangler 1989). However, conditions in these second and third tiers of employment are frequently far worse than those in large companies, which come under the purview of labor legislation.[3] Small enterprises employing a hundred employees or fewer tend to elude regulatory control and are hosts to a variety of labor problems, including low wages, late or nonpayment of wages, work targets, and lack of employment security. Home-based workers, a majority of whom are women and immigrants, are paid a piece-rate that falls far below the local minimum wage. To increase payments and meet deadlines set by companies or middle-men, they often involve their underage children and family members in assembly work.[4]

Production workers in electronics manufacturing are subjected to a range of acute and chronic forms of damage to their bodies (see LaDou; Hawes and Pellow, this volume; see also Fox 1991). These industrial health hazards are distinctly gendered due to the labor processes predominately undertaken by women and the high-pressure environment in which they work (Theobald 2002). Resigning from hazardous employment is not a viable option for most workers, particularly migrant women. Their marginalization in the local labor market underscores their dependence on jobs that are harmful to their health, even if they are not aware of the risks.

The health and safety of migrant workers, especially those holding an irregular status, is a major concern, as they often avoid seeking medical treatment because of prohibitive costs, an inability to take time off work, problems with transportation, or the fear of drawing attention to themselves and losing their jobs or being deported (ILO 2004). Sahabat Wanita, a national feminist workers' organization in Malaysia that supports the rights of electronics workers in EPZs, has documented cases of migrant workers who are sent home to die without any explanation or compensation for their medical conditions (Papachan n.d.). In addition to corporate negligence, linguistic barriers, poor access to health care, and a lack of familiarity with local health care systems compound migrants' work-related risks (ILO 2004).

FIGHTING AGAINST THE ODDS

Although the global electronics industry thrives on the labor of young, migrant women workers, these workers' rights are consistently violated with impunity, as the contemporary global electronics manufacturing workforce remains largely unorganized. In Bangalore, for instance, unionization is limited to the public-sector plants that were established in India's post-Independence era,[5] whereas forming a national union for electronics workers in Malaysia remains virtually prohibited (Wangel 2001). In 2000, the electronics industry had only eight enterprise-level unions, representing just 5 percent of the country's 150,000 workers—80 percent of whom are women—and leaving the rest unprotected (ICFTU 2001).

Recent union-organizing efforts in the high-tech industry have been limited to the male-dominated, professional occupations. For example, the Union Network International (UNI), a Global Union Federation, has launched a campaign to organize software programmers and financial, executive, technical, and consultancy workers in Bangalore and Hyderabad in India.[6] The Communications Workers of America (CWA) has been involved in organizing contingent workers, including long-term temporary workers (or "perma-temps") in white-collar career occupations at IBM in Alliance@IBM and WashTech, the Washington Alliance of Technology Workers.

Because organizing migrant workers is tremendously difficult due to the temporary nature of their employment and the ways in which managers use ethnicity and place of origin to pit workers against each other and against unions (see Hossfeld 1990; Kelly 2002), unions are being forced to find new ways to extend collective bargaining rights to migrants. Although some countries reserve the right to organize for nationals (ILO 2004), there are additional structural challenges to overcome. In the Guangdong Province of China, contrary to the national trend, women outnumber men among the 10 million migrant workers (estimated at 60 percent) who are drawn to the labor-intensive industries, including electronics (*China Labor Bulletin* 2004). Here, the Guangdong Federation of Trade Unions (GFTU) rejected the Ruian Migrants' Management Association (RMMA), which was established in 2002 to support the rights of migrants, particularly temporary workers, in Ruian City, and, considering it a rival workers' organization, declared it illegal (*China Labor Bulletin* 2002).

Many unions, both nationally and internationally, support women's participation and have clear policies to make organizing women workers a high priority. However, it is unclear to what extent these unions have been able to move beyond rhetoric to accommodate women workers' specific employment conditions and issues in their action agendas. The Iron and Steel Trades Confederation (ISTC) in Scotland and the General Confederation of Italian Labor (CGIL) in Italy are examples of positive union responses at different levels to the changing structure of employment and unfair managerial practices.[7]

Recognizing the increases in home working and self-employment, the CGIL set up a new union organization to organize and represent these workers, whereas the ISTC doubled its membership in two years and has the highest female membership of any ISTC branch due to its active organizing agenda (May 1999; Rigby 1999).

Reports from various parts of the world, such as Japan, Italy, Thailand, and Taiwan, suggest that, once organized, women workers' interests are not given high enough priority within the male-dominated culture and leadership of union structures (see Hossfeld 1991b; WWW 1991, for examples). Without women's participation in critical decision-making processes and in leadership positions, unions risk a male bias in organizing priorities and strategies. As long as they are seen as "special interests" or as being divisive, migrant women workers' issues will remain unaddressed by labor unions.

Forms of Resistance

Contrary to the stereotypes of women workers as meek and docile, they continue to struggle for justice in the workplace, often in the face of tremendous corporate hostility (Fuentes and Ehrenreich 1983; Mitter 1986). As a result, they are frequently fired, demoted, assigned to night shifts, or transferred to factories in other locations that have worse working conditions (CAFOD 2004; Ferus-Comelo 2005; WWW 1991).

Women workers also have been physically attacked for their trade union activities.[8] In the walkout described at the beginning of this chapter, management harassment of workers started immediately after the first open union meeting. Managers were able to mobilize the state machinery against workers. On the second day of the strike, the police beat the workers so viciously that some could hardly move; one woman miscarried. Throughout the strike, hundreds were arrested on trumped-up charges. A union leader elected during the strike was threatened about having acid thrown on her face and having her legs broken if she testified on behalf of the injured workers in hospital. She was illegally fired immediately after her election. Police harassed other women activists at home during the night, causing them a great deal of anguish due to the social stigma they suffered as a result.

Despite such virulent opposition, workers deploy a range of strategies to challenge and subvert management. Some women are finding ways to deal with unfair management practices without directly confronting their bosses or risking their jobs. For example, coworkers of a six-month-pregnant woman in Mumbai's Santa Cruz Electronics Export Processing Zone (SEEPZ) surreptitiously rotated places with her because she was forced to stand for hours at a stretch without a break and was refused light work by the manager (Cecilia 1992). Similarly, Asian women workers in Silicon Valley circumvented the manager's divide-and-rule tactics when a Mexican coworker was assigned to their workstation to "learn speed" by deliberately slowing down their work and setting a lower average quota than usual (Hossfeld 1990, 174). In general, workers draw inspirational tactics from their cultures to respond to hegemonic relations of accumulation and domination in the workplace (Ong 1987; Sargeson 2001).

Women also have waged militant campaigns using hunger strikes and slow-downs of production as tools. For example, the striking workers in Bangalore lay down in front of the company gates to prevent scab workers from being bussed into work. Small groups of four or five women took turns on a hunger strike to protest against the false arrests and police brutality (Ferus-Comelo 2005). Similarly, women workers in Silicon Valley, who were predominately immigrants from Mexico, held a hunger strike to protest against poverty wages, a lack of benefits, and unsafe working conditions at Versatronex (Bacon 1993). Hundreds of 20- to 23-year-old women workers in a South Korean electronics firm occupied the factory to prevent relocation when the company threatened to move (Hamilton 1991, 31–32).

Recourse to the law is another way workers seek justice. About 890 migrant workers organized and filed a grievance against Seagate Technology in Shenzhen, China, for cheating them of their pensions worth thousands of dollars each (Schoenberger 2002). However, a few landmark cases demonstrate the bitter defeats that many workers face. For instance, production worker Mayuree Taeviya made history in 1994 when she accused the Japanese-owned Electro-Ceramics Ltd. in Thailand of poisoning its employees. After a four-year legal campaign, which resulted in her being socially ostracized, almost cost her husband his job and sapped her not only of all her savings but also of her will to live, Mayuree lost her case (H. M. Chiu 2003; see also Foran and Sonnenfeld, this volume).

Organizational Support

A number of organizations have emerged to support women workers who do not have access to union protection. Women's associations, church groups, and university-based labor advocates attempt to bridge the divide between the workers and the general public and to provide workers with much-needed moral support (WWW 1991). Through various service-based projects, such as legal advice forums, these organizations strive to build long-term relationships with workers and foster a sense of trust and collectivity that may result in further action. For example, women members of the Malaysian Trade Union Congress (MTUC) run two hostels for women who work in the EPZs in the suburbs of Kuala Lumpur (David 1996; Rosa 1994). Besides providing workers with safe, decent, and affordable housing, these hostels create a space within which women can discuss their problems and raise their awareness of the benefits of unions. Not only has this initiative been replicated elsewhere, but also a small group of women who lived in these hostels have helped create a new union in the electronics industry.

Similarly, the work of community-based organizations in different parts of the world has been effective in the absence of local union representation. The Center of Reflection and Action in Labor Issues (CEREAL) is involved in popular education among electronics workers in Guadalajara, Mexico (CAFOD 2004). The Hong Kong-based Christian Industrial Committee (CIC), an independent, church-supported workers' support center, has collaborated with the Electronics Industry Employees General Union to organize workers at Digital Equipment Corporation (DEC), who were mostly young women with children. These workers succeeded in convincing the company to provide either transportation or severance pay to workers when it relocated its assembly plant to a different site (Wilson 1986). Workers in Philips Hong Kong also have managed to make significant improvements in their workplace environment with the assistance of the Neighborhood and Workers' Service Center (WWW 1991, 73–75). In Thailand, the Centre for the Advancement of Lanna Women (CALW)[9] at Chiang Mai University organized study groups and seminars to encourage electronics workers to discuss their concerns and strategize about how to tackle them (Theobald 1996). CALW also played an important role as a workers' advocate by circulating a petition to demand that the government reopen an investigation into the deaths of electronics workers in the Northern Regional Industrial Estate (NRIE) in Lamphun in 1993 (see Foran and Sonnenfeld, this volume).

CONCLUSION

This chapter provides some explanations for the prevalence of women, especially foreign and internal migrant workers, in global hotspots for electronics production. It is the industry's drive toward flexible production that makes the control and replacement of workers, as well as the expansion and contraction of the workforce, high managerial priorities. Although migrant workers' prospects and terms of employment may be better than those in their places of origin, they often face conditions far inferior to those available to local nationals. Electronics manufacturing not only provides women with jobs that may pay relatively higher wages than some other occupations but also fosters economic insecurity. Migrant women workers typically experience wage discrimination, job casualization, and considerable health problems. Despite existing international labor standards to protect them, their rights as workers are too often undermined. Combined with their weak labor market position, the limited collective bargaining strength of electronics production workers worldwide translates into a double jeopardy for migrant women workers.

Examples of labor action illustrate workers' belief in collective action and their ability to unite against unjust managerial practices. Although women and migrant workers fight hard for more control over their work lives, it would be wrong to romanticize their efforts for workplace improvements. Despite their courage, determination, and solidarity, production workers' actions often end in defeat. Under the threat of production relocation and the termination of production contracts, workers have been forced to either compromise or surrender. In most cases, the fight for justice is a long, drawn-out process that demands tenacity and endurance, but holds no promises (see chapters by Ku; McCourt, this volume). Organizing workers, especially women and migrants, in electronics manufacturing is a critical task whose time is long overdue.

NOTES

I am grateful for comments and encouragement from Matt Griffith, Sean Gogarty, Paul Bailey, Jenny Holdcroft, Molly Kenyon, Dr. Jane Wills, the participants of the Wageningen editorial workshop, the editors and three anonymous reviewers; and for the financial support of the Department of Geography, Queen Mary, University of London; *Antipode: A Radical Journal of Geography*; the Developing Areas Research Group of The Royal Geographical Society; and the University of London Central Research Fund.

1. Information about this strike was compiled from interviews with strikers and union officers (see Ferus-Comelo 2005).

2. *Financial Times*, February 5, 1985, p. 22, cited in Elson and Pearson (1989), p. 2.

3. Working in large factories that are covered by labor legislation does not necessarily protect workers' rights, as working conditions are most often determined by managerial practice and not by state regulation.

4. See Ewell and Ha (1999a, 1999b) regarding an investigation into home-based work in Silicon Valley.

5. See Ferus-Comelo (2005) for a fuller account of the state of the local labor movement.

6. UNI refers to the sector as Industry, Business and Informational Technology Services Sector. See www.union-network.org/unisite/Sectors/IBITS/IBITS.html, for a current report. I am grateful to Andrew Bibby for this information.

7. The *Confederazione Generale Italiana del Lavoro (CGIL)* is a national federation of unions in Italy.

8. See Hamilton (1991) for an account of the violent resistance to unionization that women workers faced at an electronics assembly factory in South Korea.

9. *Lanna* means "Northern Thai."

5 "Made in China"

Electronics Workers in the World's Fastest Growing Economy

OVER THE PAST two decades, China has emerged as the fastest growing economy in the world. With an annual growth rate of more than 8 percent, it is emerging as the world's manufacturing hub. China's industrial production has reached unprecedented levels. Despite the global economic slowdown and health scares of the first few years of the twentieth century, China, more than any other country, continues to both grow steadily and attract foreign direct investment. Its utilized foreign direct investment for 2002 was US$52.7 billion.

Hidden beneath the marvelous economic statistics are China's millions of workers who toil on the production lines of the various industries. With 1.28 billion people, China is not only the most populated country in the world but also the country with the largest number of workers (about 700 million). Although most of its workforce still is engaged in agriculture, the trend is changing quickly, with thousands of peasants moving out of rural areas to work in urban manufacturing centers.

The Chinese government estimates that nearly 100 million migrants from rural areas work in the country's cities, accounting for about 30 percent of the industrial labor. However, unofficial figures are much higher, and according to Guo Wencai, director of the Grassroots Organization Department of the All-China Federation of Trade Unions (ACFTU),[1] "The makeup of China's manufacturing workers has undergone great change, the number of farmers-turned-workers has surpassed that of workers in traditional terms, or those born in urban areas with household registration." Most work in the private sector or foreign-funded enterprises and often are exploited by investors to derive maximum profits; many are women (see Ferus-Comelo, this volume). In sum, they do not earn a fair wage for their hard labor, and their labor rights are not truly respected. The same observation holds for electronics workers. Table 5.1 displays China's major economic indicators.

The electronics industry has been identified as a "pillar"[2] industry of the Chinese economy. The country's information technology (IT) sector has seen phenomenal growth during the past decade. Presently, China's information and electronics industry, with total sales revenue of 1.88 trillion Yuan (US$227 billion) in 2003,[3] increasing 34 percent over the previous year, is the third largest in the world, after the United States and Japan.

TABLE 5.1. Major Economic Indicators for China, 2004–05

Major Economic Indicators	2004 Value	2004 Growth (%)	January to July 2005 Value	January to July 2005 Growth (%)
Area (sq km, mn)[a]	9.6			
Population (mn)	1,299.9			
Gross Domestic Production (RMB bn)[b]	13,651.5	9.5	6,742.2	9.5
Urban Per Capita Income (RMB)	9,422	7.7	5,374	9.5
Rural Per Capita Income (RMB)	2,936	6.8	1,586	12.5
Added Value of Industrial Output (RMB bn)	5,480.5	16.7	3,812.3	16.3
Urban Unemployment Rate (%)	4.2			
Exports (US$bn)	593.4	35.4	407.9	32.0
– By FIEs (US$bn)[c]	338.6	40.9	232.9	32.5
Imports (US$bn)	561.4	36.0	357.8	13.7
– By FIEs (US$bn)	324.6	40.0	205.7	15.1
Trade Surplus (US$bn)	31.9		50.1	
Foreign Direct Investment				
– Number of new projects	43,664	6.3	24,652	−2.0
– Contracted amount (US$bn)	153.5	33.4	98.6	9.2
– Utilized amount (US$bn)	60.6	13.3	33.1	−3.4
Foreign Currency Reserves (US$bn)	609.9	51.3	711.0	51.1

[a]mn, million.
[b]RMB bn, billion Yuan.
[c]FIE, foreign invested enterprise.
Source: National Bureau of Statistics, Ministry of Commerce, and General Administration of Customs, Government of China, as referenced in Hong Kong Trade Development Council (2005).

THE INDUSTRY'S DEVELOPMENT

China's electronics industry developed late compared to the rest of its manufacturing sector. Electronics imports exceeded exports greatly, and in 1989, the ratio was 2 to 1. In the Eighth Five-year Plan (1991–95), the electronics industry saw rapid development. The industry's key economic goals, set for the next five years, were achieved in just two years. By 1995, the volume of the export exceeded the input, with increasing surplus favorable to the China side. The industry also became increasingly sophisticated. In addition, the government organized three "Golden Projects" in 1993,[4] in a bid to develop IT infrastructure locally and to upgrade the industry from low-end, low-skilled manufacturing to the high-technology sector.

In the Ninth Five-year Plan (1995–2000), the electronics industry was recognized as key to China's economic growth; thus a special emphasis was placed on electronics as a "pillar industry." Since then, electronics in China has become a leading industry in the world. The domestic consumption of electronic products also has risen a great deal. China has more mobile phone users than anywhere in the world. Today, personal computer (PC) shipments have grown to over nine million per year in China. Tremendous growth in the local consumption of electronic goods has led many international companies to seek to capture the domestic market. China has attained a unique position as both a major producer and exporter, as well as a major consumer of electronic goods.

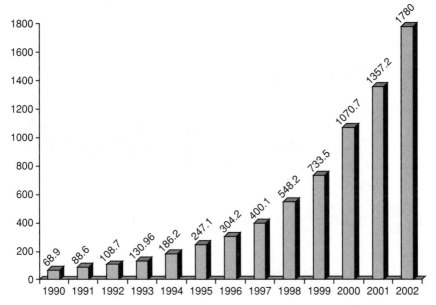

FIGURE 5.1. Growth of IT Production in China, 1990–2002 (RMB bn).
Source: Lou (2003).

It is projected that China's share of global electronics production will rise from 8.1 to 14.3 percent by 2005. By then, China's share of world electronics manufacture will nearly double, making it a hub for the IT industry, according to a recent World Bank study. Its growth rate has been three times higher than the gross domestic product (GDP) growth rate during the past decade (representing 24.2 percent of the national GDP in 2001). The IT industry leads national industrial production and occupies the number one position in the export industry (28 percent of the national total). Electronics and IT production in China has grown more than 21-fold since 1990 (see Figure 5.1 and Table 5.2).

STRUCTURE OF THE INDUSTRY

Local enterprises had dominated IT production in China, but this has been overtaken by foreign enterprises and joint ventures. According to 2002 data

TABLE 5.2. IT Industry Indicators Compared, 1989–2001

Indicator	1989	2001
Gross Output (RMB bn)	63.4	1357
Sales (RMB bn)	49	824
Profit (RMB bn)	3.7	48
Export (US$bn)	2.76	65

Source: MII (2002).

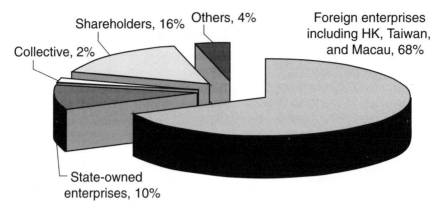

FIGURE 5.2. Types of Ownership in China's IT Sector, Percentage Share in 2002. *Source:* MII (2003).

provided by Ministry of Information Industry, foreign enterprises, including Macao, Hong Kong, and Taiwan, constituted about 68 percent of the total ownership (Figure 5.2).

In terms of product categories, home appliance equipment was the largest segment in 2002, accounting for about 28.7 percent of the total output. Prominent, foreign-invested enterprises in this section include JVC, Samsung, Matsushita, Kenwood, and Philips. Some of the Chinese corporations in this field are Changhong, Konka, TCL, Panda, Haxin, and Zhongshan Jiahua. The recent strategic alliance created between TCL and the French Thompson illustrates both parties' ambition to capture national and international markets. Together they form the world's largest maker of televisions, with an expected annual output of 18 million sets (Figure 5.3).

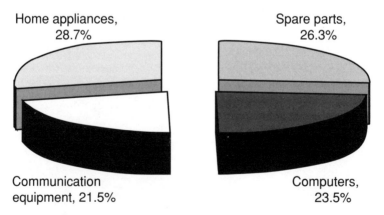

FIGURE 5.3. Sectoral Composition of China's Electronic Industry in 2002. *Source:* MII (2003).

Components or spare parts equipment is the second largest segment, which constituted 26.3 percent of the total output in 2002. The third most important sector is computer products, which accounted for 23.5 percent of the total output in that year. Major products include PCs, notebooks, printers, monitors, modems, and network apparatus. The industry relies on the importation of the core components, but a number of local enterprises have successfully developed their local brands in China. Legend is the largest PC manufacturer in China and also the leading PC supplier to the world market. Other prominent local players include Stone, Founder, Great Wall, and Haxin. Many of these mega-IT enterprises built on their technological capabilities accumulated during the planned economy period. Foreign firms setting up operations in China also have grown. IBM, Compaq, Hewlett–Packard, Dell, Acer, Toshiba, NEC, LG Electronics, and Siemens all have built production facilities and research and development centers in China. Suzhou, a coastal city in Jiangsu province in East China, has become the largest laptop computer production center in the world, with an annual output close to 10 million units, about one fourth of the world's total. The top nine computer companies in Taiwan have set up factories in Suzhou, including Uniwell Compute Corp., Acer Inc., and Mitac International Corp. (*China Daily*).

Communication equipment with a total output share of 21.5 percent constituted the fourth major segment. Both local and foreign enterprises, including joint ventures, are major players in the communications industry. These include Motorola, Siemens, Matsushita, Nokia TCL-NEC, Ericsson, Fujitsu, Shanghai Bell Telecom, Shenzen Huawei Technology, Beijing Telecommunication, Haxin, and Panda.

Although China has achieved leadership in producing home appliances and computer hardware, it does not produce its own core technology. Almost all the chips (80 percent) used in manufacturing are imported from other countries. According to the China Semiconductor Industry Association (CSIA), China's US$15 billion semiconductor market represented 13 percent of the total world demand in 2001, making it the third largest market after the United States and Japan, and China is projected to pass Japan by the end of the decade. China is also trying to develop its capacity in chip manufacturing and as per CSIA, as of June 2002, China had six foundries and 40 other silicon wafer fabrication facilities. Production is spread across several regions within China, but Shanghai and Beijing are by far the most significant areas for semiconductor production. Investors include Advanced Micro Devices and IBM, which are expanding their current operations. Other new investors include Toshiba, Singapore's Chartered Semiconductor Manufacturing, and Taiwanese tycoon Winston Wong.

INDUSTRY CONCENTRATION

The structure of China's electronics industry has become more concentrated in recent years with the advent of giant local players and the national brands in the market. As per the Ministry of Information Industry,[5] the revenue

TABLE 5.3. China's Electronic/IT Production Percentage by Region, 2002

Region	Production Percentage
Central and Southern China (includes Guangzhou)	38
Southwest (includes Sichuan)	4
Northwest (includes Shanxi)	2
Northern China (includes Beijing)	14
Northeast China (includes Dalian)	4
East China (includes Shanghai)	38

Source: MII (2003).

from China's top 100 electronics IT enterprises almost topped 572 billion Yuan (US$68.9 billion) in the year 2002, up 15 percent from the previous 12 months. The top 100 enterprises had revenues of more than 780 million Yuan (US$93.9 million), which had grown from 2001's base level of 510 million Yuan (US$61.4 million). The top ten groups comprised about 22 percent of the entire sector's total, with sales reaching more than 307 billion Yuan (US$37 billion). The leading brands included Haier, Putian, Changhong, Legend, TCL, Hisense, Huawei, Konka, and Panda. Changhong and TCL sold 11.29 million and 7.92 million TV sets, respectively, accounting for 37 percent of the country's total. Legend sold 3.26 million personal computers; and Founder, 1.75 million units, which accounted for 35 percent.

In terms of production regions, Pearl River Delta, Yangtze River Delta, Fujian, and Bo Sea Bay regions are the four major players, with South China, which includes Guangdong as the largest production base, which accounted for about 38 percent of the industry total in 2002. Table 5.3 provides the regional output for electronic products in 2002.

Exports

Foreign-invested companies dominate exports. The total exports from the electronics sector stood at US$92 billion in the year 2002 (see Figure 5.4). As per government statistics,[6] machinery and electronic products made up more than half of China's foreign trade during the first six months of 2003. Combined imports and exports rose 45.2 percent from the previous year, to US$194.49 billion. Most trade was dominated by foreign-invested establishments.

The recent entry of the World Trade Organization (WTO) has accelerated growth, as more transnational corporations (TNCs) aspire to exploit China's cheap labor[7] and government incentives. The Ministry of Commerce has released a list of the top 200 exporters for 2002, which was dominated by foreign companies, with the Taiwan-based computer parts maker, Honhai Electronics' Foxconn, holding the number one title, a historical record of US$4.38 billion. Electronics and IT accounted for more than one third of the top 200 export enterprises and about half of the top 20 export firms as well.

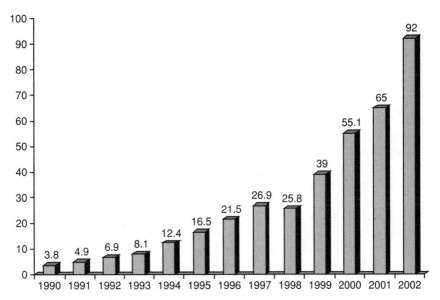

FIGURE 5.4. Growth of China's IT Exports, 1990–2002 (US$bn).
Source: Lou (2003).

EMPLOYMENT GENERATION

It is very difficult to have a clear picture of employment generation, because of conflicting figures by various bureaus and definitions. Some reports claim that 200,000 jobs were created in 2001, and the total work force was 3.26 million people or 6 percent of all industrial labor (MII 2002), and another report claimed that seven million people held jobs in related industries.

According to Chinese researchers, three major factors contributed to this phenomenon:

1. *Domestic demand:* For example, TVs, DVD players, PCs, and mobile phones are nothing new for most urban dwellers, and the saturation rate is quite high in large cities, such as Beijing, Shanghai, and Guangzhou;
2. *The emergence of large domestic IT companies:* For example, the Changhong Holding created employment for 200,000 workers, including its suppliers. In 2001, Changhong produced six million TV sets. Haier (which has plants in the United States), Huawei, and Legend are popular names throughout China. Some of them also have subsidiary plants and operations outside China; and
3. *Export of spare parts/components:* As China is already labeled the "world factory," the volume of contract manufacturing and original equipment manufacturing (OEM) occupies 90 percent of electronics exports.

WORKING CONDITIONS

Generally speaking, two major camps dominate the IT industry. On one hand, there are many talented IT experts earning high salaries with good benefits; on the other hand, there is an enormous number (constituting a majority) of nameless frontline workers on assembly lines (see Photo 5.1), as well as other supporting staff in various departments and outsourcing workers at home and other places. The first camp is frequently cited as the "winners" because they easily can become millionaires or hard-working heroes or heroines in the industry. But the undeniable fact is that most IT industrial workers earn low wages, suffer from hazardous working conditions, experience harsh factory discipline, and have little technical training or career advancement. The latter are mostly migrant workers from rural areas who do not enjoy the same political, social, and economic rights as city dwellers. The vast difference in wages is illustrated by a report released in August 2003, showing that IT workers' annual incomes ranged from 2,111 Yuan to 384,142 Yuan. As one China expert based in Hong Kong (HK) noted,

> In Guangdong, many HK and foreign-owned companies spend very little in research and development, and they are ill-treating their workers. Many factories have no training and no human resources investment. They are just using it as some sort of slave labor. Workers face long hours, low pay and have little motivation to improve quality. (*South China Morning Post*, December 2002)

More documentation is available from the Asia Monitor Resource Centre (AMRC), the *China Labour Bulletin*, the Hong Kong Christian Industrial Committee, and China Labour Watch (see the Web sites listed at the end of this chapter); and items in this book's reference section.

In the industrial zones, visitors easily can identify many small- and medium-size factories that employ a few dozen or maybe a hundred workers. Some larger firms, however, occupy such a great amount of space that they look like a small town, with rows of dormitories for migrant workers who work together in an environment like an army base. The Flextronics plant in Zhuhai, for example, employs some 20,000 workers (AMRC 2003).

Working hours

As per the Chinese Labor law, an employee's normal working hours should be eight hours a day, five days a week, with weekly working hours not exceeding 40. However, this is hardly observed in practice. Workers generally work more than 40 hours a week, often without overtime payment. Migrant workers are generally ignorant about the five-day working rule and usually work for six days without any overtime payment. Workers also tend to work overtime because their wages are too low. Most contract manufacturers in China run their factories on two, 12-hour shifts, enabling them to lower costs by hiring fewer workers. Overtime abuse in China's electronic factories is just as bad as that in the garment industry. In Winstron Corporation, a subsidiary of the Taiwan-based Acer group, some workers work for more than 72 hours in a six-day week. The labor law restricts monthly hours, including overtime, to

PHOTO 5.1. Women assembly workers in an electronics factory in northeastern China. Courtesy of Apo Leong, Asia Monitor Resource Centre.

249, but some of them work a minimum of 312 hours a month. Similarly, at an electronics factory in Nanshan, Shenzhen Special Economic Zone (SEZ), workers complained that they were forced to work overtime. If they objected, they would be seen as neglecting their duties or fined. At another factory, in Huizhou, employees worked an average of 80 to 90 overtime hours per month.

The other problem is that if a company reduces the number of hours employees are required to work, bowing to pressure from various groups or due to its compliance to codes of conduct, the workload is not necessarily reduced. Workers must complete their quotas in the stipulated time frame, and consequently, may perform extra work without additional pay.

Wages

The Chinese government has established minimum wages for the manufacturing sector, which varied across regions and ranged from a low of 160 Yuan (US$20) in the Sichuan province to a high of 574 Yuan (US$72) in the

Guangdong province in 2002. However, the minimum wages are not living wages based on the present cost of living in Chinese cities. For example, in Guangdong province, workers may have to pay about 200 Yuan for room rent (shared accommodation) if the company does not provide them with subsidized accommodations (i.e., dormitory rooms; see Photo 4.1, previous chapter). The company also will charge them about 40 to 100 Yuan for food (subsidized). Because most workers are migrants, they need to send a major portion of their earnings to their families; thus, they are left with practically no savings or may work overtime to make their ends meet. Moreover, most workers are not aware of the legal minimum wages, as the government usually publishes them once a year in the newspapers, to which workers may not have access. In addition to normal wages, workers are entitled to overtime wages, which are 150 percent of their normal wages by law. Wages are unfairly deducted from, withheld, or cheated. In one Dongguan electronics factory, workers were paid nearly one third less than the minimum wage. Another plant in Zhongshan paid workers more than 10 percent less than the minimum wage. In many cases, workers need to pay a one- to three-month pay deposit before taking a job. Recently, there have been many cases of employers running away and disappearing after owing workers three to six months of wages and then refusing to pay any compensation for closure.

In a survey carried out by the China Labor Education and Information Center of Hong Kong in 1996, in 14 foreign-invested electronic enterprises in Shenzhen, Zhuhai, and Dongguan in Guangdong Province, eight of such enterprises (51.4 percent) offered wages far below the minimum level. On average, the wages were 17.86 percent less than the statutory minimum. The lowest wage level was found in Guanya Electronics Factory in Dongguan City, which paid 32.2 percent less than the minimum wage. The companies with the "best" record were in Zhuhai, where wages were 9.4 percent less than the statutory minimum. One foreign-owned electronics factory manager openly admitted that, when there is a raise in the minimum wage imposed by the local government, the management complies by giving the exact amount to the workers. However, they then deduct or withdraw subsidies or benefits to the workers, such as meal allowances. In the end, workers would receive approximately the same level of wages as before the increase in the minimum wage.

In another notorious case that occurred in the Baoan district, Shenzhen in August 2003, a British boss in an electronics factory openly tore up a labor-law document the local district union officer had given him. The dispute was about a failure to pay workers the minimum wage and the legal overtime payment. Two thousand workers stopped work in protest. Finally, the British boss apologized and agreed to abide by the law.

Punishments

In many factories, workers are fined or punished for what employers call "improper behavior" and even some minor mistakes. In one Japanese electronics factory, workers who violate factory rules are served a yellow card, followed by a one-day wage deduction. Workers said that most violations are trivial matters, such as putting their name tags in the wrong position or chatting at the workplace. One of the most extreme cases was in Zhuhai, where a Korean female owner ordered more than 100 workers to kneel down as a punishment for falling asleep while working and refusing orders. In fact, these workers had been working continuously for four days without proper sleep or rest time.

One electronics worker in Dongguan was unfairly detained for 100 hours by local security guards for not carrying a temporary resident permit. In fact, he was trying to buy a bowl of noodles after finishing overtime at 10 P.M. and was caught within 100 meters from his factory. In March 2003, one unfortunate young migrant worker from Hunan was beaten to death in a detention center after local police accused him of not being able to produce his temporary resident card. This incident created an uproar throughout the country through highly publicized media exposure and direct actions by his family and legal advocates. These cases are too numerous. Despite the central government's repeated calls, the local authorities still impose all kinds of ridiculous fees and fines on migrant workers.

Workers Organizing and Organizations

There is only one union federation legally recognized in China, the ACFTU; thus, workers' freedom of association is very restricted. Moreover, due to the rapid investment in China and the expanding manufacturing units, even the unions under the ACFTU constitution do not exist in many of the units. However, this has not stopped workers from protesting against the injustices against them. Management resorts to any measures necessary to curb opposition. The union or government officials (if any) also offer little help or may even oppose protests. When workers in one Japanese electronics factory organized a strike, the local public security officials warned them not to spread the news to Hong Kong reporters, which would "negatively" affect the foreign investment environment. Another strike in a Japanese-owned camera factory was initiated by the young women workers themselves. However, the local union chair promptly appeared, scolded the striking girls, and coerced them back to work, so as not to upset the investors, and demanded that they behave well. Last, in a strike against a Japanese factory, the local labor bureau officer did a quick inspection tour, but did not bother to ask any workers about the situation. He proceeded directly to the management to have a conversation.

The Taiwan Business Association in Dongguan circulated a "black list" of 39 workers to alarm other employers when interviewing any one of them, for they had joined a strike and demanded unreasonable compensation from one of their members. After mediation, the local Taiwanese Business Association apologized and removed the said circular.

The most recent case irritated the complacent ACFTU, when the former union chair of a Beijing-based joint venture, Sanhuan Sagami High-tech Company, was dismissed. He claimed that the company dismissed him because he had organized workers to protect their legal rights, and this was not in the venture's interests. According to the Chinese Trade Union Law, a trade union officer cannot be dismissed during his or her contract unless there is a serious breach of duty (*China Daily*, September 14, 2004).

Occupational Health and Safety

The electronics industry is known for its hazardous nature worldwide; in a bid to lower operational costs, safety standards are often ignored. This also is due to weak inspections by the authorities, who are more interested in obtaining investments by offering the workers' "cheap lives." Most workers have no idea about the chemicals being used in the work process and their hazards. There are no material safety data sheets (MSDSs) available on the shop floors, even though this is required legally. Chemical poisoning is very common in these factories, and the long-term impacts are unknown, as workers may not work very long in the factories, and when chronic symptoms appear, workers may not relate their diseases to the work. Furthermore, the IT industry involves supporting or downstream work processes, such as plastic molding and metal-case stamping, which may share the same factory premises. The following are some examples that depict the health and safety situation in China's electronics factories:

- From 2000 to 2002, 38 cases of industrial accidents with 39 serious injuries were recorded in one Taiwanese-owned factory producing computer cases in Dongguan, Guangdong province. Most of the victims suffered hand injuries (while operating pressing machines) or fire burns. When workers reported these cases to the media, the management insulted, intimidated, and even beat the victims. Thirty-five workers suffered from benzene poisoning in one home appliance factory in Dongguan because the glue exceeded the safety limit. Another factor was poor ventilation and a lack of protective equipment.
- In 2002, an electronic appliance factory fire in Shenzhen killed 16 workers and injured 18 others. It was discovered that flammable materials and a lack of fire safety measures had risked workers' safety. The doors and windows had been barred or locked. Workers had no safety training at all. Furthermore, local officials ignored these problems.
- In 2003, Chen, a female electronics worker, discovered that all her teeth had turned blue gradually, but the management refused to provide her with any medical treatment. Her doctor found that she was suffering from lead poisoning because her bed in the dormitory was too close to an exhaust fan of the factory where safety standards were not observed.

It is rather difficult to assess the environmental impact of China's electronics industry, as the field work and reliable information are so scarce. But the recent GP Battery case provides a good illustration. About one fourth of its workers had suffered from occupational diseases resulting from cadmium poisoning. Follow-up field work by Greenpeace confirmed that the factory had polluted the neighborhood as well (*Globalisation Monitor* 2004).

CRITICAL ISSUES

China's IT industry undeniably has many underlying problems; the key ones are as follows:

- *As most (90 percent) of the factories are assembly/processing facilities*, they are mostly labor-intensive oriented, with weak internal links, as they still depend on the core technologies of developed countries. An article in *Taipei Times* (November 18, 2003) argued that China should be called the "world's processing plant" rather than "the world factory." It argued, "The competitiveness of Chinese products in global markets is basically built on trading and processing, and a major part of it is due to product processing by foreign manufacturers in China." Of the US$325 billion high-tech exports in 2002, China's Ministry of Commerce rated only 20 percent as genuinely high-tech (*The Economist*, December 20, 2003).
- *Upgrading China's IT industry* is a top agenda, as the country's high-tech production technology is 5 to 15 years behind that of international standards. The major reason for this trend is that China is seen as a major destination for low-cost, labor-intensive production, which may be mostly low- or medium-level assembly. It is not that China is not developing its high-tech or capital-intensive sector. In fact, the Chinese government has been making a conscious effort to develop its high-tech sector (by establishing high-tech development zones), Science Parks, and research and development (R&D) facilities and offering huge incentives for high-tech industries.
- *High-tech exports have been increasing* steadily and constituted about 20 percent of the total exports in 2002. However, the absolute majority of high-tech exports were made up of processed products. In 1993, processed products constituted 70.2 percent of high-tech exports, and by 2003, this figure had increased to 89.6 percent. As already stated, China still exports 80 percent of the chips needed to fuel its electronics industry.
- There also has been a steady increase in China's *development of the semi-conductor industry*, mostly through Taiwanese investments (even though the Taiwanese government does not allow Taiwanese companies to invest in chip R&D in China for strategic reasons, as the chips may be used for military purposes). Yet, it will take years for China to attain a core techno-logical competence comparable to that of Japan, Korea, or Taiwan. China provides not only cheap labor but also a potential market to be exploited. Thus, companies shift their industries to China with a view to produce cheaper goods for international markets, as well as to capture local mar-kets. Core design and high-end production remain centered in developing countries, which profit by exporting these components to China.
- *China is heavily dependent on international market and monetary fluctua-tions*, as foreigners and locals own an increasing number of IT companies. The foreign direct investment (FDI) in this industry amounted to US$7 billion and is growing. There are more than 10,000 joint ventures and wholly owned foreign-owned enterprises.

- *There are few earnings for foreign exchange* as major income depends on labor wages. In fact, from 1996 to 2002, the average price of low-end consumer electronics products dropped by 7 percent, and for PC and telecommunications equipment, it dropped by 35 percent.
- *Low-end products dominate the market.* High-end products are in great demand, but this is controlled by overseas TNCs. Of the top 100 IT companies in the world, only two are from China—China Mobile and China Unicom, far fewer than those in Taiwan, Korea, and Japan (*Business Week* 2003). The so-called "high-valued" productions in China are "low-valued" ones that developed countries have discarded.
- *Localization overrides the national interest,* creating overlapping development zones and intracompetition between cities and regions in regards to their overproduction/capacity; for example, Guangdong province generates 54 percent of the total IT exports.
- *Digital divide:* poorer regions, especially in Western China, cannot even afford to have electricity, and many more children, particularly young girls, are out of school.
- *China has become a dumping ground of e-waste* from other countries, particularly the United States (BAN et al. 2002). Many forms of e-waste are not properly dismantled or recycled under strict regulations, supervision, or monitoring. The scavengers and their family members are easy victims, as well as the environment.

CONCLUSION

On October 6, 2004, nearly 4,000 electronics workers at Computine, a Hong Kong-China joint venture in Shenzhen, blocked the street in protest against low pay and harsh working conditions. The strike paralyzed traffic for four hours, and workers won a 170 percent wage rise. According to participants,

> Our basic salary is only 230 yuan a month [Guangdong minimum wage is 574 Yuan]. We have to work 14 hours a day, seven days a week....
>
> Each time you go to the toilet you have to apply to the squad leader first and then sign your name on a logbook. If you spend more than five minutes in the loo, you will be fined. (quoted in Chow 2004)

The local government has admitted that major labor disputes have increased more than 12 percent compared with previous year.

Industrial relations was not a major concern for many smaller companies in China, and the better managed firms are now quite concerned to learn about complaints and deal with them through the human resources department, as some researchers have noted. The abundant supply of migrant workers seems to make the exit of disgruntled workers a substitute for improving labor relations. If workers are upset by the poor pay and working conditions, they usually choose to leave the factory and look for other jobs, rather than organize or seek help from the government or union officials. The more desperate ones may use physical violence against their supervisors, employers, or their family members. Sabotage is another trick that disgruntled workers frequently use.

In recent years, the more popular approach has been to channel their complaints and appeals through local, national, or Hong Kong newspapers. In a market economy, local newspapers compete by doing investigative stories to attract more readers, even though the government censor limits such stories. Also, individual journalists who are sympathetic to the workers' suffering demand the authorities or the management to address these issues. More labor-oriented, nongovernmental organizations (NGOs) are being established in various industrial zones and city centers in China to provide legal assistance and workers' education. They fill a vacuum where unions are pro-management, pro-government, or virtually absent, but the demand to respect workers' rights is growing. For example, Wu, an IT worker, lodged the first case against his enterprise union for failing to protect his rights when he was unfairly dismissed. He demanded to recover all his union dues for the past four years. Workers are becoming more assertive and more willing to take their employers to court. Here, NGOs can play an effective role in facilitating the legal process. International NGOs and labor organizations must be prepared to respond positively and actively to these workers' struggles.

NOTES

1. "China's Farmers-turned Workers Outnumber Urban-born Counterparts," *People's Daily*, December 19, 2002.

2. Under the 9th Five-Year Plan, five pillar industries were designated: machinery, electronics, petrochemicals, automobiles, and construction.

3. *People's Daily*, February 4, 2004. China's currency is known interchangeably as the Yuan, or Yuan Renminbi. Elsewhere in this chapter, it is abbreviated as RMB. In April 2006, RMB 1 = US$ 0.12497 (eds.).

4. The "Golden Bridge" (also known as information superhighway project) aimed at constructing state-of-art high-speed economic information communication network across the country. The "Golden Card" aimed at promotion of cards (magnetic and IC) and all kinds of electronic currency for financial transitions. The "Golden Customs" project aimed to connect foreign trade companies with banks and China's customs and tax offices. There are many more "Golden Projects" since the start of the three projects.

5. "Top IT Companies Revenue Reach US $68 billion, up 15%," *China Daily*, May 13, 2003.

6. *China Daily* August 2, 2003.

7. "China's labor cost is nearly one fourth that of Korea or one twentieth that of US or Japan," *Economic Observer*, December 2003.

USEFUL WEB SITES

Asia Monitor Resource Center (www.amrc.org.hk)
Asia Trans-National Corporation Monitoring Network (daga.dhs.org/atnc)
China Labour (www.chinalabour.org.hk)
China Labour Watch (www.clw.org)
Hong Kong Christian Industrial Committee (www.cic.org.hk)
Hong Kong Confederation of Trade Unions (www.hkctu.org)
Ministry of Information Industry, Government of China (www.mii.gov.cn)

6   Corporate Social Responsibility in Thailand's Electronics Industry

INTEREST IN CORPORATE social responsibility has grown during the last two decades, particularly among nongovernmental actors and citizens in industrialized countries. That interest stems, in part, from a growing recognition that the relations among nation-states, corporations, and civil society have changed. The modern industrial corporation is transnational in its scope and impacts; its power has arguably grown: Given a context of emerging consumer markets, increasingly flexible production, and an expanded geographic search for cost-effective production, the power of states and societies to dictate the conditions of production to corporations has changed in complex ways (cf. Held et al. 1999; Sassen 1996). The current popular movement to demand increased transparency and public accountability from large corporations is one such relational change.

This chapter examines corporate social responsibility in Thailand's electronics manufacturing industry, focusing on environmental management, occupational safety and health, and labor relations. It focuses primarily on the multinational sector of Thai electronics firms, firms making hard-disk drive components, and assembling and testing semiconductors for export around the world. In the 1990s, "Thailand [was] one of the world's largest production sites for hard disk drives and related components" (Doner and Brimble 1998). During that decade, one firm alone, Seagate Technologies based in Silicon Valley, California, employed more than 40,000 workers, more than any other private company in the country (Chowdhury 2002).[1]

Research questions included: What practices do firms use to reduce environmental impacts, comply with laws, and build trust with their neighbors? What state agencies regulate electronics manufacturing? Who are the civil-society actors that are currently involved in defining corporate responsibility in Thailand's electronics sector? What kinds of interactions (e.g., adversarial and cooperative) have occurred between these actors and these firms?

The findings are based on interviews and site visits conducted between 1998 and 2002, as well as on secondary materials. Interviews were held with representatives from firms, government agencies, labor unions, and nongovernmental organizations (NGOs). The chapter ends with recommendations for continued improvements in the sector's social responsibility.

THE REGULATORY ENVIRONMENT

Regulating environment and occupational health and safety in Thailand's electronics factories is complicated for several reasons (Bundit 2000).

Most significantly, current statutes have overlapping provisions, which create ambiguities and hinder their interpretation and compliance. For example, the Industrial Estate Authority of Thailand (IEAT) regulates firms within industrial estates that otherwise would be regulated by the Pollution Control Department (PCD) and Department of Industrial Works (DIW).

The PCD holds the primary, overall responsibility for regulating some of Thailand's pressing and recurrent environmental problems, including the illegal dumping of industrial waste; chemical accidents—either sporadic releases or chronic nuisance emissions; and the non-point-source biological pollution of rivers (Sukran 1999). A combination of factors appears to have caused these problems: rapid expansion of industry, firm-level cost minimization, weak regulatory oversight, and a lack of industrial zoning (Bello, Cunningham, and Poh 1998).

The PCD faces an enormous set of enforcement challenges. During the last decade, the agency has promulgated twenty-five new environmental quality standards, including standards for general air quality, general coastal and surface freshwater quality, waste incinerators, factories, vehicles, and residential communities. In addition, the agency has generated, and appears to give priority to, action plans to reduce air pollution (i.e., urban dust, vehicles, and coal-fired plants).[2] A second set of PCD action plans attempts to improve water quality, particularly in problem rivers, such as the Nam Pong and the Chao Phraya, whereas a third set of action plans covers solid waste (including usage of hazardous chemicals by farming households and industry). All action plans combine command and control methods, outreach to citizens and firms, new initiatives to train regional inspectors in solving air-quality problems, and new investment in wastewater treatment plants. In addition, the agency has been studying ways to facilitate the adoption of clean technology and establish a "polluter-pays principle." However, other agencies have argued that attempts to implement this principle have met with little success in communities, organizations, or government agencies (cf. Department of Civil Works and Planning 2004).

Potential problems also arise in the area of workplace safety and health from weak linkages between employees and information to which the firm is privy. Thai law, like that of many countries, does not guarantee employees the right either to know about occupational hazards or to decline work if it is hazardous. When employees are given physical exams, they can neither choose the physician nor determine the scope of examination (Bundit 2000).[3] They also have no right to access their employers' medical records for them. At all but the few unionized workplaces, employers choose which employees sit on the mandated, joint-safety committees. Employees have no right to participate in plant inspections by the government safety inspector. The Ministry of Labour has argued that one barrier to effective inspections is the low number of government inspectors (approximately 800) relative to the number of factories (about 300,000). Labor rights advocates have pointed out that the chief problem is not a lack of inspectors, but weaknesses in enforcement management (Bundit 2004).

TABLE 6.1. Presence/Absence of Corporate Responsibility Practices in Thailand

Type of Governance	Thailand		Examples
	Electronics	Apparel	
Internal Occupational Health and Safety, and Environmental Management Processes			
– ISO 14001	Yes	Yes	AMD Thailand Co., Ltd.
– BS 8800	Yes	?	Agere Systems
Corporate Code of Conduct with Human Rights Provisions	No	Yes	Reebok Corp., Thailand
Good Neighbor Agreements	No	No	Chevron Corporation, Richmond, CA
Technical Monitoring by Independent Nonprofit Third Parties	No	No	Nike Corporation, Vietnam Labor Watch
Research/Fact-Finding Collaboration with Civil Society	No	No	

Note: Reebok's activities include: health, safety, and labor rights training and awareness raising, conducted in collaboration with NGO partners.
Source: Authors.

VOLUNTARY CORPORATE PRACTICES

In the context of Thailand's weak state-regulatory apparatus, corporate social responsibility increasingly takes place via voluntary practices. Worldwide, such practices range from internal procedures and codes of conduct, to third-party expert certification (e.g., the International Organization for Standardization [ISO]), to various forms of agreement negotiated with communities (see Table 6.1).

The electronics firms we visited were proud of their in-house health clinics. Some firms used the hall space surrounding their clinics to report statistics on occupational illness by plant subsector or work group, as well as to disseminate preventive health information. In addition, firms took certain health precautions. Employees at Agere Systems'[4] integrated circuit plant, just outside of Bangkok, receive an annual "special" blood test for lead, and the firm disallows women from performing certain tasks once pregnant.[5] Employees have access to translated versions of U.S.-sourced material safety data sheets (MSDSs) for the substances with which they work. The firms also displayed a pattern of investing in international third-party certified voluntary standards: environmental management systems (ISO 14001) and occupational safety and health management systems.

Managers interviewed stated that their firms had decided to pursue ISO 14001 certification for two main reasons: because of their corporate customers' demand for it and because it was a priority for those with a parent company. Many multinational subsidiaries were the first in their corporation worldwide to receive ISO certification. This suggests that firms perceive such voluntary measures as important and that efficient supporting organizations (e.g., certifiers) exist in Thailand. All firms interviewed had obtained ISO 9000 quality assurance certification prior to undertaking

ISO 14001 certification, for which they typically took 6 to 12 months to prepare.

Firms mentioned a variety of benefits of becoming certified: substantial savings on energy and process water (e.g., via conservation and recycling), an ability to meet customer demands, and a positive public image. As an indirect benefit, some corporations affirmed the importance of environmental management programs and systems. Managers felt that the main challenge of the ISO 14001 certification process is that it requires "continuous improvement" to become recertified. "Getting certified the first time was not so difficult," said one interviewee, "getting recertified gets more difficult each time, because you are audited for your success in obtaining goals specified the previous time."

The process of developing environmental management systems and certifying them under ISO 14001 seems to have allowed all firms to identify opportunities to reduce solid, liquid, and airborne material throughput (influx or emissions to the environment). All firms interviewed implemented changes, beginning with the easiest ones (e.g., using spent potable water on grounds and gardens in the plant, reducing purified water on the line, and recycling printed circuit board scrap for resale as opposed to disposing it in a hazardous waste landfill).

Firm interest in occupational safety and health management systems (e.g., British Standard 8800, the Thai Industrial Standard 18000) was evident at only two of the firms visited, Agere Systems (mentioned previously) and Philips Semiconductor. The managers we interviewed gave three reasons for their hesitation in obtaining third-party occupational safety and health certification. First, they cited the adequacy and effectiveness of existing internal Occupational Safety and Health Service (OSH) procedures. Second, some managers noted that the ISO had not finished developing this standard (see ISO 2000). Finally, lack of customer or parent-company interest also was mentioned as a reason.

In terms of physical dimensions, economic activity, and workforce, the electronics manufacturing plants we studied all exhibited an obvious presence at the local level. Notwithstanding their industrial sector's traditions of being "closed" (for competitiveness reasons), it was somewhat surprising that community interactions appeared to be the exception rather than the norm. Some firms, such as Agere Systems, Seagate, and AMD, stressed a willingness to meet with community members, as part of the environmental management (ISO 14001) process they chose. Others did not mention it. None of the firms studied appeared to have stakeholder consultations or monitoring in place, nor was there evidence of environmental monitoring by nongovernmental, "public interest" third parties.[6]

Worker Illnesses and Deaths

The California-based multinational, Seagate Technology, had opened two plants in Thailand in 1988 and 1989.[7] In 1991, Seagate confronted a union organizing drive. It eventually fired a total of 708 workers who were publicly calling for union recognition (e.g., by staging demonstrations in front of the U.S. Embassy). A union leader in the Federation of Electrical Employees mentioned that Seagate's human resources director at the time staunchly resisted the union drive. Union leaders could not enroll the 20 percent of employees needed to officially represent the workforce. According to Seagate, when it became clear that the company would not recognize a union, most of the fired workers asked to go back to work, but all were denied the opportunity to do so. The dismissed workers appealed to the tripartite national Labor Relations Committee over unfair labor practices. Seagate chose to compensate the workers (as ordered by the Committee) in lieu of reinstating them.

Four workers at Seagate's Teparuk plant, south of Bangkok, died in 1990 and 1991. According to their coworkers, they all had experienced headaches, fatigue, muscle aches, and fainting. Almost 200 others were diagnosed as having chronic lead poisoning, possibly aggravated by solvent exposure. The plant made components for low-margin, 3.5-inch disk drives.

In August 1991, Dr. Orapan Metadilogkul, Thailand's most prominent and active practitioner of occupational medicine, was asked to investigate the deaths. She sampled blood from 1,175 workers and concluded that blood levels in approximately 200 employees were high enough to suggest chronic lead poisoning, which perhaps had been aggravated by solvent inhalation. Her clinic (the National Institute of Occupational and Environmental Medicine [NIOEM]) treated some workers from a group of 200 that had complained of headaches, insomnia, fatigue, and muscle aches. At least two of these workers showed common symptoms of seizures, cramps, and limb numbness, and had blood lead levels exceeding the Thai standard of 40 micrograms lead per 100 milliliters of blood (Kedrick 1994).

Seagate disputed the vast majority of the findings. In 1992, it commissioned Mahidol University's Department of Occupational Health and Safety to measure levels of airborne lead and dust concentrations in Teparuk workspaces, as well as in the exhaust ventilation ducts that release outside the plant (see Chalermchai and Vichai n.d.). The Mahidol team found workstation lead levels ranging from nondetectable to 0.0504 mg/m^3, surpassing the Thai standard, set by the Department of Labor Protection and Welfare, of 0.2 mg/m^3. In the vent ducts, Seagate's highest exhaust air lead concentration was measured at less than 0.002 mg/m^3, surpassing the Thai DIW standard of 30 mg/m^3. Seagate's highest dust concentration was 67.7 mg/m^3, compared to the DIW's standard of 100 mg/m^3. Having found no compliance problems, the Mahidol University report recommended precautionary follow-up and review of that particular exhaust duct.

Workers Compensation Dispute

Seagate was taken to Thailand's administrative Central Labour Court to resolve a worker's compensation claim made by some of the group of 200 workers identified by Dr. Orapan as having occupational illnesses. However, according to Dr. Orapan, only one worker was willing to go to the Labour Court, where she successfully won compensation from Seagate prior to 1993. (By 1993, the two-year statute of limitations had expired for any others in this group who may have wanted to seek worker's compensation.) However, in 1994, Seagate initiated a suit to reverse the compensation verdict.

That same year, Seagate also wrote to the Medical Council of Thailand, Thailand's highest level medical board, asking them to review Dr. Orapan's suitability to continue directing her clinic and practicing occupational medicine. She was reviewed and cleared; however, the Ministry of Public Health reassigned her staff to other offices. In 1996, Seagate withdrew its suit from the Labour Court, anticipating, according to one observer at the time, a court dismissal due to insufficient evidence. Seagate's actions against Dr. Orapan brought to a standstill a leading center of occupational medicine in Thailand, damaged the career of one of the country's leading advocates for worker health and safety, and wrought a heavy personal toll on Dr. Orapan, as well—a chilling reminder of the power of large, multinational corporations to harass, intimidate, and punish their critics throughout the world.

Incidents at the Northern Region Industrial Estate

In 1993, while the "Seagate affair" was still heading toward litigation, a separate pattern of illness and death among electronic workers occurred at the Northern Region Industrial Estate (NRIE), in Lamphun Province, about 30 km from Chiang Mai city. A wide variety of domestic and foreign firms employed about 29,000 workers within the NRIE; the most common sectors were food processing (for which the estate was designed) and electronics component manufacturing and assembly (Valiya 2000). Two thirds of all firms in the NRIE were classified as "exporters," which were eligible for five to eight years' worth of tax exemptions from the Board of Investment. Of the total workforce, an estimated three-fourths were women. The exporters hired almost 80 percent of the total workforce. Half of the companies in the NRIE were in the electronics sector. Japanese capital appears to have had a significant presence.

In 1993, a pattern of illness and deaths became evident among workers at electronic component makers Murata, Electro Ceramics, Hoyo Opto, KSS Electronics, Tokyo Coil, Tokyo Try, and F.M. Brush. All except F.M. Brush are Japanese owned. By September 1994, there were numerous reports that people had died after working in electronics factories (Forsyth, 1994; Tara 1998; see also Theobald 1998). The number of reported deaths ranged from 10 to 23. The exact number was uncertain, possibly due to workers dying after going on sick leave and losing contact with their employer; receiving medical care from a number of clinics and hospitals; having no health status follow-up or reporting requirements once no longer employed; and no organization systematically tracking down an exact number.

When the head of the IEAT held a press conference in late 1993, he denied that the deaths were firm related. According to Forsyth (1994), the firms distanced themselves from the dead workers by noting that: all of the deceased were no longer employed, they were not working directly with lead, or they were HIV positive. Although there is a high rate of HIV infection in northern Thailand, the medical and academic sources that Forsyth interviewed noted that only three of the workers who died were HIV positive.

Also, they mentioned that the deceased did not have typical HIV/AIDS symptoms (such as marked weight loss and opportunistic infections). Rather, their symptoms included headaches, fatigue, occasional fainting, and occasional seizures.

When more deaths occurred during the six months following the IEAT press conference, the government sent a team of Ministry of Public Health epidemiologists to investigate (Forsyth 1994). Their report was never released. Dr. Uthaiwan Kanganakamol, a professor of dentistry and public health, and a prominent activist based in Chiang Mai, participated in a high-level review team whose report was not released. Tara (1998) argued that "there has been no significant independent study of health and safety conditions in the estate." Neither government agencies nor researchers have been able to obtain permission to conduct research on the estate's health and safety.[8]

In 1998, researchers from Mahidol University conducted an extensive study of environmental conditions at NRIE, resulting in the publication of a three-volume report. Although useful as an introduction to processes used at the almost 70 firms in the estate, the study contained no safety and health or epidemiological data. Tara (1998) speculated that at least one of the deceased had symptoms of trichloroethylene (TCE) poisoning. Another sick worker, Mayuree, had been employed by Electro Ceramics and worked intensively with alumina powder. When she sought treatment on her own initiative, her doctor (whom she had already seen, but through the company) diagnosed her as having aluminum poisoning. According to Forsyth (1994), Electro Ceramics intervened with the doctor's employer, McCormick Hospital, which had the diagnosis "retracted."

More recently, beginning in 2002, an independent team led by Thanpuying Dr. Suthawan Sathirathai, of the Bangkok-based Good Governance and Social Development and Environment Institute, sampled the blood of employees working for companies at NRIE, on a private, voluntary basis. Firms at NRIE have not allowed this NGO project to work on their premises. Sampling detected elevated concentrations of alumina among some employees; however, no medical practitioner has yet ventured a diagnosis of work-related poisoning.

Common Themes

The Seagate and NRIE cases differ in their details, but the overall pattern contains striking similarities. The cases show how, in the early 1990s, firms could withdraw from their responsibility by appealing to scientific or medical uncertainty regarding the complex epidemiology of work-related illness and death (see also LaDou; and Hawes and Pellow, this volume). In addition, the firms at NRIE relied on certain norms of property to refuse access to a state-sanctioned investigation. Because employees could not present timely or effective cases before the Labour Court, firms were ordered to pay compensation in only a handful of the compelling cases (see Kedrick 1994). Furthermore, assisted by pressure from the governmental Board of Investment of Thailand (BOI), firms were able to cast aspersion on the quality of occupational medicine in Thailand, including through litigation.

Sadly, but not surprisingly, the worker illnesses and deaths in Thailand in the early 1990s were pivotal grievances that helped spur activism. This activism aimed to transform the politics of occupational health. Dramatic episodes—at Seagate, Lamphun, the infamous Kader toy factory fire,[9] and elsewhere—appear to have emboldened Thai civil society activists to form new advocacy networks. By campaigning for greater worker participation in occupational health policymaking, these NGOs seek to realign the balance of power and the structure of state-business-civil society relations, which they see as central to the problems reviewed previously.

CIVIL SOCIETY INTERACTIONS

By the late 1990s, Thailand had a new constitution, drafted with the partici-pation of progressive academics and their NGO allies. The 1997 Constitution redistributed certain important powers to citizens (cf. McBride 2002). In do-ing so, it has been regarded by activist NGOs as a source of new structural opportunity. The NGO network for occupational safety and health consists of a small number of nodal organizations tied together by relationships and alliances that date back at least to the early 1990s (Voravidh 2000). The name for this network—Network of People Impacted By Industrial Devel-opment (NPIID)—conveys that its interest extend beyond workplace health and safety.

NPIID consists of more than two dozen organizations in Bangkok and the provinces, including the *Arom Pongpa-ngan* Foundation (AP), the Friends of Women Foundation (FOW), and the Work and Environment Related Patients' Network of Thailand (WEPT). Of these organizations, the AP is the oldest, dating back to 1975. AP is a resource center for protecting and promoting labor rights. For instance, AP lawyer, Bundit Tanachaisaetawut, publishes the monthly *Labor Review* (*Raeng-ngan Paritat*), along with a useful year-in-review special edition. He also has published an edited a volume discussing problems in the new Labour Relations Act of 1998 (Bundit 1999), and a recent analysis of the problems in Thailand's fragmented occupational safety and health laws (Bundit 2000). The AP is one of Thailand's most prominent nonacademic labor law and policy think tanks.

The FOW, a larger nonprofit founded in the late-1980s, works closely with the AP on labor rights issues. In addition, it lobbies for women's equal rights under the law and provides training and human resource-building services for other groups, including legal and medical professionals. Its first major political campaign, in 1991 to 1993, was for employees' rights to a 90-day unpaid maternity leave. The FOW publishes *Ying Chai Gao Glai (Women and Men Advancing Far)*, a biannual news magazine that covers a variety of health and political topics. Senior staff member, Jaded Chaowilai, has published on female labor rights issues and Thai labor law and sits on the advisory boards of several smaller NGOs.

The WEPT is a grassroots organization that is now partly funded by the Ministry of Public Health. It began in 1993 as a support group for eight women whose lungs were injured by persistent exposure to cotton dust in textile factories and were struggling to win worker's compensation through the Labour Court (*Bangkok Post*, April 28, 1998). The WEPT's membership has grown substantially in recent years. Most members have occupational health grievances. The WEPT's distinctive identity comes from drawing on its membership for a variety of activities, including contributing art and poetry to its monthly newsletter. It has established a mutual aid fund levied from its members (B 100 per person per month) and organizes plaintiffs—and lately, it has initiated action in Labour Court cases. The WEPT's advisory board includes academics and professionals, but the organization maintains considerable autonomy.

Dr. Orapan Metadilogkul's clinic at Ratchvithi Hospital remains one of the few independent centers for treatment and public health education on occupational and environmental disease in Thailand. In addition to seeing patients, Dr. Orapan has been personally active in the NPIID. She is an effective public speaker and has reached out to leaders from Thailand's labor federations, a set of organizations that previously had not actively pursued occupational safety and health issues.

Campaign for a Safety and Health Institute

Following the Kader fire, a number of civil-society organizations participated in a protest movement to lobby Thailand's powerful BOI for increased transparency in foreign-owned workplaces (e.g., the right of community inspection—similar to Good Neighbor Agreements devised in other places like the United States). However, the BOI apparently denied that it had the authority to issue new policies. In 1994, the FOW, together with such NGOs as the Assembly of the Poor (AoP), began to air proposals to create an independent institute for occupational safety, health, and the environment, with a broad set of mandates, including occupational safety and health research, inspection, and the management of comp funds.

In June 1997, a committee composed of civilians and public servants submitted a new bill to the Thai cabinet, under Prime Minister Chavalit, for consideration. Pressure on the state increased significantly during 1997, following a three-month protest led by the AoP (Missingham 2003). But in the wake of the 1997 to 1998 financial crisis, the subsequent Chuan Leekpai administration gave the bill a much less sympathetic reception. The Ministry of Labour issued alternative draft legislation proposing more modest reforms. Not pleased with what they viewed as the government preemption of their proposals, the NGO coalition decided in 1988 to launch a citizen petition campaign to force parliament to consider their version of the bill.[10]

Both versions of legislation involve consolidating the government's existing occupational safety and health promotion offices into one new organization. In addition, the NGO version assigns responsibility for extra-judicial review of worker compensation cases and includes a medical and occupational therapy unit. The NGO version invests interest collected from the national workers' compensation fund in health education and includes more senior civil servants in the proposed institute management council (including the

Prime Minister and the Ministers of Labour, Environment, and Industry). In this version, four segments of the public are represented in the council: employers, employees, the sick and injured, and those with special expertise. The government's version, by contrast, follows the traditional tripartite formula of state, employer, and employee representation.

The NGO version contains several radical reforms, including a greater scope (the clinical medicine unit), independent review, and settlement of workers' compensation cases; as well as more power sharing between powerful office holders and the sick and injured. The budgetary and organizational implications for the new institute are clearly not trivial and will likely be contested. Competing versions of the bill still exist, and the debate continues, with the government and NGO coalition divided over who should have the final authority over workers' compensation.

In the years since the Kader fire (now National Safety Day), the NPIID has made dramatic inroads in marshalling public support for its policies, as well as forging closer ties with relevant state agencies and politicians. The government conducts occupational safety and health education workshops through the Thai Industrial Standards Institute (TISI) and the Office of Environmental Policy and Planning (OEPP).[11] Industry associations (e.g., the petrochemical industry association) do the same. The TISI has coordinated planning for small- and medium-sized enterprises interested in the new Thai Industrial Standard 18000. At the same time, relations between civil society actors and electronics firms (domestic or foreign subsidiaries) remain strained. Civil-society actors distrust electronics firms, partly because of the legacy of conflicts at Seagate and Lamphun, as well as their lack of progress in initiating recent invitations for firms to participate in such activities as collaborative health and safety action research. Meanwhile, they are largely unaware of the nontrivial environmental and safety gains that firms have achieved through their own efforts. Firms distrust civil society actors: Perhaps they fear that more open engagement will increase their vulnerability to collective labor action. Electronics firms may be hampered by a lack of staff assigned to community relations.

Multinational apparel makers that operate in Thailand, such as Reebok and Adidas, offer a revealing example of what can be achieved when voluntary measures include more active community engagement. Reebok has a Corporate Code of Conduct and, since the year 2000, has maintained a Human Rights staff person in Thailand. It gave funding support to NGOs organizing National Safety Day activities in 2004 and organizes training sessions on safety, health, and labor rights for the workforce employed by its subcontractors, some of which are nonunionized (Voravidh 2004).

Certainly, civil-society labor-rights actors today are more effective than they were in the early 1990s, the period of early campaigns for maternity leave, unexplored worker illnesses, deaths, and—arguably—more dangerous workplaces. In pressing for social change, civil society actors have found it much easier to work with governmental officials than with electronics firms.[12]

CONCLUSION

The Thai government's ability to regulate corporate environmental health and safety practices, including in electronics, remains weak. Voluntary measures remain important—yet they are not always transparent. Modes of quasi-regulation, such as those related to the adoption of ISO standards for environmental and occupational health and safety (OHS) management systems, create customized discourses and procedures, respectively, at the firm level. These practices may diverge from the best practices of risk assessment and minimization that could be produced via more open processes, including dialog with such third parties as independent OHS researchers and community health organizations (both public and private) dedicated to improving industrial workers' health.

Without such dialog and collaborative fact-finding, several basic questions remain unanswered:

- How do workstation levels of lead and other toxic chemicals today compare to levels measured in the mid-1990s (e.g., at Seagate)? How do they compare among firms?
- Firms keep records on employee health indicators—what do they record? How do worker-health indicator levels change over time? Does data collection improve worker health, and if so, how? Is there a need for data-sharing systems conducive to longitudinal health monitoring and evaluation?
- What evidence is there that today's emphasis on voluntary corporate environmental health and safety systems reduces the risk to workers of chronic occupational illness?

In light of the public controversy in Thailand in the early and mid 1990s regarding the deaths and occupational illnesses in electronics-related manufacturing, the environmental- and health-monitoring practices that firms conduct, both inside their plants and among their workers, deserve to be specified, standardized, and publicized. We believe it is possible to devise programs to answer questions, such as those previously cited, in a manner acceptable to all parties. Models of participatory, scientific research methods do exist (e.g., in public health and sociology), as well as examples of multi-stakeholder processes among firms, government agencies, and NGOs (e.g., the World Commission on Dams).

Civil-society actors, both issue based (e.g., labor and women's NGOs) and locality based (e.g., neighborhood associations), are two of many potential "third parties" that have an incentive to participate in improving corporate social responsibility. Unfortunately, as we have shown, these actors' interactions with firms have been structured by conflicts over responsibility in the wake of industry-related illnesses, deaths, and accidents, such as those at Seagate, the NRIE, Kader, a more recent Cobalt-60 radiation leakage incident, and a Chiang Mai fruit-processing-plant explosion. The long campaign for an independent institute for occupational safety, health, and the environment is an important, high-stakes advance. Regardless of which vision of the new institute prevails, citizens' and workers' ability to engage firms'

PHOTO 6.1. Participants at a workshop on occupational and environmental health and safety in electronics manufacturing, Chiang Mai, Thailand, October 2003. Courtesy of Phongtape Wiwatanadate.

efforts to improve occupational safety, health, and environmental conditions via alternative, complementary channels remains important.

Because it is not clear whether the regulatory system has improved or led to improvements for workers and the environment, we recommend more research, including collaborative research among specialists, firms, workers, and community-based organizations.

NOTES

The authors appreciate the genuine cooperation and helpfulness of many individuals, organizations, and firms in the collection of data for this chapter. It is updated and substantially revised from a report prepared by the first author for the Nautilus Institute for Security and Sustainable Development, Berkeley, California, April 2001.

1. The number of employees in Thailand's electronics manufacturing sector dropped dramatically in the first years of the twenty-first century due to a variety of circumstances, including the super-miniaturization and automation of electronics component manufacturing, regional and global economic downturns, and global overproduction of electronic components. By 2002, Seagate employed fewer than half the numbers of workers in Thailand than it did a few years earlier (Chowdhury 2002). Tens of thousands of especially young women workers remain employed in the sector in Thailand, however.

2. See PCD's Web site: www.pcd.go.th.

3. This is not unique to Thailand. California, for example, recently restricted the ability of workers compensation plaintiffs or victims to choose their own physicians.

4. Agere Systems was spun off from Lucent Technologies, formerly part of AT&T, in June 2002. See the firm's Web site: www.agere.com.

5. While firms test new applicants for pregnancy, it is not clear whether pregnancy constitutes grounds for rejecting an application. By contrast, in Mexican maquiladoras where workers make television sets, pregnancy does constitute grounds for rejection (see García and Simpson, this volume).

6. Third-party or community monitoring is not required under the ISO 14001 guidelines.

7. The following information is from Forsyth (1994).

8. Researchers associated with Chiang Mai University have conducted several interesting community surveys, however. See Tara (1996) and Theobald (1998).

9. On May 10, 1993, more than 400 people were injured, and almost 200 people died in a fire at the Kader Industrial Toy Company, in an industrial estate outside Bangkok. Greider (1997, p. 337–339) notes that locked doors, barred windows, illegally narrow fire escapes, and unreinforced structures contributed to "the worst industrial fire in the history of Capitalism."

10. Article 170 of Thailand's 1997 Constitution grants citizens the right to introduce legislation for consideration by the legislature, if endorsed by 50,000 registered voters.

11. OEPP is an environmental agency with planning and problem-solving responsibilities. Its regional offices have assumed greater responsibility as a result of the country's decentralization efforts.

12. Various campaigns in Thailand for improved working conditions and other labor rights have been conducted almost exclusively by domestic actors. There has been limited support from international trade unions and development assistance missions, such as through the Danish-supported Asian Workers Occupational Health, Safety, and Environment Institute (see www.ohseinstitute.org). Thai labor activists assertively emphasize the national character of their movement, however (cf. www.thailabour.org).

7   Electronics Workers in India

Sheela[1] can feel her head reeling. She works in the soldering section of a printed circuit board factory in Mumbai. She has been working for more than eight hours on a very hot and humid day. She could not get a lunch break as she had taken a day off the previous day, and there is a pending job she is supposed to finish. The noxious fumes are giving her stomach cramps, and with an empty stomach she is feeling even worse. Her co-worker, Rajni, looks at her with sympathy, but Rajni can do little to help her. With no union in the factory (as unions have never been allowed), any sort of "indiscipline" (as management calls it) could result in a worker being punished, or even fired. Sheela thinks of her family and tries to concentrate on the work, but it is becoming increasingly difficult. Suddenly, a dark cloud appears in front of her eyes, and she collapses on the factory floor.

SHEELA IS ONE of the thousands of invisible workers who toil night and day in India's electronics sweatshops, remaining untouched by the sector's apparent prosperity. The industry's total production figure of US$21 billion (in both hardware and software) for the 2002–2003 fiscal year did not mean much to her or to the many other thousands of workers, who find it difficult to make ends meet.

This chapter conveys a picture of India's electronic hardwarek manufacturing industry and the condition of its workers. After a brief overview of India's electronics sector, including its extent and geographical spread, this chapter provides insight into the working conditions and lives of the workers that it employs. India often is called "the IT [information technology] destination." This chapter analyzes the reality and hype of this claim, as well as problems associated with future growth of the country's hardware sector. Finally, this chapter examines the Indian government's role and ambitious claims in terms of this industry's growth and employment and its deliberate denial (in the name of investment) of any kind of social security for the workers.

INDUSTRY OVERVIEW

Currently, the Indian electronics industry is classified into six main categories: consumer electronics, instrumentation and industrial electronics, data-processing systems and other office equipment, communication and broadcasting equipment, strategic electronics, and electronic components. Table 7.1 provides the five-year production figures for the different electronics sectors, and Figure 7.1 shows the percentage value of each of these sectors for the year 2002 to 2003. As Figure 7.1 clearly indicates, consumer electronics

Table 7.1. IT and Electronics: Sectoral Production Datasheet (Sales Million Rupees)

Item	1998–99	1999–2000	2000–02	2001–03	2002–03
Consumer Electronics	92,000	112,000	115,500	127,000	144,000
Industrial Electronics	33,000	37,500	40,000	45,500	47,000
Computers	23,000	25,000	34,000	35,000	39,000
Comm. & Broad. Eqpt.	44,000	40,000	45,000	45,000	56,000
Strategic Electronics	13,000	14,500	17,500	18,000	22,500
Electronic Components	47,500	52,000	55,000	57,000	62,000
Subtotal	**252,250**	**281,000**	**307,000**	**327,500**	**370,500**
Software for Exports	109,400	171,500	283,500	365,000	475,000
Domestic Software	49,500	72,000	94,000	116,340	124,000
Total	**411,400**	**524,500**	**684,500**	**808,840**	**969,500**

Source: MoCIT (2003b). (US$1 = 45.6 Rs).

is the single largest sector (nearly 40 percent) of the electronic hardware sector's production.

India's hardware sector accounted for about US$7.93 billion (MoCIT 2003b). India has yet to become a preferred electronic and IT hardware manufacturing site. In 2001, the country's total hardware production accounted for a meager 0.6 percent of the global electronics/IT hardware production of US$1.2 trillion. Most electronics manufacturing in India is low-wage, labor-intensive assembly with low capital investment. This can be illustrated by the simple fact that there is no semiconductor fabrication in India (even though Intel recently announced plans to set up a fabrication plant there). However, India is a major destination for researching and designing chips. Intel has one design facility in Bangalore, employing more than 1,000 people. Much of the hardware manufactured in India is for domestic consumption. However, only 25 percent of India's IT hardware needs are met by domestic production, and the share is expected to fall to 20 percent in the future, as India moves to a

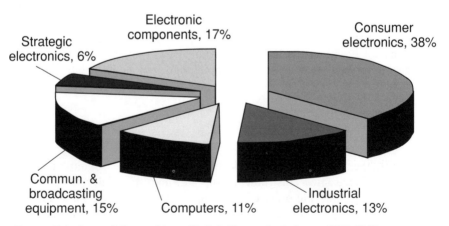

Figure 7.1. Sectoral Composition of India's Electronics Industry, 2002–2003.
Source: MoCIT (2003b).

zero-duty regime (by 2005) for IT product imports in line with the Information Technology Agreement (ITA) of the World Trade Organization.

Approximately 3,500 firms were engaged in electronics production in India in 1997 (DoE 1999). Of these, 71 were public-sector firms, 625 were in the organized private sector, and more than 2,800 were registered small-scale and tiny firms.[2] Many unregistered smaller firms, many of them home based, also were engaged in the assembly of consumer electronics, instruments, and electronic components. The top-200 firms, including 50 small-scale firms, accounted for nearly 73 percent of the industry's production.

India's electronic hardware industry is concentrated in three main regions. The northern region, around the national capital of Delhi, accounts for 37 percent of the output. The western region, around Mumbai and Pune, accounts for 25 percent of the output; and the southern region, mainly around Bangalore, accounts for 32 percent of the output. Bangalore has a concentration of large, public-sector units and organized, private-sector players, partly linked to the presence of the defense establishments in the city. Pondycherry, a small union territory in southern India, has become a major IT hardware assembly location for both Indian and multinational corporations (MNCs), including IBM, Acer, and Compaq.

Electronics manufacturing employed 365,000 people in India in 1999 (MoCIT 2000).[3] This figure seems grossly understated, as it does not take into account the thousands of those working in very small units and home-based workers. The electronics manufacturing sector constitutes 7 to 8 percent of the total value added in the manufacturing sector in India (Bhavani 2002), and the manufacturing sector employed 40 million people in 2000 (GoI 2003). The number of persons employed in India's electronics/IT industry in hardware and software is projected to become 7 million in 2008, of which 4.8 million will be employed (directly or indirectly) in hardware manufacturing (MoCIT 2003a). The present electronics manufacturing workforce seems to have been completely ignored in the production and growth statistics.

Forms of Employment and Employment Relations

The employment patterns in electronic hardware manufacturing vary widely in India depending on both the type of unit and, also within the unit, the worker's status (temporary, permanent trainee, etc.). As described earlier, electronics production in India is carried out in home-based and small-, medium-, and large-scale, organized units. Small-scale units employ the largest number of workers. In 1997, small-scale enterprises employed about 47 percent of the total workers in the electronics manufacturing sector. However, they contributed about 35 percent of the total produced value (DoE 1999).

In small- and medium-sized units, workers are employed predominantly for the assembly of components or parts, which in turn are used in larger units. This sort of subcontracting has been a hallmark of the Indian electronics industry, and with the industry's globalization, it is becoming increasingly prominent. The workers in smaller units do not have any sort of formal contract with their employers. They receive only wages, no other social benefits. The "Factories Act" of India applies to units employing ten or more workers and does not cover any unit employing fewer than ten. However, even the units employing ten or more workers will not provide benefits, such as provident funds,[4] to the workers, as the law prescribes.

LABOR FLEXIBILITY AND SUBCONTRACTING

In larger, organized units, workers may be employed as permanent workers who receive wages and other benefits. However, there is a trend toward having fewer permanent workers. Instead, larger units are increasingly relying on contract workers, who also may be employed for night shifts and to replace workers on leave. In some factories, the level of contract workers is as high as 80 percent. In the Okhla industrial area in New Delhi, electronics companies do not recruit permanent workers, only temporary or casual workers (Chhachhi 1997a). Permanent workers often are retrenched legally (by offering voluntary retirement schemes) or even illegally. Some units employ only casual workers for a period of time, and then they rename the unit and reemploy the workers on a temporary basis.

This trend is still prevalent, though the exact forms may differ. An interesting scenario exists in Pondycherry, where many Indian companies and MNCs have computer assembly plants. All use contract workers. The contract can last from three to six months, and then the workers are either reemployed on a new contract or just thrown out. The most surprising aspect of this arrangement is that the workers are highly skilled. Most have either diplomas or degrees in computer engineering. Their wages range from 1,500 to 3,000 rupees per month[5] (without any other benefits) depending on their degree. However, all do the same job. The workers take these jobs because no others are available. They work for six months to one year with this arrangement, hoping to be offered better employment. IBM issues a certificate to such workers, and this, the workers say, helps them find better jobs due to IBM's reputation.

Within the units, job flexibility is common and may involve either multitasking or job rotation. This management strategy is intended to achieve the maximum productivity using the fewest workers. This is more prevalent in small- and medium-size enterprises. A unit for assembling televisions can shift to making cellular phones in a few months (Chhachhi 1997b).

Larger units or brands, both in both consumer electronics and hardware IT units like computers, often subcontract part of their production or procure components from other units, which may be large or small. Calcom India, for example, is India's largest manufacturer of picture tubes, and most brands, like Samsung, Onida, and Sony, procure picture tubes from them. The subcontracting chain in the electronics sector is very complex, and it usually is very difficult to trace or even map.

THE FEMINIZATION OF LABOR[6]

Kamla is waiting again outside a major consumer electronics factory, situated in Greater Noida, near New Delhi. Kamla has been coming here for a week. This company often hires casual workers, who outnumber the regular ones. She is among many others who wait every day outside the factory gate, hoping to get work. No one knows whom will be picked. She must walk six km every day in the scorching heat of summer, as the factory is located at the city's far outskirts and the buses are infrequent.

However, a few months ago, Kamla had decided that she would never work for this company again. She had been hired for three months as a casual worker and that was the beginning of her miseries. The authoritarian management treated all the casual workers very badly. She had to work for 12 hours every day, without proper breaks, and was paid for only 11 hours. The supervisors were brutal, often shouting at the workers. Kamla still remembers when one worker lost his arm in the molding unit. The worker was not paid any compensation: Only the hospital charges were paid and then he was sent home.

During Kamla's third month of work, her supervisor told her that she needed to work overnight, as the company had to produce more for the festive season. She worked for more than 18 hours and her feet became swollen. She did not have enough time to eat properly. When she went home, she collapsed and could not get up the next morning. She was down with a fever, and it took her a week to recover completely. When she went to the factory again, her supervisor started to abuse her and told her to get out. She felt insulted in front of the other workers and decided not to go back again.

However, with her two young children to feed and no other jobs available, she has completely forgotten all the insults and horrors, and is hoping to get work again—whatever the costs may be.

India is not exempt from the global trend toward employing young women for most assembly jobs in the electronics sector (Kumar 1986). The annual report of the Ministry of Information and Technology stated that the "IT sector provides flexibility to its employee to operate from home and in working time which enables women to carry on jobs with their family life" (MoCIT 2002). The report also acknowledged the preference for women over men in the assembly sector. The industry generally prefers young, unmarried women because they can work flexible hours and can be controlled easily. Women carry out most of the home-based work in the electronics industry.

Although women constitute a major portion of the labor force, their jobs are always the unskilled or low-skilled ones. They never are preferred for the skilled jobs, and they mostly occupy the bottom of the occupational hierarchy. Indian women, rural women in particular, seldom enjoy the same education and training as do men. Thus, they find it difficult to get jobs in skill- and capital-intensive industries. Employers also are reluctant to invest in developing women's skills, as they feel that it may be a waste of investment because women may leave after marrying or having children. Therefore, women have to be satisfied with low-skilled jobs in a labor-intensive industry.

WAGES

Wages vary widely depending on the type of the unit (small or large), the worker's status (temporary or permanent), and the worker's skill level (skilled, semiskilled, or unskilled). The general trend can be explained based on the pyramid depicted in Figure 7.2.

Most of the workers in India's electronics industry attain the base of the pyramid and receive much lower wages, with no social security or any other benefits. These workers include temporary and casual workers in both small- and large-scale enterprises. Wages are paid based on a piece rate, as well as on a time rate, and they range from 800 to 3,000 rupees per month.[7] Home-based workers receive the lowest wages among all the electronics workers. They are paid mostly on a piece-rate basis and earn about 500 to 800 rupees a month.[8] Skilled and permanent workers working in large, organized units generally earn 2,000 to 10,000 rupees per month.[9] In addition, workers may receive retirement benefits and some medical allowances. However, this category of workers is very small, and, as stated earlier, the industry has been making concerted efforts to get rid of these workers and replace them with casual laborers, to whom they do not need to pay other benefits.

In India, the government fixes the workers' wages, based on the Minimum Wages Act. Minimum wages vary across both states and cities, and they also vary based on the workers' skill level (skilled, semiskilled, or unskilled). However, the management widely abuses the workers' designation as skilled

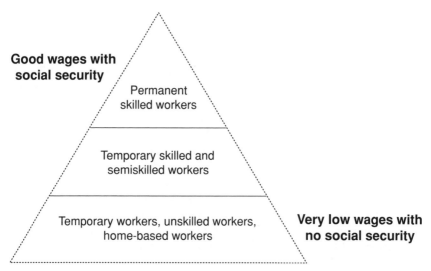

FIGURE 7.2. Structure of Employment, Wages, and Social Security in India's Electronics Industry.
Source: Author.

or unskilled. For example, one worker designated as an operator would be skilled worker, and another worker performing a similar job, but designated as a helper, would receive an unskilled worker's wages. Companies even may change the workers' designation from skilled (like fitters, operators etc.) to unskilled (general workers) so that they can pay them the lowest wages allowed by law.

The minimum wages set by the government are not living wages, yet many workers do not even receive even the minimum wages. In Chhachhi's (1997a) sample of 66 workers, almost 57 percent did not receive even the minimum wage in 1995, which was 15 to 44 rupees a day at the time. Living costs in cities like Delhi, Mumbai, and Bangalore are very high, and minimum wages barely cover workers' basic expenses. A wage of about 2,000 rupees (the average minimum wage is about 1,500 to 2,000 rupees) a month is too little in these cities. Rental housing costs are very high, and the cheapest accommodation, which consists of just a room, costs between 800 and 1,000 rupees a month. If workers also have to pay their commuting costs, then they are left with very little money.

Work Hours and Leave

As per the Factories Act of India, workers are not supposed to work for more than eight hours without proper overtime payment. However, workers usually work for more than eight hours, sometimes even more than 12 hours, without receiving it. In many assembly lines, workers must achieve some target (which can be monthly or daily), and they must finish the target irrespective of the time. In India, overtime payment, by law, is normally double that of what the worker earns normally. However, in practice, workers seldom are paid for their overtime work.

Workers generally are paid according to the number of days they work. They may receive a paid weekly day off. However, in smaller units, no such rule is observed. Very few workers in larger, organized units receive some sort of paid annual leave; most do not receive it. As per the law, women are entitled to maternity leave; however, in practice this is hardly observed. Women normally lose their jobs if they become pregnant. In some places, women are recruited with the condition that they will not marry or get pregnant.

Occupational Health and Safety

It was a very happy day for Ramesh. He got a new job in a switch gear manufacturing unit in the Madras Export Processing Zone. This unit was a German venture, and his dream to work in a MNC finally had come true. Ramesh had been offered a job in the plant's manual electroplating section. The factory looked very clean, and the whole unit was air-conditioned (which is a luxury in India). He soon learned, however, that this was due to the product's requirements, rather than for the workers' comfort.

Ramesh's unit was in the backyard of the main unit and contained two hot, electrolytic baths. His job was to dip the metal plates manually into the bath of hot hydrochloric acid. Ramesh soon realized that he had to work in a hell. The fumes from the acid made him dizzy, and dipping the metal in bubbling acid was not an easy job. Any small error could be fatal. He thought of running away, but getting a new job was impossible, and he was paid 50 rupees extra every week as a hazard allowance.

On the fateful day, Ramesh remembers only that he was being carried to a hospital. The fumes had made him dizzy, and he lost his consciousness. When he opened his eyes, he found that acid from the electrolytic bath had spilled over his body, and his abdomen and legs were badly burnt. He was lucky to be alive. Fifty rupees a week is the price of a human life as valued by the management.

Even though occupational health and safety is a very serious problem in India's electronics industry, it is not yet regarded as a serious concern, nor has it attained any prominence in the eyes of the government or the industry. There is hardly any doubt about the hazardous nature of the electronics industry, with numerous chemicals (solvents) and gases being used in the work process. Workers have few, if any, work opportunities from which to choose. With such limited opportunities, they are compelled to take hazardous jobs, so that their families can survive.

India has very good laws on paper to prevent workers' exposure to hazards. However, these laws are poorly implemented. No statistics are available on the accidents and diseases that occur in this particular sector in India. The more general occupational accident and disease reporting system that does exist is very inefficient, and governmental statistics (often lower than actual numbers) hardly reveal the true picture.

The other major problem is implementing the law. The number of factories far exceeds the prescribed International Labour Organization (ILO) limit of 150. In a survey conducted by the Society for Participatory Research in Asia, few units comprised of mostly women had any written health and safety policies, and injuries due to the splashing of chemicals were quite common. The fumes in the soldering operations caused frequent headaches, watery eyes, dizziness, and even respiratory problems (Pandita and Kanhere 1998).

India's Factories Act requires employers to provide information about the chemicals to the workers, in a local language. However, in practice, almost none of the workplaces have material safety data sheets (MSDSs)[10] for any chemical. Most of the time, workers do not even know the name of the chemicals they are using or the short- and long-term hazards associated with them. Only workers in some large units are provided with personal protective equipments. Even in these units, sometimes only the permanent workers are provided with such protective gear (such as masks, gloves, safety goggles); casual or temporary workers are not. Also, sometimes the protective gear provided does not protect the workers. For example, most of the masks provided to workers are made of cloth or cotton, and thus they are useless for working with chemicals.

Workers must spend a substantial portion of their incomes on health every month. Very few electronics factories provide health services to their workers.

Some of the permanent workers in the larger units are covered by the Employees' State Insurance (ESI) provided by the state. However, the ESI is in a bad state in India; thus workers often go to private doctors for treatment.

Overall, employers are not very interested in improving workplace conditions. Both skilled and unskilled workers are abundantly available, and the tendency is to replace sick or injured workers, rather than to improve workplace conditions.

LABOR UNIONS

Apart from some large units and some public-sector units, labor unions are almost absent in India's electronics sector. The number of organized workers has been steadily declining since the reforms of 1990s. Only 6 to 8 percent of the workers are organized, mostly in the public sector. The absence of labor unions in India's electronics industry can be explained with many reasons. Globally, unions have very little presence in the electronics industry, and the emerging IT hardware industry is virtually free of trade unions. The new forms of labor relations in the electronics/IT sector (using a high level of casual and flexible labor) hardly provide an enabling environment for the formation of any sort of trade union. Employers take any measures necessary to prevent the formation of unions, which includes firing the workers who join. In most units, employers create an atmosphere of fear, and workers even fear to talk to any outsider, as they might lose their jobs.

THE COST OF ORGANIZING

In January 2004, Asia Monitor Resource Centre (AMRC) staff visited Bangalore to meet the workers from the BPL group of companies' workers

PHOTO 7.1. Activists attending the "Waste Not Asia" conference in Taiwan, July 2001, signed the Computer TakeBack Campaign platform calling on electronics producers to "take it back, make it clean, and recycle responsibly." Courtesy of Leslie Byster, International Campaign for Responsible Technology.

union (BPL Group of Companies Karmikara Sanga), affiliated with the Centre of Indian Trade Unions (CITU). The union has been fighting for BPL workers' rights since 1998 (see Ferus-Comelo, this volume). In the union office, about 22 BPL workers, most of them women, greeted us. "Our leaders have been sentenced to life imprisonment," said Lata, a BPL worker and an active member of the union. We were shocked to hear this. Soon, all of them were eager to share their stories with us. It was evident that they have been fighting an uphill battle with the management. They have faced problems from the beginning, when their union registration was cancelled under the company's pressure. However, they won the case in the court, and their union was declared legal.

"Because of the union we have dignity now," said Laxmi, who has worked in the company for about 30 years,

> I have been toiling in the company for the past 30 years and was not even paid even the minimum wages. Only because of the union, now I can get decent wages and other benefits. However, we all feel bad because many of our colleagues have lost their jobs in this fight and some of them are in jail serving life sentences.

All of them had similar story: The company had hired them as trainees and never made them permanent. After they formed the union in 1998, they went on a strike in November 1999. The struggle was tough, and they had to face the wrath of the police and management toughs. In January 1999, they even went on a hunger strike. In February 1999, 400 to 500 women were arrested as they demonstrated outside the Chief Minister's house, and they were put in different lockups outside Bangalore for about a week. Ten to 12 of the arrested women were breast-feeding their babies at that time.

The situation took a dramatic turn on March 25, 2004, when some people (believed by the union to be management goons) burned the BPL staff bus. Two women died in the incident, in mysterious circumstances according to the union. The police said that, before dying, the women told the names of the people who had burnt the bus, which the police claimed included trade-union leaders. Forty-four workers were arrested and were put in the jail for about two and a half years. On October 13, 2003, seven of them were convicted and sentenced to life imprisonment, among them Mr. Srinivas, president, and Mr. T. K. S. Kutty, general secretary.

On the following day, we went to the Bangalore Central Prison to meet the convicted arrested leaders, Mr. Srinivas and Mr. Kutty, both in their late fifties or early sixties. "This is all because of globalization," said Mr. Srinivas, who seemed not to have lost his vigor despite the tough sentence,

> All the multinationals have started to move to Bangalore and our
> government has been promoting the investment at all costs. Our strike was at
> a very critical juncture as more and more investors were coming to invest in
> Bangalore and our government was promoting it as the IT capital of India.
> Any sort of labor unrest would have been bad for the investors, so
> government was very tough on us. . . . BPL has been making huge profits as it

was a market leader for a long time. Now they may have been pushed behind, but they have already reaped the benefits from the sweat and blood of the workers.

It is really hard to believe that these people had taken part in burning the bus, as declared in the court of law. When we left, we met some of the women workers again in the prison compound. "We come here regularly to provide our moral support to our leaders. We also bring some food and books for them," said one of them. When we asked how they were able to take a day off, they said that the company had told them to stay at home, as there was no work, but they would pay their wages. "We feel scared, as we have heard they might shut the units," they said. "They have already moved into different sectors and the money they made all those years, they will invest it in something else and close these units and they are no longer profitable for them." And this is quite visible, as BPL has been providing mobile phone services in many Indian states, spanning about 209 cities with about two million subscribers in this lucrative business.

THE GOVERNMENT

The Indian government's approach to developing the country's hardware sector has been very interesting. Many policy documents discuss at length opportunities for India to capture the global market. Very little is mentioned regarding the workers' welfare. India is offering its "cheap and skilled workforce" for exploitation for profits, which in turn may never reach the workers and may provide jobs to women that are low-paying, hazardous, and without any social security. This is illustrated by two excerpts from the brochure prepared by the Noida Export Processing Zone (NEPZ) authority, which is under India's Ministry of Commerce:

> Make your mark in the international market... with abundant low cost labor.
> A wealth of human resources... the city of Delhi and adjoining areas are home to a vast skilled & semi-skilled labor force. Plus, an experienced & highly productive workforce is available at relatively low wages.

CONCLUSION

Many economists have been predicting a phenomenal growth in India's hardware sector. The Ministry of Communication and Information Technology predicts that hardware production will reach US$30 billion in 2008, which is nearly five times the current production (MoCIT 2003a). In a similar study carried out by Ernst and Young (2002) in association with the Indian Manufacturers Association for Information Technology (MAIT), it is estimated that India's electronics hardware industry has the potential to reach US$62 billion by 2010, 12 times its existing size. In the area of contract manufacturing, the study says, India can garner 2.2 percent of the global market, which would be a US$11 billion opportunity.

There are some serious problems with these speculations. India's hardware industry has shown growth mainly in consumer electronics, and it caters to the domestic market predominantly. Industry experts believe that there is huge overproduction in electronics hardware manufacturing globally, and India has yet to develop a manufacturing capacity that can be compared to that of any of the major hardware destinations. Electronics manufacturing in India is still low-end assembling. In this scenario, it is not clear how hardware manufacturing in India can reach the predicated levels. Also, because India is a signatory to the Information Technology Agreement (ITA) of the World Trade Organization and will be moving toward zero duty by the year 2005, with huge overproduction elsewhere, it seems conflicting that manufacturing will be established in India at the scale perceived by government.

Similarly, India's government has predicted an employment figure of 4.2 million by 2008 (MoCIT 2003a), which seems very ambitious, considering that present levels are many times less. Anyway, generating the employment will not solve the problem if the quality of employment is not good. At present, it seems that workers are just a "miscellaneous" entity that is needed to generate the requisite figures and to capture local and global markets. Government, under pressure from business, is already relaxing labor laws in India's Special Economic Zones with almost no social security for the workers. Unless immediate steps are taken, India's hardware industry threatens to continue producing its "hazardous sweatshops" employing workers (predominantly women), who work unorganized in oppressive environments at very low wages and with no social security. Job creation should not be the government's only aim; workers should be offered decent jobs that do not require them to risk their lives and that offer full labor rights.

In India there is still a notion that electronics is a nonpolluting industry, and many organizations have carried out environmental studies about this sector that predominantly focus on the problems of the toxic waste the industry generates and the problems this waste causes (see Agarwal and Wankhade, this volume). There is a need, however, to look at the industry's complete life cycle and the hazards that the industry poses on all levels, both to the workers and the community. This book contains many such insights. Such action-based research needs to be replicated in India (with local adjustments) in order to portray a correct picture of this industry, thus contributing to the movements for both environmental and labor rights.

NOTES

1. Name has been changed. The case stories and much of the rest of this chapter were collected as part of a research project on electronics sweatshops in India conducted jointly by Asia Monitor Resource Centre (AMRC), Hong Kong, and Center for Education and Communication (CEC), New Delhi. Interviews were conducted outside factory gates and in workers' homes.

2. A small-scale unit, as per the definition of the government of India, is a unit with investment not more than 10 million rupees and a tiny industry is one with investment not more than 2.5 million rupees.

3. The most recent report available when this chapter was written provides a figure of 650,000 workers/professionals in the IT software and service industry, but does not present data on total employment in the hardware sector (MoCIT 2003b).

4. Workers compensation, disability insurance, and retirement funds (eds.).

5. In 2004, US$34 to $68 per month.

6. For detailed discussion on feminization of the electronic industry, please see Ferus-Comelo, this volume.

7. In 2004, US$18 to $68 per month.

8. In 2004, US$11 to $18 per month.

9. In 2004, US$45 to $227 per month.

10. A Material Safety Data Sheet (MSDS) is designed to provide both workers and emergency personnel with the proper procedures for handling or working with a particular substance. MSDSs include information such as physical data, health effects (both short and long term), first aid, reactivity, storage, disposal, protective equipment and spill/leak procedures. These are of particular use if a spill or other accident occurs.

ANDREW WATTERSON

8   Out of the Shadows and into the Gloom?

Worker and Community Health in and around Central and Eastern Europe's Semiconductor Plants

FOLLOWING THE COLLAPSE of the former Soviet Union in the late 1980s, international high-tech companies moved into Central and Eastern European (CEE) countries with histories of technical expertise in semiconductor production. This chapter explores the available data regarding occupational health and safety in semiconductor manufacturing companies in the region.

Sources consulted include various types of reports (official, labor, industry, and environmental) and publications available through libraries, the Web, and direct contact (i.e., phone, fax, and e-mail) with researchers, organizations, campaigners, and government bodies, both within the region and internationally. Russia, Slovakia, the Czech Republic, and Belarus provide brief case studies because they have had and still have semiconductor plants. Poland also was selected because it had such an industry until relatively recently. Country-specific inquiries were made to the national governmental organizations dealing with occupational health and safety in each of the six countries, and to relevant research institutions and national trade unions. After identifying the towns and cities where the wafer plants were situated, further inquiries were sent to local trade unions, environmental groups, and city or district public health departments about the health of workers in the plants and the public health status of the communities near them. Altogether, 105 inquiries were sent, primarily via fax and e-mail. Only two responses were received, however: a particularly helpful one from a Polish scientist and another from a Russian occupational physician. One additional response was received from a regional public health agency requesting money to provide the data requested.[1]

COUNTRY EVIDENCE

This chapter presents a brief account of each country within the CEE region that has had a significant semiconductor industry, and it identifies influential, and sometimes generalizable, factors relating to workplace health and safety in those countries. Several themes, trends, barriers, and obstacles that cross national boundaries in terms of influences on wafer production health and safety also are discussed.

Several countries lying on the western side of the region share common characteristics in terms of past technical and educational skills bases that make them attractive for investment. For example, their trade unions are weak, a direct result of both past history and a lack of public support for them, and free-market and deregulatory thinking dominates the region's governments. The existing environmental groups have addressed major, "old industry" polluters, such as lead and copper smelters and the nuclear industry, but have not focused on the newer high-tech industries, unlike some of their Western counterparts.

Caution should be exercised, however, to not overemphasize the similarities among countries. The countries do not represent a homogenous entity historically, culturally, politically, or economically. Belarus appears to be the most politically and socially unstable, and it is also the most aggressive in dealing with workplace organizations. Slovakia, Poland, and the Czech Republic are the most organized societies, and are closest to Western Europe and perhaps the United States in terms of market influences and established occupational health and safety structures.

The decline of states in regions clearly has led to heterogeneous developments in their features associated with "civil society" (Habermas 1974), building community beyond the direct domain of government, although not through economic influences. This has been positively influenced by an increasing number of new CEE environmental organizations. When measured by trade unions' ability to identify, address, and resolve occupational health and safety problems in the semiconductor and other industries, however, the strength of civil society is arguably much weaker in the region (Watterson and Constantinoaia 2004).[2]

"Post-transition" Poland has developed strong environmental groups and has had politically active trade unions (EIROnline 2003; Polish Ecological Club 2003); Belarus has a weak and shrinking trade union base; Romania has a mixture of environmental organizations that sometimes contain government scientists and reflect official views and sometimes do not; and the Czech republic has trade unionists who simultaneously may hold senior management posts in organizations where they represent the workforce (ILO 2001). Table 8.1 shows the countries involved in semiconductor production in Central and Eastern Europe during the 1990s, as well as their health and safety activities.

Russia

Information about the occupational health status of Russian workers is sparse and may not be accurate. The longitudinal data now available about the state of Soviet occupational health also appear to be limited (Matveev 2003). There are many reasons for this: political pressure to constantly reduce annual occupational disease figures, leading to the nondiagnosis or re-categorization of occupational diseases; a lack of information available for workers; workers' lack of understanding about their health and safety rights; and a shortage of occupational physicians legally entitled to treat occupational diseases—currently fewer than 1,000 (Matveev 2003, 7).

Research on occupational health began during the early Soviet period, and Melanie Ilic (1999) has investigated the position of women at work in some depth. For instance, in the 1930s, efforts were made to exclude women

TABLE 8.1. Semiconductor Production in Central and Eastern Europe during the 1990s

Country	Chip Mfg.	PCs	Companies Involved	Health and Safety Reports/Activity
Czech Republic	✓	✓	Motorola Compaq R&D in Roznov ON Semiconductors (1,500 workers)	Industry summaries of ISO activity
Hungary	?		InterMOS & Interbip chip companies Moved out of chip production in 1990s	?
Russia	✓	✓	Mikron (linked to Hua Ko/Hong Kong) Angstrem Electronika Svetlana Vostok Planeta	Toxicology reports in scientific journals
Belarus	✓		Integral	
Slovakia	✓	✓	Motorola (1,500 workers estimated to come to the plant in 1998)	
Slovenia				Industry summaries of ISO activity
Poland	✓	✓		Technical reports in conference proceedings

Source: Various news, scientific, and industry intelligence reports.

from hazardous occupations that involved working with heavy metals and chemicals. "Working with toxic substances, as scientific research identified, increased the likelihood of miscarriage, premature births, stillbirths and infant mortality" (Ilic 1999, 135–136). As Ilic described, the health and safety legislation in the 1930s intended to protect women was based on their perceived weakness due to physiological differences. Later in the century, such restrictions apparently disappeared when the semiconductor plants emerged because women certainly worked in those plants. Lists of prohibited occupations for women were drawn up, but the state argued that as its occupational hygiene controls increased, the size of the list would be reduced. In practice, however, this did not appear to happen.

The period after the demise of the Soviet government was also highly problematic. Black market labor was used for hazardous work, and there were problems associated with criminal activity in the labor market, deregulation drivers, and a desire to seek Western investors by offering a low-wage economy with few if any constraints on capital. All these things had serious consequences for occupational health and safety. Indeed, evidence exists that occupational health and safety disappeared from the agenda completely in some instances, whereas in Soviet times, it had only been distorted. Matveev observed that "virtually no information on occupational health and safety is available on the Web sites of the Russian trade unions or any political parties" (2003, 9).

The situation has been compounded by the reform-period changes, in which the old trade unions lost their rights to fund trade-union inspections concerning occupational health and safety and to penalize those who broke occupational health and safety laws (Hoffer 1997, 9). Trade-union membership in Russia has plummeted in recent years, so a weak organization with some powers and a significant membership has become even weaker and smaller, and with less power. "Given today's occupational safety conditions in Russian companies, the unions can (however) justly maintain that the general situation has worsened by comparison with the past" (Hoffer 1997, 39). Also, concerns about working conditions have risen among employees. The Russian Federation of Independent Trade Unions views the state occupational health and safety inspectorate system as having collapsed in 1991 to 1992 (ILO 1996, 1).

During the transition period, employers believed that legal safety regulations should not apply to private companies (Hoffer 1997, 27). Trade unions may well have survived the transition period through "social partnership" (Ashwin and Clarke 2002). However, the unions' capacity to improve, or even stop, the decline in workplace health and safety seemed decidedly limited in 2003.

The Russian privatized semiconductor fabrication is based in Zelenograd with the Mikron and Angstrem companies, which are both involved in international trade. Mikron was making 30,000 four-inch wafers monthly in the late 1990s, and it has received investment monies from Hong Kong's Hua KO Electronics Company to build a new semiconductor wafer fabrication factory that will produce 10,000 six-inch wafers a month. Angstrem made several thousand six-inch wafers a month in the late 1990s, and the German company, Meisner and Wurst, built a new clean room for the company. Altogether, the Russian plants had the capacity to supply a total of 100,000 wafers a month. Smaller fabrication companies exist in Voronezh (Elektronica), St Petersburg (Svetlana), Novosibirsk (Vostok), and Novgorod (Planeta).

The industry developed to supply the Soviet military (Popov 1997). This fact may explain the apparent continuing reluctance of Russian trade unions, workers, and environmental groups to investigate what, if any, adverse health effects are linked to the industry. Commercial press coverage of working conditions in Russian semiconductor plants is low, if not nonexistent (Popov 1997; Sandford 2000b). Indeed, as in the Czech Republic, the view is that most companies interested in Russian semiconductors that visited the country (primarily from China and Russia) did so "to find a cheap workforce and brain power" (Simonov 1997). The mayor of Moscow also signed a law to create a "special industrial zone" in the so-called Russian Silicon Valley, Zelonograd, to attract favorable investment conditions for foreign companies "including tax exemptions, payment preferences and government backed credit guarantees" (Telford 1998).

However, a number of scientific publications in Russia since at least 1984 have flagged the occupational health problems, both toxicological and ergonomic, that electronics workers face, including semiconductor production workers exposed to a range of toxic chemical and ergonomic hazards (Salangina et al. 2001; Semenova et al. 1986; Soldatenkova and Prilutskaia 1987). More recent papers have examined semiconductor workers' exposure to dust from copper, boron, silver, and lead (Ianin 2000). Zelenograd is also one of the few centers where such gases as sucharsine, phosphine, silane, and silicon tetrachloride are produced with high levels of purification. These highly toxic gases are produced by Horst Ltd., an offshoot of the Research Institute of Materials Technology, and the EMA semiconductor plant.[3]

Other researchers have explored the specific problems that female microelectronics workers in the country face, including reproductive health hazards (Ailamazian 1990; Datsenko, Semenova, and Novak 1984; Frolova 2001; Ishenalieva 1994). These studies have reported occupational diseases, as well as reproductive disorders, linked to the "combined effects of complex low intensity factors and intensive work" due to chemical exposures (Frolova 2001). However, it is difficult to establish the extent to which these studies were widely available and acted on elsewhere in CEE. Castells and Natalushko conducted a study of the Zelenograd semiconductor industry between 1991 and 1993 and found a large technological gap between Russia and the United States. "Russian enterprises did not have the capability to design sub-micron chips and their 'clean rooms' were so 'dirty' they could not even produce the most advanced chips they could design" (cited in Castells 1998, 522). This suggests, but does not confirm, that occupational health and safety in these *de facto* "dirty" rooms were poor, although paradoxically, a dirty clean room for products might have proved a safer clean room for the workers.

It is very difficult to establish the extent to which Russian occupational exposures were accurately recorded, diseases were diagnosed, and engineering and other controls were introduced and applied because of the political pressures to reduce disease numbers on an annual basis in official reports. It should be noted that the problems of data verification and disease assessment were and are not unique to the CEE. In Scotland, for instance, in 2003 it was not possible to check industry data about worker exposure to toxic substances in the clean rooms of Silicon Glen, and government agencies have not been a good source of independently validated occupational hygiene or occupational health data. Other studies have indicated that efforts were made to carry out biological monitoring of workers' exposure to heavy metals in the electronics industry.

With the decline in Russian public health, occupationally caused and related diseases may not be picked up or prioritized in the health care system, adding to the difficulty of identifying any diseases that may be cause by or related to working conditions in the semiconductor industry. Some limited work has been done on public health in Zelenograd, but it does not appear to have identified workplace health and safety as a factor (Denisov 2000a, 2000b).

Belarus

Belarus has been one of the countries most hard hit by plummeting public health during the 1990s. Post-Soviet reforms have led to far greater economic and social inequalities in all ex-Soviet countries. Women workers in Belarus have been extensively affected by poverty during this period, with women's poverty for the city of Minsk, which includes the semiconductor factories, running at 65 percent, and in the Minsk region at 80 percent

(Alexandrova 2001). There is much international evidence to indicate that socioeconomically disadvantaged populations may be more vulnerable to adverse health consequences in the workplace (Watterson 2003). If Belarus semiconductor workers were more prosperous, such effects would be reduced, but neither poverty nor affluence protects against some basic toxicological exposures: solvents, acids, and heavy metals remain serious occupational threats to all who come into contact with them.

The city also demonstrates cross-cutting and countervailing forces that may impact its occupational health and safety activity. The ILO developed a project that included Minsk City, with the mayor's full support, to develop occupational health and safety training for small- and medium-size enterprises in the city. The project highlighted the lack of data about accidents and occupational diseases available in the city (ILO 2001, 4). It was widely publicized among key stakeholders and trade unions, as well as among business people, and those trained in the project seminars often joined regional labor protection committees. In 2001, however, the Belarus government also was involved in suppressing trade unions in the country, and this has continued into the twenty-first century (cf. Amnesty International 2004). Thus, its efforts have produced negligible results.

During Soviet times, the Belarus semiconductor industry produced chips, though the highest quality chips were produced only in Russia. By the mid-1990s, the main Belarusian semiconductor consortium, Integral, was the largest Eastern European semiconductor company. All six key plants were based in Minsk. At one point, Motorola was planning a joint venture project with Integral, but this plan was abandoned in 1998 (Virtual Guide to Belarus 2003).

Slovakia, Czech Republic, Poland, and Romania

During the 1990s, Slovakia had an expanding, but very small semiconductor industry, with 250 people working in fab production. This led to further external investment with ON Semiconductor, a former division of Motorola based in Phoenix, Arizona, which announced that it would build a second fab at their plant in Piestany, Slovakia, in 2003. Like other large, multinational semiconductor companies, ON gained ISO 14001 environmental management systems certification for its plants in the United States, as well as in Piestany, Slovakia, and Rostov, in the Czech Republic (ON Semiconductor 2005). What this means for working conditions in the latter plants has not been documented.

Czech trade unions faced similar obstacles and challenges to those in post-Soviet Russia. In the late 1980s and early 1990s, there was little evidence of any effective action in regards to workplace health and safety (Myant and Smith 1999, 272).

The Czech microelectronics industry has been one of the most advanced in the region and dates back to the 1960s. Motorola (United States) had subcontracted work from the Tesla Sezam factory and linked wafer suppliers from the 1990s. In 1997, the U.S. company bought a controlling interest in the plant (Linden 1998, 6). ON Semiconductor (Phoenix, AZ) separated from Motorola and now runs the Roznov plant. Tesla Sezam had more than 800 employees involved in making semiconductor chips in 1997 (Radosevic 2002). Around 1,200 employees work at the Tesla Roznov, where there is a 2,400-square-meter clean room for analog-integrated circuits (ON Semiconductor 2005). The Tesla plant received a health, safety, and environment award in 2001 from the Czech Business Leaders Forum, which was apparently based on the awarding of the ISO 14001. So little other detailed evidence of the company's work has been provided that is difficult to assess the validity of such awards (Radio Praha, April 18, 2002).

The Terosil plant at Roznov, which also developed from Tesla and supplies silicon wafers and single crystals to the semiconductor industry, has 300 people working on growing silicon ingots and shaping and polishing silicon wafers. The wafers grown at the plant are doped by boron, arsenic, antimony, and phosphorous. In 2002, Terosil produced an environmental, health, and safety policy with the usual commitment to "continually improving environmental health and safety performance," but data about the policy's implementation and the success of the company's practices do not appear to be available within the public domain (Terosil 2002).

In 1999, government ministers recognized that the electronics industry, including chip manufacturers, presented environmental challenges and economic costs to the Czech Republic, although very little weight was given to occupational health and safety matters. They anticipated that future problems would be addressed through the use of European (EU) directives on integrated pollution and best available technology and that the Health Protection Act of 2000 would address occupational health and safety issues. For ministers in the late 1990s, the Czech workforce, with its experience in electronics, including chip-integrated circuits, provided the best guarantee of foreign investment and the sector's maintenance (Malik 1999, 1–4).

Trade unions have had a major impact on political developments in twentieth-century Poland, but they appear to have a far more limited workplace occupational health and safety role (EIROnline 2003). Several Polish environmental groups have been working since 1980 on issues relating to pollution and sustainability, including actions on major polluting industries, such as aluminum smelters near Krakow, nuclear plants, and road transport. Links with trade unions do not appear strong, but the nongovernmental organizations (NGOs) have pressed for the use of environmental impact assessments in the context of assessing people's health. This may prove a very useful tool for investigating the electronics industry's past and its possible performance in the country (Polish Ecological Club 2003). In Poland, trade unions have been politically active nationally, but seem to have been far less active at a local level on working conditions (Watterson, Silberschmidt, and Robson 2001).

The Polish semiconductor industry was effectively demolished by competition from Western companies, although research institutes still work in the field. Cemat Silicon SA in Warsaw produced unpatterned silicon wafers for the semiconductor industry with three-, four-, five-, and six-inch wafers. In 1998, Motorola searched for a joint venture partner to build a fabrication facility in Krakow (Lineback 1998). Past Polish studies of the electronics industry have focused on electrical, ergonomic, and lighting hazards, although papers on toxicological threats to semiconductor workers were published in a Polish occupational health journal during the same year (Bauer et al. 1992; Weiss, Kaluzny, and Lesiewwska-Junk 1992).

The Romanian semiconductor industry effectively relied on the establishment of the Research Institute for Electronic Components founded in 1968 and Baneasa SA, the first Romanian semiconductor plant (Sandford 2000a). By 2000, Microelectronica SA was a modern Romanian semiconductor facility.

OCCUPATIONAL HEALTH AND SAFETY STANDARDS

Table 8.2 shows data in the public domain on the paper standards established to control chemicals in wafer production processes in the United States,

TABLE 8.2. Substances Widely Used in Semiconductor Manufacture Up to the 1980s, and National Occupational Threshold Limit Values, Maximum Allowable Concentrations

	USA			RUSSIA 1984
	NIOSH 2005	OSHA 2001	GERMANY	unless 1993
Substance	ppm unless stated		MAK ppm 1992	(a) MACs mg/m^3
Acetone	250	1000		200
arsenic	C^a			0.01 mg/m^3(b)
– arsenic pentafluoride	0.2 mg/m^3	0.05		n/a
– arsine gas	0.002 mg/m^3	0.05	0.05	0.05 ppm(a)
				0.1 mg/m^3 STEL(a)
beryllium oxide	0.002 mg/m^3 C			0.001 mg/m^3
boron trichloride	None		1	n/a
boron trifluoride	1.00	1.00		1.00
chloroform	10			50 ppm (a)
	2 C	50		
diborane	0.1	0.1	0.1	0.1 mg/m^3 STEL(a)
glycol ethers				
– ethylene glycol acetate	5 ppm			
– 2-ethoxy ethanol	5 ppm		20	
– GMEEA	0.5	100		
– GMME	0.1	25		
– GMMEA	0.1	25		
methylene chloride	100		100	50
	C	25		
perchloroethylene	50 ppm		50	10
(tetrachloroethylene)	C	100		
phosphine	0.3	0.3	0.1	0.1
toluene	100	200	100	50
trichloroethylene	50		50	10
	C	100		
xylene (o,m pisomers)	100	100	100	50

^{a}C, potential occupational carcinogen.
Source: International Register of Potentially Toxic Chemicals (IRPTC) (1984); LaDou (1986); Bauer et al. (1992); NIOSH (2005).

Germany, and Russia, respectively in the 1980s through early 2000s. Russian standards were sometimes higher than those in North America and Western Europe and were set tighter much earlier. These standards were adopted in all Soviet bloc countries, and were influential across the CEE region for controlling chemical exposures of substances used in semiconductor manufacturing. A number of substances used in the industry apparently were neither approved nor available for use in such places as Zelenograd, Russia. However, little, if any data exist to demonstrate that such standards were ever applied effectively (Watterson, Silberschmidt, and Robson 2001). Rather, the existing evidence indicates the opposite (Matveev 2003). Also, because military rather than commercial interests dominated the Soviet industry's early development, it seems possible that substances not approved or recognized for use in the region, but essential for semiconductor wafer production, would have been used. In the 1990s, a number of Russian company and technical institute reports indicated that they had been developing and refining materials for wafer production in the 1960s that did not appear in the maximum allowable concentrations lists of Soviet chemicals in the early 1980s.

DISCUSSION

Globally, there are common and basic needs regarding occupational and environmental health and safety practices and standards. Some solutions to high-tech industrial production problems are not high tech; sometimes these solutions may be relatively inexpensive. The lack of detailed reports on semiconductor plant health and safety systems, operations, and practices (and the lack of access to them) makes it difficult to assess problems and good practices in the industry. The CEE may be beset by job blackmail arguments that falsely play health and safety needs against environmental and production needs. There also may be an issue of employment "carrots" being used to justify unsustainable and hazardous work in some towns, regions, and countries. Hence, economic and political problems must be resolved before technical solutions can be introduced, and these factors may be deeper and stronger within the region than they are outside of it.

Good databases on materials and processes used in the semiconductor industry are needed globally, and the best occupational exposure limits available should be disseminated. Now is the time to provide this information to the CEE community and environmental NGOs, trade unions, and scientific institutions. For instance, Californian exposure levels for beryllium oxide[4] were closer to Soviet control standards than were the U.S. and UK ones, but they were still 100 percent weaker than Soviet standards. Accurate data about effective engineering controls, occupational exposures, and accurate job classifications also are needed. This would help prevent the endless cycle of new workers and communities facing the same hazards and paying the same human health price as their predecessors in countries where the industry has withdrawn or relocated.

Opportunities are available to establish, if not the best practices in the industry, at least better, and at the very least, good practices. This hinges on freedom of information, good regulatory standards, regular inspections, rigorous enforcement, and meaningful worker organization backed by legal rights, education, information, and training. For the EU and its candidate countries, it means establishing standards in a consistent and uniform way and then monitoring and enforcing them effectively.

There already are troublesome signs that health and safety practices within the EU vary significantly among countries. The problem is that the CEE countries that enter the EU may have even less enforcement and even worse working practices than the existing countries, which Brussels will ignore. A transitional period to bring health, safety, and environmental standards within the CEE up to those of EU member states is envisaged, but how this would work out in practice is unclear. Multinational companies already are working with lower health and safety standards in some CEE countries than in their own (Watterson, Silberschmidt, and Robson 2001).

Globally, there are real differences in the occupational and environmental health constraints, checks, and balances that affect the semiconductor industry, especially regarding environmental matters. Paradoxically, there are now U.S. semiconductor companies in Western Europe and the CEE that do or will need to fulfill EU occupational health and safety controls in Poland, the Czech Republic, Hungary, and Romania; whereas Russia, with its Asian semiconductor investment, will not.

There are remarkable similarities in the basic problems and failures documented in the CEE, Western European, and North American track records on semiconductors, but the problems seem far more extensive in the CEE. In addition, in the past, the social position and well-being of CEE production workers appeared to have been better than those in some other parts of the world. But the degree of transparency; the extent of the information available about the hazards, risks, and follow-up regarding long-term employees, ex-workers, and retired workers; the limited activity of labor inspectors; the weakness of trade-union organizations; and environmental groups' focus on non-workplace environmental problems appear to be worsening.

Taking the international quality of the semiconductor industry into account, there must global thinking if local actions to address the workers' problems are to be successful. Local, national, and international rights, standards, and operational practices need to be created or activated to ensure that workers in the semiconductor industry—be they in Novosibirsk or New Jersey, Minsk or Merseyside, Piestany or Paris—are not only informed about the hazards and risks they face but also equipped with the power and skills to deal effectively with those threats.

NOTES

1. In parts of Western Europe, similar charges in some circumstances would be made for similar data extraction and provision.

2. Yet I would argue that similar weaknesses exist in "civic society" and trade unions within that society in Western Europe and North America, perhaps not in identifying and campaigning on those hazards but definitely in successfully resolving them.

3. Web site of the Horst Firm Ltd., Zelenograd, Russia, www.horst.ru/english/zel.htm, accessed August, 2003.

4. California's standards for exposure to beryllium oxide were consistent with those promulgated in the 1970s by the U.S. National Institute of Occupational Safety and Health (NIOSH), and were both technically achievable and health based.

II. Environmental Justice and Labor Rights

Andrew Watterson and Shenglin Chang

TWO DISTURBING PHENOMENA are generally found where clusters of electronics manufacturing, assembly, and disassembly operations are located: the generation of serious occupational and environmental hazards for workers and nearby communities (Byster and Smith 1999: Fox 1991; LaDou 1984; Sonnenfeld 2002) and the intensification of social inequalities through low wages and labor disempowerment (Hossfeld 1988; Nash and Fernández-Kelly 1983; Park 1992; Robinson and McIlwee 1989). These problems of *labor rights* and *environmental injustice* (Pellow and Park 2002; see also Asia Monitor Resource Center [AMRC] 1998: Ong 1987) have been the focus of substantial efforts by workers, community members, health professionals, and government regulators, among others, for several decades. These stakeholders have placed the industry's anti-labor, anti-social, and anti-ecological practices on the public agenda to effect progressive change.

Part II of this volume gives voice to the compelling experiences of workers, families, and communities in centers of electronics production in North America, Europe, and Asia. Despite different economic, institutional, cultural, geographic, and ecological factors, there is remarkable similarity across political boundaries with regard to how and why the electronics industry has manipulated and exploited labor forces and ecological resources. Community, trade union, and other civil society responses to challenges posed by such global-industrial processes and companies often have been similar. However, at the same time, there have been important national and local differences in how labor rights were established or eroded and how local communities struggled to improve and defend environmental and community health.

The economic, political, and public health threats posed by the global electronics industry to workers, families, communities, and regional and national institutions are richly and graphically presented in this part of the book. Authors who are involved in or close to these issues document the struggles of:

- Migrant laborers, women, and communities in California's Silicon Valley (Byster and Smith; Hawes and Pellow; Pellow and Matthews);
- Women and trade union advocates in Scotland's "Silicon Glen" (McCourt);
- Electronics workers in Mexico on its border with the United States (García and Simpson; Partida Rocha); and
- Former RCA workers (Ku), and employees and residents of one of the largest "high-tech industrial parks" in Taiwan (Chang, Chiu, and Tu).

Part II concludes with an overview of the prospects for and the challenges of international trade-union organizing in the sector, along with electronics companies' overarching threats and other responses to employees (Steiert).

Though sometimes considered separately, environmental justice and labor rights struggles are integrally related, for four reasons: First, the foundation of any environmental justice battle is the unfair exposure of vulnerable or marginalized groups to environmental harm. In the electronics industry, most frontline production workers exposed to the industry's worst hazardous conditions are women, immigrants, and ethnic minorities earning low wages. Second, the workplace is where people in many communities are first exposed to toxics and where exposure is often the most intense. As Hawes notes, in the United States this is largely because regulations of toxic chemicals are less stringent in occupational settings than outside the workplace. In Scotland, public health officials have taken a somewhat more assertive stance in response to labor advocates' organizing efforts, but still there is much room for improvement (McCourt).

Third, environmental justice activists and scholars have long defined the "environment" as where people "live, *work*, and play" (Alston 1990), underscoring the direct links between toxics in communities and those on the job (see Appendix A). This rearticulation and broadening of what is traditionally meant by "environment" critically acknowledges that toxics produced in workplaces often migrate into homes and communities, thus framing the problem so that it unites workers and environmentalists in their efforts to promote change. Fourth, the workplace is a site where people often begin to resist environmental toxins and injustices: Workers thus may be a community's first environmental activists. Linking occupational and community aspects of environmental justice struggles lays the foundation for bridging the "work–environment divide" (Gottlieb 2001) that persists in many cultures. It also exposes a gap in assumptions that hides or obscures workplace and ecosystem—and worker and environmentalist—connections. Part II of this volume directly challenges such a divide.

Several common themes run throughout this part of the book: poor working conditions; polluted land and water; exploitation of migrant, ethnic, and female workers; targeting of workers and advocates; and the related reluctance, inability, fear, and hostility of many scientists in addressing occupational and environmental problems that often characterize the global electronics industry's social relations. The efforts of labor, community, and other nongovernmental organizations (NGOs) to establish basic civil society rights in their encounters with electronics firms often have been rebuffed, but sometimes have been successful. Unfortunately, failures in state regulation and inspection and in the human-rights and living standards of those engaged with the industry have been the norm to date. The "race to the bottom" in some segments of the electronics industry in terms of wages, hours, working conditions, and environmental pollution has emulated trends in the global shipbuilding and steel industries, which currently also contain both highly skilled and unskilled workers. Paradoxically, the electronics industry too often has produced deskilled and degraded workers in a high-tech industry.

Such agencies as the International Labour Organization (ILO) and the World Health Organization (WHO) have a role in protecting the health of individual workers and their communities, as well as environmental quality. Their efforts have had limited success and sometimes have been quite ineffective, as this section clearly illustrates. International free-trade regimes, including the World Trade Organization and the North American Free Trade Agreement (Byster and Smith; García and Simpson; Partida Rocha; and Steiert) have yet to demonstrate that they can establish effective frameworks for controlling such industries and preventing labor and pollution abuses (see also Watterson; and Geiser and Tickner).

Trade unions across the globe have been faced with employers who, as Donald Roy (1980) aptly observed, used the "fear stuff, sweet stuff, and evil stuff" on their employees over many decades. In the electronics industry, trade unions and activist workers have experienced the sweet stuff and the fear stuff all too often, as the chapters in this section and elsewhere in the book reveal all too vividly (McCourt; García and Simpson; Partida Rocha; Ku; and Steiert). Yet labor and community organizations have shown that they could ratchet up and improve conditions when access to legislators was possible and supportive legislation followed (Pellow and Matthews). Civil society groups can produce powerful results by working together with progressive legislatures. Labor traditions linked to historically strong, urban-based unions could contribute to economic and social improvements in electronics workforces with many migrant, ethnic, and female workers.

Environmental justice movements also have played a role in this drama, with mixed success. They have proved strong in some parts of the United States (Byster and Smith; Pellow and Matthews) and significant in such countries as South Africa. Despite the green political parties, however, such movements have been surprisingly weak in Europe, where concerns for "nature" rather than the impact of work and wider environments on people have dominated. In Taiwan, illegal toxic dumping had devastating effects on local populations and the environment (Chang, Chiu, and Tu; and Ku) on a scale beyond anything seen in Europe or the United States. Although redress for such human-rights breaches remains grossly inadequate, powerful social forces have arisen in Taiwan to conduct public education and organizing. Fortunately, the International Campaign for Responsible Technology and its partners have had notable successes in proposing and passing progressive legislation in the European Union, the United States, and even in parts of Asia regarding environmental dimensions of electronics production and waste management (Byster and Smith). To what extent these successes will translate into benefits for workers and their communities over the long term remains to be seen.

Labor rights, including the right to a healthy and safe workplace, are central to human rights (Partida Rocha; see also Leong and Pandita; Pandita; and Watterson). Industries such as electronics target the most vulnerable working populations in terms of gender, race, skill, and sometimes history of unemployment. Without effective labor rights gained through activist and governmental pressure, there can be no environmental justice for workers, their families, and the wider community. Such justice would intrinsically enhance worker rights by focusing on cleaner production and greater corporate accountability.

Part II of this volume provides carefully documented evidence that a range of environmental and labor solutions and indeed victories—albeit often small ones—are possible and have been achieved in widely different settings. At the same time, this section clearly demonstrates the need for international action to develop effective and just standards to promote sustainable conditions within the transnational electronics industry, both in the workplace and in the surrounding communities.

9   From Grassroots to Global

*The Silicon Valley Toxics Coalition's Milestones in
Building a Movement for Corporate Accountability
and Sustainability in the High-Tech Industry*

MISSION STATEMENT

The Silicon Valley Toxics Coalition is a diverse organization engaged in
research, advocacy, and grassroots organizing to address human health and
environmental injustice caused by the rapid growth of the high-tech industry.

VISION STATEMENT

We envision a toxic-free future, where each new generation of technical
improvements in electronic products includes parallel and proportional
advances in social and environmental justice. Our goal is environmental
sustainability and clean production, improved health, and democratic
decision making for communities and workers most affected by the
high-tech revolution.

FOR MANY YEARS, Santa Clara County, California—an area once
known as the Valley of the Heart's Delight—flourished with bountiful fruit
orchards and boasted the largest concentration of fruit canneries in the United
States. Starting in the 1970s, however, the area was irreversibly transformed.
The orchards were cut down and the canneries were closed, as semiconductor
fabrication ("chip") plants sprouted on the landscape and workers in "bunny
suits" replaced cannery workers. Today, this area, located 50 miles south of
San Francisco, is known around the world as Silicon Valley, the birthplace of
the global electronics revolution.

For more than 30 years, Silicon Valley has exported not only circuits and
chips, but also the hard-learned lessons of the industry's impact on human
health and the environment. The rise of the electronics industry seemed like
the perfect success story, with brilliant engineers and innovative companies,
fueled by American ingenuity. It was viewed as an industry without pollution,
with workers in "clean rooms" and factories without smokestacks. In fact,
industry leaders promoted it as the "clean industry."

In the late 1970s, however, the clean-industry myth began to dissolve. After
learning that manufacturing computer chips required more than 1,000 chemicals, worker-safety advocates formed the Santa Clara Center for Occupational
Safety and Health (SCCOSH; see Hawes and Pellow; Smith, Sonnenfeld; and
Pellow, this volume) to address the high-tech industry's occupational health

hazards and to advocate for humane and safe working conditions for the industry's low-wage, migrant, and immigrant workforce. When SCCOSH began to document patterns of reproductive health damage, these production workers—primarily women of childbearing age—provided the "proof" that serious problems existed. These early high-tech pioneers became the "canaries" in the high-tech coal mines.

POISON IN THE WATER WE DRINK

In 1981, Silicon Valley received an alarming wake-up call when it was discovered that the circle of poison had seeped from the factories into neighboring communities. Lorraine Ross, a woman living in south San Jose near the Fairchild semiconductor factory that had polluted the drinking water supply, gave birth to a daughter who had a serious heart defect that required several surgeries. When she learned about the water pollution, Lorraine went door to door in her neighborhood and identified other families with members suffering from similar health problems, including cancers and miscarriages.

Her efforts and the investigative work of Susan Yoachum, a reporter for the *San Jose Mercury News* (cf. Yoachum, Izumi, and Wisdom 1983; Yoachum and Malone 1980), led to the shocking discovery of substantial drinking-water contamination in Silicon Valley caused by the improper handling of toxic chemicals and leaking underground storage tanks at Fairchild Semiconductor and IBM. The pollution from the IBM facility spread several miles in the underground aquifer northwest of the original spill site. Before clean up began, the contaminated groundwater plume was over three miles long and 180 feet deep (Smith 1984a). Authorities tested the drinking water and found that it was contaminated with 1,1,1-trichloroethane (TCA), 29 times above the state's action levels (California Regional Water Quality Control Board 1995; Smith 1984b).[1] In 1985, a California Health Department Study reported significantly higher than expected rates of miscarriages and birth defects in the area near the leaking storage tanks (Rudolph and Swan 1986; Wrensch et al. 1990).

Community activists organized a series of community meetings that brought together community residents, high-tech workers, union members, public health advocates, firefighters, SCCOSH supporters, and policymakers who recognized that they needed to form an organization to protect the environment and the community's health and to monitor the high-tech industry's practices. In 1982, the Silicon Valley Toxics Coalition (SVTC) was founded as an outgrowth of these meetings. Although SVTC started as a project of SCCOSH, it later became an independent organization whose mission was to protect residents from toxic exposure in their communities.

SVTC members realized that leaking underground storage tanks at IBM and Fairchild were only the tip of the high-tech iceberg and called for further investigations at the Valley's other high-tech facilities. Residents were shocked to learn that most of these facilities also had leaking underground storage tanks. SVTC organized in many of the valley's most polluted communities to demand a cleanup of all toxic sites. In response, the Environmental

Protection Agency (EPA) identified 29 sites that were so polluted that they were placed on the National Priority List as "Superfund" sites. This action gave Silicon Valley the unwanted distinction of having more Superfund sites than anywhere else in the country.

As SVTC researched the processes and chemicals used to manufacture semiconductors, it became frighteningly clear, as Dr. Joseph LaDou, a noted expert on occupational safety and health, wrote, "what was once thought to be the first 'clean' industry is actually one of the most chemical-intensive industries ever conceived" (LaDou and Rohm 1998, 1). "Thousands of different chemicals and other materials have been used in this industry" (ibid). These include acids, solvents, chlorinated and brominated substances, heavy metals, and toxic gases.

RIGHT-TO-KNOW

Since its inception, SVTC has advocated for greater "community right-to-know" to provide more information to workers and residents about potential toxic chemical exposures. SVTC organized to pass the toughest safety standards in the country for preventing gas releases and helped win national community right-to-know laws that require companies to disclose the chemicals they discharge into the community. In 1983, less than a year after its founding, SVTC won its first victories when two new laws—the nation's first community right-to-know law and a Hazardous Materials Model Ordinance, which required secondary containment and strict monitoring for underground storage tanks—were passed throughout Silicon Valley. Later, a cutting-edge Toxic Gas Model Ordinance also was developed and passed (see www.unidocs.org/members/deh.html for more information). These local laws established powerful community right-to-know disclosure rules about toxic chemical storage, which led to the subsequent passage of similar laws by the State of California and the U.S. Congress.

During 1986, SVTC campaigned to persuade the U.S. Congress to pass the right-to-know provisions of the Superfund amendments that created the Toxics Release Inventory (TRI). When the first TRI[2] data were made public in 1988, SVTC was the first group to publish a report exposing companies that released the greatest volume of toxic chemicals and challenged the "clean industry" to clean up its pollution. In 1989, SVTC used TRI data to document that IBM-San Jose emitted nearly 1.5 million pounds of chlorofluorocarbons (CFC)—a principal cause of ozone-layer destruction. Working with many other organizations, SVTC organized a large Earth Day "IBMad about Toxics" rally in front of the San Jose IBM plant (see Photo 9.1). After these other groups joined SVTC in challenging IBM to phase out its use of CFCs, IBM soon agreed to substitute soap and water as a safe, alternative solvent.

SVTC was also an early adopter of cutting edge electronic tools—such as Internet mapping technology. In the 1990s, SVTC developed its family of interactive eco-maps documenting the Valley's groundwater contamination, which showed that communities of color were disproportionately located near polluting high-tech industries domestically, and—where the industry

PHOTO 9.1. Thousands protest at IBM's disk drive plant in San Jose, California, on Earth Day, 1989. This facility discharged more than one million pounds of ozone-destroying chlorofluorocarbons (CFCs) into the environment during the previous year, according to the company's own Toxic Release Inventory (TRI) reported data. Courtesy of Howard Beck.

expanded to other parts of the world—globally. These point-and-click maps earned SVTC several awards, including the Yahoo! Award of Excellence for providing information in new and engaging ways.

EXPANDING BEYOND THE BORDERS OF SILICON VALLEY

As the high-tech industry began its exodus from Silicon Valley in search of lower costs and higher profits, chip companies began pitting city against city, state against state, and eventually country against country in a hunt for the lowest cost opportunities for its new factories. In response to this new trend, SVTC launched a new national network in 1990, the Campaign for Responsible Technology (CRT). One of the main goals of CRT was to raise public awareness and to expose industry demands for tax breaks, environmental and safety concessions, cheap labor, and other forms of corporate welfare as "prizes" for locating new semiconductor plants. The CRT helped arm high-tech communities with information, strategies, and activities so that they could fight to avoid repeating Silicon Valley's toxic legacy.

During this time, U.S. chipmakers lobbied loudly for federal government subsidies—claiming they were "losing" the international competition to Japanese chip firms. Congress responded by providing US$100 million per year to support Semiconductor Manufacturing Technology, Inc. (SEMATECH), an industry-led, high-tech research and development consortium developed to maintain U.S.-based high-tech corporations' global competitive edge. In 1992, the CRT organized a national campaign and won a major victory when Congress expanded the mission of SEMATECH to include developing cleaner production and directed that 10 percent of Federal funds be dedicated for this purpose. Activists throughout the United States began to realize that CRT's diversity was a key element of its success. This was highlighted when Frank Squires, Chief Executive Officer of SEMATECH, acknowledged in remarks to his employees: "They were not just environmentalists, but also labor, and social justice activists. That made it especially hard for us to deal with them" (SEMATECH 1992).

In the early 1990s, the CRT and the Southwest Network for Environmental and Economic Justice (SNEEJ) launched the Electronic Industry Good Neighbor Campaign (EIGNC), a community-based, multi-racial, collaborative effort to strengthen the work of local organizations in high-tech communities, which included SVTC in California, People Organized in Defense of Earth and Her Resources (PODER) in Texas, the SouthWest Organizing Project (SWOP) in New Mexico, and Tonatierra in Arizona.

In 1997, the CRT and the SNEEJ published *Sacred Waters: Lifeblood of Mother Earth* (Plazola 1997), four case studies of high-tech water resource exploitation and corporate welfare. The book became a major organizing tool for activists, who were working to protect their communities. Judith Espinoza, the former Secretary of Environment in New Mexico, said, "This study does not argue for holding back technology...but examines our obligation to advance a moral corporate commitment that meets the needs of today without wasting resources for future generations" (Plazola 1997, back jacket).

BUILDING ALLIANCES WITH WORKERS

From its outset, SVTC made a conscious decision to develop as a labor—community—environmental coalition. It has worked with the labor movement and SCCOSH to protect high-tech workers who suffer "double exposure" to toxics, both on the job and in the community. SVTC founders knew that this strategic alliance was necessary to challenge the industry argument that choices had to be made between jobs and the environment. Examples of this collaboration permeate SVTC's history.

SVTC's Board of Directors historically has included key representatives from the community, labor unions, and faith-based organizations. This broad cross-section of individuals and groups has enabled SVTC to lend its support to a variety of movements for environmental and economic justice.

OUR WORST FEARS

For more than 20 years, workers, their advocates, SVTC and other organizations, public health professionals, and medical doctors have urged the high-tech industry to phase out the use of known or suspected carcinogenic and reproductive toxins (see Photo 9.2). This perspective was forged in the early 1980s, stemming from the discovery of the groundwater contamination and the California Health Department's finding in 1985 that documented high rates of birth defects and miscarriages in the affected neighborhoods (Rudolph and Swan 1986; Wrensch et al. 1990).

In 1986, the first U.S. health study on electronics workers at the Digital Equipment Corporation revealed that its female production workers experienced higher rates of miscarriages than women in the general population (Pastides et al. 1988). In response, SVTC formed a partnership with SCCOSH and launched the *Ban Toxics, Not Workers* campaign advocating that toxic chemicals, not workers, should be removed from the workplace.

In 1992, two more epidemiological studies documented that women exposed to reproductive toxins had a 33 percent higher rate of miscarriage than those who had not (Schenker 1992; Schenker et al. 1995). Again SVTC and SCCOSH responded, launching the *Campaign to End the Miscarriage of Justice*, which called for phasing out all reproductive toxins in the workplace (see Appendix B, this volume) and criticized the Semiconductor Industry Association's (SIA's) decision to phase out use of ethylene-based glycol

PHOTO 9.2. Erin Brockovich, world-renowned champion for corporate environmental responsibility and community empowerment, giving the keynote speech at SVTC's 20th anniversary benefit, November 2002. Courtesy of Benjamin DeAsis.

ethers as overdue and insufficient. SVTC and SCCOSH met with SIA leaders to urge them to take more comprehensive steps to protect their workers' health. This issue attracted more attention when a 1998 *Wall Street Journal* story revealed a cancer cluster among women workers at National Semiconductor's plant in Greenock, Scotland (Richards 1998). SVTC continued to track the industry's occupational health impacts and built relations with occupational health professionals, worker organizations, religious shareholder activists (see Appendix C, this volume), and others throughout the world.

Although SVTC has campaigned successfully to persuade the industry to phase out some of its most harmful chemicals, many highly toxic chemicals are still used in electronics manufacturing. Semiconductor companies have resisted undertaking comprehensive health studies of their workers for many years, even though evidence has indicated that exposure to toxic chemicals results in increased birth defects and occupational cancer. After many years of pressure, the SIA finally has agreed to conduct more health studies of its workforce. Activists remain skeptical that the new studies will be comprehensive and credible.

FROM PRODUCTION TO DISPOSAL: HIGH-TECH'S TOXIC TRAIL

SVTC spent its first 20 years urging the high-tech industry to clean up its production processes. More recently, a new threat has emerged: the growing mounds of toxic electronic waste (e-waste). Growing concerns about protecting people from end-of-life toxic chemical exposure generated from discarded electronic products has prompted many European governments to adopt health protective measures (see Geiser and Tickner, this volume). SVTC became the leading U.S. nongovernmental organization (NGO) on these issues and organized support for the European Union's Directive on Waste Electrical and Electronic Equipment (WEEE) when the U.S. Trade Representative attempted to argue that it was a trade barrier (see Raphael and Smith, this volume).

In 2001, more than a dozen U.S. environmental and recycling organizations joined with SVTC and formed the Computer TakeBack Campaign (CTBC) to promote sustainable production and extended producer responsibility (see Wood and Schneider; Appendix D, this volume). In 2002, SVTC and the Basel Action Network released "Exporting Harm: The High-tech Trashing of Asia," which documented the dumping of toxic electronic waste in Asia (see Puckett; Wood and Schneider, this volume; see also BAN's 2005 report "The Digital Dump" on e-waste exports to Africa).

SVTC activists have traveled to countries throughout the world to share their experiences and to document the conditions of global, high-tech production. In 2001, the Taiwan Environmental Action Network (TEAN) invited SVTC to participate in its first high-tech environmental exchange. This provided SVTC with an opportunity to see first-hand high-tech production in one of the fastest growing regions of the world (see Chang et al. 2001).

FROM GRASSROOTS TO GLOBAL

SVTC, SCCOSH, and others recognized that as the high-tech industry was expanding globally, it was exporting not only its technology but also its toxic practices, especially to low-wage countries with inadequate environmental and occupational health standards. They recognized that this was an important aspect of globalization and that it needed a grassroots response. The seeds for creating the International Campaign for Responsible Technology (ICRT) were planted in the late 1990s. In 1997, at the European Worker Hazards Conference, SVTC delegates successfully passed a resolution to form an international network to address the global electronics industry. Two years later, at a meeting in Soesterberg, the Netherlands, an international gathering further developed the ICRT's vision by adopting a new "electronics sustainability statement":

> Each new generation of technical improvements in electronic products
> should include parallel and proportional improvements in environmental,
> health and safety as well as social justice attributes.

Since then, the ICRT has become a clearinghouse and resource center for technical advice, organizing strategies, and information. A global Listserv and Web site have been established, and inquiries from around the world now flood the ICRT's e-mail box. By developing organizing and advocacy models based on SVTC's successes in Silicon Valley, the ICRT is in a unique position to provide its research and experience to a vast network of organizations. The ICRT links a wide array of global activities by supporting the struggles of cancer victims in clean rooms from Scotland to Taiwan to the United States, and it is joining allies to demand studies of the health effects on high-tech workers throughout the world.

In November 2002, SVTC hosted the first "Global Symposium for a Sustainable High-Tech Industry" in San Jose, bringing together 50 leading community members, activists, electronics workers, health and safety experts, and academics from more than a dozen countries for a three-day conference (see www.svtc.org/icrt/index.html). Participants developed creative strategies for addressing the myriad problems associated with electronics manufacturing, assembly, disassembly, and disposal. During the meeting, delegates went to the headquarters of the SIA to present their stories and concerns about occupational and environmental health to the head of the chip industry trade association (see Photo 9.3). Participants committed to further develop strategies for organizing and empowering workers and communities and to identify opportunities for approaching regulatory institutions. At the same time, participants recognized the need to continue efforts to compel firms to reduce their toxic impacts and promote sustainable solutions. At the end of the symposium, the participants adopted an ICRT Mission Statement:

> We are an international solidarity network that promotes corporate and
> government accountability in the global electronics industry. We are united
> by our concern for the lifecycle impacts of this industry on health, the
> environment and workers' rights.

PHOTO 9.3. Delegates from the International Campaign for Responsible Technology (ICRT) assemble at offices of the Semiconductor Industry Association (SIA), San Jose, California, prior to meeting with SIA President, George Scalise, November 2002. Courtesy of David Sonnenfeld.

> By sharing resources we seek to build the capacity of grassroots organizations, local communities, workers and consumers to achieve social, environmental, and economic justice.

SVTC has grown over the past two decades in large part because of support from its board of directors, volunteers, interns, funders, and the broader community. Through its work in networks like the ICRT and CTBC, SVTC continues to work with groups worldwide, by sharing expertise and lending mutual support to improve the industry's environmental and health record. SVTC is working toward the day when the next generation of chips does not threaten the next generation of children, in Silicon Valley or anywhere else.

NOTES

1. TCA, a chlorinated solvent, used by the semiconductor industry, eventually was phased out and replaced with another toxic substance, trichloroethylene.

2. The Toxic Release Inventory (TRI) database provides information to the public about releases of toxic chemicals from manufacturing facilities. See www.epa.gov/tri/.

AMANDA HAWES WITH DAVID N. PELLOW

10   The Struggle for Occupational Health in Silicon Valley

A Conversation with Amanda Hawes

INTERNATIONAL BUSINESS MACHINES (IBM) came to dominate and embody the personal computer industry during the early 1980s, when its first desktop model became an instant global-market blockbuster. Not long after that, IBM broke its traditional "no layoff pledge" to its workers, as the recessions of the 1980s raged on and unemployment spiked to new heights. By the 1990s, attorney Amanda Hawes was making life even more difficult for this global electronics giant, as it was discovered that scores of its workers were succumbing to environmental illness and dying of cancer. In addition to the occupational health concerns being raised about Big Blue's manufacturing processes, the firm was also responsible for a host of environmental pollution problems outside the plants. By 2004, IBM had sustained public relations damages from a high-profile trial for Jim Moore and Alida Hernandez, two of fifty manufacturing workers with cancer from IBM San Jose, all represented by Hawes. Though the jury decided in favor of IBM, important parts of the largely untold story of how high-tech treats its manufacturing workers were at last starting to reach a global audience. That same year, the company announced that it was getting out of the PC-manufacturing business altogether, as other firms had become much more adept at this, while remaining profitable and lean. The toxic legacy is still with us, however, as workers continue to suffer from illnesses they allege were caused by exposure to chemicals while employed at IBM.

In late 2003, James Moore and Alida Hernandez, two former clean-room employees in an IBM factory in San Jose, California, took IBM to trial. For the first time, workers were charging IBM with illegally exposing them to toxic chemicals that caused them to get cancer, and also with concealing from them that their work was harming them for years before their cancers developed. Both worked at IBM from the late 1970s to the early 1990s. Moore and Hernandez claimed that if IBM had told them that clean-room chemicals at their workplace were poisoning them, they would not have remained there. The medical monitoring tests that IBM had performed on Hernandez's liver showed clear signs of chemical harm, but she was never told that her job was causing these problems. Hernandez worked with lots of cleaning solvents and a witch's brew of chemicals known as "disc coating." Her clothes were often soaked through with chemicals. Moore thought his headaches and sinus problems were "allergies," unaware of how many other IBM workers were being seen at the industrial clinic for similar "allergic" responses to their chemical environment. Moore worked with trichloroethylene (TCE) and lots of epoxy resins. His TCE exposure was orders of magnitude higher than what the state of California now recognizes as the threshold of cancer risk.

Hernandez came to IBM after decades of work in fruit processing. Moore started at IBM as a young man from the Central Valley. Both thought they were lucky to work in IBM clean rooms—each a closed system with recirculating air that, according to UC-San Francisco clinical professor of occupational medicine Joseph La Dou, continuously exposed workers to a broad array of chemicals (see LaDou, this volume). Moore, who died in October 2004, suffered from non-Hodgkin's lymphoma, whereas Hernandez, 73, was diagnosed with breast cancer in 1993. The lawsuit represents one of more than 200 cases brought by former workers against IBM for chemical poisoning resulting in cancer or other chronic disease. In addition to claims by IBM workers, there have been more than 50 cases brought by children of IBM workers who were born with disabling birth defects. By early 2006 this whole tragic saga appeared to be inching toward what corporate publicists typically refer to as "resolution"—the bittersweet and long-overdue kind.

The following is a conversation between David Pellow and the plaintiffs' attorney, Amanda Hawes (a partner in the San Jose law firm Alexander, Hawes & Audet) that took place on September 27th and 28th, 2003, and again in 2004. Hawes specializes in representing people exposed to toxic chemicals, and has done so for more than two decades, especially within the electronics industry. She is also a founder of the Santa Clara Center for Occupational Safety and Health (SCCOSH; see Pellow and Matthews, this volume) and of WorkSafe; both organizations advocate for workers' health protection.

DNP: *IBM makes the claim that there is no credible evidence to link cancer among its employees to the workplace. Yet, the epidemiologist Richard Clapp has concluded that the cancer death rates are significantly higher among IBM employees than what is commonly found in the general population. How do you sort all of this out?*

AH: Dr. Clapp did extensive analyses on IBM's "Corporate Mortality File" (CMF)—a comprehensive record of the cause of death of IBM employees over the past 35 years—and found that the proportion of IBM worker deaths due to cancer was much greater than you would expect among the general population. He also discovered that IBM workers were dying of cancer at much younger ages than the general population. IBM says its own CMF is not "a representative data set." Yet, the data set represents 99 percent of all the deceased employees who were eligible for death benefits. IBM reasons that there may be other deceased former employees who quit, left, or went someplace else and suggests that they may be alive and well, so that the deaths in the CMF are unrepresentative. That is the claim they were still making in 2004, but I'm not persuaded. IBM's claim that, compared to the general population, IBMers have no more cancer overall, does not mean much, especially when we consider that IBMers are not heavy smokers and have a lower than average incidence of lung cancer. Unfortunately, this "deficit" is more than made up for by the scary number of deaths from brain cancer, non-Hodgkin's lymphoma, leukemia, and breast cancer—particularly among manufacturing workers, scientists, and engineers, compared to IBM office workers, for example.

It was a good thing that IBM created its Corporate Mortality File; it is very unfortunate that they did not use and consult their own data sooner because unusual patterns of cancer mortality were already starting to show up by the early 1980s. If they had shared their data the way these kinds of data are routinely used in the field of epidemiology, there would have been a lot of useful, possibly life-saving information available for high-tech workers years ago. Not only did they fail to consult these data, their attorneys successfully excluded the CMF from consideration in the jury trial for Jim Moore and Alida Hernandez. That jury never heard about all the other manufacturing workers at IBM who died of breast cancer, and never heard how common non-Hodgkin's lymphoma was as a cause of death at IBM compared to the general population. When I started working on these cases, I thought that IBM probably did not have useful information to share with its workers about adverse health impacts. Once we were able to obtain the Corporate Mortality File through our discovery, I came to believe that not only have they had it, but they have never wanted to share or disseminate it because of the message it sends about the risks of working in the so-called clean industry.

DNP: *You referred to the Corporate Mortality File. It has been established that IBM has kept such files since 1969 on nearly all of its 30,000 employees. Yet, the company denied that these files even existed and later claimed that they could not be accessed or used to track employee health. How do you respond to this claim, and were there other examples of the ways the company was withholding information?*

AH: It is very frustrating to hear those denials made, especially when you then get the data and see how important they are. We filed a motion for sanctions because they withheld ventilation documents, but they are so good at covering their tracks. Months earlier, the discovery judge—a kindly, elderly man—had said in so many words, "If they are found to have been withholding documents, I can't think of a sanction too heavy for them, disbarment wouldn't be enough, castration maybe." They clearly have always had ventilation documents that relate to the different buildings and units in their facilities, but when we sought them last year they did not produce them: It was cat-and-mouse for months.

Then they turned around and produced 300 blueprints for their experts. In the same way, they tried to keep us from getting the Corporate Mortality File by saying, "It's too impossible to make any sense or use of it, it's a total waste of time." So I said, "We're willing to take that chance." IBM's lawyers liked to play judge and decide what documents and what information we would get, while they are sitting on thousands and thousands of pages of relevant material. And, of course, you have to call a document by the "right name" or it will never show up. Even then you will have a huge fight, and they say, "Tell us exactly what you want," so then they can say, "Well, they didn't quite call it by the right name so we can continue to hide that." I know this sort of game seems clever to some people but it is not funny when we are talking about workers' lives.

Another frustrating thing is realizing that medical files and key data are maintained electronically, but not being able to access them even though it is very clear that IBM created its system with that purpose and function in mind. They set their system up so that they have the capacity to sort not only an individual person's history, but also everybody in the same work area and how their health compares to "the norm." We discovered that they kept injury and illness cards, but the card does not go in your file; it goes down to the data processing center. And that is how they are supposed to make reports under the OSHA reporting system. When IBM workers got sick from the job, IBM's injury and illness cards required the medical staff to specify what systems in the body had been affected: the central nervous system, the respiratory system, the gastro-intestinal system, etc. And this is a company that told the jury they never heard of "*systemic chemical poisoning*" and that there is no such thing!

It turns out that IBM was keeping track of a huge amount of health data. For instance, if you are gone for three days and come back to work, they have you fill out a form, and they are supposed to code the reason for your absence and your illness into their database. If you are the company and you are watching the information trends, then you can make improvements and changes, so that is perhaps a good reason to keep tabs. But IBM didn't do the follow-up to address the problems their system was finding. When people were diagnosed with cancer, it got entered into the database using the standard codes, but they sent you back into the clean room anyway. So we have been looking at how many of the women who had breast cancer were sent back into the area to work in the same kind of environment and who then died, and it is a lot. It is disgusting. And they kept track of all that. We wanted the jury to hear about it too, but the judge ruled that this kind of evidence was more "prejudicial to IBM than probative" in our case for Jim and Alida.

If IBM management were more candid about what their data showed, they could probably have written a definitive study on cancer risks in high-tech manufacturing. Back in the 1970s everybody thought, "Well, IBM, they are very sophisticated; they are on the cutting edge of occupational medicine." A paper written in 1982 chronicled how detailed their system was for tracking health information, chemical information, and making it available for the people in the medical department. After we sued them and got access to the data through our discovery, IBM's lawyers began to claim that IBM's ECHOES system (Environmental Chemical Occupational Evaluation System) never worked. Well, I don't believe it. Some of our clients' medical files have questionnaires from the ECHOES program that they were answering as late as 1990. So it is misleading to say that the ECHOES system did not work; what is more likely is that it worked quite well, but along the way somebody decided that their system could collect and manage more information than IBM wanted to manage (based on their liability concerns), so it was used less and consulted less, when from the start it had great potential to aid in the early detection of patterns of disability and death.

By the mid 1980s, one of IBM's doctors whom we were able to depose testified that the head of the medical department told him when he got there about a company-wide repository. He was talking about the same thing I was describing—this computer system that revealed that the San Jose IBM plant had higher rates of injuries and illnesses than IBM facilities did on average. That was a concern.

At the same time, a chemist from the IBM San Jose plant named Gary Adams approached the corporation to say, "Several of my co-workers have died of cancer and I'm concerned about the place where we work." At that point, there were three people who were dead of cancer and two more with the diagnosis and the company did nothing. They said, "Well, we don't see any problem here and we're not going to do any medical monitoring." They argued then that since not all of Mr. Adams' coworkers died of the same cancer, what's the difference?

But the cancers they died of are ones that chemists die of more often than non-chemists: brain cancer, lymphoma, and digestive-tract cancers. Studies from the 1960s that show this pattern are repeatedly cited in Schottenfeld and Fraumeni, an authoritative text on cancer epidemiology. So there was no huge mystery why Gary Adams' fellow chemists were dying of these cancers. And IBM didn't just have a simple corporate mortality file; they were also tracking illnesses among chemical workers. They were keeping track of when people were diagnosed with a liver problem, or when they were out of work for an operation, or when they were diagnosed with cancer. They had all that in the same database.

All of an employee's health information at IBM is connected to their IBM number, which is a unique number that follows you wherever you go. So if you are in the medical department, you have access to the database. So it is easy to access the entire health history on any employee, and the medical personnel can get a report and an analysis of what illnesses (except cancer) have been reported in this population of people—for example, working in a specific building, working in a department, working in one location for five years. It was designed that way.

In the 1980s, IBM published *Think Magazine*, and in one 1983 issue they quoted a doctor from the corporate medical department (who later became the managing physician at San Jose). He was describing this great medical system that was an advancement over the old methods, where "we used to have to wait until the health problems got to a really serious stage before we could do anything, but now with our system we have the ability to detect the early signs, not just in one person, but in two places." He declared that if IBM saw the same complaints being reported in two places, they had the availability to check out what they are being exposed to and tackle the problem much more rapidly.

That is exactly what they were supposed to be doing and that was what they told people they were doing. And *Think Magazine* was sent to the employees, and people developed a lot of faith in IBM because they had that capacity.

People thought that if any company would be the first to write such a program and develop such a system, it would be IBM because they are masterful at data management—that is what they do. So it seemed pretty incredible when the IBM lawyers treated us to what I call a disinformation campaign saying "You know that the system never worked." When I think they meant, "IBM didn't bother to look at it."

DNP: *I was thinking about IBM in particular, not only as one of the most important pioneers of information gathering and processing machines, but also this concept of the "Big Blue family." The notion of the industrial paternal family must impact people at home. I'm wondering if some of the IBMers are feeling betrayed.*

AH: A friend of mine in Houston said that when IBM came to that city, they said that their policy was they never hired more than 3 percent of the available workforce in the community because they did not want to be like the company store. That's creepy. Did you ever hear anybody say something like that? Well, that sort of sounds like, "We're just going to pick the people that fit our image and nobody else." And I have always heard of it that way, that it is a big honor to work there. But the company's logic is that when times are tough, and they pull right out, they only manage to mess up the lives of 3 percent of the population.

DNP: *You have been able to demystify this whole science of epidemiology and toxicology. You've broken this very complex stuff down so that people can understand it. You have developed a real skill to the point where you seem to know this better than anybody. When I read that at least 250 people with various illnesses are suing the same company, that sounds like pretty damn good statistical significance to me. To manage this public relations problem, IBM has highly paid spokespersons—nice women, mostly—who are paid to create a warm fuzzy image for the company, but I assume that IBM has scientists to back up their countering arguments. How do they do that?*

AH: IBM and its attorneys mounted a very intense campaign to try to discredit epidemiologist Richard Clapp's analyses (see LaDou, this volume) and are now asking the public to believe that fewer IBMers died of cancer than you would expect, so that must mean it's a really safe place to work. But they don't mention what is called the "healthy worker effect." In general, the people who work are healthier than the entire population thrown together. There are people who are not healthy enough to work; therefore, it is not a surprise if you look at the overall patterns of illness and death among a working population that that population would be alive longer than a population that includes people who, during ages 21 to 64 (primary working years), are not working full-time because their health doesn't allow it. So that's the healthy worker effect. The researchers hired by IBM to look at patterns of death at the plants where there have been claims are always finding some way to dismiss any indication that there is, in fact, a different pattern of disease among high-tech workers than one would expect.

DNP: *Is there any indication that the semiconductor industry is becoming more environmentally responsible?*

AH: I believe that on some issues there have been substantial improvements because of the environmental pressure to do so, and industry officials have gotten rid of chlorofluorocarbons as degreasing agents, primarily freons, but also other chlorinated solvents because they are all ozone-depleting chemicals. I'm glad that they got rid of them; not only because of the ozone depletion, but also because of the health effects those compounds are capable of causing people who are working with them. However, they tend to be replaced by a family of materials that are characterized as surfactants, some of which are nasty chemicals, some of them containing Proposition 65 carcinogens. So the issue is that it's another replay of "Well, they managed to get rid of a problem that caused contamination or pollution in the air outside the plant, but let's talk about what's going on inside the plant." I think that the full impact, in terms of health consequences for the alternative materials, has not been studied at all. I would like to think in the grand scheme of things that these materials are less hazardous and can be better controlled. In the semiconductor industry, there is one way in that they are becoming ecologically more responsible, but it is almost by accident. And that is because their increasing need for cleanliness in the manufacturing process has meant that they have modified their new manufacturing facilities, and robots are doing a lot of the work that people used to do. So it's an unintended consequence, or serendipity, but workers are no longer exposed to chemicals to the extent they were 10, 20, and 30 years ago.

DNP: *What is IBM's legacy in Silicon Valley?*

AH: During the trial for Jim Moore and Alida Hernandez, the *San Jose Mercury News* ran a front-page story about Sammy Burch, this wonderful woman who retired from the IBM plant maybe 12 years ago, but who keeps in touch with a lot of her former coworkers. She talks about how after her retirement, a lot of what she was looking forward to was organizing baby showers and parties for employees getting married, but what she is spending her time on is funerals because people are dying.

I think in IBM's philosophy, there is only one source of authority and that's IBM. They have had their own fire department and their own medical department; they have had their own everything and so nobody needed any outside information. But in the last several years, workers, attorneys, environmentalists, and doctors have slowly but surely challenged this attitude and we are getting results. Jim Moore and Alida Hernandez lost their trial against IBM, but plenty has happened as a result of their courage. First, in taking on Big Blue it was a little like Lewis and Clark's expedition into the unknown; we turned up and shared information about how this industry operates that won't ever be secret again. Jim Moore died knowing that he did shed light on some of the dirty secrets of the so-called clean industry. Because the jury said they weren't convinced that Alida Hernandez and Jim Moore had been poisoned by their jobs, they never actually reached the BIG question: Did the jobs cause Jim's lymphoma and Alida's breast cancer? Right after the verdict,

Alida said, "I was born poor and I'm not afraid to die poor. I am proud of having had this opportunity to uncover some of the secrets of this industry so that others may not have to suffer what Jim Moore and I and many others have gone through."

The next day, we got deluged with messages of encouragement and thanks, but also of outrage. Here are some of them:

- "Just because we have a legal system doesn't mean we have a justice system."
- "This kind of trial reminds us why it's always good to swing for the fences."
- "Duh, everybody out here got what was going on—where was that jury?"

Then we got a call from one of the alternate jurors who wasn't part of the deliberations, but was paying attention. She called when the news was announced that IBM had just "concluded" a birth defects case we had brought for a New York plaintiff, the child of an IBM employee. She said that reading that was like hearing IBM say "guilty" even though officially they were saying nothing. What I thought was this: When a large corporation is facing an injured person on a level playing field, things go very differently than when the injured person happens to be an employee and the law says your only remedy is workers' comp *unless* you can prove what is a virtually impossible thing to prove.

DNP: *What lessons do you draw from this experience, and what do you think needs to happen in order to provide better health protection for workers who toil in toxic workplaces?*

AH: There is another important part of IBM's legacy that provides a lesson we learned through the trial of Jim Moore and Alida Hernandez. We took IBM to court under a section of the Labor Code that allows a worker to sue the employer when there has been concealment of an industrial injury and the concealment leads to an aggravation of the original injury because the worker, unaware of the harm that is taking place, keeps working and the continued exposure turns a small, fixable problem into a huge, pretty unfixable one— like cancer.

It's clear that our laws don't create any incentive for employers to be proactive about workplace hazards; they can be very confident that the "worst that will happen" is a claim for workers' compensation, which has never, ever, been enough of a "stick" to encourage precautionary steps to protect workers' health. So I've been thinking about how to get the precautionary principle incorporated into our legal system in a way that does protect workers. After all, I have never had a client with cancer who was glad they had me as their lawyer instead of having their health.

So here are some proposals that could make a real difference in workers' lives:

- If an employer uses any chemicals known to cause cancer, the maximum permissible exposure limit must be no greater than it is for environmental uses. This change would bring an immediate benefit to thousands of workers who are currently at risk for exposures thousands of times higher than the level that California acknowledges poses a cancer risk.

- An employer who continues to use these cancer-causing chemicals must do routine air sampling, must send the results to a government repository, and must tell the workers the results. If a worker develops cancer and wasn't given his or her test results and had them explained—or if the employer just didn't bother to do air sampling—those failures would be assumed to be intentional withholding of potentially life-saving information—and would make the employer liable for civil damages for a cover-up.

If an employer says that doing all these things would create too stringent a set of requirements—too much work to control cancer-causing chemicals at these lower health-protective levels, too much bureaucracy, too much record keeping—there are some obvious responses. First, this sort of rigorous documentation of exposure is done all the time in Scandinavian nations—from whom we have a lot to learn. And second, if you don't like being required to take these important steps to protect workers from cancer-causing chemicals you have an obvious alternative: stop using the cancer-causing chemicals now. That's right, "just say no" to the carcinogens and nobody gets hurt.

11   Immigrant Workers in Two Eras

Struggles and Successes in Silicon Valley

CALIFORNIA'S SANTA CLARA VALLEY, now world famous as Silicon Valley,[1] was also famous during an earlier period as one of the world's leading fruit-growing and processing centers, home to thousands of acres of orchards and several dozen canneries and dried-fruit packing plants. In this chapter, we compare and contrast the struggles to improve production workers' labor conditions in both the fruit and electronics industries; these workers were predominantly immigrant women. Ultimately, the cannery workers achieved considerable success in improving their situation by forming and defending a union, whereas the electronics workers have yet to unionize, though they have struggled valiantly and have won battles in other arenas, such as the fight for environmental justice. It is important to acknowledge and understand the cannery workers' unionization victories because these successes challenge those who believe it is impossible to organize vulnerable immigrant women workers, either in labor unions or for other purposes.

ONE VALLEY/TWO INDUSTRIES

Business Unity/Disunity

There are, of course, many dissimilarities between the agricultural and the high-tech eras. During the fruit era (early 1900s to the 1970s), two competing sets of interests comprised the business community—growers and processors, both of whom were powerful and well connected. With tens of thousands of acres in such fruits as prunes, plums, apricots, and cherries, Valley growers counted on a good price for their fruit—to say nothing of its role as a cornerstone of local prosperity. However, the canneries and dried-fruit packing plants were run by men—processors—who strove to pay as little for fruit as possible. Such is the logic of capitalism, and during the Great Depression, the inherent conflict of interest between these two groups flared into open conflict and prevented the business community from presenting a united front against workers. Now, in the electronics era (1970s–present), just the opposite is true. Though firms compete, the electronics industry is characterized by many powerful trade associations, which, above all, have united to keep out labor unions (Eisenscher 1993; Robinson and McIlwee 1989).[2]

Industry leaders repeatedly have gone on record declaring to the community and elected officials that the electronics sector can survive in Silicon Valley only if it remains union free (Pellow and Park 2002). Consequently, community activist organizations, such as Asian Immigrant Women's Advocates (AIWA), the Santa Clara Center for Occupational Safety and Health

(SCCOSH), and the Silicon Valley Toxics Coalition (SVTC), have stepped up to perform tasks normally associated with union leadership. This includes waging protests and lawsuits against firms for violations of wage standards, labor laws, and occupational safety and health regulations; leading educational activities to inform workers about their rights under the law; and advocating safer and more equitable workplace conditions.

Although all other unions were inactive in the electronics sector during the 1980s and 1990s, the United Electrical Workers Union (UE) made unique, continuous efforts s to organize Valley electronics workers. In 1993, the UE successfully organized the first electronics-based union in several decades in the Valley at Versatronix. The foundation for this victory was laid years before by Michael Eisenscher, a longtime UE activist who arrived in the Valley in 1980. Through his union drive at National Semiconductor, Eisenscher put the question of collective bargaining rights on the agenda in the Valley's electronics sector for the first time.

The State's Role

In the 1930s, the cannery workers' successful struggle for a union came at a time when the power of the American state was harnessed on behalf of the dispossessed as never before or since. The economic collapse that began with the stock market crash of 1929 generated the political will and President Franklin Delano Roosevelt's leadership provided the catalyst for the New Deal programs, including path-breaking labor legislation that guaranteed workers the right to collective bargaining.

In the decades since, the idea that government can and should be a major source of help to its citizens has eroded precipitously. Republican Party politicians now routinely run for office on a platform of "social conservatism" (dismantle social welfare programs), "small government" (roll back the New Deal legacy), and "free trade" (anti-union)—and Democratic Party politicians run scared. Through the North American Free Trade Agreement (NAFTA), the Free Trade Area of the Americas (FTAA), and such related organizations as the World Trade Organization (WTO), the state has willingly abdicated much of its regulatory power in favor of protections for investors and corporations, both here and abroad. In short, the context for worker organizing is much more hostile today than in the past because the state's power is much less likely to be deployed on workers' behalf.

Related to this is the fact that unions in the United States have been steadily losing ground since their glory days, which were primarily during the 1930s, World War II, and the immediate postwar period. Indeed, as of 2003, only about 13 percent of American workers belong to labor unions, down from the high of 35 percent in 1953. This is the direct result of corporations' union-busting efforts, severely weakened regulatory mechanisms, and the impact of deindustrialization and globalization, which encourage jobs to move to domestic and foreign locations where unions are often nonexistent and illegal (Bluestone and Harrison 1982).

Last, we need to compare the nature of civil society in both eras, and here the differences are more complicated than in the other areas. Anyone who has read the great novels by John Steinbeck—*The Grapes of Wrath* (1939) and *In Dubious Battle* (1936), stories that accurately capture the social history of the period—knows that California in the 1930s was a violent place, where local authorities came down hard on dissident workers. In the Santa Clara Valley, vigilantism was directed against the radicals, who were, for a while, the only ones attempting to organize cannery workers. Yet in the Valley there also had long been a public culture of dissent, with a variety of radicals meeting in St. James Park in downtown San Jose and giving speeches to the residents who gathered there.

By contrast, people today are much likelier to stay in their homes than go out to listen to speeches in public places. There was an extraordinary decline in the state of civil society and volunteer associations in the late 20th century (Putnam 2000). This is all the more troubling, as the *Third Force* (Florini 2000) of civil society was what Alexis de Tocqueville (1835) viewed as the key ingredient to the success of the society he described in *Democracy in America*. For a number of reasons, Americans today are less likely to join churches and Parent Teacher Associations (PTAs), sign petitions, join unions (as noted previously), or vote in elections.

Reliance on Foreign/Global Markets

Both the fruit and electronics industries have relied on immigrant women as the bulk of their production work force. A scholar who studied the Valley's canning industry nearly 100 years ago, for example, found that the workforce was only about 10 percent "American," whereas the other 90 percent consisted of immigrants (Matthews 2002). Jumping forward many decades, a Valley electronics employer told social scientist Karen Hossfeld that his firm's chief criteria for selecting a new employee were the categories "small, foreign, and female" (Hossfeld 1990; Matthews 2002). And statistics on the industry's composition in the late 1990s bear out the accuracy of this statement.[3]

From the earliest stages of European American settlement, the Santa Clara Valley always has been tied to a world market, first for hides, then cattle, then wheat, then fruit, then semiconductors—and beyond.

The electronics industry is also deeply tied to global economic patterns. More than 900 semiconductor fabrication plants (fabs) are operational world-wide. Electronics manufacturing has expanded from Silicon Valley and the electronics corridor along Route 128 near Boston (and a few areas in western Europe and Japan) to the U.S. Southwest, and to nations throughout Asia, Europe, Latin America, and the Caribbean (see Leuthje; and Steiert, this volume).

In each era, Valley workers have benefited from their proximity to San Francisco, arguably one of the most liberal cities in the United States, with a long and proud tradition of citizen activism. A 1930s' militancy known as the "march inland," generated by San Francisco longshoremen who wanted to organize collateral industries, was critical to the success of the cannery work-ers' drive to unionize in the Santa Clara Valley because the San Franciscans provided both a powerful example and resources (Matthews 2002). In 1978, when activists founded the SCCOSH, they enjoyed a more favorable context to recruit supporters than had they been part of a less liberal, regional culture. The San Francisco Bay Area was then, and remains, a nationally recognized training ground for progressive, left-leaning social movements, based on university campuses, churches, small offices, and homes throughout the area. Affordable housing, labor rights, immigrant rights, health care, public health and environmental quality, corporate accountability, student rights, and racial justice movements have all seen exceptional development in this area, so it was ripe for the emergence of SCCOSH in the late 1970s.

Finally, another important similarity lies in the fact that, during both eras, workers, whether formally or informally, engaged employers in struggles over wages and working conditions. Beginning with unions like the Cannery and Agricultural Workers' Industrial Union (CAWIU), UCAPAWA, and International Workers of the World (IWW) in the 1930s and continuing with worker advocacy organizations like SCCOSH and AIWA today, the continued militancy of workers rights has been a hallmark of the Valley (Matthews 2002). We now turn to a fuller discussion of a few of those struggles, both in the 1930s and today.

THE VALLEY OF HEART'S DELIGHT: SILICON VALLEY IN THE 1930S

In the late 1920s, just prior to the Great Depression, there were approximately 20,000 fruit-industry workers in the Santa Clara Valley at the height of the summer season. They toiled in some three dozen canneries that were interspersed among the fruit trees.[4] In the off-season, when work consisted of maintaining the machinery and warehousing, men predominated in the workforce. But as soon as the fruit ripened, a workforce consisting mainly of women arrived to cut and pack it (Anthony 1928). The work was physically demanding—in this time before refrigeration, the length of the workday was determined by the quantity of fruit on hand—and the women workers faced a number of unpleasant circumstances, such as being subject to capricious and unfair floor ladies and being vulnerable to abrupt terminations. With no union, the workers lacked recourse. The skilled trades-oriented American Federation of Labor (AFL) showed no interest whatsoever in organizing the canneries.

When the massive economic downturn of the early 1930s plunged the regional California economy into turmoil, workers were hit hard. They saw their already low wages plummet, and their working conditions deteriorated. It did not take long for them to respond. In late July 1931, hundreds of cannery workers staged a strike in San Jose, California. On one particular day, there was fighting in the city streets between striking workers and police—with the police receiving support from community members sympathetic to employers. Though the strike resulted in no permanent gains for the workers—and no union—it was, nonetheless, important. In the first place, it demonstrated that large numbers of workers were angry about their situation (Matthews 2002). Second, it marked the Communist Party's first visible role in the Valley's labor struggles, with Party organizers declaring the formation of the

Cannery and Agricultural Workers' Industrial Union during the course of the strike. Further, the strike antedated the passage of New Deal legislation, inasmuch as Herbert Hoover was in the White House at the time, rather than FDR. In the end, legislative change was very important to worker success in 1937, but it was not a prerequisite for triggering the decade's opening salvo of worker militancy. Finally, the strike mobilized a group of activists, including the eight or nine local Communist Party members, to organize tirelessly until there was a major cannery workers' union in Silicon Valley in 1937.

The period between the cannery worker strike of 1931 and the emergence of a cannery union in 1937 saw many developments that were antithetical to social movements and labor organizing. These included the AFL's persistent reluctance to invest in organizing cannery workers—until the birth of the rival Congress of Industrial Organizations (CIO) in the mid-1930s, suggested that others might be taking these workers seriously. Even more damaging was the growth, throughout California, of the proto-fascist Associated Farmers, an employer group dedicated to combating food-industry unions with heavy-handed tactics. Whether the group was directly responsible for the vigilantism there—which showed its most aggressive face when anonymous thugs invaded the homes of known radicals—is impossible to prove. There was enough local violence directed against militant workers and radicals to warrant an article in *The Nation* entitled, "The Terror in San Jose" (Terry 1934).

Yet cannery workers in northern California *did* join the ranks of organized labor.[5] The full story has too many labyrinthine twists and turnings to recount fully in this chapter. A brief summary is as follows. In the early summer of 1937, a San Jose cannery local union seemed to be emerging under national AFL auspices, the AFL having "got religion" on this subject owing to CIO interest in cannery workers (Ruiz 1987). But the AFL abruptly revoked the charter of the first local and sponsored another, clearly with employer connivance. It seemed that all the workers would get would be a company-backed union; however, the officers of the second local plotted to reclaim it from company control, which they did so successfully that it staged a victorious strike in 1941 (which netted a significant pay raise; Matthews 2002).

In trying to fathom how this worker victory could have happened, one first must acknowledge the crucial role played by the passage of the major New Deal labor law, the Wagner Act, which established the National Labor Relations Board in 1935.[6] Cannery workers were within its purview and got a union. Local factors also must have played a significant role because even in the 1930s—a period that saw the greatest spate of labor victories in U.S. history—such successes were unusual among seasonally employed, semiskilled, immigrant women. We already have delineated the most salient local factors, which included the public culture of dissent and the proximity of San Francisco, with its militant labor movement (Nelson 1988).

From the early 1940s, cannery workers had a union that genuinely protected their interests. Evidence for this, in addition to the successful strike in 1941, is contained in the contracts negotiated on their behalf during World War II. One item for which the union worked, for example, was to guarantee to female piece-rate workers the right to rotate on the line, so that everyone would have a fair chance at the same quantity of fruit. Moreover, the union held annual elections. But the national AFL, which had always taken a dim view of these workers, refused to grant them an international charter, and as a result of a complicated series of events, turned them over to the very conservative Teamsters' Union shortly after the war (Matthews 2002). Within the Teamsters, the interests of the female production workers suffered, and these interests would not again be adequately addressed until a lawsuit in the 1970s, as discussed later.

The tide of union militancy that had drawn upon the cannery workers' own strengths and the infusion of energy and resources from the march inland came to a close because conservative unionists, in connivance with employers, were able to use the anti-Communist fervor following World War II to roll back the tide. The Teamster takeover of the northern California cannery union involved both unfair elections and strong-arm tactics. When workers turned to the National Labor Relations Board (NLRB) for help, however, that agency's ability to protect workers was undercut by red-baiting charges made by employers against NLRB staff (St. Sure 1957, 227–29). In effect, this tactic greatly impeded the Wagner Act's ability to guarantee workers' rights. When the *Alaniz* lawsuit was filed in the 1970s, plaintiffs would employ Title VII of the 1964 Civil Rights Act as the basis for their suit, rather than labor law.

By the 1970s, there had been a transformation in the ethnic nature of the cannery workforce. Predominantly southern European (primarily Italian and Portuguese immigrants) prior to World War II, the industry opened up new employment and became overwhelmingly Mexican-American by 1945. But the union offices remained in the control of Italian American men. Mexican American women could thus plausibly complain about unfair work rules and allege discrimination, as they did in the *Alaniz* case of the 1970s, a complaint for which a civil rights law provided a remedy.

Though the workers did not receive everything they optimally might have wanted as a result of *Alaniz*, they did achieve a marked improvement in their status. The court ordered that an affirmative action program be set up in the canneries, for example. Moreover, the rules regarding seniority were to be rewritten so as to be fairer to seasonally employed workers. The only problem was that this legal victory came at a time when canneries were dwindling in number and diminishing in their significance to the local economy: *Alaniz* was fought out in the mid-1970s, but by that time the Valley already had been dubbed "Silicon Valley." Though the last cannery did not close its doors until 1999, the 1970s can be seen as the twilight of fruit as a way of life in what is today Silicon Valley. Generations of women and their male allies had struggled with a fair amount of success for justice in the canneries. Now there were women workers in a new industry, but with the same need to struggle.

THE VALLEY OF TOXIC FRIGHT: SILICON VALLEY TODAY

We want to challenge some of the myths that have grown up around Silicon Valley, flourishing especially in the days before the economic downturn in the high-tech industry after 2000. Then we will explore the role of SCCOSH.

There are three pervasive, but misguided notions regarding Silicon Valley today. Myth number one is the notion that the Santa Clara Valley is some kind of land of milk and honey that confers riches upon most of its inhabitants. Owing to a combination of low wages for electronics production workers and sky-high prices for homes, it is a tough place for newcomers. Myth number two would have it that electronics is a clean industry, a preposterous distortion of reality, given the heavy use of toxic chemicals used to manufacture its products (see Hawes; Byster and Smith, this volume). From a different part of the political spectrum comes a third myth that we also would like to take on: the contention that Silicon Valley arose where it did because the Valley possessed no history of a vital labor movement. Not widespread in popular culture, this myth has nonetheless been perpetuated by many progressive scholars. We argue that an important reason that the history of women cannery workers' successful struggle has gone so unrecognized by those who study the origins of Silicon Valley lies in the concept of female invisibility; such lack of recognition is not an isolated phenomenon. Feminist scholars have used the concept to explain why female accomplishment is so often trivialized or even leached out of the historical record. We believe that it is important for today's electronics workers to know that they have Valley foremothers, immigrants like them selves.

SCCOSH

Although there are a number of other grassroots groups in the region (Asian Immigrant Women's Advocates, Silicon DeBug, and Silicon Valley Toxics Coalition), the SCCOSH has been one of the most visible forces in the effort to make clear the links between toxic workplaces and contaminated communities. In this section, we focus mainly on SCCOSH because it was the first such organization and because other chapters in this book emphasize the role of SVTC (see Byster and Smith "From Grassroots to Global," this volume).

The founders of SCCOSH were three women, each of whom was connected to the electronics industry in some way. Amanda Hawes was an attorney representing electronics workers in compensation cases, Robin Baker worked for a local university's occupational health program, and Pat Lamborn was an activist and electronics worker. Amanda Hawes began her work in the region in the early 1970s, representing workers seeking better conditions in the canneries. SCCOSH was established in 1978, and at that time it was a combination of two projects: the Electronics Committee on Safety and Health (ECOSH) and the Project on Health and Safety in Electronics (PHASE). These groups led the effort to monitor Silicon Valley industries, and they achieved a number of accomplishments, including: the formation of the Silicon Valley Toxics Coalition (SVTC) in 1982; starting a support group called Injured Workers United; helping found the Occupational Clinic at Valley Medical Center; creating a Hazards Hotline for Electronics Workers; and launching the Campaign to Ban TCE (trichloroethylene) as a reproductive hazard. Recollecting the founding of SCCOSH, Amanda Hawes emphasized the workplace-community environmental links:

> A big success for ECOSH was our campaign to ban TCE. The TCE campaign was noteworthy because it brought the spotlight on the chemical-handling aspects of the so-called clean industry at the same time TCE contamination of local water supplies was coming to light. But it was mainly noteworthy because its origin and focus was always the workplace. If hazards faced by workers are not made a priority, we will all suffer the consequences. (Hawes 1998)

SCCOSH's work has evolved since the 1970s to encompass women, immigrants, and others in two segments of Silicon Valley's electronics industry: semiconductor manufacturing and electronics assembly.

Semiconductor Plants

The environmental justice movement is a phenomenon that emerged from working-class communities and communities of color in the United States in the 1970s. The movement sought to target government and industry for concentrating a disproportionate volume of toxics in workplaces and communities populated by people of color and poor persons. Silicon Valley was no exception. One of the first steps the environmental justice movement in the Valley took was to prove that there was indeed a problem with the electronics workplace. This involved encouraging government, industry, and health officials to conduct health studies of electronics workplaces throughout the United States. In October 1992, the preliminary results of a five-year study at IBM were released. In that study, 10 of 30 pregnant women exposed to glycol ether at an IBM semiconductor plant experienced miscarriages (Pellow and Park 2002, 104). The Semiconductor Industry Association (SIA) recommended to its member firms that they accelerate efforts to eliminate the use of ethylene-based glycol ethers (EGEs). Although environmental justice activists were pleased at this turn of events, they also were disappointed because many of them had recognized this problem and had called for a phase-out of EGEs long ago. Amanda Hawes charged that the industry "has been stalling the adoption of safer alternatives until there is a body count" (Smith 1992).

The 1992 IBM report shook the semiconductor sector and challenged the three-decade-old myth that this was a "clean industry." Activists viewed these scientific affirmations of their claims as both a vindication and a window of opportunity for organizing to reform the electronics industry. For example, in response to the 1992 study of miscarriages, SCCOSH announced the launching of the Campaign to End the Miscarriage of Justice, calling on the industry to phase out glycol ethers and other reproductive toxins. Representatives from this campaign led workshops on environmental health and safety at the annual conferences of the American Public Health Association and the Committees on Occupational Safety and Health (COSH) in San Francisco in 1993. In 1994, after campaign members met with SEMATECH—the tax-payer-subsidized consortium of semiconductor chipmakers—the industry began phasing out its use of ethylene-based glycol ethers. Thus, SCCOSH and its allies had a major influence on regulators, universities, and the industry in that its protests and negotiations led to the commissioning of several health studies and a national change in company policies regarding the use of certain toxins.

Organizing Resistance

Most workers in computer and printed circuit board assembly shops are women, people of color, and immigrants. SCCOSH has stepped up to the challenge of providing services to these populations. Beginning in the late 1990s, SCCOSH's Working Women's Leadership Project (WeLeaP!) focused on educating and empowering women workers in Silicon Valley's low-wage jobs. The program is a multiethnic, multilingual effort to provide participants with technical and practical information about the hazards associated with their jobs and the skills needed to negotiate with management regarding these issues. Classes have been conducted for Korean, Latino, Vietnamese, Cambodian, Filipino, and several other ethnic groups (at least 12 in all). Workers are encouraged to participate in what SCCOSH calls the Worker Stories Process—wherein participants tell "their story" about who they are, their challenges and opportunities at work, and their plans for improving their situations. Raquel Sancho, the Acting Executive Director of SCCOSH and founder of WeLeaP!, is a Filipina activist who emigrated to the United States in 1987. She has been active in the GABRIELA Network, a Philippines-U.S. women's activist alliance, and regularly travels to Southeast Asia to work with women's groups on social justice issues. The WeLeaP! project attracted and graduated more than 200 Silicon Valley workers in its first two years of operation. SCCOSH became a major, grassroots political force in Silicon Valley over the years.

CONCLUSION

From the Valley of the Heart's Delight to the Valley of Toxic Fright, Silicon Valley has seen more than a century of labor strife; racial, ethnic, and gender exploitation; and continuous damage done to ecosystem. Land and labor always have been at the center of this drama. In the 1930s, when the valley was viewed as a place of great natural beauty, land was being monopolized for agricultural production and the oppression of immigrant workers. Since the 1970s, that same land has changed hands and has been paved over; it now houses electronics firms that claim to value the environment, while engaging in great harm to natural systems and placing their employees at risk, as they confront highly toxic working conditions.

Today, building on the region's long history of labor activism, a range of decentralized, innovative organizations is pursuing labor and community empowerment in the Valley. SVTC, SCCOSH, AIWA, Silicon Valley DeBug and various "worker centers" have spearheaded the struggle. The AFL-CIO-affiliated South Bay Labor Council is closer to the "worker center" model of organizing than a union and has assisted non-union workers in gaining access to benefits that electronics firms have denied them. Through WeLeaP! and SCCOSH's Campaign to Ban TCE, these groups have led mobilizations to empower women, immigrant, and youth workers in the Valley, to provide basic rights and health care access to temp workers, and to pursue employer liability for a host of wage violations and the impacts of chemical production and exposure. Ranging from the reformist to the radical, these campaigns remain the best hope for strengthening labor rights and environmental justice in Santa Clara Valley. Workers in the Valley today have a great challenge ahead of them in this era of economic globalization, a corporate-state alliance, and the declining role of unions in particular and civil society in general.

NOTES

1. Today the Valley includes the cities of San Jose, Santa Clara, East Palo Alto, Palo Alto, Menlo Park, Mountain View, and many others.

2. See also Lüthje (this volume) regarding the electronics industry's contemporary structure.

3. In the April 16, 1999, issue of the *San Jose Mercury News* there was this figure: 77 percent of the blue-collar jobs in contract manufacture in Santa Clara County were held by Asians, most of whom are known to be relatively recent immigrants.

4. The vast acreage in orchards and the extensive number of canneries made this area the world's largest center of fruit growing and processing at the time.

5. The San Jose local of the AFL union that emerged was by far the largest in the region.

6. The National Labor Relations Act, also known as the Wagner Act after New York Senator Robert Wagner, gave workers the right to form unions and bargain collectively with their employers. The act also created the National Labor Relations Board to oversee union certification, arrange meetings with unions and employers, and investigate violations of the law.

12   Worker Health at National Semiconductor, Greenock (Scotland)

Freedom to Kill?

THIS CHAPTER EXAMINES INDIVIDUAL, political, and societal issues associated with the occupational health, safety, and welfare of the current and former employees at National Semiconductor in Greenock, West Scotland. Also included is a discussion of civil society groups that have advocated on these employees' behalf: a community group named PHASE Two (People for Health and Safety in Electronics), the Inverclyde Advice and Employment Rights Centre, and local trade unionists. The chapter raises the possibility of negative occupational health outcomes created by National Semiconductor UK (NSUK) and examines the impact that raising these issues has had on the local community. It draws heavily on the personal testimony of employees who have worked in the industry.

Key questions posed are as follows: Does the fact that National Semiconductor is a major employer in a small town influence the power relationship between the firm and the local residents? Does this employer have any genuine concern for its current and former employees' health and safety? Is the minimal information gathered under the guise of occupational health used as the first line of serial defense in corporate, legal personal injury cases? Regarding a wider issue, should self-regulation, as is the case here, be allowed, especially for companies using such toxic substances?

This chapter reveals that the apparent laissez-faire attitude that the company, state regulators, and local and national health professionals exhibit toward occupational and community health has contributed to a grim situation.

THE SEMICONDUCTOR INDUSTRY

Semiconductor Chip Manufacture is a major international industry. Its explosive growth has resulted in a world market for semiconductor chips that is valued at US$175 billion per year. These high-technology devices are crucial to the manufacture and sales of about US$1 trillion in electronics products each year. The microelectronics industry has a worldwide workforce of around one million workers.

The manufacture of microchips involves many complex and chemically intensive processes. LaDou and Rohm offered a vivid description of the cynical macro strategies developed and continued by the industry as a whole:

> The migration of European, Japanese and American companies accommodates regional markets. Low wage rates and limited enforcement of environmental

regulations in developing countries also serve as incentives for the dramatic global migration of the industry. The manufacture of microelectronics products is accompanied by the high incidence of occupational illness, which may reflect the widespread use of toxic materials. (LaDou and Rohm, 1998, 1)

How important was the prospect of the limited enforcement of regulatory requirements when National Semiconductor decided to locate a plant in Scotland? If not the foremost consideration, it certainly has been to National Semiconductor's benefit.

HOW THE ELECTRONICS INDUSTRY ARRIVED IN INVERCLYDE

Inverclyde is an area about 20 miles northwest of Glasgow, with a population of 85,000. It consists of three main areas: Port Glasgow in the east of the region, Greenock in the center, and Gourock to the west. Like many other areas in Scotland, it has seen a transition away from traditional industries. In the 1950s, Inverclyde's main industries were ship and boat building and sugar production, along with their suppliers. These industries were characterized by nearly all-male workforces. National Semiconductor arrived in 1970, and by the mid-1980s, the Greenock plant was the largest semiconductor manufacturing site in the world (*Scottish Enterprise* 1989), supplying silicon chips to the European market.

WHY MICROELECTRONICS ARRIVED IN GREENOCK

There are undoubtedly many reasons why National Semiconductor located in Inverclyde. At the time, the Prestwick airport was the main gateway to the United States, and generous government grants were made available. Another key reason was the availability of water. Silicon wafers use on average 2,270 liters of water (SCCOSH 1998), and a mini reservoir was built next to the plant, ensuring a plentiful supply.

The type of labor available may have been a contributing factor. An interesting theory regarding the factors contributing to location is that when NSUK located in the West of Scotland (Greenock), it was at a time when male employment was high—National Semiconductor was guaranteed an all female (production) workforce. These women, as wives and daughters of shipyard workers, would have been "subject to patriarchal domination" all of their lives (Henderson 1989, 129). In the same work, Henderson accurately alluded to the fact that the senior management structure was, *and still is*, exclusively male. Dolly, a senior supervisor, stated:

Women only got to supervisory level. I was a senior supervisor for around 20 years. Latterly, my male counterparts went on to senior management. I did not. I never ever considered it was possible. Ability had little to do with it. I was as good as, if not better, than some that moved on. I did not question it; it was the done thing and that was that. It did not bother me. I had a family that was enough responsibility for me.[1]

INDUSTRIAL RELATIONS AT NSUK

There are no trade unions at NSUK. At the time of location, nonunionized employers were a rare phenomenon in the Inverclyde area. In fact, prior to the location of the electronics sector, all major employers on the Lower Clyde Reaches had trade unions. Various trade unions have made sporadic attempts to recruit at National Semiconductor, the last attempt having been made in 2001. Evidently, the trade union movement implicitly accepts that electronics workers are not receptive to unions and that they are too difficult to recruit (see Pellow and Matthews, this volume). During one recruitment campaign in the 1980s, Jane, a clean-room worker, thought of joining the union:

> My father had been a steward in the Klondyke (shipyard). I knew you were not allowed to join the Union in Semis. I happened to mention to my supervisor in the canteen that the union men were outside the gate trying to get us to join and that I was thinking of taking up their offer. Minutes later I was took into the office to see my manager and told the paper lying on the desk was a warning with my name on it; any talk of unions and my feet will not touch the ground. I told him I did not give a shit for him. I would join the union if I wanted to. He could take his warning and stick it up his ass. I worked beside the wee bastard and the only reason he got the job was because he had [testicular] cancer. I never joined, my weans [kids were young] and I did not want to get sack[ed] through it. And my man was not working either.[2]

Jane was diagnosed with breast cancer at 28 years of age.

At the National Semiconductor site, there was an Employee Representative Committee (ERC) with mainly supervisors, which discussed things like social events, peripheral safety matters, and company sales data. The operators had little or no input. Indeed, the ERC had such a bad reputation that a later attempt in 1998 to set up a worker representative committee and a works council was disallowed. Similar dynamics occurred at the National Semiconductor plant around the same time in Santa Clara, California, when unions tried to organize the workers there.

To comply with government legislation, National Semiconductor was compelled to set up an employee representatives consultative safety committee in 1996. This meant that there was a safety committee required by law. It was the first time in the United Kingdom that a non-unionized employer had a specific duty to consult with its workers on matters relating to heath, safety, and welfare (under the Health and Safety Consultation with Employee [HSCE] Regulations of 1996). The HSCE regulations came from a European directive of the same name.

EARLY WORKER, UNION, AND COMMUNITY ACTIVITY AND GOVERNMENTAL AND AGENCY RESPONSES

In the early 1990s, trade union activists Pat Stuart and Jimmy Swan of the Lothian Trade Union & Community Resource Centre in Edinburgh; Duncan

McNeil, Health and Safety Officer of the GMB[3] (and now a member of the Scottish Parliament); and Bill Speirs, then Assistant General Secretary of the Scottish Trade Union Congress (STUC), met with the HSE (the UK Health and Safety Executive) to discuss possible detrimental reproductive health effects being experienced by semiconductor workers throughout Scotland.

Their concerns were based on important, anecdotal evidence from clean-room workers, who had voiced their concerns about the number of workers who had experienced negative reproductive outcomes while working in clean rooms. This led to the development and publication of the HSE Spontaneous Abortion in the Semiconductor Industry Study (Elliott et al. 1999), which had been undertaken by the HSE's Epidemiology Department. Participation, which was voluntary, involved five semiconductor manufacturers at seven sites throughout the UK. Among other findings, the study conclusion implied that it was actually safer to work in the clean rooms whilst one was pregnant. This flew in the face of three previous studies conducted in the United States, all of which found excess miscarriage rates among clean-room workers.

CONTESTING THE INDUSTRY TERRAIN ON HEALTH AND SAFETY: GATHERING MORE INFORMATION

In 1996, the local Greenock and District Trades Union Council accessed the STUC's Scottish One Fund for All (SOFFA) fund. The fund, supported by contributions from trade union members over and above their weekly contributions, is used for a variety of good causes. SOFFA donated a sum that allowed me to locate in Greenock, primarily to undertake administrative duties for the Trade Union Council, Inverclyde's Occupational Health Project (IOHP).

THE NEXT STEP: MEETING THE WORKERS

In April 1997, John, a male semiconductor worker (now deceased) visited me and complimented me on my work with shipyard workers, but said I was missing the whole point. "Semis son, that's what you want to be . . . concentrating on, there's a . . . holocaust going on up there and not a bastard is giving a toss." I asked him to provide me with more details. He advised that he had been on full sick pay for around five years and did not want to do anything that would jeopardize that. We arranged to meet the following week in Glasgow, 22 miles away, "this is the only place I feel I can talk to you," he said. John went on:

> I have been involved in the engineering side for many years and the place is a total shambles. In the mid-seventies it was blatant murder. Those lassies did not have a clue what was going on, they had no chance. We used to unplug the chemical alarms if they were working against a production deadline, and there were women vomiting all over the place. We used to get

it as well: When we were working the extraction ducting we used to get chemical blowout and this caused temporary neck and facial paralysis. It was ... weird, your whole world used to slow down, but you could hear your heart racing.... If you reported it they never put it in the accident book. They told us to go to the canteen for a drink or see the nurse, but she was hopeless. I was never tested for any chemical exposure in the 22 years I was on site, even after I was overcome [with chemicals].[4]

John connected me to another three or four former workers whose stories were equally powerful. I decided that I would examine matters more closely. I made it known throughout the town that I was interested in speaking to current and former workers. Between April and August, about 60 workers visited or telephoned me. The stories ranged from fairly routine to almost unbelievable. By this time, I had managed to research the chemicals with which they probably had worked. Very few workers could provide any detailed information, as most were familiar with trade names only.

The Birth of PHASE Two

In 1997, I decided to establish a support group for the workers who had visited me so that they could tell about their experiences in and out of work. I felt that these workers would derive a psychological benefit from sharing their experiences. Previously, they had visited as individuals, and, to my knowledge, they had never publicly discussed their experiences. It is my view that their experiences should be shared.

I sent a mailshot[5] out confirming my intention to form a group. This effort was met with a relatively favorable response, and at the first meeting on January 26, 1998, about twenty people attended. We took the name, PHASE Two, in tribute to our American colleagues, who started PHASE, in Silicon Valley in the 1970s.

The media began expressing an interest—cancer victims are news after all—and soon afterwards, BBC Frontline Scotland produced the program, "Shadow over Silicon Glen," which aired in February 1998. Members of Parliament began demanding health data on the area's workers.

This combination of group activities and the resultant media coverage led to the first-ever, independent study of a UK semiconductor site. The subsequent interest was significant. I received a telephone call from Dr. Gunneberg, Public Health Consultant with the Argyll and Clyde Health Board. He was keen to speak to Amanda Hawes, the lawyer who spoke at the first PHASE Two meeting. He was invited to and attended a PHASE Two meeting in April 1998. He conveyed the need for the group to bring the Health Board hard evidence to back its anecdotal claims.

The PHASE Two group has campaigned continuously since on the matter of semiconductor worker health and safety and welfare. We believe that our work has raised the industry's profile to such a degree that the HSE will never take it so lightly again. About 200 workers citing a litany of health complaints, ranging from cancer to Crohns Disease, have contacted PHASE Two. There is a core of about 30 consistent members.

In May 1999, the group launched a legal action on its members' behalf. The class-action lawsuit was filed to ensure that workers still coming forward are protected should they wish to pursue matters. We are represented by Thompsons Scotland and, in the United States, by Alexander, Hawes, and Audet.

INTERNATIONAL PERSPECTIVE

Several international links emerged along with PHASE Two's formation. The Silicon Valley Toxics Coalition (SVTC) proved to be an important source of information and resources, in particular, the connection to an effective, existing network of activists who had experiences similar to those of PHASE Two. This led to a visit by Ted Smith, SVTC's Executive Director, in July 1998. The critical exchange of information and visits by activists traveling between Scotland and Silicon Valley led to the development of key networks, such as the International Campaign for Responsible Technology, and this has been of great comfort to the PHASE Two members (see Photo 12.1).

Of course, practical benefits have manifested. PHASE Two's link with Dr. Joseph LaDou, an occupational physician of the University of California, San Francisco, has been critical. Few such physicians exist in the UK, and even fewer have shown a commitment to worker health. Twice traveling to Scotland at his own expense to meet with the group, his input has been an effective way to publicly demonstrate that credible professionals, not influenced by the industry or the need for work, believe in PHASE Two.

PHOTO 12.1. Participants from the "Global Symposium for a Sustainable High-Tech Industry," sponsored by SVTC and ICRT, on a "toxic tour of Silicon Valley," visit the National Semiconductor site in Santa Clara, California, a U.S. Superfund site with groundwater contaminated from solvents used in microchip manufacturing, November 2002. Courtesy of Silicon Valley Toxics Coalition.

At the local level, Professor Andrew Watterson of Stirling University, Scotland, has provided ongoing, technical advice, which has been vital to deciphering the pretentious language of medical science. The assistance that both men provide is more welcome than they could ever imagine, and what they see as second nature has galvanized the campaign during some of our darkest times.

HEALTH PROFESSIONALS: ARGYLL AND THE CLYDE HEALTH BOARD

Unfortunately, despite my early attempts to convince the local Health Board of the urgency of these matters, it has been, in my opinion, wholly unsupportive of our activities. In fact, I would go as far to say they are resolutely against PHASE Two on this matter. I say this because they have repeatedly been unavailable for the meetings that we have arranged, even when in April 2001, PHASE Two held a seminar featuring Dr. Joseph LaDou. One aim of the seminar was to help local medics understand the complex processes and the chemicals used therein. Of the 66 local general practitioners who were invited, not one attended.

I believe Argyll and Clyde Health Board has ignored the community it is paid to serve. Public and environmental health is clearly part of its mission. At no time have its members done anything other than avoid the issue, however. They may perceive that it is not their role to become involved. The "public" in public health should include people who are injured or diseased as a result of work.

Does this mean that, as a society, we leave the discovery of such matters to community groups? Recent events have demonstrated that if PHASE Two had not formed, the excessive rates of cancer in the National Semiconductor workforce would have gone undetected. Who else would have raised it? Neither the company nor the HSE had previously shown any interest.

STATE REGULATORS: THE HEALTH AND SAFETY EXECUTIVE

NSUK Greenock is under the HSE's jurisdiction for health, safety, and welfare regulatory purposes. As permitted under the Open Government Act, an employee can ask for the HSE records for inspections that took place while they were employed at the site. One PHASE Two member requested this data, and the HSE produced a brief description of its regulation activities at NSUK during the period.[6]

The report, which took about three months to forward, revealed that, among other things, the company had been fined $200 for failing to properly seal a radioactive reactor. The report included details of one reportable accident, a gas leak (arsine), which led six workers to be hospitalized. It stated, rather alarmingly, that the company did not have a workable Control of Substances Hazardous to Health (COSHH) system until 1994, some five years after the COSHH Regulations had been enacted and some years after the initial briefing papers had been distributed. The HSE offered no explanation as to how the company regulated chemical, use, handling, storage, and disposal in the absence of complying with the law. Despite extensive use of many carcinogenic and suspected carcinogenic substances, no measures, legal or otherwise, have been taken against the company for failing to comply.

During an interview, an HSE Officer stated:

> We did not know what National Semiconductor was. We thought it was the electronics industry. The company [was] not going to advise us any differently. It was only in the early 90s, when there was some publicity over miscarriages and birth defects, did our bosses take things seriously. You will see [from the HSE report] that the fine coincides with the early days of the concerns being raised. They [HSE] shit themselves. They had taken their eye off an industry that had crept up on their blindside.[7]

In November 1999, the HSE announced that it was going to undertake a cancer study at NSUK. The study was initiated because "concerns have been voiced by local campaigners about the possibility of cancers arising from employment in current and former [workers] at National Semiconductor, Greenock."[8] The Cancer Study Protocol further stated (p. 4, par. 5): "In addition those cancers not already included in 7.3 which are the concern of the campaign group PHASE Two will be tested in the analysis. These are (i) Malignant neoplasm of the stomach (ii) Malignant neoplasm of the uterus (iii) Leukemia."

This suggests that the HSE undertook the cancer study as a result of publicity generated by the PHASE Two campaign. Before the study, the fact that there was no scientific evidence of harm, in their view, validated the company's stance that our claims were anecdotal. As it stands, the HSE's Cancer Study, published December 11, 2001, revealed excess rates in many cancers. Thus, the HSE's actions challenged National Semiconductor's standard corporate response.

In their actions to quell what they believed to be a financially motivated and publicity-seeking, unmerited campaign, they overlooked the possibility that we could be right. What drives state regulators to act like this? Should the HSE be asked to undertake retrospective studies, which, in effect, examine a workforce for which it had a responsibility, but evidently failed to protect? It may be more prudent to use reputable, independent international academic institutions with no links to the industry to undertake such work. The HSE frequently uses subcontractors, and it should have done so in this case.

NATIONAL SEMICONDUCTOR: THE RESPONSE

In 2001, a document entitled, "National Semiconductor Communications Plan" (Anonymous 1998) was left at the premises of the Inverclyde Advice and Employment Rights Centre. It highlighted the company strategy for dealing with the rise of PHASE Two and the questions we were raising. Under the heading of "Progress to Date," it read: "establish contact with possible supporters of National such as Argyll and Clyde Health Board." In this context, it is interesting how the authors should view the Health Board as their possible allies, but did not see community members working to protect health and safety in the same way. Another section titled, "Strategy" contained the statement, "Use discreetly and sensitively, all available information to undermine the credibility of such individuals and groups." The document further recommended that National Semiconductor "utilise Beattie Media female staff members to pose as clean room workers to elicit information." Beattie Media is a large public relations company that was subject to publicity involving alleged access to Labor politicians.

The "National Semiconductor Communications Plan" was the subject of a police investigation. Contained in the document, dated January 19, 1998, is the directive, "Begin to gather as much information as possible on Inverclyde Occupational Health Project and Jim McCourt." On March 17, 1998, my office was burglarized, during which my personal documents and house keys were stolen. On April 3, 1998, we had just completed a PHASE Two meeting, when two cars were discovered outside the building with cameras being used to survey our activities.

Upon approaching one car, I was verbally abused as it drove off. The second car had no one in it, but a video camera was mounted on the passenger-side dashboard. As the driver approached, I asked him what he was doing, and he said, "You have already been warned, fuck off." Dr. Gunneberg of Argyll and Clyde and Bill Richards, a reporter for the *Wall Street Journal* who was doing a story on PHASE Two, both witnessed these events and were addressing the PHASE Two meeting that day.

I immediately reported these incidents to Greenock police, yet no action was taken. Upon discovering the "Communications Plan," I visited the police. They investigated those involved and have submitted a report to the Procurator Fiscal. I have been informed that no charges will be pressed, and that I have no right of appeal.

National Semiconductor has since engaged Jack Mandel of Exponent, "a PR Solutions company." Mandel addressed the National Semiconductor workforce the day the damaging HSE Cancer Study results were announced. As reported by a National Semiconductor worker:

> All of a sudden this guy appeared. We did not know who he was and I was getting agitated with him. All we could hear was an American accent and a load of figures. I asked him who was paying him, and the plant Director, Gerry Edwards stood and said it was the company. After that we just switched off because he was just another company man.[9]

CONCLUSION

The experiences in Greenock, Scotland, detailed above, highlight the corporate influence on small and vulnerable communities everywhere. It also implicates the politicians, health professionals, and state regulators, who are often complicit in this process. As described by Ulrich Beck (1992, 71) "they [injured, diseased or dead workers] do not exist—at least not legally, medically, technologically or socially and they are not prevented, treated or compensated for." Beck further argued that there is an inherent, brutal resistance in our society to accepting the links between chemical exposure and illness. His statement is entirely appropriate.

There is a systemic failure in health agencies that are not set up to detect properly the existence of cancer clusters. Health professionals too easily ignore the activities of community groups like PHASE Two.

In the present case, the key stakeholders did not show the slightest inclination to assist the community members who found themselves in the situation that PHASE Two and the local community in Inverclyde are facing. That lay people (as opposed to public health officials and government regulators) have to play the pivotal role in driving this type of issue demonstrates the depths of the problem. In this respect, the greatest allies have been the media. I thank them all, because without them, the medical profession and HSE would have taken even less notice.

The HSE's role has been shameful. It went directly to the company to assist in dealing with our "allegations." At no time did the HSE attempt to consult with PHASE Two prior to the announcement of the Cancer Study protocol.

The HSE's role needs to be closely examined. Rather than doing effective proactive inspection and enforcement when necessary, it seems that it exists to create favorable conditions for prospective and current employers. Despite its actions, the HSE have failed to quell PHASE Two. This has highlighted its systemic failures and their highly political nature.

It is my view that the stakeholders involved with the National Semiconductor workers accept *preventable* death as an inevitable consequence of work; there can be no other conclusion from their silence and inactivity. The type of fatal occurrence that has taken place in National Semiconductor has highlighted this very point. "The victims of course are not a random group. There is an undeniable correlation between employment in lower-status, lower-social-class jobs and an increased risk of developing a work-related cancer" (O'Neill 1997, xi).

All of the PHASE Two members I have had the opportunity to know meet this description, and they are the very population that the state has failed most. The typical PHASE Two member has been a victim of chronic, low-dose, chemical exposure. There is a clear strategy in the system that puts the onus on the workers and their families to prove (1) that the exposure has taken place, (2) which employers caused it, and (3) that the exposures alone caused the ill health. With no company data available, a pitifully inadequate health support system, not to mention a dreadfully difficult and expensive legal process to enact, the employer and powerful insurance companies have the clear advantage.

National Semiconductor is fully aware of the situation that these employees face. The company's ostracization of injured former employees, in my view perpetuates an ongoing abuse of power and ensures that justice, in the form of recognition, compensation and future prevention, is denied to those affected and with the potential to be affected, with no hope of closure of any kind. PHASE Two will continue to struggle against these abuses and seek justice for deceased, diseased and injured workers and their families.

NOTES

1. Interview, February 20, 2002.
2. Interview, March 28, 2002.
3. The GMB is "Britain's General Union." According to the union's website, "For the historically minded the **G** derives from General, the **M** from Municipal and the **B** from Boilermakers but GMB is not an abbreviation for these titles. So many unions have merged with GMB that the initials are its official name" (see www.gmb.org.uk).
4. Interview, April 1997.
5. [Postal mailing—eds.]
6. The report was dated September 20, 1998.
7. Interview, February 1, 2001.
8. Page 1, par 1, Protocol of NSUK Cancer Study 1995 (as cited in McElvenny et al. 2001).
9. Interview, October 15, 2003.

13 Community-Based Organizing for Labor Rights, Health, and the Environment

Television Manufacturing on the Mexico-U.S. Border

During the 1990s, Tijuana, Mexico, became the "TV Capital of the World." More televisions were produced in this bustling town on the Mexico-U.S. border than in any other city in the world. TV plants were a key component in the electronics maquiladora (assembly) sector on the Mexican side of the border. Yet by the end of the decade, that thriving TV manufacturing industry began leaving Mexico for lower wage countries, including Vietnam, Thailand, Malaysia, and especially China. China offered investors tax breaks, low energy costs, and other incentives—their labor force was earning wages one third or less of what workers earn in Tijuana. This chapter details the environmental and health consequences of both the boom and the decline of border electronics manufacturing in Mexico and considers the efforts of local citizens to fight back and regain greater power over their lives and communities.

The Free Trade Agreement

Starting in the 1960s, Mexico and the United States established free-trade arrangements that encouraged companies to send materials to Mexico for workers to assemble and return to the United States for sales. Reduced tariffs, lower wages in Mexico, and fewer environmental regulations gave companies an advantage, allowing them to produce goods more cheaply. Finalized in 1994, the North American Free Trade Agreement (NAFTA) expanded free trade between the two countries and established new rights for corporations. Easy access to the huge U.S. consumer market contributed to the phenomenal growth of the TV maquiladora industry at the border. Of more than 500 *maquiladoras* in Tijuana, the largest are the Japanese-owned Sanyo, Sony, and Panasonic plants; and the Korean-owned Samsung factories.[1] Adding the Japanese JVC and Hitachi facilities, more than 20,000 workers were employed in TV manufacturing in Tijuana in 2001 (*Guía de la Industria Maquiladora* 2001; see Photo 13.1). More than 11 million sets were assembled there in 2003 (Nudelstejer 2000).[2]

Laborers come from all over Mexico to assemble TVs in Tijuana. NAFTA triggered the largest migration within the nation since the 1960s (Kraul 1996). Typical jobs are soldering, inserting screws, connecting wires, testing, inspecting, painting, and packaging. Other workers are employed at plants like Xpectra, a plastic injection molding facility in Tijuana with 1,000 employees

Photo 13.1. Maquiladora consumer electronics factory in Tijuana, Maxico, just across the border from San Diego, California. Courtesy of Amelia Simpson, Environmental Health Coalition.

that supplies the Sony, Panasonic, Sanyo, Samsung, and Hitachi factories (Goldsberry 2002).[3] Across the border in San Diego, the TV industry maintains warehouses, and high-tech manufacturing, research and development facilities, sales, distribution, and administrative offices.

NAFTA was hailed as the first trade agreement to link trade issues and the environment. U.S. Trade Representative Carla Hills declared in 1991: "We think the North American Free Trade Agreement that liberalizes trade will create wealth and enable [Mexico and the United States] to more adequately address the environmental problems that currently exist at the border" (Eckhouse 1991). NAFTA's Commission for Environmental Cooperation (CEC) touted enhanced levels of protection, particularly for the border region, and improved public participation (see Table 13.1).[4]

An Inadequate Agreement

But by NAFTA's 10-year anniversary, a different picture had emerged. Mexico's average amounts of soil erosion, solid-waste generation, and air pollution increased 63 percent since 1988 (Brown 2002). Air pollution alone grew by 97 percent between 1985 and 1999, whereas government spending on the environment fell 45 percent (Wise 2003, 5). Authorities admit that unaccounted for are many millions of tons of dangerous industrial waste (Turati 1999). The government estimates that environmental degradation since NAFTA has cost Mexico $36 billion annually (Wise 2003, 2). The Environmental Health Coalition (EHC) and the Colectivo established the failure of the CEC to

TABLE 13.1. NAFTA Countries Toxic Release Tracking Systems

Mexico	United States	Canada
Registro de Emisiones y Transferencia de Contaminantes (RETC)	Toxics Release Inventory (TRI)	National Pollutant Release Inventory (NPRI)
104 substances[18]	667 chemicals (three of which are not currently reportable).	245 substances
Since 1993	Since 1987	Since 1997
Initially voluntary, but mandatory since December of 2001	Mandatory	Mandatory

Source: NACEC (2002, Annex 1).

protect the environment through their work on the landmark case of *Metales y Derivados*.[5]

Mexico's toxic pollutants registry, the "Registro de Emisiones y Transferencia de Contaminantes" (RETC), is inadequate as a toxic chemical right-to-know mechanism. The RETC is designed as a tool for companies to report chemical substances that are discharged into the air, water, or soil during the manufacturing process, and which could impact human health and the environment. Yet the infrastructure is not yet in place for reporting or enforcement. In the United States and Canada, the registries give the name and geographic location of the reporting industry, whereas this is not the case in Mexico. Moreover, the U.S. Toxic Release Inventory lists 667 chemicals, the Canadian system has 268, but Mexico's lists only 104.

From its inception in 1997 until June 2004, reporting toxic releases to the RETC was voluntary. In 2004, only 5 percent of companies required to report industrial toxic discharges were doing so. Currently, Mexico has yet to fully implement the RETC and make the information available to the public.

During the NAFTA debates, one of the common arguments used by proponents was that the agreement would provide mechanisms to standardize environmental legislation throughout North America. Yet after ten years of NAFTA, the disparity continues and allows businesses to avoid costs by operating where environmental legislation is more lax. Requiring a comparable right-to-know system in all three countries, one of the foremost and most frequent demands of fair trade advocates, was never considered by the trade negotiators or included in trade talks.

Transport of Hazardous Materials

There is no centralized system tracking the millions of tons of industrial chemicals, toxic and explosive compounds that move by truck every year through San Diego and Tijuana to and from the assembly plants (Cantlupe 2003). The La Paz agreement, signed by Mexico and the United States in 1983, established a mechanism for management of hazardous waste along the border. Waste generated by *maquiladoras* is designated to be returned to its country of origin. But the La Paz agreement has never been systematically implemented. Similarly, the Haztrak system, created in the mid-1990s to address concerns about repatriation of hazardous waste, never functioned in any meaningful way and was cancelled in 2003. Currently, critics, inspectors, or federal officials cannot say with certainty how much hazardous material and what kind is being transported across the border, either southbound or northbound.

THE BORDER ENVIRONMENTAL JUSTICE CAMPAIGN

EHC is a 25-year-old social and environmental justice nonprofit organization with offices in San Diego, California; and Tijuana, Baja California. EHC began working on border health and pollution projects in the early 1990s. EHC's Border Environmental Justice Campaign (BEJC) and EHC's Tijuana affiliate, the *Colectivo Chilpancingo Pro Justicia Ambiental*,[6] work together to reduce toxic pollution caused by the *maquiladora* industry in Tijuana and to promote fair trade and globalization for justice. The *Colectivo Chilpancingo Pro Justicia Ambiental*, a group of residents of a Tijuana neighborhood called *Colonia Chilpancingo*, was formally inaugurated in May of 2002. Colonia Chilpancingo is a community of about 10,000 people, adjacent to the largest complex of industrial parks in Tijuana. Four of the six TV corporations with maquiladoras in Tijuana operate plants next to Colonia Chilpancingo. The *colonia* has been severely impacted by a free-trade regime, in particular, by NAFTA. BEJC and the Colectivo work with allies on issues critical to their border community, where corporate globalization has left workers and their families facing extreme poverty, illness, and a severely contaminated environment. By uniting to demand the right to safe workplaces and toxic-free neighborhoods, communities challenge a free-trade regime that ruthlessly and routinely violates rights and undermines democracy. BEJC and the Colectivo engage in organizing and advocacy to bring about real improvements in people's lives, as well as policy changes.

In response to pressures to expand the NAFTA model through other trade agreements, BEJC and the Colectivo documented the impacts of ten years of NAFTA on the San Diego/Tijuana border region. The report, "Globalization at the Crossroads: Ten Years of NAFTA in the San Diego/Tijuana Border Region,"[7] is a community document on what is missing from the pleasant picture of globalization painted by the corporations that benefit from it. The report focuses on the TV manufacturing industry as representative of corporate globalization.

JOBS WITHOUT DIGNITY

Wages in the electronics and other manufacturing plants in Tijuana are so low that two full-time workers can cover only two-thirds of the basic needs of a family of four. Full-time workers often cannot afford medical care or school fees. It is common not to have money to buy a birthday cake for a child; to pay for a baptism, a funeral, to make a dress for a *quinceañera* coming-of-age party, or other important cultural events and celebrations.

Families lack telephones, toys, sports equipment, books, or newspapers (Rosenbaum 2000). Many live in squatter settlements where disease thrives because of the lack of piped water, sewage service, or garbage collection. A study by the Mexican government determined that over 67 percent of houses in Tijuana have dirt floors (INEGI 2000). Unpaved roads and footpaths contribute to illness and the spread of disease.

Since NAFTA was implemented, poverty among Tijuana's factory workers has grown worse. "In real terms of earnings and purchasing power, workers in the maquiladoras of Baja California earn less in [$]2000 per month than they did in 1994," according to one economist who studies the border region (Gerber 2000a). In Tijuana, "the minimum wage buys approximately one-fifth of what it could in the early 1980s. This represents an enormous decline in the purchasing power of the least well-off residents" (Gerber 2000b).

Women Maquiladora Workers

Interviews with women workers create a portrait of what it is like in the TV plants for them. Now in her twenties, Lupe began working in the assembly plants at the age of 13. In her job soldering at Panasonic's TV plant, she worked from 8 o'clock in the morning to 6 o'clock in the afternoon, five days a week, and earned 650 pesos a week (or about US$65, approximately $1.45 an hour). One complaint about the job was that workers are only allowed to use the bathroom twice during a ten-hour shift.

> You have to ask the supervisor for permission, so they can get a replacement to sit in your place. Sometimes there's a waiting list, so you never know when you're really going to get to go. If you leave without permission, you get written up. The bathroom is a five-minute walk each way. Sometimes when you get there there's fifteen women waiting in line. Women try not to drink water to avoid having to go to the bathroom. A lot of women in the plant suffer from bladder and kidney infections. At lunch break, you can also use the bathroom, so when the time comes, women are literally running through the plant, trying to get a chance to use the bathroom and have time for lunch, too. It's horrible.

Other common observations by women assembly plant workers in Tijuana refer to sexual harassment and a stressful, degrading workplace:

- "Sexual harassment is constant."
- "They were very rude. They would call us 'pendejos' [assholes]."
- "They try to fire anybody who speaks up in order to have a more obedient labor force."
- "The company lawyer used to be a prison judge. He told me, 'I'm used to dealing with people like you,' as if we were criminals."[8]

Pregnancy Testing

A negative pregnancy test is a condition of employment in the TV *maquiladoras,* although the practice is illegal. A 1996 Human Rights Watch report (updated in 1998) on labor force sex discrimination in Mexico led to a U.S.

Labor Department investigation under the auspices of NAFTA's labor side agreement (HRW 1996). The Labor Department found that mandatory pregnancy tests constitute a form of discrimination based on gender that occur routinely in the assembly plants. The practice violates Mexico's labor law, as well as international human rights obligations to guarantee the rights to equality before the law and to nondiscrimination. HRW labels as "questionable" the ensuing agreement signed October 21, 1998, by the three NAFTA countries to address the problem (Jefferson and McKinney 1998).

Among the factories investigated for the HRW report were three of Tijuana's TV plants: Samsung, Sanyo, and Panasonic. A physician hired by Panasonic (then Matsushita-Panasonic) in 1993 testified that her job was to administer pregnancy tests to job applicants so that pregnant women would not be hired: "Any applicant labeled as pregnant was told by the personnel director that she was not qualified, or that all the positions were taken."[9]

By not hiring pregnant women, the *maquiladoras* avoid benefit payments required by law for six weeks before and after childbirth. The *maquiladoras* also avoid taking responsibility for health consequences, since a fetus is especially vulnerable to chemical exposure. Yet male reproductive capacity is also very sensitive to industrial solvents and metals. Workers who have been exposed to lead while soldering or performing other activities can also easily contaminate their families by bringing home deposits on their bodies and clothing. All workers have the right to a clean and safe shop floor.

Unions

For workers and labor rights defenders in Tijuana who seek to organize for better conditions in the factories, the environment is hostile.[10] The full exercise of trade union rights protected by the Mexican Constitution and the Labor Law is undermined by a number of restrictions, acts of intimidation, and the lack of accountability, including government collusion with employers who violate workers' rights. There are no independent unions in Tijuana's TV plants. Workers sign contracts with the factories directly, or with employment agencies.

The industry perspective toward union organizing in the *maquiladoras* is captured in a document for businesses looking to establish themselves in Tijuana:

> Organized labor in Tijuana does not represent a major impediment to new starts or expansion.... The large Japanese and Korean manufacturers in Tijuana have resisted the unions successfully by hiring new workers from Tijuana's abundant labor pool.[11]

Management-friendly, or "ghost," unions do operate in Tijuana, but workers know not to turn to them for help, or to ask too many questions.

JOBS WITHOUT HEALTH AND SAFETY PROTECTIONS

As other chapters in this volume attest, electronics manufacturing involves a series of chemical processes that can negatively impact the health of workers

TABLE 13.2. Cathode Ray Tube (CRT)
Manufacturing Processes

Glass Fabrication
Screen Preparation
Shadow Mask Fabrication/Assembly
Funnel Preparation
Bulb Joining
Electron Gun Fabrication
Final Assembly

Source: U.S. EPA (2002, 7).

(see LaDou; Ferus-Comelo; Leong and Pandita; Hawes and Pellow; Agarwal and Wankhade, this volume).

Health Impacts of Lead

A report prepared for the U.S. Environmental Protection Agency (EPA) discusses the health risks posed by lead used in the manufacture of cathode ray tubes (CRTs; USEPA 2001). Lead is found in the glass of traditional CRT displays, in the printed circuit boards used in TVs and in the components of these boards. Swallowing or inhaling lead causes health problems ranging from reproductive harm, including miscarriages and birth defects, to developmental harm in children, to cancer and even death. Many workers employed in the Tijuana TV maquiladoras spend the entire workday exposed to lead solder (see Table 13.2).

Residents who live in Tijuana's Colonia Chilpancingo are extremely concerned about lead exposure from the nearby electronics plants and other maquiladoras. A *Washington Post* article in February 2003 reported that rates of anencephaly and hydrocephaly in Tijuana are abnormally high. In one two-block area of Colonia Chilpancingo, at least eight babies have been born with those birth defects since 1994 (Sullivan 2003). Evidence suggests that lead is one cause of neural tube defects, including anencephaly (Bound et al. 1997). A sample of children living in Colonia Chilpancingo found all had elevated blood lead levels.[12]

A study in the *New England Journal of Medicine* in 2003 indicates that current international guidelines labeling 10 micrograms per deciliter of lead in blood as "safe" are not so. A drop in IQ of up to 7.4 points can occur in children whose blood lead level is within the 10 micrograms per deciliter "safe" guideline. "The fact is," one of the leaders of the study declared, "we found no evidence for a safe level. There is no safe level of exposure" (Canfield et al. 2003; Maugh 2003; see also LaDou, this volume).

Occupational exposure to lead can be minimized through the use of protective equipment like masks, gloves, and air extractors; or advanced equipment such as an enclosed vented solder machine. Workers interviewed for this article described soldering without protective equipment. Government inspection of *maquiladoras* is irregular. None of the TV manufacturers in Tijuana agreed to the authors' request for information and a tour of the factories. Although both Sony and Panasonic have announced programs to switch to lead free solder, the health effects of the lead substitutes have not been evaluated.[13]

Cleaning

Workers in manufacturing facilities in Tijuana are at the front lines of exposure to chemicals used for cleaning in the electronics industry, including solvents, acids, and alkalis. Little is known about the long-term health effects of these chemicals on humans. Next in line of exposure are the nearby communities, where residents are at risk from storage tanks leaks, vapor emissions, and improper handling of chemical wastes (Gassert 1985, 14). Workers interviewed indicated that trichloroethylene is routinely used to clean machinery in the plants. One former Samsung worker described the cleaning process as follows:

> Trichloroethylene was used in the rework area to remove epoxy spots in the fly back cables. This was done with rags, without gloves, and without mouth and nose masks. The trichloroethylene would eat up the latex gloves, so we did not wear them. Workers were given masks but they did not use them because they were the white masks—the type that don't protect you anyway. We also used trichloroethylene to clean our work area the same way, without any protection and without proper ventilation.[14]

Workers at Sanyo and Sony reported similar experiences. According to the Agency for Toxic Substances and Disease Registry, trichloroethylene has the following effects on human health:

- Breathing small amounts may cause headaches, lung irritation, dizziness, poor coordination, and difficulty concentrating.
- Breathing large amounts of trichloroethylene may cause impaired heart function, unconsciousness, and death. After long periods there may be nerve, kidney, and liver damage.[15]

Storage of solvents and cleaning agents presents another risk. Accidents involving chemicals in the maquiladoras are a constant concern for workers and residents of nearby communities. The cities of Tijuana and San Diego were put on alert, in one instance, when a toxic waste processing and recycling facility at the Mesa de Otay industrial park caught fire, causing 200 tons of toxic waste to burn up. Much of the water used by firefighters to control the flames ended up flowing through Tijuana's Colonia Chilpancingo and into the Río Alamar, whose waters ultimately end up on the San Diego coast. In addition, a large puddle of contaminated water formed at the entrance to Colonia Chilpancingo's kindergarten (*La Jornada* 1997). In another case, 26 workers were hospitalized when acetylene gas was accidentally released at a maquiladora in the same industrial park (*Frontera Norte-Sur* 2001).

The health hazards associated with common chemical compounds used in the electronics industry represent a small sample of the potential dangers that Tijuana's workers and residents face in their jobs and homes near the TV plants, which operate with little transparency and inadequate accountability.

Informal Recycling of Electronics

Informal recycling operations, an ongoing danger around the world (see Agarwal and Wankhade; Puckett, this volume), are also common in Tijuana. Entire families make a living scavenging from landfills and other dump sites, and are routinely injured from handling hazardous materials by improvised methods, such as burning wires or circuit boards over open-air fires to recover metals. Computer equipment, like TVs, also contains hazardous materials that require proper recycling. Under NAFTA, all tariffs on importing used computer equipment into Mexico were eliminated on January 1, 2004. There is great concern that many of these computers could end up discarded in Mexico.

JOBS WITHOUT SECURITY

TV plants can move on short notice. Compared to auto assembly plants, standard TV assembly involves relatively simple technologies. Factories are smaller and cheaper to equip, and they rely on a smaller network of suppliers (Kenney 1999, 49). Because most of Tijuana's TV subassembly plants are foreign owned, the "TV Capital of the World" label never described an economically sustainable model for development there (UNCTAD 2001, 135). Most of the materials and components that go into building a TV in Tijuana come from other countries, including the United States, Thailand, Japan, Korea, Taiwan, Malaysia, and Germany. The TV industry, like the other free-trade factories on the border, operates on a hit-and-run basis, creating economic insecurity.

Tijuana Manufacturing Jobs Lost

In Tijuana's TV factories, 3,000 Sanyo workers lost their jobs in 2001 and 2002 when the plants moved to China and Indonesia (*Business Week*, April 2002; Iritani and Boudreaux 2003). Panasonic trimmed operations, and Sony consolidated its four Tijuana plants into one. Although JVC opened a second plant with 432 new jobs in 2003, and Hitachi announced in 2002 that it would open a new factory making plasma TVs, the industry overall is shrinking in Tijuana. From October 2000 to June 2002, the Mexican *maquiladora* industry lost more than 240,000 jobs. As a July 2003 U.S. General Accounting Office (GAO) report concludes, "the decline was particularly severe for certain industries, such as electronics, and certain Mexican cities, such as Tijuana" (GAO 2003).

Now, as Tijuana plants close and move to Asia, many uprooted workers wonder what they will do to support themselves. In July 2003, Mexico's president and economy minister addressed the nation in the weekly government radio program, "*Fox Contigo*" [Fox With You],[16] after figures were released showing unemployment levels at a four-year high. Economy Minister Fernando Canales recommended that people "set up a taco stand" or "bake cakes at home" (*Los Angeles Times*, July 2003).[17]

Mexico now has a $600-billion economy, the ninth largest in the world. Yet there is greater per capita income disparity at the U.S.-Mexico border than at any other major commercial border in the world (Rothman 2003).[18] More free trade has meant more poverty and economic instability. The Mexican government estimates that 54 million out of the country's 100 million people cannot meet their basic needs. In the past 20 years, 19 million more Mexicans have been classified as living in poverty (Jordan and Sullivan 2003). At least 42 million live on less than $2 a day, and 10 million live on less than $1 a day (Ferriss 2003). Fully 63 percent of the population has no health insurance coverage (Ferriss 2003).

FIGHTING BACK

Tijuana's Colonia Chilpancingo, once a pretty neighborhood filled with trees and gardens and a beautiful clean stream, is now a highly contaminated site. Biological and industrial wastes blow, flow, and seep into the lives of everyone who lives in the colonia. But this situation is not inevitable. Through community organizing and policy advocacy, BEJC and the Colectivo achieved an agreement with the Mexican government for clean-up of the *Metales y Derivados* toxic site. That victory and a series of other successful activities revolving around social and environmental justice issues related to the maquiladoras are having an impact. Awareness is growing for the need for the electronics and other industries in Tijuana to adopt clean production and pollution prevention principles to reduce the amount of toxic chemicals used and disposed of; to provide adequate protective gear for workers who are using or exposed to toxics; to increase enforcement of environmental regulations to avoid dangerous, illegal emissions and disposal; and to guarantee basic human and worker rights.

Community activists and supporters are demanding that trade instruments like the Free Trade Area of the Americas (FTAA), be replaced with agreements that are fair to workers, safe for communities, and clean for the environment. The FTAA, currently under negotiation, is intended to expand the NAFTA model to the rest of the hemisphere (except Cuba) by 2005. It has been called "NAFTA on steroids" (Barlow and Clarke 2003, 16). EHC's BEJC and the Colectivo are calling for trade agreements that, at a minimum, have enforceable environmental protections, comply with International Labor Organization standards, put citizens' rights over corporate rights, are negotiated and function with transparency and public participation, and provide economic resources to reduce inequality between signatory nations.

CONCLUSION

For the people of Colonia Chilpancingo, the dream of a clean, safe, and prosperous community depends on raising the floor for everyone through enforceable global minimum standards for living wages, worker health and safety, and environmental protections. They want to see transparency and democratic participation in trade-related decisions and accountability among the institutions that oversee global trade. A decent future for their children means building real, sustainable economic development and reducing inequality. Community organizing and advocacy is their hope to bring about social change for justice.

NOTES

1. Panasonic and JVC are subsidiaries of the Matsushita Corporation.

2. See INEGI (2000) and Baja California state governmental statistics from 2000 (www.teamnafta.com/cities/Tijuana/TIJUANA.html).

3. Additional source: interview with Xpectra representative at NAFTASHO trade show, September 18, 2003, Tijuana.

4. [See Sanchez (2002) for background on NAFTA's environmental dimensions—eds.]

5. See www.environmentalhealth.org for background on *Metales y Derivados.*

6. [The Chilpancingo Environmental Justice Collective—eds.]

7. The report is available at www.environmentalhealth.org.

8. Interviews with authors, Tijuana, July 5, 2003. The names of workers have been changed to protect their identities.

9. Human Rights Watch telephone interview, Dr. Moreno, Tijuana, July 9, 1995, published in HRW (1996, 14).

10. Authors' interviews with workers in Tijuana. The story of efforts to organize Tijuana's Hundai plant illustrates the difficulties of labor organizing in that city.

11. See www.teamnafta.com/cities/Tijuana/TIJUANA.html.

12. Tests conducted in 2003 by Environmental Health Coalition and the Colectivo Chilpancingo Pro Justicia Ambiental of 17 children living in homes adjacent to the industrial park where Metales y Derivados, as well as the TV plants, are located.

13. See www.boblogar.com/marzo_22_2002/panasonic_de_mexico_en_pro_del_medio_ambiente.php, where Panasonic announced that they do not use lead and www.panasonic.com.mx/index_flash.html, where Panasonic announced soldering without lead.

14. Authors' interview with Rosa, August 8, 2003.

15. Agency for Toxic Substances and Disease Registry Web site: www.atsdr.cdc.gov/tfacts19.html.

16. [Named after Mexico's president, Vincente Fox—eds.]

17. Transcript of the Mexican government's weekly Radio Program, "Fox Contigo," July 26, 2003.

18. World Bank estimates show the U.S. per capita gross national income is $34,870, whereas in Mexico it is $5,540.

14 Labor Rights and Occupational Health in Jalisco's Electronics Industry (Mexico)

HUMAN RIGHTS is a relevant topic for both labor rights campaigners and social scientists. The concepts and models associated with human rights may help activists and communities understand how and why their human rights are shaped and possibly restricted. This chapter addresses the issue of human rights in the context of the electronics industry, using a quantitative approach. This chapter presents some of the preliminary findings of a survey of Jalisco electronics industry workers, conducted in December 2002 and June 2003, on labor rights issues in the electronics sector. The first section provides a brief discussion of the sociological theory of human rights to set the stage for discussion; the second presents a profile of the workers in Jalisco's electronics industry; and the third section presents major concerns regarding labor rights, concluding with several final reflections.

SOCIOLOGICAL THEORY OF HUMAN RIGHTS

The sociology of human rights shows a lack of any particular tradition. As a result, researchers dealing with this topic mix legal, moral, and historic points of view into their analyses, a mix that does not correspond to the purpose and methodology of the social sciences. At least six approaches to human rights can be identified, and they are discussed next.

The dialectic of the civil society-state model rejects an analysis of human rights that centers on the result of a divine will, the natural order, or a universal human nature, and instead, tries to understand human rights as the result of processes that take place in a given social system. This approach links the origin of human rights to the rise and fall of social inequality. Human rights arise as an answer to central social problems. This approach's main foundation is that human rights must be analyzed sociologically from a civil society/state perspective.

The relativist model is based on several fundamental lines of research. Among the most important is the study of social genesis, which grew out of the different foundations of the philosophy of law, which is necessary to demystify the metaphysical and naturalist concepts of human rights. The relativist model does not address many phenomena relevant to the sociology of the human rights, which leaves it insufficient for explaining their origin, development, and pertinence.

The model of legal normativeness argues that sociology cannot have a purpose of its own or define human rights unless legal science has set legal standards. If the concept of law is intrinsically normative, it cannot be defined in explanatory terms. This perspective's approach is to accept the normative definition of human rights, taking it in a strictly legal sense.

The moral normative model centers on the idea that social action is largely conditioned by socially shared moral representations. As was mentioned in regards to the relativist model, sociologists should not judge these theories, but if applicable, they can review them, provided they keep these theoretical systems of norms to direct their behavior.

In Niklas Luhmann's *structural-functional model*, human rights are not the rights of individuals; rather, they are structural demands of contemporary social structures. Luhmann's hypothesis reduces the entire development of human rights to one mechanism: social differentiation.

Weber's model of the rationalization of law approaches human rights as typical claims for legitimacy of the political system that meet a series of social conditions. A key aspect of Weber's sociological methodology is the doctrine of neutrality, which is closely related to the methodology of "ideal types." For Weber, the purpose of sociology is to study social actions, that is, actions that occur in relation to the behavior of other individuals. Scientific knowledge is the basis of decision making. According to Weber, sociological methodology cannot assume that natural laws are scientific facts. However, at the same time, sociologists cannot ignore the fact that human rights have different validities, as collective representations, in different cultures.

This chapter adopts a scientific approach to decision making, based on Weber's idea that structures of the dominant system and claims for legitimacy create a system of interdependencies that provides a base for understanding the modes of social media where human rights become typical claims for legitimacy (Aymerich 2001, 243). Therefore, labor rights are oriented toward meeting individual and collective demands that satisfy and guarantee full development and dignity on the job. There are at least five basic principles of labor rights that guarantee human rights: a stable job, a fair salary, healthful work conditions, gender equity, and legal rights. These principles are analyzed here in relation to the electronics industry workers in the state of Jalisco, explaining the origin and efficiency of human and labor rights, based on Weber's theory of social rationalization. A general description of the electronics workers in Jalisco follows.

JALISCO'S ELECTRONICS WORKERS[1]

With the implementation of the North American Free Trade Agreement (NAFTA), Jalisco entered a new process of industrialization, and large-scale investment projects oriented to the international market began. According to the Economic System of Information Jalisco (SEIJAL), Direct Foreign Investment (DFI) in the electronics industry is the most dynamic in the state. In the last five years, the DFI in the electronics sector accounted for approximately 40 percent of the US$4.7 billion invested in all of the state's sectors. According to the Secretary of Economic Promotion (SEPROE), the total investments in 1999 in the electronics and telecommunications sector were US$359 million,

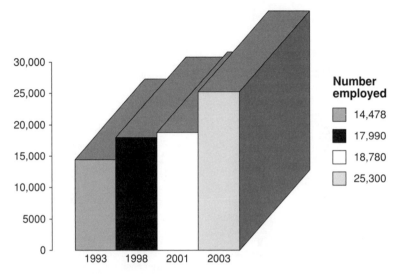

FIGURE 14.1. Total Employment in Jalisco's Electronics Sector, 1993–2003.
Source: Author, based on the *Encuesta de los Trabajadores de la Electrónica* (Survey of
Workers in the Electronics Industry).

with another high-tech industry—photography—adding US$29 million. This
increase in investments created an important growth in the number of workers,
with a estimated labor force of 30,000 (see Figure 14.1).

In the second half of the 1990s, after NAFTA was signed, many contract
manufacturers (CMs), electronics manufacturing services (EMS) firms, and
support supplier (SS) companies; and some original equipment manufacturers (OEMs) arrived in the state. The OEM companies such as HP, IBM,
Kodak, and Siemens created 9,800 jobs. These firms' brand names and logos
are stamped on the equipment, part of a wide variety of productive functions
(Lüthje 2003b, 63). Jalisco's plants led the electronics boom and promoted
the consolidation of the cluster. The electronics firms that arrived at the end of
the 1990s were mostly built with American investment and include Solectron,
Flextronics, and Sanmina-SCI, the largest employers.

The EMS firms supply manufacturing input or services and are related
to computer and telecommunications companies like Mti, Pemstar, Usi,
Yamaver, and Telect. This group had a strong presence at the end of the
1990s, with 17 companies—many of them American—employing nearly
5,000 persons.

The SS companies in Jalisco's electronics cluster provide materials for
manufacturing: from cardboard boxes, labels, and packaging to plastic injection. This group includes firms such as Acoustic Control, Estatec, and
Sistemas y Accesos Controlados. Generally, these are supplying companies.
This is a group of at least 17 companies with approximately 1,000 jobs.

The OEM companies manufacture original equipment with regional capital. Among them are BTC, GPI Mexibal, and ATR. These companies assemble

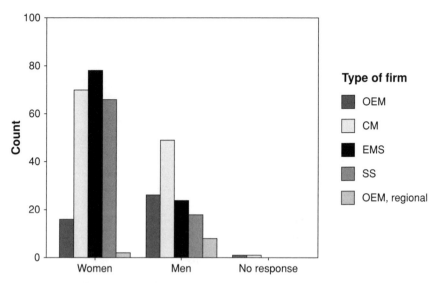

FIGURE 14.2. Type of Firm Where Jalisco's Electronics Workers are Employed.
Source: Author, based on the *Encuesta de los Trabajadores de la Electrónica* (Survey of Workers in the Electronics Industry).

computers, produce capacitors and other components, and design power sources.

The workers surveyed worked for companies from the above five categories. One finding is that CMS companies hire more men than women, whereas in the other categories, we find that female work is predominant, as shown in Figure 14.2.

Working conditions and labor relations have changed dramatically with the region's recent growth in electronics, and this impacts electronics workers' human rights. The growth requires a massive labor force, most of which centers on the production lines.

At the same time, labor relations are changing (Olmedo and Murria 2002). With the restructuring of the world economy, workers have become increasingly marginalized and their jobs are more precarious. Consequently, some labor rights have diminished.

LABOR RIGHTS

At least seven elements guarantee labor rights, namely: stable jobs, salaries, working conditions, trade unions, collective contracts, gender equity, and gained social rights. I discuss the relative presence or absence of these elements in Jalisco's electronics industry next.

Loss of Stable Jobs

Some of the fundamental characteristics of a good job are the capacity to freely choose work, not being discriminated against, being trained to perform the job, being guaranteed a stable job, having protection against unemployment, being compensated when unjustly terminated, and being promoted based on seniority. Workers see their jobs as relatively unstable, since most jobs in the electronics industry are considered temporary, being almost as common as permanent jobs. Our survey revealed that 64 percent of the workers were employed for between 1 and 1.5 years and the rest for much less than that.

Salary Reduction

Labor rights indicate that, in theory, fair pay must be received to guarantee the worker and his or her family a decent living, supplemented, if necessary, by other means of social protection; to receive the same salary for the same work; and to guarantee workers a living after retirement with a pension system. This survey found that salaries are insufficient, because the majority of workers surveyed earn between US$40 and $60 a week. And because most workers spend a considerable percentage of their income (34 percent) on home utilities, this income barely covers their needs. Not surprisingly then, we found that most workers work overtime to increase their salaries.

Working Conditions

Adequate working conditions include reasonable working hours; sufficient rest to recover spent energy; a labor environment free of moral and sexual harassment; safe and healthy working conditions; and compensation for labor risks. The typical workday in Mexico consists of eight hours, and apparently this right is respected because most workers reported working that long each day.

Ninety-two percent of the electronics workers spend between one and two hours each day commuting between work and home, because they live in the poor areas of the city. Nevertheless, company vehicles transport 35.5 percent of the respondents, 34.8 percent take urban transportation, and 18.8 percent uses both (company and personal vehicles), as shown in Table 14.1.

Health problems are another issue in electronics companies. Sixty-nine percent of the individuals presenting more problems of this type are women. Prevalent among diseases and health problems in this industry are work accidents, which include fractures, sprains, and cuts to lesions on workers' hands, among others.

TABLE 14.1. Means of Transportation for Jalisco's Electronics Workers

Type of Transportation	Percentage
Company's transportation	35.5
Urban transportation	34.8
Urban and company's	18.8
On foot	4.2
Did not answer	7.7
Total	100.0

Source: Author, based on the *Encuesta de los Trabajadores de la Electrónica* (Survey of Workers in the Electronics Industry).

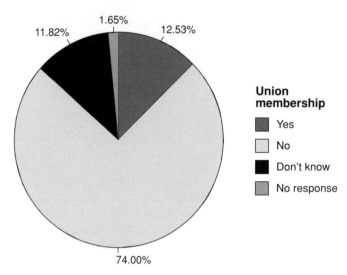

FIGURE 14.3. Trade Union Membership among Jalisco's Electronics Workers.
Source: Author, based on the *Encuesta de los Trabajadores de la Electrónica* (Survey of Workers in the Electronics Industry).

Union Rights?

Unionizing represents the possibility of associating or affiliating with a union to defend the workers' interests, with no participation of authorities or employers in union activities; the freedom to choose their representatives in a democratic process; protection from harassment because of affiliation or leadership (see Steiert, this volume, for more discussion of this topic). Seventy-four percent of the surveyed workers have no right to be unionized, because many of them are hired through employment agencies, as shown in Figure 14.3.

Collective Recruiting

The right to collective recruiting is understood as taking into account the workers' will and interests, as well as the companies' interests and environment for the bilateral determination of appropriate work conditions. It implies that workers organized as a union can negotiate with employers to receive more and better benefits than required by law. This right has all but disappeared, as shown in Figure 14.4.

The lack of bilateral contracts is explained by increases in the growing indirect hiring (subcontracting) of workers through a third-party or employment agency. Most electronics companies use outsourcing firms. Thirty-two percent of the workers in the survey indicated they had been hired through an employment agency.

Another important fact is that 31 percent of the workers knew about a job with an employment agency via friends or relatives, and 28.7 percent went directly to the employment agency. The vast majority (98.8 percent) said they

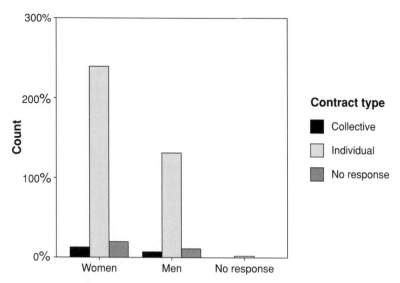

FIGURE 14.4. Types of Employment Contracts for Jalisco's Electronics Workers.
Source: Author, based on the *Encuesta de los Trabajadores de la Electrónica* (Survey of
Workers in the Electronics Industry).

were sent to more than one electronics company. Also, 35.5 percent stated
that the employment agency renewed their contracts every three months, and
59.7 percent indicated that an employment agency's foreman paid them inside the plant. The subcontracted workers said there were differences between
subcontracted and contracted workers. For instance, 34.4 percent mentioned
that permanent workers have more stability in their jobs, while 21.8 percent
said they received a Christmas holiday bonus; 20.6 percent said contracted
workers have seniority, whereas subcontracted workers do not. Only 3.4 percent of subcontracted workers were unionized, while 81.6 percent were not,
and 13.7 percent did not know whether they were union members. Most of
the subcontracted workers (93.1 percent) indicated that they had individual
contracts, and only 4.3 percent had a collective contract. In 53.3 percent of
the cases, the contract term was between one and three months; in 1.4 percent, it was more than four months and up to six months; in 5.2 percent, it
was from seven months to one year; and only for 1.4 percent was the term
for more than a year. This shows the precariousness of labor relations, because these are unstable jobs with the minimal social benefits and no union
participation.

   The electronics companies indicated that subcontracted workers have no
unions, do not work under collective contracts, and have no strikes or conflicts,
because employment agencies control and manage the human resources area
and the company is only in charge of the manufacturing. The subcontracting
model guarantees an abundant and controlled labor force that generates no
labor conflicts. Also, many traditional and subordinate union organizations
are characterized by a policy of reconciliation (Quintero 2001a, 168).

Gender Equity

Labor rights are related to the guarantee that men and women will have equal job opportunities and measures to promote effective gender equity. This implies specific prohibitions and rights that protect certain special conditions that enable individuals to perform their jobs. Even though there is a special emphasis on gender discrimination, because of its importance and seriousness, the right to equity must be understood in a broader sense in any case of job discrimination.

Among the computer electronics industry workers, 62.2 percent is female, and 35.1 percent is male, with a declining number of jobs for women. In other words, there is a trend toward the masculinization of work, for both qualified and non-qualified workers. This can be explained by the fact that traditional industrial activities (related to machines, footwear, and foods, among others) have been affected by NAFTA, and men had to work in export activities in the automotive and electronics industry. At the northern border, the ratio of male to female workers is 50:50. According to studies by Delgado (2001) and Gabayet (1990, 1994), in Jalisco in the past, women performed 70 and 80 percent of the work in these industries.

It is critical to recognize that men are assigned the most important positions. Although women have the right and ability to hold managerial or supervisory positions, most are operators. This indicates that the trend of using female labor in manufacturing work because of its delicacy prevails.

Gained Rights

As to gained rights, 94 percent of respondents said they had Social Security, 43.5 percent received profit bonuses, and 36.4 percent received vacation time. Among the benefits that few received were nurseries/day care centers for workers' children (4.8 percent). Also, 73.8 percent were not affiliated with a union and 11.8 percent did not know whether they belonged to a workers' organization.

Clearly, globalization has led to new labor conditions and relations. Globalization has spread and deepened the precariousness of work, understanding work as a responsibility exercised under inconsistent (or insufficient) conditions to guarantee the survival of the worker at minimally accepted levels (Sotelo 1999, 125–26). This has led the quality of jobs to deteriorate, thanks to subcontracting, the unfair extension of working hours, and the reduction of labor rights.

CONCLUSION

The labor rights discussed in this chapter are more or less legally recognized as indispensable to any society that respects human rights. Violations in the length of the work day, unreliable wages, a lack of democratic unions, sexual and labor harassment, and gender discrimination in salaries and working conditions, as well as the impunity with which the government and law enforcement agencies protect managers and union leaders are seen as legal acts that may violate the constitution, but do not violate human rights.

All societies must respect human rights. Thus far, many nations have limited respect for international law and the concept of human rights. This must be challenged in Mexico, as well as in other parts of the world where electronics industry sector clusters have emerged.

We must take into consideration, however, that human rights have different meanings across cultures. At the same time, there must be some global standards that all nations and industry sectors should follow. In the meantime, in Jalisco, state policies play a more significant role than international protocols. This is something that, without a doubt, has made labor rights more vulnerable, and consequently, the most fundamental human rights are violated.

NOTE

1. See author's survey for further details on many of the items presented here—eds.

15 Breaking the Silicon Silence

Voicing Health and Environmental Impacts within Taiwan's Hsinchu Science Park

Hsinchu Science-based Industrial Park (HSIP) is located northeast of Taiwan and about forty-four miles south of Taipei, the capital city. It stretches for 632 hectares over both Hsinchu County and Hsinchu City. The newly developed 138-hectare Chunan base is located in Miaoli County, south of Hsinchu (see Figure 15.1).[1] The HSIP is Taiwan's first science-based industrial park, established in 1980 as part of the state's strategic plan for promoting high-tech industries. It started with 17 firms in 1981, and, as of June 2003, there were 348 companies with 98,725 employees. Companies in the Park are engaged primarily in the design, manufacture, and research and development of high-tech products. The major industries within the Park can be categorized into six basic groups: integrated circuits, computers and peripherals, telecommunications, opt-electronics, precision machinery, and biotechnology.

This chapter reveals the environmental and occupational consequences of this electronics boom at the HSIP, and questions why and how local residents and high-tech employees have remained silent about these problems over the past two decades. Why does the information technology (IT) industry have such power over politicians and society in Taiwan? The chapter argues that a unique IT dominance, cultivated by the HSIP's success, has constrained local residents and IT laborers who otherwise might have voiced their concerns on the adverse impacts of IT development and manufacturing. The following three sections explain the concept of IT dominance, provide an overview of the environmental impacts of the high-tech firms in the HSIP, and discuss stories of resistance, as told from the point of view of local residents and high-tech employees. The chapter concludes with a discussion of the lessons learned from the HSIP experiences.

The "IT Dominance" Complex in Taiwan

The sociopolitical and economic context of post-Martial Law Taiwan has provided a unique environment that has nurtured the HSIP's success. As economic growth and success often indicate the coveted status of a "developed country," Taiwan's resources and policies that promote IT development have been prioritized over environmental, labor, and other social concerns. The power of IT is legitimized in the name of international competitiveness, especially as this particular industry is embedded in the global network of

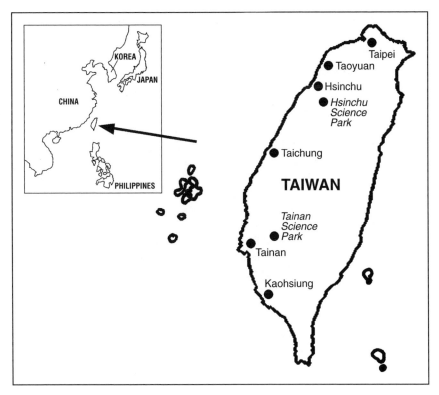

FIGURE 15.1. Map of Taiwan.
Source: Authors, with the assistance of Ichun Kuo.

production that results in enormous capital mobility and flexibility. We argue that this IT dominance has greatly altered social dynamics.

State economic agencies provide favorable treatments for the industry through a set of national IT promotion plans and the construction of centrally regulated IT parks, which are outside of local jurisdictions. Strong partnerships among state economic agencies, local authorities, and IT industries are formed to pursue policy goals that provide regional advantages.

We also see the emergence of IT workers who possess a distinctive corporate identity and a sense of privilege associated with working in prominent, high-tech firms. The high-tech firms build a close partnership with their employees by offering stock options and shared revenues. Sharing common financial and personal interests with the industry, many IT workers, who also live near the industrial park, may become reticent when confronted with their concerns regarding health issues, out of fear of undermining the glitzy IT image. Threats of capital flight further reinforce such trends. In this way, IT dominance operates to maintain a hegemonic power over workers who might otherwise seek reforms when problems arise (Tu 2004).

To demonstrate the foregoing argument, below we provide an overview of IT's environmental impact. The HSIP administration's protection and defense of the IT industry has shown how the Taiwanese state plays a vital role in nurturing the IT dominance complex.

THE ENVIRONMENTAL IMPACT OF THE IT INDUSTRY IN THE HSINCHU AREA

In the past two decades, few Hsinchu residents publicly expressed concerns about the environmental impacts brought forth by the IT industry. It was not until 1997 that the public finally received a rude awakening, following a fire incident at Lien-Dian (aka UMC), a semiconductor company located inside the Park. Why did the fire shock Hsinchu residents? Community people shared the following story. They said that the fire chief reported no knowledge that the smoke was toxic. After the fire was extinguished, he walked into the factory without wearing a mask. He fainted and then was sent to the hospital where he remained for a week. The fumes emitted by the Lien-Dian fire constituted the first shock for Hsinchu residents, leading them to realize how toxic the IT industry is. However, when the same incident was mentioned to high-tech engineers who had worked at Lien-Dian, one response was, "By all means, we were running away from the fire. You couldn't believe how toxic the fire was. Only those dum-dum firemen who knew nothing about the toxics were trying to get into the fab and [put out] the fire!!!"

In retrospect, the story of the 1997 Lien-Dian fire incident that local residents and high-tech employees revealed was the historical moment when local people broke the silicon silence. Lien-Dian's story is very similar to what happened in Silicon Valley in the early 1980s. Based on the authors' investigation, toxic releases, land use, and water planning and allocation are the three major issues threatening the Hsinchu region's environmental quality. Exploring the IT industry's environmental impact reveals how it has exercised its dominance in Taiwanese society.

Toxics Releases

Although the Lien-Dian fire incident led to local residents' first realization that the IT industry was not as safe as its promoters had claimed, the Shengli Toxic Dumping Incident further demonstrated a loophole in regards to the handling of waste solvents generated from IT production that threatened the Taiwanese society as a whole.

The story was uncovered on July 18, 2000. Kaoping River was found to contain illegally dumped toxic wastes that had left Kaoshiung City without safe drinking water for two days. More toxic dumps were found in several streams in northern, central, and southern Taiwan. A couple of days later, the Shengli Chemical Company (henceforth, Shengli) was identified as the source of the illegal dumping. However, Shengli has been one of the largest, licensed, toxic-waste treatment companies since 1996, and it had been approved by ISO 14001. The company had contracted with 80 percent of the integrated circuit (IC) companies in the HSIP for handling their toxic organic chemical waste. Each IT factory, on average, produces 250 to 300 gallons of solvent waste per day. Because of the illegal dumping, the Environmental Protection Agency

(EPA) decided to cancel Shengli's license, and, as a result, the Park's IC firms faced difficulty in treating waste solvents (C. L. Lee 2000).

The Shengli incident revealed the IT firms' inability to monitor the toxic-waste handling process. The incident also showed how government agencies (in this case, the Science-based Industrial Park Administration, or SIPA) defend IT firms by taking responsibility for the clean-up, including paying for waste treatment and constructing an incinerator for hazardous substances management (Tu 2004).

Land Use

Local authorities are actively involved in either developing large-scale new town planning projects or advocating the relaxation of land use control. Local residents support these developments because they believe that, under the name of "high-tech" or "IT," their home villages and towns will receive better land use value, economic prosperity, and quality of life (Fan 1997).

In these circumstances, massive clusters of land development led to further resource-use conflicts because the industry's site selection is not based on sustainable land use or regional environmental objectives. The environmental agencies have been powerless in stopping inappropriate land development in watershed protection areas and on hillside land. Violations of the Environmental Impact Assessment (EIA) law have never become a major concern of the public or policy makers. Rather, the focus generally has been on how to protect the corporate sector's financial health.

Quanta's EIA review process is a well-known phenomenon that showcased the high-tech sector's power with its commitment of investment,[2] and how environmental laws could be set aside to accommodate business demands. President Chen Shui-bian openly criticized local EIA standards as too stringent and as the cause of business development delays. He declared, "This tripping stone [the slow EIA process] should be removed; otherwise I shall kneel down for that."[3] Chen's criticisms forced the local EPA agencies to change the EIA review process. The central government discouraged the local EIA committee from examining the environmental carrying capacity of Nankan Creek, which received 3,000 tons of wastewater per day discharged by Quanta Display, Inc. Chen's special advisory committee made sure that the EIA process was favorable to the corporation (C. Y. Lin and Chen 2001).

Water Planning and Allocation

The Quanta EIA review of the Nankan Creek's chemical carrying capacity relates to the issue of watershed planning and water allocation. In Hsinchu, water shortages have occurred repeatedly since 1995.[4] In 1999, the shortage was so severe that the HSIP firms spent NTD $100 million to have water delivered.[5] The situation became worse in 2002. In the spring, the Ministry of Economic Affairs (MOEA) implemented emergency measures that diverted water from farms to HSIP in response to the drought. About 15,000 hectares of Hsinchu farmland were left fallow, but high-tech firms, like those in IC manufacturing, were exempted from restricted measures.[6] At the end of 2002, the Cabinet ordered 3,000 hectares of farmland to be left fallow in order to reserve water supplies for industrial and residential uses (Y. T. Chiu and Ko 2002).

In the face of a water shortage, the IT firms complained that unstable water and electricity supply had impeded their investment in Taiwan. They blamed governmental incapability, making comparisons to such competitor states as China and Singapore, in providing production elements.[7] Out of fear that the drought would threaten the nation's "international economic compet-itiveness" and "economic prosperity,"[8] the government took two measures to ensure water supplies for the high-tech sectors: they reallocated agricultural water for the HSIP's use and invested infrastructure for this purpose. In 2002, proposed plan for increasing water supply included overland water shipping, a fallow project, dam construction,[9] and desalinator construction to insure an ample water supply to Hsinchu Science Park. Local communities raised environmental concerns regarding the new dam proposals, although there are three existing dams located in Baoshan village and the village surrounding the HSIP.

Vice-premier Lin openly stated, "the government will come up with a plan to put rice fields out of commission in favor of keeping computer chips and other products rolling off production lines at the Science Park . . . " (Lu and Tan (2002), February 28, 2002). Besides farmers' protests and requests to increase compensation, little has been done to challenge the uneven distribution of water resources and related environmental impacts.

MAINTAINING OR BREAKING SILENCE?

From the previous section, it is clear that the Taiwanese central government has directly supervised and authorized the HSIP since 1980. Hsinchu local government authorities and local communities seldom have a chance to par-ticipate in the decision-making processes. Chen Chi-nan, an anthropologist who served as the vice-minister of the Cultural Affairs Committee, stated that, "Hsinchu is colonized by the Science-based Industrial Park." Local residents have echoed Chen's sentiments. They feel that Hsinchu is a "Colonial Town." Jing-shan, a community activist, told us, "inside the Park is Heaven; outside the Park is Hell." Neighbors of the Park must endure traffic jams, air pollu-tion, toxic water discharge, and groundwater pollution. Even worse, their cost of living has increased significantly because the numbers of high-income IT professionals are soaring in their neighborhoods.

Local residents agree with Jing-shan's "Heaven and Hell" metaphor be-cause there is a physical wall that divides the Park and the rest of Hsinchu into two separate worlds. However, the census data indicate that members of one out of four households in Hsinchu work in the Park.[10] Eighty percent of the employee population (77,828) consists of native-born Hsinchu residents (see Table 15.1).

These census data help shift perception of the relationship between the Park and the local communities in Hsinchu. There are intertwined networks among those who work inside the Park and those who do not. They might be close family members, relatives, neighbors, old classmates, or high school

TABLE 15.1. Hsinchu Science Park: Employee Age, Sex, and Foreign Labor

	Male	Female	Average Age	Foreign Labor	Total
Employees	58,175	55,154	31.81	9,922	113,329
Percent	51.33%	48.67%		8.76%	

Source: SIPA (2004).

and college alumni. Then why do most people have little understanding of the risks associated with IT development, particularly after the Lien-Dian fire, a series of water pollution problems, and the Shengli incident? Why is there so little public awareness and community mobilization surrounding these concerns?

In fieldwork conducted in 2000 and 2003, we found that high-tech employees suffer from both potential occupational disease and environmental dangers; yet they remain silent. Shu-ing, a Hsinchu native community planner and organizer said, "My younger brother and sister-in-law both have worked in the Park for about nine years. They only [began to] talk about the toxic issues and occupational health problems at home very recently." Shu-ing's brother and sister-in-law were afraid of losing their jobs if they shared their work stories with other members of their family at home because they had signed contracts with their company that forbade them from releasing any information concerning their work environments.

Why the Silence?

The issue of the high-tech industry's environmental and health impacts remains of marginal interest among the members of the high-tech professional community within the Park. In a conversation with Paul, a process integration engineer, he said cynically, "Environmental concern? People care more about the fluctuation of the stock market, indeed!" At the same time, however, the high-tech employees do know that they are working in a very sensitive environment, whose daily operations require the handling of hundreds of chemicals in the so-called clean room. Brian, a process engineer, confessed, "You don't know for how many years and how much amount of chemicals you absorb will really affect you. At least, we all know that it is not good to expose yourselves to such a chemical environment. The only effort we can make is to protect ourselves; finish risky work as quick as we can."

Peter, an equipment engineer, explained:

The most scary part is that the process has been changed so quickly. The treatment technologies cannot really follow up the new manufacturing process. To catch up to the demand of production, we don't have any choice but run the process. There is no clinical experiment. We may gradually get hurt in such an environment. My feeling is, we may finally discover that we were the experimental mice in the IC fab.

The gender division of labor in the Taiwanese high-tech industry is as strict as that of India (see Ferus-Comelo, this volume). Almost all of the assembly workers are women with a high-school diploma or an equivalent amount of education from a vocational school. Although there are few female engineers, the female assembly workers work with machines for long hours daily. Although their bodies are not directly exposed to chemical materials, their health is always at risk. Ma-li,[11] an operator, said:

> We don't touch toxic materials directly. Only engineers, who take care of the machines, have to take the risk. In this sense, we are safer. But who knows? Many high-tech employees found difficulties in fertility. I had to take Chinese medicine to get pregnant. Many of my colleagues are taking medicine for increasing their fertility.

There are no trade unions in the Park. The only labor organizations formed in these companies are the employees' welfare committees. Most of these high-tech employees have made no attempts to organize their own trade unions.[12] One common policy among these high-tech companies is sharing stocks with employees as a bonus; thus, the relationship between high-tech employers and employees is more cohesive.[13]

Is there any alternative way for employees to break this silence and voice their frustration? IT employees have developed passive approaches to handling the situation. IT engineers have more autonomy, whereas assembly workers remain relatively powerless. Many engineers reveal that they have quit their old jobs and started new ones when they were not satisfied with their managers or situations in their working environments. More often, the individual engineers stealthily publicize their concerns on their own websites.[14] However, few comments relate to environmental and health issues, whereas the stock market and the critiques of infamous senior managers are predominant issues.

In contrast, most female assembly workers are not so lucky. It is not easy for them to switch jobs from one company to another. Shu-ing, the community planner mentioned earlier, told us that the typical path for female workers seeking to change jobs is to achieve the standard of outstanding performance; then they might have an opportunity to work in an office, not in the fab. Shu-ing declared, "My sister-in-law followed this path. She was in the assembly line for several years, and just moved to the office two years ago." She added, "Of course, marrying an engineer is always another alternative."

Breaking the Silence: Taking Action to Voice Discontent

Although environmental groups in Taiwan are not identified as a strong sector, they have been able to generate support from expert/volunteer recruitment and public resources to successfully challenge some environmental polluters and unsustainable projects, such as polluting chemical factories. However, the grassroots movement for sustainable high-tech development is still limited in its influence, as the strength of conventional environmental mobilization has been altered in the context of IT dominance. Compared to some successful environmental mobilizations, community empowerment strategies that mainly rely on community bonds and proximity to the land are not effective here because the IT growth imperative has dramatically changed the social, political, and economic landscape at the local level.

Specifically, the highly connected job opportunities among the high-tech IT Park, local communities and high-profile economic development interests not only diminish environmental critiques, but also hinder potential alliances between local environmental groups and high-tech workers.

However, several first-ever local initiatives indicate new grassroots efforts in response to the adverse impacts of IT development. Several community activists initiated negotiations with the Park Administration regarding the illegal wastewater discharge and groundwater pollution. Since 1999, the Park Administration began communicating with local communities via the Environmental Monitoring Group (EMG) in response to increasing environmental concerns. The EMG provides a formal channel to involve environmental professionals, resident representatives, and environmental groups. However, its efforts only have limited impacts in the Hsinchu region, because its participation is confined to committees without allowing the general public and the media to participate.[15] In addition, Professor Tea-Yuan Hwang, the EMG's director, reflected, "operation of the EMG is constrained by its committees' time, energy and limited budget." He admitted that the EMG has a hard time monitoring the Park Administration's environmental practices (EMG 2002). He claimed that it is crucial to create mechanisms that foster substantial citizen participation.

In such a difficult situation, more organized cooperation between local residents and pro-environment scientists was established in June 2001. The community-based Environmental Supervision Network trains local volunteers to monitor high-tech pollution with the help of university scholars.[16] This progressive approach highlights the value of "ordinary knowledge" and "practical knowledge"—which is rooted in villagers and farmers' everyday experiences—for understanding environmental problems (Chiu 2001).

In addition, global cooperation among environmental nongovernmental organizations (NGOs) demonstrates the possibility of challenging locally and globally dominant businesses. Due to a lack of domestic resources, the Taiwan Environmental Action Network (TEAN)[17] arranged the first Annual Taiwan High Tech Environmental Exchange at the end of March 2001 (see Photo 15.1). It invited the Silicon Valley Toxics Coalition (SVTC) to Taiwan for an information exchange with local government agencies, industrial representatives, and grassroots environmental organizations. The exchange enriched both sides. On one hand, it fostered international collective efforts to hold the IT industry and government accountable for environmental and social sustainability; on the other hand, local grassroots organizations increased their leverage by sharing information and movement strategies to attain more equal footing in negotiating with IT promoters.

Conclusion

Within the particular context of IT dominance in Taiwan, laborers, communities, and the entire society have long struggled to break the Silicon Silence

PHOTO 15.1. Delegates from the Taiwan Environmental Action Network (TEAN) and the Silicon Valley Toxics Coalition (SVTC) meet with community members near Hsinchu Science Industrial Park, Taiwan, March 2001. Courtesy of Ching-Po Kao.

at the dawn of the information age. We conclude that the Taiwanese anti–IT pollution campaigns have been confronting three major challenges: (1) a lack of public concern about environmental and occupational health information, (2) a lack of citizen participation in planning and monitoring mechanisms, and (3) a lack of trade unions for high-tech employees. In general, scholars have argued that there has been a lack of labor union and industry-wide bargaining structures (Benner 1998; Lüthje 2002a; Pellow and Park 2002). Studies in high-tech development also have shown low levels of community involvement and social interaction (Nautilus Institute 2002). The Taiwanese experience echoes these findings. In particular, the first challenge—the lack of public concern about environmental and health information—has bottle-necked the anti–IT pollution campaigns. Alternative media (i.e., the Internet and grassroots networking) might engage, facilitate, and assist future steps toward speaking out about the IT industry's environmental and health impacts.

In the context of Taiwan, even though the environmental and social issues have been widely revealed in Silicon Valley (see Smith, Sonnenfeld, and Pellow; Byster and Smith, "From Grassroots to Global"; Pellow and Matthews; Hawes and Pellow, this volume), little effort has been made to address the negative impacts of high-tech development in Taiwan. Even worse, IT companies aggressively lobby the mainstream media to neglect health and environmental effects of their operations. Some reporters who released information regarding severe effects from the HSIP have received tremendous pressures and threats from IT companies to retract or bury those reports. Under such conditions, therefore, Web-based alternative media may yield greater opportunities for public access. Although, as stated earlier, most engineers only visit Web sites and chat rooms for financial investments, Web-based reports and information centers for environmental and occupational health information may provide better access for laborers, community residents, and members of the general public who are eager to seek environmental and health-related information.

Meanwhile, the grassroots-based environmental initiatives shed light on local struggles with IT dominance, as community members try to empower themselves through cross-sector discussion, community organizing, and transnational exchange to increase information flow and to seek solutions. We believe that the IT industries, the Park, and local communities should actively collaborate on their effort to manage the environmental and occupational health impacts within the Hsinchu region.

Taiwan's case demonstrates that the campaign against high-tech environmental and health impacts has yet to be maneuvered away from the business sector's interests. Overall, mobilizing high-tech employees and local residents to act for the foregoing demands remains a real challenge.[18]

NOTES

1. Background available at www.SIPA.gov.tw/guide/2001e/index.html.

2. According to the Ministry of Economic Affairs, Quanta Display Inc. invests NTD 200 billion and is the important investment case in these five years.

3. C. Y. Lin and Chen 2001.

4. According to Hui-min Chen (2002), the water shortage became an issue in Hsinchu Science Park after 1996.

5. Industry leaders declared that unstable water supplies would hurt the industry's ability to "keep roots in Taiwan." They appealed to the government to take actions because it would cost 200 million NTD per day without a water supply.

6. The related news was covered in major newspapers from February 2002 to April 2002.

7. Complaints are often aired in newspapers when water shortages occur (e.g., C.W. Lee 2002).

8. Whenever government indicated it would cut water supplies in the north of the country, home of many electronics factories, stocks often would fall to their lowest in several months.

9. The second Baoshan dam will store 32 million tons of water, six times the volume of the first Baoshan dam.

10. According to the Ministry of Finance in Taiwan, in 1993, 3.8 out of 10 of the manufacturing employees in Hsinchu City and County work in the HSIP.

11. Mary, an operator, had a miscarriage when she was working for one IC fabrication factory. In order to conceive, she left her job and then succeeded in being pregnant. She is now working for one IC company in HSIP.

12. According to two of interviews, some engineers have tried to found trade unions in one IC company but failed. It happened in the early 1990s.

13. Chang et al. (2001, Section 2, p. 22).

14. Chang et al. (2001, Section 2, p. 20).

15. NGO representatives proposed to open up the EMG meetings to the general public and media, but the proposal was criticized by some committees. There was no conclusion as no consensus was reached (field note, July 25, 2002).

16. See the Web site of Hsinchu Foundation (www.hsinchu.org.tw/).

17. The Taiwan Environmental Action Network (TEAN) is made up of young Taiwanese environmentalists strongly connected to each other through the Internet. The network was founded to save the habitat of the Black-faced Spoonbill and oppose development of the Bin-nan Industrial Complex. Among its aims are "to increase Taiwan's involvement in

international efforts on diverse environmental issues that concern all people" and to "work on collecting first-hand information to assist Taiwanese society in moving toward sustainable development" (see http://tean.formosa.org/).

18. Despite the efforts of Hsinchu activists and residents since 1997 or earlier, most members of the general public and IT employees remained unaware of the problems. A conversation with night shift IT employees during the summer of 2003 indicated they have few ideas about local residents' complaints about environmental pollution produced by the Park. Many night shift workers have only a vague impression of the inappropriate treatment of water discharge several years ago, or of the Shengli incident. Everyone may mention one or two local environmental issues without confirmation. No one heard about the environmental monitoring group founded in 1999. Indeed, IT dominance has tuned out all the cries and screaming from recent years' horrible environmental incidents.

16   Human Lives Valued Less Than Dirt

*Former RCA Workers Contaminated by Pollution
Fighting Worldwide for Justice (Taiwan)*

BASED ON ACTION RESEARCH and in-depth interviews, this chapter reveals the Radio Corporation of America's (RCA) illegal toxic dumping practices in Taoyuan, Taiwan. RCA's two decades of misconduct have seriously contaminated people, soil, and groundwater in Taoyuan. When Taiwan's Environmental Protection Agency (EPA) revealed that RCA's Taoyuan plant had been permanently contaminated in the 1990s, 216 former RCA employees already had died of cancer. In addition, 1,059 people were suffering from various kinds of cancer and 102 others developed tumors, with the numbers increasing every year.

The RCA story demonstrates how developing countries have served as sites for manufacturing and assembling plants and how the flow of international capital prioritizes capital over labor and profits from exploiting human lives. This brings into question whether RCA's economic development model should be pursued. The former RCA workers' struggle should be taken as a warning against the effects of international capitalism.

The following story describes Mr. Bon-Tsu Liu's family tragedy and what happened to his wife, a former material management worker at RCA. When we first met Mr. Liu in January 2001, he told researchers from the Taiwan Association for Victims of Occupational Injuries (TAVOI):[1]

My wife started to work in the RCA factory soon after she graduated from high school. During the 11 years of her RCA career [1979–1990], she was assigned to material management. Every day she would have to work in a closed environment, handling all sorts of disposal buckets previously used for containing plastic materials and organic solvents.

She was laid off in 1990 because of the recession. She became a full-time mother. When my third daughter, Wen-Shen Liu, was about four-months old, her belly started ballooning to the size of a basketball. Later diagnosis by doctors confirmed she had hepatoblastoma. In a series of operations and chemotherapy treatments for three years, Wen-Shen became skinnier day by day and it was unbearably heart-breaking for us, but more painful for her. She died at the age of three from multiple organ failures caused by fulminant hepatitis. This marked the beginning of the great sorrows and terrible pains that will never escape us.

After the death of our baby, I started to worry about my wife's health and kept asking her to get a medical examination. She did so and unfortunately, the examination report suggested she had breast cancer at a critical stage.

She had surgery immediately, hoping that all cancer cells could be completely removed. During the following three years, she was given regular chemotherapy treatments, but it was all in vain. Bone cancer had developed, and she lost her hair and physical strength. Even her muscles were totally destroyed from the side effects of chemo treatments. Every movement was a torture for her. In her last six months, she had to rely on morphine to kill the sudden pain that would strike without warning.

My doctor told me that my girl might have contracted cancer cells while still in her mother's womb, and that breast-feeding might also have come into play. It was 1995 before my wife was diagnosed with breast cancer, and it took years to develop into the critical stage. This means that my wife could have contracted cancer while she was still working for RCA. Nobody in my family or her family has ever had cancer; even her 90-year-old grandmother is still very healthy.

It was during the period of time that we witnessed the takeoff of Taiwan's economic miracle that my wife was still working. She sacrificed her most precious time of youth to a society that exploited her when she was still capable of contributing, but then totally forgot her and deemed her useless. RCA denied any negligence or wrongdoing, and said it has never made its workers use groundwater. The Council of Labor Affairs was reluctant to identify the whole situation as a vocational disaster and continued researching in order to be sure about the underlying causal relation, before it would agree to our legitimacy claim for compensations.[2] Medical treatments were so expensive. Even worse, there was no National Health Insurance Program as we have now. Even now, with the Insurance Program, we still have to shoulder the full costs for drugs and treatments.

People said, "The poor have no right to be sick. Even with the national health care, only the rich people have the right to be sick." I strongly feel that I have been alienated and deserted by our society. Nobody would recognize my wife's contribution to Taiwan's economy. My wife and daughter's sacrifices are totally irrelevant in today's world.

FEMALE LABORERS AND INDUSTRIAL POLLUTION

Mr. Liu's wife's story is not a random case. During the past three decades, RCA's Taiwanese female workers have shared many painful experiences—menstrual irregularities, early menopause, miscarriages, stillbirths, ovarian tumors, and uterine illnesses—in secrecy. Within the Taiwanese cultural context, such painful experiences are considered too private to disclose to others. These female workers blamed themselves for this suffering, as if it were their own fault. In the second section of this paper, I explain how, not until the mid 1990s did the news about cancer cases occurring in large numbers among RCA's former workers become public knowledge. I address how female workers suddenly realized that most of them had experienced one or two miscarriages and some even gave birth to babies born with cancer. Finally, in the third section, I discuss how the former workers united and protested against RCA. Since 2001, TAVOI has joined RCA Workers' Self Help Group

(RCA-WSHG) to conduct a series of protests to fight for workers' compensation.[3] During the protest, sad, middle-aged female workers angrily stood up to declare that, after contributing the best 30 years of their lives to RCA, they had been unjustly laid off without pensions (Ku 1996).

These tragedies and protests lead TAVOI to investigate the relationship between industrial pollution and RCA female laborers' health problems. Taiwan's economy made its transformation in the 1960s, attracting direct foreign investment with policies like tax breaks, low wages, and virtually zero environmental regulations on land use, hoping that outside investors would set up plants and employ local workers. One reason that global capitalists prefer to invest in Taiwan is because of its compulsory middle-school education. Many middle-school-educated, young, diligent rural female workers with delicate skills look for jobs within industrial parks (Cowie 1999), providing a pool of cheap labor. As the leading manufacturer of consumer electronics (TV sets, VCRs, hi-fis, stereos, etc.), RCA began searching for investment opportunities in third-world countries around 1970, and decided to invest in Taoyuan, Chupei, and Yilan in Taiwan. The Taiwanese government regarded RCA as a model company, as well as its best exporting company for many years.

At its peak, RCA had more than 30,000 workers. In RCA's Taoyuan plant, female employees worked in three shifts around the clock. The company had ten buses to bring them from the nearby countryside and poor veterans' communities every day. RCA also provided nine dormitories to accommodate female workers who came from farther away (the middle and southern parts of Taiwan). All the girls living in these dormitories used ground water polluted by organic solvents from RCA's plant.

TAVOI examined the Material Safety Data Sheets from the EPA and found that the organic solvents that the electronics industry uses for dyeing, cleansing, and welding purposes can enter the human body easily through inhalation, drinking, and direct skin contact, causing severe chronic damage. Trichloroethylene can cause menstrual irregularities, and tetrachloroethylene may increase the risk of cervical cancer. Taiwan's Council of Labor Affairs also revealed that RCA's employees suffered from a higher percentage of breast cancer than the general population.

The story of RCA's Taoyuan Plant is a classic example of globalization. Developed capitalist countries locate their factories in less-developed countries to save on labor and environmental protection costs. Then they ship finished products home or elsewhere in the world to earn large profits. The RCA case makes it even clearer that, under the international division of labor, female workers in the electronics manufacturing industry are more prone to damages done by the organic solvents that it commonly uses.

THE MERGING OF PLANT POLLUTION AND VOCATIONAL INJURIES

During the past two decades, RCA has been illegally pouring toxic wastes and organic solvents into wells surrounding its Taoyuan plant. It also has left more than one thousand workers dead or suffering from vocational diseases, mainly cancer.

In 1994, the Legislative Yuan lawmakers revealed to the public that neighbors of the RCA plant had been hard hit by an unusually high rate of cancer because of RCA's pollution. Taiwanese government officials helped RCA create a "rush" running water supply system for these residents.[4] In 1998, the Industrial Technology Research Institute[5] also confirmed that ground water as far as two kilometers away from the plant site—contained excessive levels of the toxins trichloroethylene and tetrachloroethylene that were more than 1,000 times above the safety standard allowed by law for drinking water.

As mentioned earlier, RCA provided its approximately 10,000 workers in the Taoyuan plant with drinking machines using pumped ground water that was not properly treated, except for a crude filtering process. However, all the managers that worked in the office drank distilled water that the company had bought outside the plant. Recalling days past, a former RCA employee said, "No wonder all those foreign managers drank bottled mineral water, only we, the foolish workers, would drink toxic water everyday, live in the plant and eat in the plant . . . even the shower water was toxic!"

More than 1,000 former RCA workers have developed liver, lung, colon, stomach, bone, nasopharyngeal, lymphatic, and breast cancers, plus various tumors. Medical experts have indicated that the former RCA workers' cancer rate is 20 to 100 times higher than that of the general public. Taiwan's EPA declared RCA's Taoyuan plant a "permanently contaminated area;"[6] that is, the site and the ground water nearby cannot be cleaned and decontaminated.

In April 2001, TAVOI and RCA-WSHG conducted a telephone and in-person investigation with help from Taiwan's Council of Labor Affairs. The study concluded that, among those who had worked in RCA's Taoyuan plant during the previous 20 years, 1,395 had been diagnosed with cancer, of which 226 had died, and more than 100 had suffered from various kinds of tumors.

Human Lives Valued Less Than Dirt

Similar to García and Simpson's case in Mexico (this volume), RCA simply dumped waste solvents on the site of its Taoyuan plant in Taiwan. As the volume of waste solvents grew, it either pumped them into the ground or dug holes to contain them, without processing them first. As time passed, these waste solvents seeped into the ground and contaminated ground water (Meng 2000). Ah-Sin, a former female worker, confirmed:

I remember it was when I just entered the company in early 1970. Superiors told workers to pour the stinking waste solvents on the ground. In the beginning, the dumping guys did not wear masks at all. Not long afterwards however, they had to put on masks because it was impossible to stand the irritating odor. As the company's business grew significantly, the waste also grew too, so the company just dug holes and poured wastes into them. I think many people knew and had even witnessed such practices.

One former senior foreman, who now takes part in RCA-WSHG, said, "I think RCA had taken advantage of the government's inaction and the workers' ignorance, and this led to the ballooning of the seriousness of the problem." In retrospect, he understood that these international companies "were just passengers. They would leave after they had made enough money. They didn't care about the lives and deaths of the workers and the local residents."

It was not until pressure from Taiwan's EPA began mounting that RCA conducted an investigation in 1996 concerning pollution on its Taoyuan plant site and in nearby ground water sources. It spent NT$200 million (about US$6 million) for soil and water cleanups.[7] However, although the number of newly confirmed cancer cases among its former employees kept growing and many were dying of cancer every year, RCA showed no signs of accountability. A former RCA senior worker said angrily: "Our lives are valued less than the dirt!"

Ironically, RCA is now styling itself as an environmentally friendly company that focuses on protecting natural resources and promoting its "product recycling management project" for all of its consumer electronics.

The Malfunctioning State and the Arrogant Scientific Community

What makes the RCA story even more ironic is that Taiwan's Council of Labor Affairs conducted eight labor inspections at the Taoyuan plant from June 1975 to May 1991, and, at every step, it identified violations of the Rules for Labor Health Management and the Regulations for Labor Safety and Hygiene Facilities for Prevention of Toxification from Organic Solvents. Even right before they shut down the plant in 1990, there were nine violations against the aforementioned regulations on organic solvents.

Meanwhile, Taiwan's Control Yuan began investigating the RCA case in 1998. Its official report accused the Council of Labor Affairs of: "being slack on duty for taking only paperwork instead of on-site inspection in supervising the company, leaving the workers to be seriously hurt by pollution later on." The Council of Labor Affairs, the Department of Health, and the EPA examined the polluted soil and water, but left unattended the illnesses of inflicted employees and residents living near the plant. The Control Yuan thus demanded that these government agencies review their handling of the case and make improvements.

Since the RCA disaster, the Taiwanese government has distanced itself as "the impartial third party."[8] In brief, although the Democratic Progressive Party (DPP) replaced the formerly ruling Nationalist Party (the Kuomintang, or KMT) and took control of the government in 2000, the new government has made no progress on urgent issues.[9] For example, (1) it has not yet identified how individuals will qualify as victims of occupational injuries/diseases, (2) it falls short of measures intended to cover victims' future living expenses, (3) victims bear a heavy burden from very high litigation costs, and (4) victims experience complications urgently in need of medical care.

However, Taiwan's EPA and Council of Labor Affairs individually conducted studies on RCA's workers and the company's neighboring residents. Their results have suggested that the percentage of these female workers suffering from breast and ovarian cancer had increased significantly, as had death rates among RCA's neighboring residents due to liver cancer and cancer in general (Lin and Suen 2001; Wang 1999). Both findings reveal that the high cancer rate and death cases were strongly related to RCA's polluted environments.

More precisely, the EPA's Stage II Research Report, released in 2000, announced that the polluted groundwater had not improved with the clean-up treatments that had been in effect since 1994. The water still contained chloroethene, trichloroethylene, and tetrachloroethylene. As a result, residents near the plant experienced a much higher than expected frequency of cancer at 0.003,[10] and an inflicted-rate for diseases other than cancer of 16.9.[11] The same report also found that male residents had high disease and death rates from liver cancer.

However, from the EPA's perspective, these scientific data were not strong enough to argue for a "significant correlation between the workers' exposures to toxic solvents on the jobs and the cancers they had" because RCA had brought all the employment records back to the United States when they shut down the plant (Lin and Suen 2001). When Labor Affairs released Stage III Research and concluded "no significant correlation," General Electric (GE, which by that time had merged with RCA) announced to the press that the Taiwanese government had confirmed that the cancer cases had nothing to do with employment at RCA, and therefore, the company should not be held liable for compensation.[12]

Based on TAVOI's research of Taiwanese industrial development history, there is a clear relationship between cancer and the toxic environment. In 1972, the first large-scale industrial disaster occurred at the Danshui plant of the Philco Co. Ltd. (a branch company of the Ford Motor Company). This disaster led to many female workers' injuries and deaths, the cause of which was proved to be trichloroethene. The Philco accident revealed serious inadequacies in Taiwan's laws and regulations concerning labor safety. Although the incident at Philco led to the enactment of the Labor Safety and Health Law in 1974, Taiwanese workers have been paying the price of the so-called "economic takeoff" for the last three decades.

The Cost of Lives, the Price of Justice

RCA sold its seriously contaminated Taoyuan plant to Taiwan's Ever Fortune Group. The Ever Fortune Group received collateral loans and made a profit from acquiring the polluted land. By sharp contrast, the cancer-inflicted workers have never been compensated. Why? The RCA has evacuated its capital. If the 300 RCA former workers want to take legal action, they would have to pay approximately US$9 million, as required by the Taiwanese legal system, to simply process their lawsuit.[13] Where can they get the money?

Even worse, within the Taiwanese legal system, it would be the former RCA workers' responsibility to present evidence of their vocational diseases. As Foran and Sonnenfeld discussed in the Thailand case (this volume), the identification of vocational diseases must be based on epidemiological research. In RCA's case, such research is not only time consuming, but also resource driven. It needs government support and the medical profession's engagement. How can former RCA workers initiate such epidemiological research on their own?[14]

FIGHTING WORLDWIDE FOR JUSTICE

Confronting RCA's global-capital flows, former RCA workers have been fighting worldwide for justice with help from TAVOI, RCA-WSHG, and other grassroots groups (see Photo 16.1). In Taiwan, Liu's, and other RCA victim's stories have mobilized 81 lawyers, and more than 100 college students have volunteered to help prepare a lawsuit. More than 400 work-history and vocational disease cases have been compiled. Seriously ill RCA workers have protested several times to Taiwanese government agencies, the American Institute in Taiwan, and the Institut Francais de Taipei.[15] Through confrontations, public hearings, and press conferences, they have won great support from Taiwanese labor organizations and successfully exposed the RCA case to the public, which later led to the enactment of related laws and regulations on environmental and labor issues.[16] Despite bringing environmental protection and vocational disaster issues into the spotlight of public concern, they have posed no real threat to international capitalists. For example, RCA moved its production lines to Thailand and China, where labor costs are even cheaper than in Taiwan.

PHOTO 16.1. Former RCA (Taiwan) workers, their family members, and supporters gather to demand justice for colleagues who died from cancer and other illnesses they believe resulted from exposure to chemicals at the firm's consumer electronics factory. Courtesy of TAVOI.

However, the transnational mobility of capital requires an international alliance of non-government organizations and the international media's attention to escalate pressure upon company owners. TAVOI and RCA-WSHG reached a joint decision to conduct an investigation in the United States for collecting information and visiting related organizations. TAVOI successfully mobilized assistance, both in Taiwan and overseas, for fund raising, networking, and publicity for the RCA case. This support came from Taiwanese organizations (the Northwest Airlines Labor Union, the Workers' Enactment Action Committee, the Ministry of Foreign Affairs, and the Council of Labor Affairs), Taiwanese American organizations (Taiwanese student bodies and overseas Chinese organizations at the University of Southern California, the University of California at Berkeley, and New York University), and American organizations (the AFL-CIO labor federation, and Silicon Valley Toxics Coalition [SVTC]). These organizations have contributed to this investigation's success.

In May 2002, members of the RCA-WSHG, accompanied by TAVOI organizers, began a two-week campaign in the United States that sought the support of the U.S. Labor Department, members of the U.S. Congress, the AFL-CIO, the GE Labor Union, environmental groups, activist scholars, and Taiwanese student bodies. In press conferences, the GE Labor Union openly addressed its support for workers seeking compensation; it also held a public hearing in the U.S. Congress. All these efforts were aimed at a long-term, cross-border protest. Because RCA already had withdrawn from Taiwan, the RCA-WSHG was determined to bring lawsuits against RCA in the United States.

CONCLUSION

As the capitalist agenda becomes more global than ever, social movements act globally, too. In the RCA case, we have witnessed cooperation among organizations in labor movements, environmental protection, legal reform, and human rights. A transnational alliance of social movements will demand much closer cooperation across national borders so that the workers' interests in one country can join with those in others, to resist international capitalists' oppression. We need a more diversified international alliance of labor movements.

More importantly, the RCA case alerts us to the fact that epidemiological research in Taiwan is at a formative stage, while new chemical products are being introduced at a rate far surpassing our understanding of their pathological potential. Chang, Chiu, and Tu's Hsinchu Science Park case (this volume) also demonstrates this finding. In 1981, the United Nations pointed out that it may take 85 years to conduct appropriate tests to identify how the 50,000 widely used chemicals can cause hazardous damage to the human body. The clock is ticking. Mr. Liu's wife and other former RCA workers are suffering daily and dying from cancer every year. They simply cannot wait for scientific studies to produce the evidence they already know exists. Unfortunately, the Taiwanese government often requires victims to provide evidence. With the lack of relevant research, the destruction of the pollution sites, a lack of no control over the production of information that is controlled by the defendant (i.e., the employer), and without even the slightest possibility of securing such information from employers, the victims have practically no chance of winning.

NOTES

1. Founded in 1992, TAVOI was the first non-government organization formed by victims of occupational injuries/diseases and surviving family members of the victims. Its main goal is to assist such victims in bargaining with their employers for compensation; to empower the victims in an attempt to transform them into activists, movement participants, labor education instructors and policymakers; and to organize their efforts in the law-making process to try and change and improve the labor situation in Taiwan. Please refer to its Web site (http://hurt.org.tw/) for more information.

2. In Taiwan, the central government is divided by functions into five branches—the Executive Yuan, the Legislative Yuan, the Judicial Yuan, the Control Yuan, and the Examination Yuan. The functions of the Executive Yuan, the Legislative Yuan, and the Judicial Yuan can be easily seen from their names. The impeachment function normally entrusted to the legislative power in western countries is given to the Control Yuan. The Examination Yuan is responsible for administering qualification exams for public services and qualification exams for various professions such as lawyers and medical doctors, and so forth. Under the Executive Yuan, executive functions closely related to our discussions here fall into the authorities of the Council of Labor Affairs, the EPA, the Department of Health, the Ministry of Economic Affairs, and Ministry of Foreign Affairs.

3. Since 1994, the media started to report the RCA pollution case with much greater coverage. Former RCA workers who then settled in various places started to unite together and, through the suggestion and recommendation of the Department of Health of the Taoyuan County Government, incited the involvement of TAVOI. They formally registered with the government as the RCA-WSHG in 1998. In 2001, RCA-WSHG joined TAVOI as one of its group members.

4. In 1996, under the pressure from Taiwan's EPA, General Electric, which had merged RCA earlier, helped supply mineral water to residents near its Taoyuan plant for one year until their running-water supply system was completed.

5. This is a government-sponsored research institute focusing on the development and transfer of new industrial technologies for further commercial applications.

6. The RCA Taoyuan plant occupying an area of 29 Japanese pings (roughly equivalent to 95,867 square meters) was the first case to be put on the list of "permanently contaminated areas."

7. All the contaminated soil inside the RCA Taoyuan plant was dug out, washed with clean water and then put under the sun for exposure. But the underground water contamination was too terrible to clean up, so GE decided not to do anything about it and the Taiwan government also stopped looking into the case.

8. The Taiwanese government should compensate victims in the first place and then sue RCA on behalf of them. In case the lawsuit is won, the damage compensation from RCA will then be used to reimburse compensation payments that Taiwan's government had earlier paid the victims. The idea is pretty much like compensation with a subrogation clause.

9. The KMT ruled Taiwan from 1949 until it lost to the DPP in the presidential election of 2000, when the opposition camp took power for the first time. This peaceful change of

power was called "the silent revolution." Even in the days when the KMT was in charge, there was a joint commission on the RCA case that involved the participation of all relevant government agencies. Despite its ineffectiveness, the commission did provide a channel for inflicted RCA workers to have dialogue with the government. However, the commission was disassembled as soon as the DPP took power. This marked the beginning of the self-help protest by former RCA workers.

10. The acceptable range is 0.000001 to 0.0001.

11. The acceptable rate must be smaller than 1.

12. In May 2002, RCA workers traveled to the United States to visit concerned organizations and sat down with people from GE and Thomson for negotiation, hoping that an agreement could be reached. GE then made a statement to the press from the United States and Taiwan that, according to research reports by Taiwan's government, cancers diagnosed in these workers were not related to their work, therefore GE was not liable.

13. Under Taiwan's legal system, the plaintiff needs to submit an arbitration fee for bringing the lawsuit to court. For example, in a lawsuit involving 300 surviving families, with each demanding a compensation of US$3 million, the total compensation amounts to US$900 million. The 1 percent rate for arbitration fee for trials in the lower court will be US$9 million. This does not include the arbitration fee for trials in appeal courts, lawyers' fees, and the fees required for demanding a court-ordered provisional seizure.

14. Take Japan and Korea as examples. It took the Japanese government twelve years to identify its famous Minamata-byo disease resulting from mercury poisoning, and those victims' basic medical and living needs were taken care of by the Japanese government even before the conclusion was reached. In the 1987 case of chronic poisoning of carbon disulfide found in workers working for a Japanese-invested chemical fiber manufacturer in Korea, the district court returned with a verdict that the workers were entitled to compensation for vocational diseases despite insufficient epidemiological evidence to support the causal relations claimed by the plaintiffs. As a result, the Korean government—joined by leaders from the Korean medical profession—provided funds to the workers' self-help group to establish a foundation to conduct long-term medical follow-ups on these workers.

15. The American Institute in Taiwan and the Institute Francais de Taipei are, respectively, semiofficial agencies representing the U.S. and the French governments as the United States and France do not have formal diplomatic ties with Taiwan.

16. The RCA workers' protest had brought to light many loopholes in the laws and regulations, and this led to the enactment and implementation of *the Soil and Groundwater Pollution Remediation Act Enforcement Rules*, and the revision of *the Labor Insurance Regulation* to make breast removal eligible for disability compensation.

17 Unionizing Electronics

The Need for New Strategies

The London-based non-government organization (NGO), Catholic Agency for Overseas Development (CAFOD), published a report on working conditions at subcontractors for the computer industry in the *maquiladoras* in both northern Mexico and China (CAFOD 2004). The report, "Clean Up Your Computer," stirred international interest, because it was probably the first time that an independent organization described some of the inhumane conditions under which the employees of subcontractors for the computer industry, mostly women, worked. The report exposed the conditions and wages that people in industrialized countries would regard as extremely outdated. The information was not entirely new. Previously, it mostly had been furnished by trade unions, which often were purported to exaggerate, to show these companies in an unfavorable light. How was it possible for such conditions to develop largely unnoticed by the general public?

Changing Industry: Stealth Manufacturers

In recent decades, the electronics industry has seen major changes; more are expected soon, which will cause further structural shifts in the telecommunications industry and have considerable impacts on employment. The general public has hardly noticed these changes, as information technology (IT) is seen mostly as a "service industry," even by many unions. Attention has focused on specialists in the fields of system development, sales, and marketing. The IT sector has also become an experimental field for new models of industrial manufacturing (see Lüthje, this volume).

The production of IT hardware, still the core component of the products manufactured, has undergone radical changes. Top-brand companies have transferred the production of personal computers (PCs), servers, network computers, and telecommunications devices (e.g., cell phones, switching equipment, and telephones), as well as a growing number of other electronic appliances (e.g., such consumer goods as TVs, hi-fis, and other devices or electronics for the automobile industry) to a new generation of globally operating contract manufacturers.

Most importantly, these companies are far more than mere subcontractors for the large IT industry groups that wish to contract out production. They act as "global supply chain facilitators," that is, as managers of extended global production chains, providing the big companies with production facilities, engineering expertise, and logistics in all major markets of the triad. Meanwhile, they have become full-fledged transnational companies (Lüthje

2001b, 89). As their logos do not appear on the products they manufacture, these firms are hardly known to the public, despite having established dozens of production facilities throughout the world and employing tens of thousands of workers worldwide. Hence a major U.S. daily newspaper has referred to them as "stealth manufacturers." This trend is most apparent in the United States, and to a lesser extent in Europe, and it is expected to take root in Japan and South Korea soon.

THE ELECTRONICS INDUSTRY AND UNIONS

Changes in information and communications industry structure and the emergence of contract manufacturing (CM) also have led to changed working conditions in these companies' production plants. Several companies in the computer industry sell hardware, but few have their own production facilities. This segment also has seen a process of consolidation in recent years. A number of firms, such as Compaq, for example, which played a substantial role in the standardization of hardware, have disappeared from the market. Compaq first gobbled up well-known IT companies, such as Tandem and Digital Equipment Corporation (DEC), before being swallowed up itself by a global player in the IT sector, Hewlett-Packard. Dell, Hewlett-Packard, and IBM have outsourced most or all of their hardware production to CMs, and most of their remaining employees are white-collar workers. Trade unions in many companies in the "old" industries find that such employees are more difficult to unionize than are workers on the shop floor. Thus, the traditional shop-floor workers are mainly found at CMs.

Unionization varies considerably from country to country and from continent to continent. In the United States, union membership among staff of the IT companies, whether they are employees in the development laboratories of Microsoft or shop-floor workers in the remaining production plants of Intel, Solectron, or Flextronics, is virtually nonexistent.

This might partly be attributable to the working conditions that have developed mainly among CMs due to their service-oriented approach in production work. Lüthje, Schumm, and Sproll (2002, 17) summarized these conditions as follows:

- *"Work without product."* Production work is organized as "service" because identification with the company's "own" product is missing.
- *Relatively low wages with a high degree of variable pay elements.* Most of the contract manufacturers' factories are located in low-wage countries. Wages and social benefits are rather low.
- *Flexible employment.* The need to respond to changes in production quantities within a very short time have led to the extensive use of flexible and precarious forms of employment. Temporary work and agency work have become the strategically most important forms of employment in many regions.
- *An above-average employment of women and ethnic minorities.* As is the case in many electronics assembly plants, the workforces are mostly

female. In the United States, especially California, where the major CMs have their home bases, most workers are nonwhite immigrants, mainly of Asian or Latin American origin (see Ferus-Comelo; Pellow and Matthews, this volume).

The production system that is closely linked to these working conditions only could exist on the basis of industrial low-wage work, which can be adapted easily and more or less smoothly to the ups and downs of production cycles. For this purpose, it was important that no in-house regulation would prevent management from increasing or reducing working hours or quickly dismissing workers. An industry pioneer, the former chief executive of Intel, Robert Noyce, had his reasons for stating that "maintaining a union-free environment is essential to the survival of the industry"(Lüthje 2001a, 82).

In the United States, CMs mostly set up their production plants in the Sun Belt states of the South and West, where unions traditionally have had a weaker presence than in the "old" industrial centers of the North. The situation in Mexico, another important location for CM production plants on the American continent, is similar to that of the United States. The plants are mostly located in the *maquiladoras* in northern Mexico (see Partida; García and Simpson, this volume).

The situation is different in Western Europe, where the workforce of CM companies is indeed unionized. Many of these plants were acquired by other companies and already had union links before they were taken over. Experience has shown that unions and—as is the case in Germany—works councils are accepted during a transitional period, but that strong pressure is exerted on the workforce after a few years to weaken the unions or to oust them from the companies altogether. Companies often attempt to opt out of national or regional collective bargaining agreements. However, it is not as easy as in the United States to prevent unions from gaining a foothold. In "old Europe," even the large computer firms, such as IBM, Hewlett-Packard, and Microsoft, are unionized, although not to the same extent as are companies in the steel, shipbuilding, or automobile industries.

In Eastern Europe, which has become a preferred location for the European CM industry because of its low wages, the picture is different and more diverse. In some countries, companies in this industry do indeed have union structures. Again, unions often are not represented in newly established companies, but in companies that were taken over by others. A common obstacle to union organization in Eastern Europe is the experience that workers had with the unions of the Communist system. This experience often is not questioned, but transferred to all union organizations, even those that did not exist during the Communist regime (see Watterson, this volume).

Even in Southeast Asia, unions exist in a number of companies in the CM industry, but the situation differs considerably from country to country. Several Southeast Asian countries pursue a latent anti-union policy, which governments often cement in limited rights and administrative regulations. In Malaysia, for example, unions must register with a government authority. This authority also defines the affiliation of a plant or company with a particular industry. National union organizations are banned in Malaysia's electronics industry; only company unions are allowed. For companies in the electrical/electronics industry, it is very easy to "get rid" of a national union. They merely need to apply for a change in industry affiliation—electronics instead of electrical industry—and the union is no longer allowed to represent the workforce. (See also Ferus-Comelo on India, and Foran and Sonnenfeld on Thailand, this volume.)

In South Korea, the big electrical/electronics companies are partly unionized, but there are two different union organizations that do not cooperate very closely. To this day, Samsung has managed to prevent unions from gaining a foothold in its plant. In Japan, the company union system is predominant. Some, but by no means all, of the company unions are affiliates of the national union for the electrical/electronics industry, Denki Rengo. Many of the unions that have members in the information and communications industry are affiliates of the International Metalworkers' Federation (IMF), whose head office is in Geneva. Some of these unions, particularly the white-collar ones, are affiliated with another Global Union Federation, the United Networks International (UNI).

Another important location for the hardware industry and thus for many contract manufacturers is China (see Leong and Pandita, this volume), where, to this day, free unions are not allowed. The only organization that exists is an umbrella group, the ACFTU (All-Chinese Federation of Trade Unions), which is closely linked to the governing Communist party. Industrial development has clear control over the consistent representation of workers' interests, which explains their rather low wages and poor safety regulations despite the economic boom.

All in all, the worldwide rate of unionization in the electronics industry is rather low, particularly compared to the so-called old industries, such as the steel, shipbuilding, and automobile sectors. The reasons for this are manifold: from states that ban or at least severely impede the unionization of these workers, to setting up plants in free trade zones—to which unions are denied access—to intimidation by employers, governments and corporations pursue a range of anti-union policies. The high percentage of fixed-term contracts and the widespread use of employment agencies are other reasons why it is difficult to organize workforces.

UNIONIZATION: NEW CONCEPTS ARE REQUIRED

The recipes and strategies that proved successful in the past when organizing large plants in the "old" industries must be adapted to the requirements of the information and communications industry, including CM. It seems even more likely that a wealth of new strategies will have to be developed to address the different groups of workers (agency workers in CM companies and office staff in software firms, service departments, etc.) who often do not have a union "background."

Two sets of measures appear appropriate and an initial attempt already has been made to translate them into practice: establishing codes of conduct for transnational companies, known as "International Framework Agreements" (IFAs) and unionizing workers in these industries.

New Types of Agreements

International Framework Agreements (IFAs) are not direct instruments for organizing workers. However, they can create an environment in which workers may unionize without fear of reprisal. IFAs have been on the unions' agenda for some time. These IFAs are voluntary agreements between the group management of a transnational company and Global Union Federations (GUFs). One of these GUFs is the International Metalworkers' Federation (IMF), which represents about 200 affiliate unions in the metal industry (e.g., in the areas of metal-working, shipbuilding, automobile, steel, mechanical engineering, and aerospace). These individual unions, in turn, represent some 25 million workers worldwide.

By signing an IFA, the group management commits itself to a specific conduct. The basis of IFAs is the core labor standards established by the International Labor Organization (ILO), a UN organization whose headquarters are in Geneva. These core labor standards include the freedom of association; in other words, the worker's right to join a union or to set up a union, the freedom of collective bargaining, the ban on child labor, the ban on forced labor, and equality in the workplace. The core labor standards are laid down in ILO conventions, which many countries already have ratified, but not all have incorporated them into national law; sometimes they have been ignored or even deliberately disregarded at the national level.

The IMF considers a "subcontractor clause" to be a compulsory element in these agreements. Such clauses require a company to make sure that its subcontractors comply with the core labor standards or that they conclude their own IFAs. In addition to these core labor standards, IFAs often contain general statements on minimum requirements for pay, working hours, and health and safety, because there are no internationally approved standards, as is the case for core labor standards. Rules on monitoring compliance with the IFA's principles and how to handle complaints about agreement violations are other core components of this code of conduct.

To date, more than thirty transnational companies have concluded such IFAs with the relevant Global Union Federation, nine of which were signed in the metal industry with the IMF. The large majority of these companies have their origins in Europe. Thus far, Japanese and U.S. companies have concluded hardly any of these agreements. Most of the metal industry's IFAs have been concluded at automobile companies and suppliers; electronics groups have not yet been among the contracting partners. However, the possibility of concluding such an IFA with a German electronics group does not seem inconceivable. Together with a collective bargaining agreement on working hours, one company recently signed a supplementary agreement that recognized ILO core labor standards with the intent to implement them within the firm.

Most companies find it difficult to address the issue of a voluntary agreement in which they agree to respect social rights—which include the core labor standards—and to guarantee its compliance within the company. Instead, many companies treat these fundamental social rights with contempt, not only in developing countries but also in industrialized nations. In addition, workers who want to fight these practices collectively by setting up or joining a union are targeted for punishment. Unfortunately, many governments and government authorities pave the way for companies by passing labor laws that encourage their attempts to sanction such workers, and many authorities turn a blind eye to companies' violations of labor laws. That is the only way to explain some of the conditions and developments prevailing in CM companies in Mexico and China, where the computer industry's groundwork is performed (see CAFOD 2004). There are still many workers who are easily intimidated and do not defend their rights resolutely enough, even if they are covered by labor legislation. Workers often tolerate inhumane working conditions, fearing reprisals or the loss of their jobs.

It already has been mentioned that hardly any American and Japanese concerns have concluded IFAs. The only American company to have concluded such an agreement is Chiquita, and no Japanese company has done so. This is due to the companies' resistance, but it might also be attributable to a lack of pressure and support from the national unions. These organizations seem to misjudge the fact that IFAs not only affect conditions in the company's plants that are located in developing or newly industrialized countries, but also can benefit workers in industrialized countries. "Union busting" will no longer be possible in a company that has concluded an IFA because this would be a clear violation of ILO Convention 87 on the freedom of association, which is part of the core labor standards that the IFA covers.

GUFs have their reasons for attaching particular importance to independent IFAs. These agreements contrast with a number of company codes or codes of conduct formulated by the ILO, the Organization for Economic Cooperation and Development (OECD), and the UN Global Compact. Usually, these codes are only recommendations for companies and do not oblige them to act in any specific way. They use terms like "efforts" or "attempts" to comply with codes of conduct and do not require any kind of guarantee. Moreover, transnational companies' internal codes of conduct do not touch on the issues of freedom of association and freedom of collective bargaining. IFAs do not have this weakness. That is why they have top priority for many GUFs' policies vis-à-vis transnational companies.

To implement IFAs in a sustainable way, new strategies should be discussed and put into practice. NGOs and similar bodies should be included in the discussions. IFAs are not really part of the union's "day-to-day business," such as wage policies and health and safety. They lay down internationally approved fundamental social rights. "Positive advertising" should be considered for companies and their products; in other words, they should recommend that these products be bought, if companies have concluded an IFA and are implementing it consistently. In the case of subcontractors whose products are not intended for the end user, customers buying such products as components could be advised to give priority to subcontractors that have concluded an IFA. Positive advertising is easier to handle (particularly given the still small number of IFAs) than negative advertising (e.g., campaigns calling for a buying boycott), which should be reserved for particularly serious violations of international social standards.

New Organizing Strategies

Unions still need to address company workforces and convince them to unionize themselves and to defend their interests vis-à-vis the employers. At a political level, both nationally and internationally, unions must step up their efforts to achieve a general recognition of core labor standards in international treaties (including trade agreements) and their full incorporation into individual countries' labor legislation. This "lobbying" makes it necessary to look for allies at all levels and to intensify cooperation with NGOs. At the same time, the aim must be to transform existing codes of conduct for transnational companies (e.g., as laid down by the OECD and the ILO, and in the context of the UN Global Compact) from nonbinding letters of intent into binding agreements. Up to that point, particular importance will have to be attached to concluding additional IFAs.

Cooperation not only will be necessary at the level of "big policy" but also must be effective on a smaller scale at the plant level and when trying to convince workers of the necessity of unionization. To increase the chances of such unionization, unions must overcome their inhibitions about cooperating with human rights and civil rights organizations, women's and environmental groups, and other NGOs. Close cooperation with these groups can increase the chances of successful unionization, particularly in CM plants, which have workforces that mainly consist of women and ethnic minorities, as is the case in the southern United States, where most of the workers are of Latin or Asian origin.

To give these groups of workers better and more democratic participation within union organizations, a change in union structures also might be required in some cases. Most obvious in this respect is increased cooperation with human rights groups, since the right to freedom of association and the right to freedom of collective bargaining are both fundamental social rights. Human rights must not stop at the plant gates, which is why close cooperation is in both movements' interest. At the same time, social human rights cannot thrive in an environment where general human rights are suppressed and not respected.

When it comes to cooperation with environmental groups, the situation is similar. Environmental protection is important both inside and outside of the plant. Reducing the use of hazardous substances, or even eliminating them altogether from both products and the production process also will have a positive impact on the environment outside of the plant.

It is important to develop a strategy for the IT industry, not only at the national level, but also, even more so, at the international level. The IMF has taken the first steps in this direction by setting up a task force with representatives of the most important affiliates to develop common strategies, policy approaches, and activities. The development of internationally coordinated organizing campaigns for specific companies could be considered as part of such a strategy. Plants where unions are already represented would have to be involved to a greater degree. In this context, European works councils, to be established on the basis of a European Union (EU) directive, could play a special role. An internationally coordinated organizing campaign at all of the sites operated by a particular company would have the advantage of producing far better publicity than a campaign in a plant somewhere in the world that mostly goes unnoticed and gives the company the opportunity to respond with such counter measures as threats of relocation and dismissal.

To successfully carry out such international activities, however, the unions involved must commit themselves to an agreed-on action plan. So far, this has been possible only within a very limited scope, because such an approach also would mean giving certain powers to the GUF in charge. At the same time, it would be necessary to prepare the ground for such an undertaking. In countries where several unions are competing for members in IT companies, these unions would need to agree on an organization to deal with possible requests for membership. In several other countries, it would be necessary to set up new unions, because workers in IT companies do not consider the existing unions as representing their interests, given their past policies, and perhaps their present ones as well.

The fragmentation of unions in many countries is one obstacle that can make efficient international union work rather difficult, as problems of national competition often are transferred to the international level. However, looking at the potential for and the necessity of a collective representation of IT workers' interests, much closer and more focused cooperation would be necessary at both national and international levels. Many IT workers show little understanding for this competition among national unions and Global Union Federations.

Successful international union work is also hindered by the unions' structures at the national level. Many unions do not integrate workers' representatives at the plant level into international initiatives and structures. This often impedes work in the "world company councils," the union bodies at the level of transnational companies. These world company councils are supposed to establish networks to facilitate union cooperation within a company, to gather and pass on information, and finally, to develop strategies.

World councils or world company councils that were established based on an agreement with the management of a transnational company only exist in three companies so far: at the two German automobile manufacturers (Volkswagen and DaimlerChrysler) and at SKF, the Swedish manufacturer of rolling bearings. In terms of structure, the intensity of cooperation between unions and workers' representatives at the plant level, and information given by management, Volkswagen has by far the most advanced model. The IMF's aim is to establish additional world councils based on agreements, because they can be crucial in internationalizing union cooperation.

Ultimately, however, it will be necessary for unions and union members, and particularly for union officials, to adopt a more international approach in their daily work. The unions' educational policy could contribute considerably to such development by incorporating this issue in their curricula and seminars. But such an approach must not be limited to the top ranks. Without including structures and "normal" members at the plant level, international cooperation will remain superficial.

CONCLUSION

Given the state of affairs presented here and elsewhere in this volume, the creation of labor and social standards in the manufacturing of IT products and components is clearly necessary. In this age of globalization, companies operate across national borders and are global players. Unfortunately, unions are still acting "nationally," even though they are members of international union organizations. In the next few years, building these structures will be of the utmost importance. To achieve this aim, unions also will have to look for allies and partners in politics and the general public, at both national and international levels. Unions share common interests with a number of international organizations and NGOs, which should make such cooperation possible. However, it will be necessary for many to "change their spots."

III. ELECTRONIC WASTE AND EXTENDED PRODUCER RESPONSIBILITY

LESLIE A. BYSTER AND WEN-LING TU

THE WORLD'S LANDFILLS are rapidly being filled with toxic waste from obsolete electronic and electrical equipment and accessories. The mountains of "e-waste" have been growing so rapidly that they have spawned dangerous new waste-salvaging operations in China, India, Pakistan, the Philippines, and other low-income countries. The European Union (EU) is instituting its new Directive on Waste from Electronics and Electrical Equipment (WEEE) in an attempt to curtail this tide of toxic junk. Electronics is at the forefront not only of manufacturing, occupational health, and environmental justice issues throughout the world, but also of the growing movement calling on manufacturers to take responsibility for their products' entire life cycles, up to and including disposal.

Product life-cycle analysis is integral to the movement for what has come to be known as *extended producer responsibility* (EPR). Among the distinct phases in the life cycles of electronics products are design, manufacturing, assembly, consumption, and disposal. Although earlier sections of this book have focused on the manufacturing and assembly phases, Part III focuses on links between the life cycle's "alpha" and "omega": product design and "end-of-life management." Until recently, few manufacturers in any sector have taken responsibility for what happens to their products once they become obsolete. In fact, *planned obsolescence* historically has been a key feature of the market-oriented, production–consumption life cycle.

Globalization of the entire electronics product life cycle has led to a disproportionate distribution of negative environmental and public health impacts to areas far from the locations of product design and product use. Locating suppliers and assemblers throughout the world has led to manufacturing efficiencies and low-cost products. Yet, too often, as production moves down the supply chain, toward regions with weaker environmental and occupational protection and enforcement, lower income and less powerful communities face the hazards of toxic exposure, from production to disposal. Indeed, the costs and consequences of product disposal are now globally distributed in ways that artificially reduce their true costs. These so-called life-cycle costs of computers and commercial electronics remain hidden from the public so that consumers and policymakers can easily ignore them. The challenges of managing global supply chains—even in cases where management is well intentioned—is daunting and is only beginning to be understood, much less addressed by the original equipment manufacturers (OEMs).

This emerging framework is being supplemented with new strategies by nongovernmental organizations (NGOs) working in the environmental policy arena as well as on international corporate campaigns to leverage environmental commitment and performance in the high-tech sector. Such campaigns are becoming an important counterbalance to the downward pressures of economic globalization. The effectiveness of environmental strategies to promote clean production, pollution prevention, and responsible control of e-waste flow, particularly in developing countries, still relies primarily on effective local environmental practices, monitoring, and enforcement.

Part III of this volume examines how these issues are intertwined when the products created by the electronics industry are discarded, resulting in huge quantities of e-waste destined for landfills or export (Puckett; Geiser and Tickner; Agarwal and Wankhade). It also examines grassroots efforts to address these concerns and proposes a "triad of sustainability" (environmental justice, the precautionary principle, and extended producer responsibility; Byster and Smith) as a framework for more enlightened corporate practices (Wood and Schneider) and environmental policy, both in the United States (Raphael and Smith) and globally (Geiser and Tickner; Tojo).

The chapter by Byster and Smith provides an overview of the impacts of high-tech production and offers examples of groundwater overuse and contamination that occurred as the industry expanded out of Silicon Valley, California. It asserts that given the industry's projected growth, its use of chemicals and resources is not sustainable; the authors therefore propose the triad of sustainability as a policy framework. Yoshida's chapter looks at past soil and groundwater contamination by Japan's high-tech manufacturing industry, as well as more recent efforts to remediate that toxic legacy. He finds that a strong legal infrastructure and active citizen involvement are essential to environmental protection and restoration.

Puckett examines the widespread practice of exporting hazardous electronic waste (e-waste) from the United States to China, India, and other low-wage, newly industrializing countries. He argues that such practices are unsustainable and unacceptable, even when euphemistically labeled as "recycling," job provision, or economic development. Challenging the existing economics and ethics of the international e-waste trade, Puckett provides convincing evidence that, by using Asia as a global e-waste dumping ground, electronics manufacturers and "recyclers" are externalizing the health and environmental impacts of hazardous, unprotected toxic disassembly processes to communities and workers in the recipient countries.

Agarwal and Wankhade examine the fast-growing computer and electronics recycling industry in Delhi, India. Through their firsthand field survey, they reveal the substandard conditions of recycling workers who are paid subsistence wages and possess little bargaining power. This case study exemplifies environmental injustice, as e-waste flows to the less environmentally regulated areas of the world for lower operational costs, less regulation, and lax monitoring. Such environmental struggles actually go beyond India, as other case studies in this volume demonstrate. The chapter also indicates that effective local monitoring efforts are essential to hold the global industry accountable for its worldwide, product-life-cycle operation.

Raphael and Smith examine EPR policy advocacy in the United States, highlighting the efforts of NGOs and analyzing the framing strategies that have effectively advanced the campaign. The chapter suggests that NGOs' creative strategic planning and campaign implementation can help turn globalization into a positive force for environmental and labor standard leverage.

Geiser and Tickner offer an overview and analysis of three international environmental policies: the Basel Convention on the Control of Transboundary Movement of Hazardous Wastes and Disposal, the EU's WEEE Directive, and the separate Registration, Evaluation, and Authorization of Chemicals (REACH). These authors argue that globalization offers a double-edged opportunity, in that, aside from its negative economic, social, and environmental impacts, globalization also presents us with a chance to "develop new international accountability structures and to engage people and government from around the world in positive efforts to manage industrial performance for social benefits." They demonstrate how these international environmental policies create incentives for the electronics industry to promote more environmentally benign products and to consider the product life cycle during the design phase.

Evaluation of EPR programs has not been well established. Thus the chapter by Tojo, which reports the factors in Sweden and Japan influencing product design and life-cycle management, is particularly valuable. Her research indicates that the presence of EPR already has provided measurable incentives for manufacturers to incorporate products' end-of-life considerations during the design phase.

Echoing the two previous chapters, Tojo finds that international EPR initiatives are essential to reduce the electronics industry's environmental impacts.

Part III concludes with the inspiring account of the U.S.-based "Computer TakeBack Campaign" (CTBC) and its successful efforts to challenge the country's leading computer company, Dell Computer. In their chapter, Wood and Schneider show how activists influenced corporate policies through "just-in-time" organizing and well-structured campaigning activities that became an effective means to hold computer producers environmentally and socially accountable. Dell's changes, strongly encouraged by the CTBC's campaigning, suggest that the industry can move in more sustainable directions, but that grassroots activism will continue to be the key driving force in making such changes.

Leslie A. Byster and Ted Smith

18   The Electronics Production Life Cycle

From Toxics to Sustainability: Getting Off the
Toxic Treadmill

The information age has been fueled by an exponential increase in the production of high-tech electronic components, including semiconductors, integrated circuits, disk drives, printed circuit boards, video display equipment, and many other consumer products. As electronics manufacturing has expanded out of its birthplace in Silicon Valley and proliferated around the globe, so too, has the number of facilities manufacturing the materials and chemicals used in the production process, in waste treatment, and in waste disposal.

The high-tech industry's unprecedented globalization has been facilitated by the development and adoption of trade agreements such as the Multilateral Agreement on Initiatives and Central America Free Trade Agreement and institutions as the World Trade Organization. As the "incubator" of the global electronics industry, Silicon Valley served as a textbook case for other cities, states, and even nations seeking the "silicon" blueprint to recreate the wealth and prosperity of California's Silicon Valley.

Shattering the Myths

Although electronics manufacturing has carefully cultivated the image of a clean, smokestack-free industry with relatively few environmental or occupational health hazards, the reality is starkly different. During the past 25 years in Silicon Valley, as well as in other regions where the industry is operating, many production-related environmental and occupational health hazards have been identified and addressed. More recently, a new threat has been uncovered: the growing piles of electronic waste created by rapid product obsolescence.

Personal computers (PCs) and other electronic equipment are astonishingly resource-intensive to produce. Massive amounts of chemicals, water, and energy are required in the production process. Most people are astonished to learn that the manufacture of a single silicon chip requires 1.7 kilograms of fossil fuels and chemicals and 32 kilograms of water (Williams, Ayers, and Heller 2002). Likewise, it is difficult for most people to believe that about 1.8 tons of raw materials are required to manufacture the average desktop PC and monitor (Kuehr and Williams 2003).

Manufacturing a single PC involves a witch's brew of over a thousand chemicals, many of which are known or suspected carcinogens or reproductive toxins. These high-tech toxics have been linked to elevated rates of cancer and birth defects among workers and community residents in a growing number of high-tech centers around the world, and substantial groundwater contamination has become part of the "legacy" of the industry's development.

This chapter presents an overview of the environmental impacts of electronics manufacturing—inside and outside the workplace. It also proposes that a "triad of sustainability"—based on environmental justice (EJ), the precautionary principle, and extended producer responsibility (EPR)—must be integrated into business practices and become as global in the culture and conduct of electronics manufacturing as is the industry itself.

WATER USE AND CONTAMINATION

It has been well documented that semiconductor chip manufacturing requires vast amounts of water. As a consequence of the industry's insatiable thirst, groundwater reserves in many high-tech regions have been depleted and contaminated by the chip-making process. The Silicon Valley story has received significant attention and is described in more detail elsewhere in this book (see Byster and Smith, "From Grassroots to Global"; Hawes and Pellow; Pellow and Matthews, this volume).

As dozens of high-tech electronics companies established semiconductor fabrication facilities ("fabs") in Silicon Valley and later in the new "Silicons," New Mexico and Arizona (two of the most arid states in the United States), the technology boom was accompanied by the telltale footprints of electronics manufacturing—the twin problems of water contamination and overuse.

In Arizona (Silicon Desert), the groundwater near Phoenix was contaminated by a Motorola chip plant. The 15-mile-long toxic plume of trichloroethylene (TCE) is 500 feet deep in some places (Plazola 1997, 47). Three of the seven Superfund sites in the Phoenix area are the result of high-tech manufacturing pollution and 46 of the 98 groundwater wells that have been closed were due to high-tech contamination, mostly from chlorinated solvents. Based on available supplies and projected growth rates, the demand for water will exceed supply by 2010 due, in part, to this contamination, the projected population growth, and the industry's demands (Plazola 1997, 42).

The Intel plant near Albuquerque, New Mexico (Silicon Mesa), has used nearly 1.6 billion gallons per year (Harttranft 1996). The projected increase to 2.1 billion gallons may impact water sources, including the Colorado River, and threatens to deplete the traditional irrigation canal, or *acequia*, system. Polluted groundwater sites in Albuquerque contaminated by electronics plants include Sparton Technology and GTE Lenkurt (Plazola 1997, 77–88).

WORKER HEALTH

Electronic equipment is manufactured from a complicated mixture of thousands of materials, including chlorinated and brominated substances, photoactive chemicals, toxic gases, acids, solvents, heavy metals, plastics, and plastic additives, many of which impose a heavy burden on the environment and worker health. Microelectronics is considered "light" manufacturing because it causes fewer injuries than in heavy manufacturing. However, occupational *illnesses* occur at a much higher rate among electronics workers than among those working in heavy manufacturing (LaDou 1994; see also LaDou, this volume). This high rate of occupational illnesses is due to the widespread use of toxic chemicals that have both additive and synergistic effects that are still neither well characterized nor understood. The chemicals that workers are exposed to include known and suspected carcinogens, and reproductive, neurologic, and immune system toxins. Cancer clusters for such diseases as brain tumors, non-Hodgkin's lymphomas, testicular cancer, and advanced uterine and cervical cancers have been discovered among engineers and manufacturing employees at IBM's facilities in San Jose, California, and Fishkill, New York (see Hawes and Pellow; LaDou, this volume). Similar problems are emerging in Scotland, Taiwan, and other high-tech centers around the globe (see McCourt; Chang, Chiu, and Tu; Pandita; Watterson, this volume; see also Fox 1991).

As global competitiveness increases and the rate of change (the acceleration in the design and development of new chips) in the electronics industry escalates, the challenge of protecting the environment and workers' health likewise grows. Developing the ability to anticipate and prevent problems in an industry that uses so many toxic chemicals is a daunting task. Dr. Myron Harrison, a former occupational health physician for IBM, has seen firsthand the human health problems in workers exposed to hazardous materials in the workplace. In his article "Semiconductor Manufacturing Hazards," he describes the profound implications of this rapidly changing industrial culture:

> The executives who manage microelectronic businesses are now demanding the schedule [of a new technology from research and development to pilot lines to full manufacturing] be compressed into a 2-3 year time frame.... Unfortunately, the opportunities for [health and safety] professionals to be involved [in understanding new or unusual health hazards] before these new processes arrive at the manufacturing floor are being diminished by the quickening pace of technologic change. Any large semiconductor facility uses several thousand chemicals. Any attempt to review the toxicology of all these materials is doomed to be superficial and of little value.... (Harrison 1992, 490)

Dr. Harrison's anxiety was prompted, in large part, by the business strategy driven by Intel, which makes each new generation of chip technology obsolete as rapidly as possible. As Andrew Grove, the founder of Intel, said at the launching of Intel's P6 chip: "This is what we do. We eat our own children, and we do it faster and faster.... That's how we keep our lead" (Ramstad 1994, B-6).

Three health studies that linked miscarriages to worker exposure to toxic chemical were conducted in the 1980s and 1990s—at the Digital Equipment Corporation (DEC; see Pastides et al. 1988), IBM (see Gray 1993), and by the Semiconductor Industry Association (SIA; see Schenker 1992), respectively. These studies notwithstanding, for many years the SIA turned a deaf ear to calls by workers, community members and occupational health professionals for the industry to undertake a thorough epidemiological study. In 2005, after years of stalling, the SIA awarded a contract to Vanderbilt University to undertake the first retrospective epidemiological cancer study among the world's semiconductor workers (Mokhoff 2005).

Although the DEC, IBM, and SIA studies showed an increase in miscarriages among women in certain parts of the semiconductor manufacturing process, the overall health of workers throughout the entire production chain—from the mining of raw materials, to the manufacture of chemicals, to the fabrication of components, to the handling of waste products, to the disposal of electronic equipment—has not been estimated. Because cancers, birth defects, and other health problems resulting from exposure to chemicals may take 30 years to manifest, health professionals and workers are concerned that we may be seeing just the tip of the iceberg (see LaDou 1994, 1996; and LaDou; Hawes and Pellow; and Watterson, this volume). To protect the next generation of children and to prevent further pain and injury, it is essential that comprehensive and credible health studies are undertaken and that the most toxic substances are removed from the workplace.

ENERGY DEMANDS

Enormous resources are required to manufacture semiconductor chips. In addition to the huge amount of chemicals used and discharged at Intel's Rio Rancho plant near Albuquerque, New Mexico (estimated at more than 1.8 million pounds of hazardous waste and 738 million gallons of waste water), it was projected that the plant would require more than 74.1 million kilowatt hours of electric power (see Table 18.1). The annual water and energy demands for one fab alone equal those for a midsize, advanced industrial city (DeJule 1998). As dozens of new fabs are constructed around the world, resource consumption and discharges of this scale will continue to grow.

TABLE 18.1. Semiconductor Manufacturing Resource Requirements

	One 6-inch Wafer[a]	Intel Rio Rancho NM[b] (5,000/Weeks × 52 Weeks)	Projected 120 New Fabs[c]
Input			
Bulk gases (cu. ft.)	3200	832,000,000	99,840,000,000
Hazardous gases (cu. ft.)	22	5,720,000	6,864,000,000
Deionized water (gals.)	2,275	5,200,000	624,000,000
Electrical power (kw/hr)	285	74,100,000	8,892,000,000
Output			
Sodium hydroxide (lbs)	25	6,500,000	780,000,000
Waste water, pH 6–9 (gals)	2840	738,400,000	88,608,000,000
Hazardous waste (lbs)	7	1,820,000	218,400,000

[a]*Source:* "Environmental Consciousness: A Strategic Competitive Issue for the Electronics and Computer Industry, March 1993," cited in Larrabee (1993).

[b]Projections by the authors, based on Larrabee (1993) and SWOP's (1995, 50) estimated full production for Intel's Rio Rancho plant of 5,000 eight-inch wafers per week. These projections should be taken as rough only.

[c]Projections by the authors, based on Larrabee (1993) and SWOP (1995, 50), plus DeJule's (1998) estimated number of new fabs.

Unless there is major shift to sustainable practices, it is anticipated this growth will continue to demand resources that may threaten workers' health, as well as their local environments and communities.

Industry Growth

The SIA argues that "because of its amazing growth and sheer size, the chip industry has become a pivotal driver of the world economy" (quoted in Barrett 1997). The electronics industry's rapid expansion in the mid- and late 1990s was accompanied by new corporate strategies which played communities off against each other. Although communities sought the "silicon prize," companies were searching for the highest level of public subsidies. Intel, in fact, developed an "Ideal Incentive Matrix," with the 100-plus subsidies and benefits it wanted from one of the six states that would be the site of the Pentium V chip plant in the late 1990s. These states, including California and New Mexico, then began a bidding war with each other in an Intel-inspired "race to the bottom." After New Mexico offered an estimated "$250 million in direct tax abatement and subsidies *in the first five years alone*" (SWOP 1995, 45, emphasis in original), Intel opted to build its new plant in the United States' third poorest state.

In the late 1990s, Intel was among the companies leading the exodus to the low-wage options found in India and China. In recent decades, high-tech manufacturing has expanded to nearly every country in Western Europe, as well as to countries in Eastern and Central Europe, Asia, Israel, Costa Rica, Puerto Rico, Mexico, Brazil, and Canada (see Lüthje; Ferus-Comelo; Watterson; García and Simpson; and Partida, this volume). The expansion over the past decade has been mostly into the developing world; this time the companies are playing off countries against each other. Although Asia at one time may have been the primary site for low-end electronics production, currently Asia is a producer of advanced products. According to SIA's Web site, "China is now the largest market for cellular handsets, representing 20 percent of demand, and the second largest market for personal computers. South Korea has the most advanced nationwide cellular network in the world" (SIA n.d.; see also Lüthje, this volume).

Planned Obsolescence

The demand for newer and faster equipment and products is being driven by the rapid expansion of the Internet- and industry-marketing campaigns that promote the latest—often unnecessary—fads and new fashions. The industry's fast-paced competition makes many high-tech products obsolete within months and is related to Moore's Law (see Wood and Schneider, this volume), which refers to Intel founder Gordon Moore's prediction in 1965 that the computing power of electronics would double every 18 months to two years (see Figure 18.1). Clearly, Intel, which controls more than 80 percent of the microprocessor market, understands that it must generate demand for its products as it creates a new product line every six to eighteen months

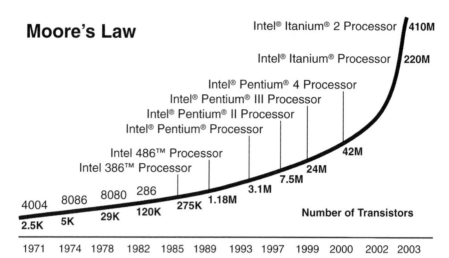

FIGURE 18.1. Moore's Law.
Source: Adapted from "Moore's Law, The Future—Technology and Research," available at http://www.intel.com/technology/silicon/mooreslaw.

to maintain its near-monopoly position. When Intel unveiled its Pentium II chip in 1997, their marketing campaign was reinvigorated with the "dancing bunnies" ads. The company spent US$100 million in one fiscal quarter alone to promote the Pentium II (Reinhart 1997).

Other commercials were used to alert consumers to the P3 and P4 processors in the late 1990s. When Intel's Centrino chip was introduced in 2003, it brought new capabilities to the wireless mobile community and attempted to satisfy the demand for "anywhere, anytime" computing access (Intel 2005a). On the fortieth anniversary of Moore's Law, Intel continues to extol the promises of economic growth and health based on their silicon expertise (see Intel 2005a).

COMPUTER DUMPING

In the United States, roughly 60 million new computers are purchased each year, whereas worldwide sales top 130 million per year (UNU 2004). However, the industry's strategy of rapid product obsolescence, which creates an endless demand for new hardware and software, also creates enormous amounts of outdated electronic consumer products that require disposal. If the full force of the electronics revolution hits the landfills, its health and environmental effects will leave no community untouched.

Electronic waste ("e-waste") is the fastest growing waste stream and already accounts for 5 percent of all solid waste in the United States, as well as approximately 40 percent of the lead, 70 percent of the heavy metals, and a significant portion of the pollutants in U.S. dumps. The threats to soil, drinking water, and human health will grow as e-waste surges into the waste stream (see Puckett; Agarwal and Wankhade; Wood and Schneider, this volume).

Today, most of it ends up in landfills or incinerators. In the United States, more than 12 million computers, amounting to more than 300,000 tons of electronic junk, are disposed of annually.

A small portion of obsolete electronics is currently refurbished and recycled in the United States, but much is shipped to China. These practices were well documented in a report and video entitled, "Exporting Harm," released by the Basel Action Network and the Silicon Valley Toxics Coalition in 2002 (see Puckett, this volume). The manufacturing by-products and the disposed products cause great concern in communities throughout the world and raise important political, technical, environmental, and financial issues that are being addressed in new policy initiatives, such as EPR (see Geiser and Tickner; Tojo; Raphael and Smith, this volume).

WHERE DO WE GO FROM HERE? THE TRIAD OF SUSTAINABILITY

Due to characteristics of the electronics production lifecycle such as those described in this volume, community organizations and NGOs view the industry's rapid expansion and push for streamlined environmental regulations with skepticism and grave concern. It is clear that there is no global governance mechanism that can effectively address the environmental and health impacts resulting from the high-tech industry's global expansion. We propose, therefore, that environmental protection and sustainable community development in the twenty-first century must incorporate and synthesize three important principles: environmental justice (EJ), the precautionary principle, and EPR.

Environmental Justice

Communities are increasingly on the defensive when industries make plans to move in, as the industries typically are promoted as the much-needed engines of economic and community development. The granting of building permits, permission to release water into the wastewater discharge facilities, may be given with little citizen involvement and participation in the permitting process. Clearly, new strategies are needed to provide meaningful community participation in the decision-making process and to ensure greater community and worker protection. It will take more authentic and informed participation and engagement from affected communities and workers to assure that new industrial development is truly sustainable.

Over the past two decades, the EJ movement has emerged in response to the concerns raised by low-income communities and communities of color, which unfairly bear the brunt of environmental hazards. The engine of the EJ movement is grassroots organizing by affected community members and is grounded in the right of people of all races, incomes and cultures to have environments where we can safely work, play, learn, and pray. EJ demands that those people who are most affected by toxic exposure have the right to effectively participate in the decisions that affect their lives. The First National People of Color Environmental Leadership Summit in 1991 brought together EJ groups from across the United States. One of the outcomes of this meeting in Washington DC was the creation and adoption of the Principles of Environmental Justice (see Appendix A, this volume). These principles have provided the basis for the work of many organizations in this volume.

In 1994, President Clinton signed an executive order on environmental justice to focus federal attention on environmental and human health conditions in low-income communities and communities of color. This order called for providing affected communities with access to public information and opportunities to participate in matters relating to their members' human health and environment. The National Environmental Justice Advisory Council—a U.S. federal advisory committee established in 1993 to provide recommendations to the administrator of the U.S. Environmental Protection Agency on matters related to EJ—developed principles to assure meaningful public participation by those most affected (Office of the President 1994). EJ groups are actively working to implement these principles throughout the United States, although under the Bush administration, the federal government has failed to live up to the executive order's promise.

The Precautionary Principle

The precautionary principle, incorporated in the Rio Declaration that was adopted at the 1992 United Nations' Conference on Environment and Development in Brazil, declares that the starting point for environmental sustainability is based on protection against "irreversible environmental damage" even in the absence of "full scientific certainty."[1] Within the chemical manufacturing culture, the absence of toxicity data is often taken to be proof of safety. The precautionary principle created a new dynamic in looking at environmental and community health by shifting the burden of proof when uncertainty exists. It gives the benefit of the doubt to nature, public health and community well-being. By serving as guide when making decisions that minimize harm, it purports that a substance or chemical should assumed to be hazardous until proven it is safe. It puts forth the practice of monitoring results, heeding warnings, and taking further action if needed to prevent harm (Montague 2005).

Five years after the adoption of the precautionary principle, the Environmental Defense Fund (EDF) replicated a study first undertaken by the U.S. National Research Council in 1984. When EDF conducted its follow-up study in 1997, it also chose 100 chemicals that were produced in quantities greater than one million pounds *and* were the subject of regulatory attention. More than half of the chemicals had not been tested for any form of chronic toxicity (see Montague 1997). The results of the survey were disturbing:

- 63 percent of the chemicals were missing carcinogenicity tests;
- 53 percent of the chemicals lacked reproductive toxicity data;
- 67 percent of the chemicals lacked neurotoxicity data;
- 86 percent of the chemicals lacked immune system toxicity data; and
- 90 percent of the chemicals had no data on their impacts on children.

As the chemical industry continues to grow, and new chemicals are introduced into commerce without adequate testing, it is ever more necessary to strengthen the precautionary principle as a cornerstone of public health. Although the chemical industry and its governmental allies continue to resist efforts to implement the precautionary principle, support for the precautionary principle continues to grow within the global grassroots movement.

Extended Producer Responsibility

EPR focuses on the responsibility that producers of products—especially those that contain hazardous materials—must be responsible for the entire life cycles of their products, especially at the products' end of life (the post-consumer stage). The model example of EPR is called "takeback"—where a producer takes back a product at the end of its useful life (i.e., when discarded), either directly or through a third party. EPR creates incentives for manufacturers to reduce environmental impacts throughout the lifecycles of their products. By extending corporate responsibility throughout the entire product lifecycle, EPR is already having wide-ranging effects on the electronics industry. The aim of EPR is to encourage producers to prevent pollution and reduce resource and energy use at each stage of the product lifecycle through changes in product design and process technology. In its widest sense, producer responsibility is the principle that producers bear a degree of responsibility for all of their products' environmental impacts. This includes upstream impacts arising from the choice of materials and from the manufacturing process, as well as downstream impacts due to the products' use and disposal. However, product take-back needs to go hand in hand with legislation to provide a level playing field and to require the phase-out of toxics used in electronics production. Europe has led the way in developing innovative legislation to promote producer responsibility with the Waste from Electrical and Electronic Products (WEEE) directive and the Restriction on Hazardous Substances (ROHS) directive. See Raphael and Smith and Geiser and Tickner (this volume), for more on the impact of the European EPR legislation in the United States.

Toward a Sustainable Future

The notion that corporate-led globalization is inevitable and unavoidable is a mantra promulgated by multinational corporations and industrialized countries; so is the idea that the ever-increasing pace of the development of technology and electronics industries is a positive pathway to the future. But globalization is human made. It reflects economic, social, and political choices and policies that need to be scrutinized and debated. When these choices do not serve human needs and community interests, they should be challenged and replaced with more people-friendly and sustainable alternatives, ones that embrace the possibility of a true bottom-up, people-led grassroots globalization based on people-to-people ties and actions to promote the global common good.

In this era of globalization, the business model of transnational high-tech growth is too often based on fundamentally unsustainable, short-term thinking that creates rapid obsolescence; depends on unrealistic and inflated, short-term profit margins; and pushes for just-in-time production schedules to avoid creating large and costly inventories. Too often these business imperatives take priority over the immediate concerns of workplace safety, wage benefits, and community health. Furthermore, they are frequently detrimental to the environment and workers' and residents' long-range health. As high-tech companies continue to expand, and trade initiatives increase corporate profits and truly globalize the electronics economy, we are likely to see the increasing social and environmental costs to communities and countries around the world unless new international cooperative and collaborative efforts emerge. The dual danger we face is due to escalating corporate subsidies and a truly international race to the bottom in terms of workers' benefits, health, and safety, as well as the quality of the environment.

To prevent such socially and environmentally disastrous outcomes of the information revolution, the electronics industry must reassess its dominant, short-term business strategy. It must face the challenge of embracing its true long-range corporate responsibilities to meet the highest standards for workers and the environment as aggressively and comprehensively as it does its new product development. It must develop sustainable manufacturing processes and a development model that can address today's needs, as well as those of future generations. As the industry plans each new generation of chips, we all have a stake in planning for the next generation of healthy children, a healthy environment, and a healthy economy.

NOTE

1. Principle 15, Rio Declaration on Environment and Development, June 1992.

19   High-Tech Pollution in Japan

Growing Problems, Alternative Solutions

THROUGHOUT JAPAN, there are plans to redevelop idled urban factory sites and vacant lots that were abandoned after land prices rose during the "bubble" years of the late 1980s. Such efforts have spotlighted a major barrier: the soil and groundwater contamination at brownfields (former factory and waste management sites; see *Japan Times* 2001). The Geo-Environmental Protection Center has estimated that Japan has 400,000 sites with soil contaminated by organic solvents, heavy metals, and toxic substances like PCBs, which would require ¥13 trillion (about US$126 billion) to remediate (Yoshida 2002).

High-tech pollution was discovered in the early 1980s. Events during the ensuing decade revealed soil and groundwater contamination from the production of electronics, cell phones, and lenses in copy machines and other office equipment. Table 19.1 lists the number of sites contaminated with solvents. Some pioneering efforts have been dealing with this widening contamination. Examples include Chiba Prefecture's Kimitsu City, which is working on remediation through exhaustive studies of pollution sources and information disclosure; and Kanagawa Prefecture's Hadano City, which passed a groundwater protection ordinance and is pursuing groundwater remediation on its own (Figure 19.1; see Hadano City 1993, 1996).

WHAT IS HIGH-TECH POLLUTION?

Japan has suffered severe pollution from traditional sources, such as chemical plants, resulting in Minimata disease, and mining sites, resulting in Itai-Itai disease. The microelectronics industry is envisioned as a clean, smokestack-free industry with few occupational illnesses. But what is the real story?

- First of all, "clean" means only "without dust," and the object is to keep the materials and parts used for making semiconductors "clean." The "cleanliness" of the workplace and the environment surrounding semiconductor factories is another issue.
- Apart from the apparent waste of water and gases, the industrial waste and garbage, as well as leaks from "storage" tanks or other abandoned sites of used solvents, are major causes of pollution.
- Groundwater plays an important role as a route for pollution.
- The semiconductor industry uses many toxic chemicals, gases, and radioactive rays, which can cause serious chemical pollution, even in very small amounts.

Table 19.1. Disclosed Cases of IT-Related Solvent Pollution in Japan, 2002

Company	Sites Polluted with Organic Solvent
Panasonic	20
Murata	14
Mitsubishi	11
Sony	11
Epson	10
Ricoh	10
Toshiba	8
Minolta	5
Sharp	4
NEC	2
Fuji Xerox	2

Source: Corporate environmental reports.

- Because high technology changes very fast and trade secrets abound, corresponding environmental protection methods tend to be delayed, as they are several steps behind the technology.

SEMICONDUCTOR GROUNDWATER CONTAMINATION

Japan's First High-Tech Pollution

Taishi-cho in Hyogo Prefecture (near Osaka) was Japan's first known case of groundwater contamination by a semiconductor plant. Taishi-cho, located

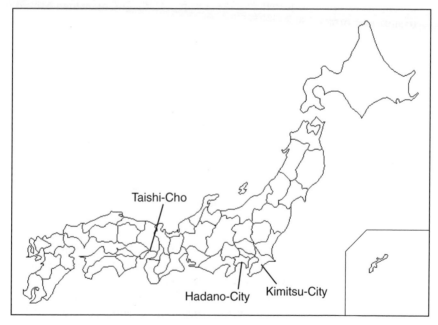

Figure 19.1. Map of Japan and High-tech Pollution Sites.
Source: Author.

west of Himeji City, has a population of 30,000 and hosts Toshiba and other companies. A large portion of Taishi-cho and its drinking-water sources became contaminated with trichloroethylene (TCE), and about one-fourth of its wells did not meet environmental quality standards (Hyogo Prefecture 1995; Ichihashi et al. 1992). Toshiba's Taishi Plant (officially known as the Himeji Semiconductor Plant), which used TCE for cleaning semiconductors and cathode ray tubes, was another source of pollution. Similar to groundwater contamination in Silicon Valley (see Byster and Smith, "From Grassroots to Global," this volume), the likely cause consisted of leaks from underground storage tanks, but the plant has not released that information. The plant remediated about 1,000 square meters of contaminated soil, but the groundwater was detected at a depth of seven meters, whereupon the digging stopped.

Removing the soil to a shallow depth lowered the TCE concentration in shallow wells on plant grounds to below the required level for drinking water quality (30 parts per billion [ppb]), but deep wells still have high concentrations of about 1,000 ppb. Tests on wells in the surrounding area revealed high concentrations of not only TCE, but also *cis*-1,2-dichloroethylene (DCE), which is believed to be formed from TCE.

Remaining Challenges

Much work remains to be done at Taishi-cho. First, contaminated soil has not been sufficiently removed. Because Toshiba could not quickly perform an exhaustive investigation to determine the reason for soil contamination, the TCE contamination will remain for a long time. In some cases it will be necessary to remediate soil after removing buildings where contamination occurred. In Silicon Valley, for example, Fairchild Semiconductor dug to a depth of 40 meters and installed barriers to prevent the pollution's spread.

Nevertheless, in its "Environment Report 2000," Toshiba announced that it will develop a "Deep Well Remediation Implementation Plan" and dig eight wells to pump up groundwater, install remediation equipment to treat the groundwater with activated carbon, and dig seven monitoring wells to observe the effects of its efforts. After groundwater contamination was revealed, Taishi-cho supplied drinking water from its wells after first air stripping it to volatilize the TCE. Private wells were replaced by tapwater in Taishi-cho. Toshiba's Taishi Plant has not officially admitted responsibility for the contamination, maintaining that the money it paid to fund the water supply switchover is a "contribution."

The case of Toshiba's Taishi Plant shows that partial attempts at finding the cause and engaging in the remediation allowed the pollution continue. This response differed from that of another Toshiba-affiliated plant in Kimitsu City because the local government's position was affected by the community's high dependence on Toshiba. Some city council members were affiliated with Toshiba and only a council member from Japan's Communist Party criticized Toshiba's response.

Japan's Remediation Experience

Tracing the Pollution Pathway

Groundwater contamination in Kimitsu City, Chiba Prefecture, near Tokyo, shocked the entire country and prompted the 1989 partial amendment (groundwater regulation) of the Water Pollution Control Law. The city's efforts to determine how soil and groundwater contamination spread and its full-blown remediation initiative became a model for the rest of the country. Toshiba Components' Kimitsu Plant (with about 500 employees) used TCE in its automobile rectifier semiconductor process. A water-quality check of Kimitsu's public water-supply source in spring 1987 revealed groundwater contamination, which was announced to the public in September 1988.

In Kimitsu's case, experts from Chiba Prefecture's Water Quality Protection Institute participated. Based on new ideas about geopollution (contamination of sedimentary strata, groundwater, and subterranean air; see Nirei et al. 1994; Suzuki 1993), they conducted Japan's most detailed investigation of the contamination route and developed a remediation technology to cope with it. The contamination's origins were traced using the Kimitsu surface-contamination investigation method, which was developed onsite. It revealed seven hot spots with high-density contamination distributions. Aerial photographs showed the year-by-year change in factories, and employee interviews revealed the following:

- Wastes were disposed in an underground dump (near Well no. 5).
- Leaks and spills occurred when filling TCE tanks (at three locations: First Manufacturing Section, Second Manufacturing Section, and Building no. 36).
- Leaks and spills occurred when transferring waste TCE (near the cafeteria).
- Leaks and spills occurred when transporting waste TCE (over the route from the Second Manufacturing Section to near the cafeteria).
- TCE discarded clean work clothing and other items (the road running by the warehouse).

The contamination was caused by aboveground leaks and spills in facilities, as well as by an underground source. These causes were probably found at many other businesses using TCE at that time.

Remediation Measures

Proper remediation measures were designed after determining the origins of pollution. Kimitsu's experience in remediation is described in the following section, as its solution is worth examining. First, to remove the contaminants, the city removed wastes, excavated, and removed contaminated geologic strata. The strata were treated by heating and air drying, which volatilized the TCE, and then removing it. To deal with groundwater contamination, the city pumped contaminated water using "catch basin" wells, blew air into the water to volatilize the TCE, and absorbed it with activated carbon. Subterranean air pollution was removed through a soil-vapor extraction method that dropped air pressure, thereby vaporizing and capturing the TCE. Recovered TCE was partly reused and partly incinerated as industrial waste.

Second, to prevent the spread of contaminants from plant grounds into the city, steel sheet piles were used to block underground contamination, and a system of barrier wells was dug to pump contaminated water before it could spread. This removed contaminants and contaminated groundwater from the soil and aquifer. Third, the city removed contaminants that spread to the aquifer by TCE air stripping. At another location, the city was conducting an experiment using bioremediation to break down TCE. This thoroughgoing remediation program considerably reduced the groundwater concentration of TCE (Kobayashi 1993).

The Experience and Lessons of Kimitsu

Kimitsu City is a groundwater contamination remediation model for all of Japan. Information on pollution is now released to the public because the citizens complained that news about groundwater contamination had been kept from the public for nearly 18 months. To date, the studies and remediation cost nearly ¥1.2 billion (about US$12 million). Following the "polluter pays" principle, the city paid about ¥5 million (about US$50,000), and Toshiba paid the rest. Health examinations for Kimitsu residents continue in an effort to investigate health damage. Examinations so far have uncovered no irregularities attributable to the groundwater contamination, but as a result of negotiations with the Uchiminowa Groundwater Contamination Committee (a community organization representing about 300 households and 1,000 individuals), in April 1992, Toshiba Components agreed to pay ¥37 million (about US$360,000) compensation for groundwater contamination. However, this payment does not cover any health damages that may arise in the future.

Kimitsu City released information on how it had found its contamination sources and remediation techniques (Kimitsu City, Department of Environment 1993), which brought a stream of visitors from throughout the country. Kimitsu's example shows that complete information disclosure, and remediation based on the scientific elucidation of pollution sources, will lead to fundamental solutions.

GROUNDWATER REMEDIATION UNDER AN ORDINANCE

In addition to Kimitsu City, there are many other municipalities throughout Japan using groundwater for their public water supplies that are working actively to solve soil and groundwater contamination problems. Hadano, a city of 160,000 people in Kanagawa Prefecture, stands at the foot of the Tanzawa Mountains and is known for the "Hadano Basin Springs," which include the "Spring of Kukai" (named after the famous Buddhist priest Kukai, who supposedly created it by striking the ground with his staff). Since 1890, when this "city of water and verdure" became the third in the nation to have waterworks, 70 percent of its public water supply has depended on groundwater. The municipality has 60 public wells, 31 water distribution stations, and many private wells.

In 1989, a photojournalism magazine revealed that the Spring of Kukai was contaminated with 34 ppb of tetrachloroethylene (PCE). Although that in itself was a shocking revelation, a national, public water-supply-quality survey showed that organochlorine contamination of the spring already had exceeded the standard in 1983. After the 1989 media story, Hadano City installed air-stripping equipment at four water distribution stations and convinced people to switch from private well water to tap water. An industrial park hosting many companies using organochlorines is located in the groundwater recharge area in the basin's center, and the contaminated zone covers about 12 square kilometers of urban land on both sides of the Mizunashi River, which flows through the city center. In 1990, the city authority began a study to determine the source of contamination, which involved taking boring samples, drilling wells, and monitoring the situation.

Meanwhile, according to pollution prevention agreements, city authorities conducted onsite inspections of companies using organochlorines. These inspections proved that the city views its responsibility for protecting groundwater quality seriously. As a result of these efforts, by 1992, 58 companies stopped using organochlorines, 28 switched to other substances, 31 improved their methods of use, and 27 improved their storage methods. In an effort to obtain a general picture of groundwater contamination, city authorities performed shallow soil surveys at the city's expense on the grounds of 131 companies that had been using organochlorines. Contamination was detected at 63 companies, most of which manufactured electric and transport machinery and tools and metal products. To determine the degree of contamination, again at its own expense, the city conducted "basic surveys" that included boring at these 63 companies in 1991. Proprietors of the 45 companies with high contamination levels then were required to conduct "detailed surveys" at their own expense to work on remediation.

Remediation has been completed at 38 companies, and the recovered organochlorine solvents amounted to about 16 tons. These groundwater remediation efforts and dialysis remediation projects (in which contaminated groundwater is pumped up, remediated, and then returned to the aquifer) quickly improved the water quality of springs in the Hadano Basin and gradually narrowed the geographical extent of groundwater contamination. Now even the water quality of the Spring of Kukai nearly satisfies environmental quality standards (EQS).

Many major high-tech manufacturers and their affiliates are located in Hadano City's industrial park, which is suspected to be the groundwater contamination source. Hadano has not released the names of the sites that are remediating groundwater because (1) groundwater contamination has multiple sources making it difficulty to determine, with certainty, to what degree each company is polluting; and (2) because Article 73 of the Groundwater Protection Ordinance stipulates that the names of "unscrupulous violators" who do not follow city guidance must be released, the city is refraining from releasing the names of business facilities that comply. Nevertheless, the polluting companies' names are a matter of public knowledge because of their remediation activities.

The Japanese Superfund

As Hadano City heavily depends on groundwater for its tapwater supply, it has a Groundwater Use Cooperation Payment System, which requires businesses using groundwater to pay a cooperation fee for helping conserve water. Groundwater contamination also led Hadano City to be the first municipality in the nation to pass a Groundwater Contamination Prevention and Remediation Ordinance (changed in 2000 to the Groundwater Protection Ordinance), which is known as the "Japanese Superfund" (*Asahi Shimbun* 2002).

Under this ordinance, when businesses use organic solvents or other regulated substances, they must properly manage those substances and prevent groundwater contamination. In the event that contamination does occur, they must perform remediation in accordance with the polluter-pays principle. Another purpose of the ordinance is to establish a fund, whose sources include contributions and city funds, to run remediation projects. This is a pioneering program in Japan that deserves a positive assessment.

From 1989 to 2000, Hadano City spent nearly ¥670 million (about US$6.5 million) on groundwater contamination studies and has built a fund of about ¥80 million (about US$800,000) for studies and remediation. The city's projects to remediate underground contamination have cost 30 times less than originally estimated in 1991; however, due to the inexpensive and efficient systems developed for the small and medium-size firms involved in the clean-up effort. Because the high-tech industrial park is located directly at the aquifer recharge area, the groundwater was contaminated with multiple substances. This situation is not unique to Hadano. If other municipalities were to conduct the same studies, they would likewise find groundwater contamination.

High-tech IT pollution is now found in plants making various electronic components, such as cell phones and office equipment. In places where high-tech pollution emerged ten years ago in Japan, there are municipalities like Kimitsu City, which fully disclosed information, performed exhaustive studies to determine contamination sources, and actively pushed remediation forward. At the same time, there are places like Taishi-cho, which economically depend on one company and have no clear prospects for remediation and recovery.

Hadano City and other municipalities with a high dependence on groundwater passed protection ordinances and remediated their groundwater because they consider it a valuable resource. However, many municipalities tend to take the easy way out by switching to tapwater systems and abandoning their valuable groundwater once it becomes largely contaminated. It is important to emphasize that contamination is not just a problem with groundwater, but one of the entire soil-groundwater system. Treating soil-groundwater system contamination requires the creation of a soil and groundwater protection law that provides the basis for studies, remediation, and information disclosure.

ELIMINATING HIGH-TECH POLLUTION

This section considers efforts that should be undertaken to eliminate soil and groundwater contamination by high-tech manufacturing; it specifically addresses the institutions and ideas that are needed.

Determining the Extent of Contamination

Some people estimate that there are as many as 400,000 locations with soil and groundwater contamination, so the first thing to do is to determine the locations and extents of contamination in order to take further remediation actions. The examples cited previously show that, except for places that rely heavily on groundwater, few municipalities actively assess the extent of their problems and carry out remediation. In addition, once municipalities discover contamination, most choose the quick fix by switching to tapwater systems. Thus the contamination remains. Even if groundwater is unused, it still poses a future hindrance to urban redevelopment.

Voluntary Information Disclosure by Businesses

Japan's Water Pollution Control Law does not require businesses to investigate and report groundwater contamination to their local governments; therefore, many companies say nothing publicly about their pollution. As the extent of pollution throughout Japan comes to light, more companies are voluntarily conducting studies and publicly releasing the results for their ISO 14001 certification and company rating. For instance, in the course of preparing to obtain ISO 14001 certification, Fuji Xerox performed a soil study and found soil and groundwater contamination. The information was released in its "Environmental Progress Report 2000."

The report explained the remediation of soil under building F and in the surrounding area of the Iwatsuki site, stating that, "the project is expected to complete in August 2001." This entailed extensive excavation and construction totaling ¥3 billion (about US$30 million), split roughly evenly toward remediation and relocating a production line. Similarly, the foreign-capital company IBM Japan, Ltd. mentioned in its "IBM Environment and Well-Being Progress Report 2000" that IBM is working on soil and groundwater contamination and remediation efforts at its Fujisawa facility in Japan. These are two examples of environmental information disclosure based on the global standard. These examples show that a company can improve its reputation by disclosing groundwater contamination and other unfavorable information instead of concealing it.

Who Will Clean Up?

In the past, Japan had no legal institutions to deal with soil and groundwater contamination caused by high-tech IT plants, small factories, waste disposal sites, and excess construction-site soil that contain hazardous substances. In 1997, the amended Water Pollution Control Law took effect, empowering prefectural governors to compel polluters to perform remediation. However, this law is limited to the contamination of groundwater used as drinking water, and governors must identify the polluters. The law does not adequately function to remediate and prevent contamination overall. The fundamental question in the remediation of soil and groundwater contamination is who will do it. It is necessary to determine the responsibility of the polluter, the landowner, and the administrative authorities, as well as who will perform the remediation and the degree of remediation needed.

New Legislation for Soil Environment Protection

In Japan, the Agricultural Land Soil Pollution Prevention Law was enacted against the background of Itai-Itai disease in 1970. However, soil pollution of nonagricultural land was not regulated, as there was no sufficient evidence that human health can be damaged unless a human being eats a sufficient quantity of contaminated agricultural products. The Japanese government finally introduced new legislation regarding soil contamination in 2002, with the major application to redevelop idled factory sites and vacant lots to stimulate the country's economic recovery. According to the new law, landowners must check the property for soil pollution and clean up polluted sites prior to redevelopment. The redevelopment includes abolished factories using toxic substances, and old factory sites developed to be residences or parks. An exemption is made for old sites already changed to residences. Also, prefectural governments will be authorized to order landowners to survey their land for pollution if any of the 26 regulated chemicals and metals are found in nearby groundwater.

Landowners carry out site inspections and report the results to the prefecture. When toxic substances, such as mercury or cadmium, are detected over the standard level, prefectures list the polluted sites in a registry that is open to the public. Also, the prefecture orders landowners to take action, including sealing off pollution underground or cleaning up contaminated sites. Once the polluters are identified, they have a duty to take action. If the toxic substances are cleaned up, the site is removed from the registry. However, if the polluted site is only contained, the listing on the registry continues (*Nippon Keizai Shimbun* 2002). The polluter-pays principle is fundamental in the Japanese environmental administration. However, the new law says that when the polluter is not identified, landowners have to pay to promote countermeasures (1) because they are responsible for the condition of their land, and (2) because they are obliged to investigate pollution on their properties.

According to the law, there is retroactive responsibility and strict liability for polluters or landowners. In Japan, it is very difficult to identify the polluters in past pollution cases. Even if the polluter is identified, it is troublesome to decide how the cost should be distributed among potential responsible parties. According to the new law, when the cost burden to landowners becomes large, a fund for cleanup (about ¥0.5 billion, or US$5 million) will be created from government and industry. However, the industry is hesitant to contribute to a fund.

The Remaining Agenda of the New Law

Any law must set forth the polluter-pays principle clearly. Pollution has spread on contaminated sites, often because these sites are on privately owned land. Few companies investigate and remediate contamination that has spread beyond the borders of their sites. Therefore, public funds often cover the costs of operating remediation wells. Soil and groundwater contamination in Japan is like a "bad debt" of the manufacturing industry. A simple mistake could lead to a huge investment of public funds. Considering Japan's current fiscal crisis, the polluter-pays principle must be followed. Furthermore, Hadano's experience provides clues regarding how to provide loans and establish a fund to help small and medium-size enterprises with cleanup costs. The liability of parent companies should be called into question (see Ohtsuka 1994). Moreover, landowners should be required to disclose information. Without provisions for studies and information disclosure, there will be no prompt response to contamination and remediation. Should such provisions become law, they would uncover the estimated 400,000 sites of soil and groundwater contamination throughout Japan, facilitate remediation, and stimulate land transactions.

CONCLUSION

To eliminate high-tech pollution, first, it is necessary to identify the extent of contamination, to trace the pollution pathway, and to take remediation measures. Second, businesses' voluntary information disclosure and initiatives are a positive response to regional citizens' and the media's criticisms. Third, the national legislation for soil and groundwater protection is an urgent agenda to promote chemical reduction and water protection. Compared to U.S. Superfund Law, the new Japanese legislation has passed more responsibility to the landowners of contaminated sites (cf. Environment Ministry. Government of Japan 2002), but the United States and Japan have a common agenda concerning the "brownfield" problems.

High tech should be used to improve individual well-being and lighten environmental burdens. However, current high-tech production and consumption add to environmental burdens and lower the level of individual well-being, thus neutralizing or even reversing many potential technological benefits.

NOTE

This chapter is an updated version of selections from Yoshida (2001).

JIM PUCKETT

20   High-Tech's Dirty Little Secret

The Economics and Ethics of the Electronic Waste Trade

IN FEBRUARY 2002, the Basel Action Network (BAN), together with the Silicon Valley Toxics Coalition (SVTC), released the report, *Exporting Harm: The High-tech Trashing of Asia.* That report, and a subsequent BAN film of the same name, revealed to the public for the first time a disturbing fact—that about 80 percent of the electronic wastes collected in North America for "recycling" actually find their way, quite legally, to dangerously primitive, highly polluting recycling operations in Asia (see Photos 20.1 and 20.2). European recycling insiders have calculated the export figures for their own continent at 60 percent despite European Union (EU) laws banning such export. The report revealed that waste "recyclers" are often no more than waste "distributors," involved in a very lucrative form of postconsumer, toxic-waste export toward which policy makers and electronics manufacturers have been content to turn a blind eye.

The investigation centered on the Guiyu region of Guangdong Province in Southern China, where displaced farmers from outlying provinces labor for about US$1.50 per day, burning wires, melting brominated flame-retardant impregnated plastics and lead-solder-laden circuit boards, and stripping chips and connectors with strong acid solutions on riverbanksways, all taking place without basic protections against occupational disease and environmental contamination.

Almost three years after the release of that report, nongovernmental organization (NGO) members and journalists have made follow-up visits to Guiyu, another scrap-processing center in the Taizhou city area, south of Shanghai, and e-waste-processing centers in India. Reports from these visits have revealed that, despite the initial shame and dismay expressed by the electronics and recycling industries, and the horrific images now well etched in the public's mind following the release of the groundbreaking exposé, the use of Asia as a global dumping ground for electronic waste from developed countries appears to continue unabated. The exploitation of low-wage, desperate communities and workforces, under the green rubric of "recycling" continues to take its toll through devastating immediate and long-term ecological and human health impacts.

THE DIRTY LITTLE SECRET

These ongoing exposés have alerted us to a "dirty little secret" of the high-tech industry. Not only did we all become aware of the previously unknown

PHOTO 20.1. Migrant child from Hunan province sits atop one of countless piles of unrecyclable computer waste imported from around the world. Guiyu, China, December 2001. Courtesy of Basel Action Network.

dangers lurking inside of our electronic equipment, but also we discovered a tacit stratagem by the electronics industry to avoid both accountability and real downstream cost for its hazardous materials use and poor end-of-life design considerations. Free trade became a mechanism that allowed these liabilities to be shunted to unsuspecting, disempowered communities and desperate labor forces. This passive strategy of convenient exploitation to boost profits created a false economic system, where the bill for the damage done is neither presented to nor paid by those most responsible. And this exploitive trade is facilitated via the green gloss provided by cooptation of the word "recycling."

Although some may be distressed that recycling's good name has been thus sullied, it is important to realize that recycling, like any industry, can be dangerous and harmful to environments and populations, and this is especially likely whenever toxic materials are involved. Although it is abundantly clear that the true solutions to our toxics crisis lie not in recycling wastes downstream, rather in eliminating them through "green design" upstream, an industry addicted to convenient cost externalization to the weak and impoverished seeks different conclusions.

THE FOURTH R: RESPONSIBILITY

The industry hopes to reduce the problems inherent in this form of toxic trade to a matter of simply accomplishing the three R's (Reduce, Reuse, Recycle)

PHOTO 20.2. Woman in Guiyu, China, about to smash a computer monitor tube to remove copper. The biggest hazard from this activity is inhalation of highly toxic phosphor dust coating inside the tube. Monitor glass is later dumped in irrigation canals and along the river where it leaches lead into the groundwater, which is so contaminated that drinking water must be trucked in. December 2001. Courtesy of Basel Action Network.

with "appropriate technology." And although espousing this catch-phrase, it is inevitable that most of the emphasis is on recycling, less on reuse, and even less on waste reduction. Moreover, what is forgotten in this view is a vital fourth R: *Responsibility*. This includes the producer's responsibility not to produce products that are toxic or that possess other environmental liabilities, and to take full financial responsibility for the entire life cycle of their wastes and products. It also includes the national responsibility to become self-sufficient in hazardous waste management, as called for in the Basel Convention (see Geiser and Tickner, this volume) and to halt all exports of hazardous wastes from developed to developing countries as called for in the Basel Convention's Ban Amendment. Finally, it includes consumer responsibility to hold corporations accountable for their actions, products, and wastes, as well as to ensure that they do not allow inappropriate disposal of their own postconsumer wastes (see Raphael and Smith; Tojo; and Wood and Schneider, this volume).

Without this greater context of responsibility, which implies upstream prevention rather than downstream exploitation and damage control, industries simply aim to apply the easiest "technofix." Just as the industry was in blissful ignorance prior to *Exporting Harm*, its new strategy is yet more denial of the real face of exploitation. Instead of calling for greater responsibility to prevent such toxic-waste trade, the answer of industry and North American governments seems to be, "Let's just give the Chinese better technology and then we can continue to send our wastes to them."

This chapter explores the larger questions of why, regardless of technologies employed, efforts to utilize weaker economies to handle environmental problems are unjust and work at cross-purposes with environmental justice and economic sustainability.

ECONOMIC "LOGIC"

In 1991, then Chief Economist of the World Bank, Lawrence Summers, now president of Harvard University, stunned the world when his leaked memo proclaimed: "I think the economic logic behind dumping a load of toxic waste in the lowest wage country is impeccable and we should face up to that" (Summers 1991). He was vilified for making such a statement and rightly so, but what few analysts mentioned at the time was that in fact he was right—according to the dictates of today's free market economics, that conveniently ignores certain real, but externalized costs, the logic of waste trade *is* impeccable. That is, as long as one can manage to get away with sending one's liabilities to those who most likely will not be able to ever present a bill—such as those living in far-off, impoverished, and desperate communities, the flora and fauna in natural ecosystems, or future generations—the logic is just lovely.

However, if we were to employ a truer economic system (e.g., "ecological economics") that is honest and *values all things valuable*—such as our health, our future, biological diversity, justice, morality, human rights, freedom—and properly accounts for what these are worth to us as human beings, the "export of harm" would fail all tests of economic "logic" and the final tally of the bill imposed by end-of-life electronics would be hefty indeed. And yes, this would be true even if "state-of-the-art" technofixes were employed for recycling in developing countries, as risks cannot be entirely eliminated via downstream technologies.

AN OBJECT LESSON IN GLOBALIZED EXPLOITATION

The lesson of e-waste trade exploitation is an object lesson in the fallacy of free trade and globalization, when such freedom of economic movement is belied by captive labor that, ironically, cannot likewise move freely across borders. With labor held captive behind national borders, globalization is a ballgame played on a field consisting of mountain ranges and death valleys—disparate economic realities—creating vast havens for the exploitation and pollution of peoples and resources. To better understand the object lesson, it is important to explore four of the fundamental reasons why the notion of exporting toxic waste from rich to poor countries is a fundamentally bad idea from both ethical and economic standpoints.

1. *Hazardous waste recycling causes damage to human health and the environment.* Indeed, hazardous waste recycling is a dangerous practice anywhere on earth, even in rich, developed countries. To this day, BAN's onsite visits to electronic waste processors in the United States reveal a very serious lack of concern and knowledge about the impacts of such hazards as brominated flame retardants and beryllium in fumes and dusts, as well as toxic cadmium and rare-earth, metal-laced phosphors released by broken cathode ray tubes (CRTs). And smelters, the final and weakest environmental link in any metals recycling operation, have been historically notorious in Europe and North America as major point-source polluters. Very few smelters still exist in North America because the costs of preventing pollution and protecting workers in accordance with legislation are enormous and the costs of upgrading facilities is not effective when weighed against using facilities in developing countries. If developed countries cannot handle the problem without substantial risk, it is no surprise that recycling hazardous electronic waste is going to be particularly dangerous in developing countries.

2. *Weaker economies lack institutional and infrastructural capacities that are even more important for protecting workers and the environment than are technological factors.* Social, legal, political, financial, and infrastructural factors are at least as important to protecting the populace and environment, as are technical criteria. These factors include adequate legislation, and the resources, people power, and political will to actually enforce such legislation, and monitor and inspect operations to ensure compliance and maintain technologies. They include the resources to create and maintain the infrastructure to provide emergency response, roads and services to ensure safe transport, and medical facilities to monitor and protect worker and community health. These factors also include a public and workforce with the political freedoms to gain access to health and environmental risk information so as to be aware of the risks they face, to be able to redress environmental and occupational concerns through legal channels, and to protest hazardous working or living conditions without fear of retribution. In practice, these factors require the freedom of speech and expression and institutionalized trade unions, as well as tort and liability law. And all of these factors need to be robust enough to counter corporate power or governmental corruption.

It would be naive to expect that most of these factors exist with sufficient force in most Southern countries where we currently find our digital detritus falling to rest, particularly because they often do not adequately exist in the global North. Even when the will exists to institutionalize these factors—the requisite resources likely do not. And without these infrastructural safety nets in place, who ends up paying the bill for the damage done? If I am a poor ex-farmer in China, India, or elsewhere, and I get cancer, where can I turn to seek compensation or assistance (see Agarwal and Wankade, this volume)?

3. *The toxic-waste trade to lower-wage communities is contrary to the principles of environmental justice and national self-sufficiency.* Even if we could magically transport all of the infrastructure, laws, policies, clinics, legal recourse, *and* the best available technology, along with the electronic waste as a nifty package deal, and the recipient country were magically able at that point to maintain relatively low wages in relation to those in developed countries, the export of such wastes to those low-wage communities *still* would be an affront to the principle of global environmental justice. In a nutshell, that principle states that no peoples should be disproportionately burdened from environmental harm simply due to their economic, racial, or other status. It is ironic that the principles of environmental justice, first developed in the United States to apply to impoverished, marginalized, and minority communities within the U.S. borders, and embraced by Democratic and Republican administrations alike, perversely, does not seem to apply once toxic waste is traded across U.S. borders.

And, such exports *still* would undermine the fundamental obligation of the Basel Convention, which calls for all nations to become self-sufficient in their hazardous waste management, to minimize transboundary movements of hazardous waste, and to minimize the generation of hazardous wastes. Even more explicit than the text of the original treaty, in 1994, the Basel Convention passed a decision banning all exports of hazardous wastes from countries that are members of the Organization for Economic Cooperation and Development (OECD) to non-OECD countries. This ban was adopted as a proposed amendment to the Basel Convention the next year applying to OECD and European Union countries, and it is now garnering ratifications for its full entry into the force of law. This ban is a complete prohibition, created with the understanding that regardless of the levels of technology employed, economically motivated waste trade, which takes advantage of low-wage countries, cannot be considered environmentally sound management.

4. *Such exports externalize real end-of-life costs, creating an economic disincentive for upstream solutions (i.e., green design/toxics elimination).* The final and perhaps most compelling reason for prohibiting the international electronic waste trade is the fact that its continuance creates a subsidy for inefficient and destructive product design. For as long as the dumping of electronic waste on weaker economies is legal and its costs remain external to the ledgers of its industrial creators, the electronics industry will not be forced to pick up the tab for the true end-of-life costs of their products. The effect will be that the importing country ultimately will pay that bill, either with its citizens' health or in exorbitant postcontamination clean-up costs, whereas those responsible for creating the problems in the first place lose all incentive to solve them at the source through green design.

PROFITS LEAVE THE INDUSTRY IN DENIAL

Leaders in the recycling industry, in government, and certainly in the electronics manufacturing industry continue to argue that strict export controls and a policy of environmental justice or national self-sufficiency in hazardous waste management are unnecessary. Rather, in their view, exporting toxic waste is acceptable, as long as developing countries are given the proper technology.

The U.S. government, for example, recently claimed that export is part of its e-waste management strategy for its national electronic-waste tidal wave. The U.S. Environmental Protection Agency's (EPA) electronic waste expert, Robert Tonetti, claims that once a minimum, global standard of technological criteria is established, waste exports should be able to proceed. The EPA's recent "Plug-In to E-cycling Guidelines" ignores the fact that the rest of the world must adhere to Basel Convention obligations and waste definitions and fails to forbid the export of hazardous e-waste in accordance with Basel Ban (Basel Decisions II/12 and III/1). It also fails to recognize that Basel Parties cannot trade in waste with a non-Party unless a special bilateral agreement is first signed between the two countries. Thus, it is currently illegal for countries like Philippines, China, India, Vietnam, and so forth that are Basel Parties to receive hazardous electronic wastes from the United States. The current situation where the United States knowingly contributes, via its free electronic waste trade policies, to promoting and facilitating illegal imports on the part of developing countries, is outrageous.

Likewise, most industry bodies, including the Electronics Industries Alliance (EIA), refuse to denounce the toxic-waste trade. In a statement following the release of "Exporting Harm," the EIA stated:

> to facilitate sustainability, exporting in a globalized economy needs to be a viable option. . . . internationally, EIA is working with governments through the OECD to develop internationally recognized guidelines for the environmentally sound management of scrap PCs. We hope this initiative will help governments ensure that recycling facilities operating within their borders are properly regulated and held to high environmental, health and safety standards. (EIA 2002)

Even the recycling industry associations, such as the International Association of Electronic Recyclers (IAER), the Institute for Scrap Recycling Industries (ISRI), and the Bureau of International Recycling (BIR), refuse to take a stand in support of a ban on the export of hazardous electronic wastes to developing countries.

LAGGARDS AND LEADERS

Unfortunately, too many of the aforementioned "waste distributors," benefiting from (and exploiting) the positive greening effect of the word "recycling," have joined the ranks of these national and international recycler associations and now represent a large part of their membership. These waste-trading interests have found undue representation within such organizations such as the

BIR, the ISRI, and the IAER. As a result, these organizations have used their members' money to lobby for deregulation, particularly as it regards defining wastes to be regulated and legislating their uncontrolled transfer from rich to weaker economies (e.g., as is now being sought in the Basel Convention).

The good news is that Europe has stepped forward with a model of a two step solution to the e-waste crisis: First, close off the cheap and dirty dumping grounds (they have banned hazardous waste exports and e-waste landfilling). Second, require producers to take responsibility for all e-wastes at end of life and to phase out the use of toxics in such products. This is a model to which North America and the rest of the world aspires.

In the meantime the good news in North America is that a growing number of recyclers and waste management officials at the local level are now beginning to take a stand against these economically distorting cost externalizations that are robbing legitimate recyclers of domestic markets and preventing the proper buildup of a domestic infrastructure to safely manage hazardous wastes at home. In 2003, North American recyclers, joining together in a series of press conferences, made the surprising announcement that in lieu of governmental action, they were going to voluntarily uphold the social and environmental waste management criteria developed by BAN, SVTC, and the Computer TakeBack Campaign (CTBC), requiring of themselves a standard of diligence far exceeding those of legal mandates. In doing so, these recyclers are very likely to incur greater business costs than their competitors.

The new alliance was forged through the creation of a document known as the "Electronic Recycler's Pledge of True Stewardship" crafted by BAN and SVTC after many months of consultation with electronic waste recyclers (see Appendix E, this volume). This pledge calls for, among other things, a full closure of the cheap and dirty cost externalization sinks for electronic wastes that are the most common destinations today: export, landfills, and prisons. As of this writing, the pledge has more than 70 signatories.[1] The intention of this effort was never to reward the status quo, but to find an elite group of concerned businesses willing to change business as usual forever.

By distinguishing the industry leaders from the laggards, and then directing those consumers—including institutions, government agencies, and original equipment manufacturers who are willing to pay a little more to do the right thing—we can work to create a growing market for responsible recycling, using market forces in lieu of adequate legislation in the United States. There are plans to convert the pledge into a certifiable program with third-party verification.

CONCLUSION

The toxic e-waste trade is an affront to the principles of environmental justice, as it targets the poor with toxic, unsustainable jobs and waste. The export "solution" also contradicts the "polluter-pays principle" and the principle of "waste prevention," as it allows very real environmental costs to be externalized by those responsible for creating them. Whenever a government allows costs to be externalized, in this case via export, it creates an unfair subsidy for industry to continue creating polluting products and wastes. This pollution subsidy then stifles the innovation desperately needed worldwide to implement preventive solutions upstream through green designs that avoid pollution in the first instance.

We all must do our part to reaffirm the principles of environmental justice and the Basel Convention's obligations to achieve national self-sufficiency in waste management through waste prevention and minimization. It is time for environmentalists, governments, and the private sector to unite in the resolve to once and for all pull the plug on the horror show that is the toxic waste trade, rather than find yet more excuses for perpetuating it.

NOTE

1. For an up-to-date list of signatories of the Electronics Recycler's Pledge of True Stewardship, see www.ban.org/pledge/Locations.html.

21   Hi-Tech Heaps, Forsaken Lives

E-Waste in Delhi

In a dark alley in Mandoli, a backyard recycling area in New Delhi, a young boy sits on the floor, dipping a high-tech, multi-layered printed circuit board (PCB) into a crumpled metal bowl containing an acid-like liquid. He is unaware that his hands hold the past 50 years of human technological advancement in the form of integrated circuits and electronic components. Probably manufactured and assembled separately in several parts of the world by high-tech facilities using new-age materials, the PCB and the boy belong to different worlds. Wiping the board clean, he proceeds to heat it on a small cooking gas stove, trying to pull out the components. The few milligrams of metals they hold are his livelihood. At day's end, he may earn 50 cents or less, another day's survival. Like the computer, of "no use" to anyone, he too could be a part of the heap. (See Photos 21.1 through 21.3.)

COMPUTERS ARE NOW at the core of every IT application and having a profound impact on business processes and life styles. Computers have become synonymous with a newly educated and technologically capable idea of the nation-state, and India hopes to become a powerful player in the information age. In this endeavor, computerization is being encouraged through all means, including the import of secondhand computers from the developed world, in hopes of penetrating price-sensitive markets. During 2002–03, India's production in this sector was approximately US$800 million, a growth of 10 percent over the previous year. Products in this category include personal computers (PCs), workstations, super computers, printers, digitizers, and networking products, such as modems and hubs (DoE 2002). The number of PCs in use in India is estimated to be over eight million, with 80 percent serving commercial segments and the balance serving residential segments. This figure is slated to rise by ten times (to 80 million computers) by 2008, as per government targets (DoE).

When it comes to computer waste, a very different picture emerges. A whole section of the population strives to deal with this waste under almost impossible subhuman working conditions, with little possibility of upward mobility in their lives. These workers, mostly in the informal sector of the economy and part of the urban poor, are India's other reality.

With more than 85 percent of its workforce in the informal sector, these people have been ignored by the major trade unions and have little power to negotiate their lives in India's political economy. These men, women, and children are the forgotten, invisible bodies who are not included in the dreams that India's leaders envision for the future. It is here that computer-waste

PHOTO 21.1. Child laborer sorts through discarded electronic circuit boards in India. Courtesy of Toxics Link, India.

PHOTO 21.2. Man at e-waste recycling facility in India, melting and extracting precious metals from printed circuit board. Courtesy of Toxics Link, India.

PHOTO 21.3. Women using simple tools to remove semiconductor chips, transistors, capacitors, and other items from electronics circuit boards at e-waste facility in India. Courtesy of Toxics Link, India.

recycling takes place, as computers sold by biggest and best-known brands in the world are finally smashed here physically.

To investigate this reality, a study was undertaken to understand the nature, economics, range, market, and trade routes of electronic waste, with a special emphasis on computer waste in Delhi and Chennai.[1] Computer-waste recycling units were surveyed in Delhi to assess the technology used and the overall conditions of recycling from both environmental and occupational health perspectives.

METHODOLOGY

This study was based on field visits and the collection of primary data at various locations in Delhi. Initially, the study adopted the survey method supplemented with detailed, open-ended questionnaires. This method did not work well, however, because electronic waste traders and recyclers were reluctant to disclose information. Subsequently, some discussions were held with workers in recycling units, but this was limited, because the workers were afraid of being seen talking to strangers without the owner's permission. Moreover, their rigorous and long working hours did not allow much time for them to talk. It soon became evident that an understanding of the waste trade was possible only through informal discussions with various stakeholders.

During such discussions, questions were asked about the recyclable components, the hazards involved, and the economics of the trade. The interviews were kept informal to engage and elicit detailed information. This approach worked better, even though answers to certain questions dealing with the pollution caused by recycling were difficult to unearth. Not surprisingly, the presence of the unit owners affected the answers, and workers were more forthcoming when managers were not around.

DELHI, INDIA'S RECYCLING CAPITAL

Delhi, the capital of India, is one center where recycling of all types of waste takes place. Over the years, Delhi's strategic location, the presence of upstream markets, local entrepreneurship, and tiny-scale industries have made it a prime spot for trading recovering, reprocessing, and selling waste. More than one million urban poor people are engaged in this activity, which includes collection and recovery, with more than 10,000 of them being part of the trade and reprocessing units (Srishti 2002).

Most of the activity occurs in the form of backyard operations, using rudimentary technology, and in an environment where labor is openly exploited. Labor and environmental laws are peripheral in such operations and not enforced. Both traders and recyclers make substantial profits, whereas the workers subsist on less than a couple of dollars a day.

This sector does not exist in isolation, but in an interdependent relationship with the other part of the economy. What are less evident are the links between the so-called informal and the organized formal sectors. Materials flow from the formal to the informal almost seamlessly, and one person's waste becomes another's livelihood. Computer waste is often routed through mainstream, institutional channels, such as customs ports, computer service centers, and registered computer dealers, and then passes onto the "gray" market. Businesses frequently auction old computers and households exchange them for newer models. With such transfers, the responsibility is also passed on, from the formal to the informal, as the computer industry and the state seem to rid themselves of any liability.

Electronic and computer waste—a relatively recent entrant in India's recycling back alleys, which have been more accustomed to plastics, paper, and industrial scrap—is now emerging as one of the more profitable activities as obsolescence rates increase, and the influx of computer scrap from local and overseas markets rises as well.

The Workforce

Over the years, there has been an increase in India's rural to urban migration. Because of its very high, per-capita investments, Delhi is a "hopeful" destination for the rural poor, especially those who are landless, from the neighboring states of Uttar Pradesh, Bihar, West Bengal, and Orissa. Of the city's 15 million people, 50 to 60 percent live in substandard and shanty housing and perform low-paying jobs (Tiwari 2003). The presence of a very active informal sector, several small-scale industries, and other cottage industries provides opportunities to find a livelihood. The recycling industry absorbs such migrants, because the skills needed for entry are low or nonexistent.

Supply being more than demand; they are exploited in the ruthless labor market.

Finding shelter is as difficult as finding employment. Without social or kinship support, a guarantee is needed to gain access to the city and find a means of livelihood to survive. The waste dealers and recycling unit owners provide migrant workers both a shelter and a livelihood, a basis for exploitation. Although all the workers stated that "poverty" was the main reason they moved to the city, 15 percent admitted that they would leave if they had options. The workers interviewed belonged to a highly varied demographic sample. Most were Muslims, but age, religion, community, or marital status revealed no singular trend for recycling workers. In some places, the recycling processes determined the type of workers. For example, women and children would segregate the products, but men would dismantle and break them.

The caste status of laborers was difficult to establish, but working in the waste sector is considered very low in the social order, even though earnings could be greater than that of jobs in local shops or roadside restaurants. Those from the upper castes feel it is beneath their dignity to engage in waste-related work. In the absence of any formal census, it is difficult to determine the exact number of people engaged in e-waste recycling.

The Materials

Sources of Computer Scrap. More than 70 percent of the personal computers in India are in the business and service sectors. It is estimated that of the eight million PCs in India, roughly two to three million are either obsolete or dysfunctional and end up as scrap. Computers are constantly upgraded because of new software and hardware capabilities. Even in India, computers below the Intel Pentium IV exit the market for spare parts and recycling. In the home sector, the obsolescence rate is slower but growing. Home users often pass on their old computers to friends and relatives. However, there is a tendency for computer sellers to "exchange" old computers and offer a discount on newer ones. Old computers often end up in smaller markets and, ultimately, the scrap heap (Toxics Link 2003).

Another major source of computer scrap is imports. Large quantities of junk computer monitors, printers, keyboards, central processing units (CPUs), mobile phones, and polyvinyl chloride (PVC) wires enter the country illegally.

Inquiries revealed that the actual process of importing obsolete PCs was well established. Details of pricing and payment are often worked out in advance and negotiated through banking channels via international letters of credit. Shipments take approximately one month to reach an Indian port of entry, where it is the importer's responsibility to clear them through customs.

Dubai and Singapore often serve as transit points for waste from the United States, Europe, and West and East Asia. At these points, waste is categorized according to its nature and coded. International traders are well aware of legal loopholes in India and routinely label scrap as "used working computers" or "metal scrap" to minimize customs' duties (see Figure 21.1).

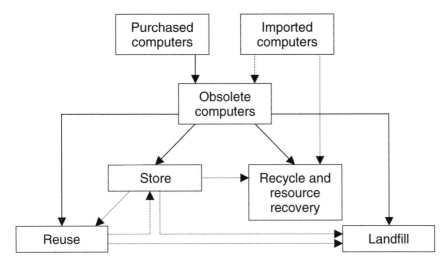

FIGURE 21.1. Flow Diagram of Computer Waste.
Source: Toxics Link, India.

THE ROUTE TO THE RECYCLER

Traders procure old computers as scrap and measure them by weight, from business users or even embassies, for as little as 50 cents per kilogram. The trader decides whether the computer can be reused or must be scrapped. A parallel and independent secondary market for reselling old computers coexists synergistically with the recycling market. If destined to be demolished, the computer's monitors, casings, motherboards, keyboards, floppy drives, different components of printers are all segregated. Sometimes, high-value integrated chips (ICs) are pulled out and sold, but most computer parts are disassembled and sold separately to different recyclers for material recovery.

Often intermediaries (*kabadis*) operating in the market collect functional items from the retailers (as well as the scrap market) and sell them to repair shops and local computer assemblers centered in Nehru Place (see Figure 21.2) and other areas of Delhi. The most popular items in demand are CPUs, parts of power supplies, and ICs. Similarly, imported, nonworking computers are sold in bulk to big traders. After extracting valuable parts like CPUs, they are sold to smaller scrap dealers, where the real PC recycling process commences.

Recycling Locations

Computer recycling takes place in various parts of Delhi, each with its "specialization" (see Figure 21.2). All markets of e-waste and recycling units for computer waste are situated in densely populated areas of the city. The recycling areas have a pattern of mixed land-use, with recycling units intermingled among residential houses. Sometimes, parts of a house end up as recycling units, with the entrepreneurs and workers living in the remaining space. At Mandoli, an industrial area in Delhi, recycling activities (metal

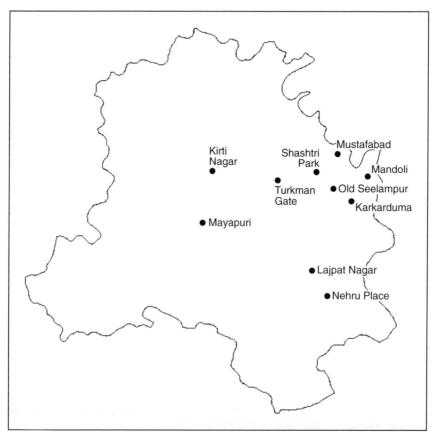

FIGURE 21.2. Map of Electronics Disassembly (Recycling) Operations in Delhi, India. *Source:* Toxics Link, India.

extraction) take place near residential areas, with little control over the fumes or emissions, which endanger the surrounding community.

Recycling clusters are found in Turkman Gate, Mayapuri, Old Seelampur, Mundaka, Mandoli, Kirti Nagar, Shastri Park, and Karkarduma (see Figure 21.2). In the "walled city" area[2] (Turkman Gate), disassembly takes place in cramped rooms, whereas in other industrial areas, such as Mayapuri, the waste is spread out. At one place surveyed, desoldering took place in a cattle shed (Table 21.1).

The Recycling Process

In the downward movement of PCs for recycling, different players specialize in recovering specific materials, as each PC component is disassembled and recycled separately. Some of these processes are detailed in Table 21.2.

Monitors. Monitors are much sought after by scrap dealers because they contain copper (in the yoke), circuit boards, and the CRT. If a monitor cannot be

TABLE 21.1. E-Waste Recycling Areas in Delhi with Specific Functions[a]

Location	Component Recycled
Turkman Gate—Delhi	Disassembly of computer, CRT breaking
Mayapur—Delhi	Disassembly of every kind of electrical goods, open and drum wire burning
Old Seelampur—Delhi	Market of every kind of electronic scrap
Shastri Park—Delhi	Computer dismantling, recharging of CRTs
Lajpat Naga—Delhi	Disassembly of computer
Kirti Nagar—Delhi	Mainframe computer disassembling
Karkarduma—Delhi	Trade and recharging of CRTs
Mustafabad—Delhi	Lead recovery
Mandoli—Delhi	Circuit board recycling
Meerut (near Delhi)	Gold recovery
Firozabad (near Delhi)	Glass recovery
Chennai (South India)	Market of circuit board and speeder motor

[a] Refer to map, except for Chennai, Meerut, and Firozabad.
Source: Authors.

reused, it is broken down to recover the iron frames found only in color CRTs. The copper recovered from yoke coils is sold to copper smelters. Copper also is recovered from the transformers mounted on the computer's circuit board.

Functional monitors or CRTs are "regunned" for local-brand televisions or screens for video games at Lajpat Rai Market in Old Delhi. The plastic casings are sold to buyers who come from Mundaka or Narela to make plastic pellets.

TABLE 21.2. The Process of Recycling E-waste in Delhi

Component	Material Recovered	Recycling Process
Monitor	CRT or glass, circuit board, copper, steel, and plastic casing	Manually, using screwdrivers and pliers. CRTs are broken with a hammer
CPU	Different metals and nonmetals from hard disk, floppy drive	Manually, using screwdriver, hammer, and pliers
Circuit board	Lead, IC, CPU, few capacitors and condensers, copper, and gold	After preheating plate, working IC chip and capacitor are removed using pliers
		Open burning to recover copper film from circuit board
		Gold is recovered through acid bath
Printer	Plastic, motor, cartridge	Motor reused in toy manufacture; cartridge refilled for reuse if possible, else smashed for plastic recovery
PVC wire	Copper or aluminum	Open and drum burning
Hard disk, floppy drive and SMPS[a]	Copper and brass alloys, aluminum, iron, and magnets	Melted after manual separation of each part
Capacitors and condensers	Aluminum	Open, or *bhatti* (small furnace), burning to melt metallic parts

[a] SMPS, switching-mode power supply.
Source: Authors.

Plastics. The plastic casings of monitors are made of PVC or acrylonitrile-butadiene styrene (ABS). PVC was used commonly in old computer models, though ABS plastic is more common now. Normally, the PVC casings were used as fuel because the silicate made them difficult to recycle. PVC is still used as an insulator of copper wires and cables, which is often burnt to separate copper.

Circuit Boards. The computers' printed circuit boards and their components contain such metals as antimony, gold, silver, chromium, zinc, lead, tin, and copper, which garner a fair market price. Recovering them is not easy, and it involves such destructive and hazardous processes as heating and open burning.

Generally, the gold-plated pins and the few inserted ICs that can be reused are removed manually. Laminated circuits, especially if they contain gold, are cut down and resold. The boards then are preheated on small household stoves to desolder resalable components like ICs and capacitors. The recovery of precious metals, such as gold or silver, occurs at a separate place.

Solder, which contains lead, is also recovered. The boards are manually held by metal tongs and heated on small kerosene burners, which are placed in a large water tub to collect the dripping molten metal. After desoldering, the circuit boards are open-burned in small furnaces or treated in acid to recover the copper.

Mechanical Components. Mechanical components such bearings, alloy, aluminum disc, and casings (called china steel) are recovered from the broken disk drives and sold to various recyclers. In the process of dismantling a computer, a considerable amount of aluminum, tin, and iron is recovered and sold to specialized dealers or to metal recyclers. Scrap leftovers, like ash, plastic residues from charred IC chips, and condensers, are landfilled. Sometimes the plastic residues from the recycling units are sold to brick kiln owners as furnace fuel, further polluting the air.

THE ECONOMICS OF RECYCLING

The medley of activities takes places in the context of the complex economics of the backyard recycling units. Each component or recovered item has a value and a market, so everything that can be sold is recovered no matter how small the profit margin.

The substantial profit margin that is possible in trading, recycling, and marketing these products prompts new entrepreneurs to enter the business. Yet, even though hundreds of small transactions take place between numerous players in a complex recycling market, the traders make the bulk of the profits. For example, a local trader buys a single PC with a color monitor at US$10 to $15 per piece and sells it for up to US$40 to $50 by selling the disassembled parts separately to different recyclers or reusers.

To understand the complexity of the operation, let us take the case of a computer monitor (CRT). Color CRTs, which are sold for re-gunning, fetch

US$25 to $30, whereas black-and-white monitors net US$2 to $3. Glass dealers purchase the broken glass from a CRT for as low as 2 cents per kilogram, but sell it for over 4 cents per kilogram to upcountry glass manufacturers in the nearby state of Uttar Pradesh. The iron frames extracted from a color computer screen, which weigh from 200 to 250 grams, are sold to an iron scrap dealer at 15 cents per kilogram. Copper from picture tube yokes is sold to copper smelters from US$1.3 to $1.5 per kilogram, a black-and-white or color picture tube yields from 60 to 200 grams, respectively. The CRT circuit tray also contains a number of condensers, and depending on their type, condition, and demand, the price ranges from 4 to 40 cents apiece. The PVC plastic casings are sold at 2 cents per kilogram, whereas the more commonly used ABS plastic ones fetch 32 cents per kilogram.

Another example is the circuit board, from which lead, copper alloy, and gold can be recovered. Recyclers buy circuit boards at 13 cents per kilogram and resell them for 10 cents per kilogram, after lead recovery. About 3 kilograms of lead is recovered from 200 kilograms of motherboards. The market price of recovered lead is US$2.17 per kilogram. The gold-plated pins (if any), locally known as *kanga*, and laminated cores of gold are sold to goldsmiths from places like nearby cities such as Meerut. Gold pins are sold at US$60 per kilogram, whereas laminated cores are priced at US$30 per kilogram. Copper recovered from the plates is sold to copper-wire manufacturers at US$1.74 per kilogram. The desoldered plates are sold at 43 cents per kilogram. The price of a single chip can range from 21 cents to US$1.08, depending on the type, size, and demand. Defective ICs, capacitors, and transistors are reduced to aluminum and then sold for between 87 cents and US$1.08 cents per kilogram.

Conditions in Recycling Workplaces

In Delhi, the operation of e-waste recycling is clandestine, as tons of e-waste lay hidden behind the high-boundary walls of recycling units. Work occurs 12 hours a day, seven days a week. Outsiders are not welcome and shunned. Within these secure quarters, workers sit on the ground among piles of computer parts, separating them with amazing dexterity, bare hands, and no masks.

E-waste recycling takes place in small, unregistered, labor-intensive units located in the industrial areas, though some also operate from houses in residential areas. Improper ventilation, excessive noise levels, high heat, and a lack of fresh air over a long period of time are some common features of the working conditions in the recycling units. Migrant and unprotected workers, including a large number of children, work in the recycling facilities, where the employers are neither aware of the hazards nor interested in the workers' safety.

Health Impacts

The recycling process is rudimentary and hazardous in nature, with a high health cost attached to it. Workers, however, are unaware of many physical hazards and routinely deal with toxic heavy metals as PVC, brominated flame retardants (BFRs), fumes, and various gases.

Heavy metals, like lead, cadmium, chromium, and mercury, can cause damage to the central and peripheral nervous systems. Lead has serious effects on children's brain development and damages human blood, as well as the kidneys and reproductive system. It accumulates in the environment and has acute and chronic effects on plants, animals, and microorganisms. Mercury, which can be absorbed in the food chain, causes damage to the kidneys and the developing fetus. It also may convert to the more lethal methyl mercury. Chromium is easily passed through cell membranes and absorbed into the body. Exposures to beryllium, barium, and BFRs could cause cancer.

THE LAWS

Various laws—including import laws, labor and factory laws, and environmental laws—impact electronic and electrical waste. These laws are enforced by different arms of the state, which do not communicate with each other, leading to unusual situations. For example, though the central government claims that no mandatory clearance has been given to any importer for secondhand computers, they are being imported regularly through Custom's ports.

Trade Policy for PCs

Computerization in India is being promoted at all levels through liberal import polices (DGFT 2003). There are various tax incentives for donating computers to educational institutions and hospitals; including a zero custom duty and an exemption from many local taxes. Interviews with the Custom's officials revealed many loopholes, which include illegally importing scrap computers. Although the hazardous nature of e-waste gradually has become recognized, only a few countries have outlawed their trade. Traders revealed that the main countries exporting e-waste to India are the United States, Korea, Singapore, Malaysia, Canada, Australia, and the United Arab Emirates.

Labor Laws

Legally, recycling operations come under the purview of various labor and industrial laws in India, as the local factories' inspectorate and the labor commissioner implement labor laws. However, almost none of the laws are applied to the informal sector. A wide range of laws, including the Factories Act,[3] provides stringent requirements for industrial operations and sets health and safety standards and working hours. The requirements for worker compensation and medical insurance fall under Employees State Insurance (ESI),[4] which includes maternity benefits and hospital care. The Provident Fund Act and the Workmen's Compensation Act provide savings for old age and joblessness.[5]

Finally, even though employing children is illegal,[6] many workers are children, supplying cheap labor for employers. Many policymakers understand this as a consequence of poverty but have failed to adopt adequate measures to counter it.

Environmental Laws. The provision of environmental protection is divided between India's various states. Although the central, state government lays down policy, national regulations, and minimum standards of various types (e.g., for permissible air and water emissions),[7] the laws are implemented by the State Pollution Control Boards, which have been known for their lax enforcement.

The classification of e-waste as hazardous is unclear within Indian legislation.[8] Its status depends on the extent to which hazardous constituents are present, and there are no specific laws or guidelines on this, except that its import needs special clearance from the central government. A lack of clarity makes applying the regulations difficult.

Local Actions

Lately, there has been an increased awareness of recycling activities and working conditions in India. This effort mostly has been spearheaded by environmental groups, who examine waste from a life-cycle approach and the health impacts of dumping, recycling, and disposal. The issue of local working conditions has been raised in an attempt to integrate the concern for livelihood with waste disposal in a framework of extended producer responsibility (EPR). If computer producers invest in upgrading recycling facilities, it is then possible to both improve working conditions and engage in safer recycling.

Trade unions are key players in implementing laws, but they have ignored both occupational safety issues and India's informal sector. Some policy conversations have emerged with the aim of providing health insurance coverage for the recycling workers, subsidized by the state, and the intent to help organize the informal-sector workers.[9] These discussions need to progress beyond pronouncements, as there is currently no action on the ground.

On a broader level, some trade unions and environmental justice groups have been trying to work together on occupational safety and health issues.[10] This is a departure from the past, because traditionally, labor and environmental groups have posited the issues in adversarial frames of "cleanliness" versus "livelihood." The effectiveness of these new constituencies has yet to be proven.

CONCLUSION

Electronic waste in India has been an unrecognized problem so far. With countries like China banning imports of electronic wastes, there is likely to be increased pressure on countries like India to accept them. Not only does India have a large backyard-recycling sector, but also its many entry ports and lax laws make the free flow of hazardous imports difficult to combat. Moreover, indigenously generated electronic waste is on the rise, as obsolescence rates become higher and newer computers become more affordable. If policies allow secondhand computer imports, the problem of e-waste flow will be ever on the rise.

The recycling sector in India is a free-floating one, operated by small, backyard recyclers. Even though the same global companies, imposed by new laws and public pressure, are improving their practices of product design and waste management in the developed world, in India, it is business as usual. In fact, one of the hardest challenges of the environmental justice campaign in India has been to bring industry on board. The consequences are borne by the poorest of the poor and left untouched by fancy statements of Corporate Social Responsibility enunciated in companies' annual reports and Web sites.

The issue requires urgent action, which includes a governmental ban on imports of such waste, and linking indigenously generated wastes with EPR. Best-practice models must be adopted locally by this global industry, leading to investments in recycling and redesign for environmentally sound products. The industry must become really "green" to be a part of a future, sustainable economy.

NOTES

1. Toxics Link has published reports on e-waste status in Delhi and Chennai. These may be accessed at www.toxicslink.org.

2. The old city of Delhi still has historical and cultural roots from the Mughal and British periods. There was a wall around it; thus it is known as a walled city.

3. The Factories Act [Act No. 63 of 1948] as amended by the Factories (Amendment) Act, 1987.

4. The Employees' State Insurance Act, 1948.

5. The Workmen's Compensation Act, 1923.

6. The Child Labour (Prohibition and Regulation) Act, 1986.

7. The Environment Protection Act, 1986.

8. The Hazardous Waste (Management and Handling) Rules, 1989, as amended 2003.

9. The Social Security Scheme, managed by the Employees Provident Fund Organization of Ministry of Labor, Government of India.

10. Organizations such as the Center for Environment and Communication, and Toxics Link are working in India on occupational health and safety issues, linking them with environmental concerns.

22 Importing Extended Producer Responsibility for Electronic Equipment into the United States

EXTENDED PRODUCER RESPONSIBILITY (EPR) is a policy approach that holds manufacturers accountable for the full costs of their products at every stage in their life cycle. EPR typically involves requiring that producers take back their products at the end of their useful lives, or pay a recycling contractor to do so, thereby internalizing the costs of recycling or disposal in a manufacturer's bottom line. When companies know that they will bear the costs of product return and recycling, they are more likely to redesign their products for easier and safer handling at each step in the life cycle. This approach "enforces a design strategy that takes into account the upstream environmental impacts inherent in the selection, mining and extraction of materials, the health and environmental impacts to workers and surrounding communities during the production process itself, and downstream impacts during use, recycling and disposal of the products" (EPR Working Group 2003, 2). In short, by requiring a company to take its products back, EPR aims to force the company to make the products cleaner in the first place.

The idea of applying EPR policy to electronics arrived in the United States in the 1990s as a welcome import from Europe. This chapter traces EPR's adoption by coalitions of U.S. environmental, labor, and health activists seeking a comprehensive policy solution to the health and safety threats posed by the high-technology industry's internationalization.

THE EUROPEAN UNION MODEL AND THE SOUL OF GLOBALIZATION

In the 1990s, American labor, health, and environmental nongovernmental organizations (NGOs) concerned about the electronics' industry's impact sought to turn the process of economic and political globalization to their advantage. Forming the International Campaign for Responsible Technology (ICRT) in the 1990s, NGOs that had worked mainly at the local level first built national and then international ties to share information and strategies and conduct campaigns across borders (see Byster and Smith, "From Grass Roots to Global," this volume). They found a promising, comprehensive policy solution in EPR, as embodied in the European Union's (EU) proposed directives on electronic waste and toxics reduction (see Geiser and Tickner, this volume). Activists recognized that by raising standards for the production and disposal of electronics in Europe, the EU directives offered the best tool for raising standards in the United States without sweeping its toxic waste under developing countries' rugs (Smith and Raphael 2003).

EPR promised to promote *higher* environmental and workplace safety benefits worldwide, rather than shift risk abroad and fuel a downward spiral in standards. By requiring producers to take back their products, redesign them for easier recycling, and phase out some of the most dangerous toxics, the EU's directives sought to reduce risk at each stage of a product's life cycle wherever it occurred in the globalized electronics industry. Rather than exerting downward pressure on environmental and labor protections, globalization could be turned into a force that conditioned access to major world markets on meeting more stringent norms for design and disposal. In the era of global markets, transnational corporations must meet the highest standards set in any major market because it is expensive to manufacture different product lines for different regional markets. In addition, if companies were to produce more hazardous and less hazardous versions of their products for different markets, they would be opening themselves up to public and regulatory criticism (as well as potential liability) for employing an environmental double standard that poses greater risks to some customers and regions.

The turn to Europe was a response to the new political realities of the 1990s, as well as a struggle for the soul of economic and political globalization itself. Many criticisms of globalization have focused on how the new international trade regime can usurp the power of national governments to maintain strong protections for their workers and the environment (e.g., Falk 1999). However, during the years of Republican presidential administrations from 1980 to 1992, the path to enacting progressive regulations rarely began at the national level. Instead, environmental activists focused on building grassroots support for legislation in the most receptive states, pressuring industry and government for national reforms to resolve a patchwork of different state rules. Because activists were accustomed to seeking the most strategic forum for advancing policy rather than fixating on the federal government, they saw that the EU's formation offered a friendlier counterweight to the rise of supranational organizations like the World Trade Organization (WTO). The route to U.S. reform now might run through Brussels, as well as through the state capitals.

As a sign of the internationalization of electronics regulation and activism, the ICRT's first step in embracing EPR was to defend Europe's ability to enact it against the U.S. government's and the industry's objections. In 1998, the American Electronics Association (AEA), a major trade association, convinced the U.S. Trade Representative (USTR) and the Mission to the European Union to fight the European directives. The trade associations argued that mandated phase-outs of toxic materials would undermine the "functionality, safety, and reliability" of their products, and "impede the development of new technologies and products, increase costs, and restrict global trade in these products" (Hunter and Lopez 1999). The trade associations also alleged that requiring producers to assume financial responsibility for collecting and processing e-waste violated the General Agreement on Tariffs and Trade (GATT) rules against trade restraints. The U.S. Mission in Brussels agreed, arguing to the EU that the directives raised "unnecessary barriers to trade, particularly the ban on certain materials, burdensome take-back requirements for end-of-life equipment, and mandated design standards" (quoted in SVTC 1999).

In response, the ICRT organized efforts to defend the directives from U.S. lobbying. After a key meeting in Europe in 1999 between U.S. activists and their allies in the European NGO community, the Trans-Atlantic Network for Clean Production was formed, with a goal to defend the European directives from U.S. industry attacks. The ICRT wrote a legal rejoinder to the industry's claims, showing how industry had erred in arguing that the EU directives were not protected by GATT's exemptions (Clean Computer Campaign 1999). The ICRT also mobilized a coalition of hundreds of labor, environmental, and community organizations expressing support for the EU directives and calling on then Vice President Albert Gore to rein in the USTR's lobbying efforts. Although industry cast the directives as a matter of "free trade" versus "protectionism," activists used the letter to Gore to transform the debate into one about corporate responsibility, sovereignty, and democracy (ICRT 1999). Later that same year, as part of the major WTO mobilization in Seattle, the ICRT organized a protest against e-waste at Microsoft headquarters to further pressure U.S. industry to back off in its efforts to undermine the EU directives (see Photo 22.1). Microsoft was chosen not only because it was a co-host of the

PHOTO 22.1. Activists protest Microsoft's role in accelerating electronics product obsolescence by piling e-waste in front of the firm's headquarters during the World Trade Organization (WTO) meetings in Seattle, Washington, December 1999. Courtesy of Jeffrey High, Image Productions.

WTO meeting, but also because its constant software updates push demand for more processing speed and drive the pace of computer hardware's rapid obsolescence and the growth of e-waste. As a direct result of this organizing, the USTR attenuated its lobbying in Europe.

IMPORTING EPR INTO THE UNITED STATES

During the years 2000–02, as approval of the EU legislation was increasingly imminent, an expanding coalition of NGOs took the lead on introducing EPR into U.S. debates. Although local and state governments, electronics recyclers, the U.S. Environmental Protection Agency (EPA), and industry began discussing how to build an electronics recycling infrastructure and allocate recycling costs, they focused on improving practices for dealing with products at the end of their lives. Had NGOs not advocated for an EU-style solution, the problem would have been seen simply as one of paying for managing e-waste responsibly, rather than as an opportunity to address the effects of electronics at each stage of their life cycle.

NGOs faced the challenge of the need to grow acceptance of producer responsibility in arid political soil. In the United States' historically pro-business regulatory context, federal regulators already had imposed a kind of conceptual tariff on the idea of producer responsibility as it entered the country. They transformed EPR into "Extended *Product* Responsibility," a voluntary approach to sharing responsibility for products by all actors, including consumers and government (President's Council on Sustainable Development 1997). This excised the notion that producers alone should assume responsibility because internalizing the full disposal costs of their products would likely force companies to redesign them for the better. The U.S. version of EPR held consumers and government partially accountable for decisions about product design that they had no power to control. NGOs opposed this definition, arguing that, "if everyone is made responsible for everything, no one is responsible for anything" (quoted in Fishbein 1996).

In 2001, a broad coalition formed the national Computer TakeBack Campaign (CTBC), which became the major voice for adopting producer responsibility policies for electronics in the United States (see Wood and Schneider; Appendix D, this volume). The CTBC developed a two-pronged strategy that combined a policy campaign aimed at fostering EPR legislation and industry agreements, with a market-based campaign, designed to build support among consumers and shareholders for producer responsibility (see Appendix C, this volume). The policy campaign supported regulatory and legislative efforts to enact producer responsibility with high environmental and worker safety standards for the recycling industry. The market-based campaign devoted much of its attention to pushing personal computer (PC) industry market leader Dell, Inc., to accept EPR, but it also generated support from recyclers for responsible recycling practices and recruited institutional buyers to adopt environmental purchasing guidelines that included demanding take-back provisions from electronics vendors.

Recognizing that there ultimately would be a need for nationwide legislation to ensure a fair, effective take-back and recycling system, the CTBC took part in national negotiations over the outlines of such a system. This began in early 2001 with the formation of the National Electronic Products Stewardship Initiative (NEPSI), a multistakeholder dialogue on resolving the e-waste problem, which represented federal regulators' main effort on the issue. NEPSI was funded by the U.S. EPA and coordinated by the Center for Clean Products and Clean Technologies at the University of Tennessee. NEPSI participants included representatives from major computer and television producers, the Electronics Industry Alliance (EIA), state and local governments, recyclers, retailers, and environmental advocates. They agreed on a goal of fostering "the development of a system, which includes a viable financing mechanism, to maximize the collection, reuse, and recycling of used electronics, while considering appropriate incentives to design products that facilitate source reduction, reuse and recycling; reduce toxicity; and increase recycled content" (NEPSI 2001). Industry representatives initially proffered a financing scheme that would have charged consumers who brought back old electronics, which the CTBC saw as a disincentive to recycling. The CTBC and its allies eventually succeeded in breaking down the industry's resistance to charging front-end fees on its products that would be used to finance the recycling infrastructure (NEPSI 2003).

During this multiyear process, following the defeat of the industry's "back-end financing" scheme, it became clear that the industry participants were split between two different "front-end financing" positions. The majority view advocated for a small consumer fee on new equipment to pay for recycling, without any additional obligations on manufacturers. The television industry and IBM supported this plan, largely because they are the major producers of historic waste, for which they would not have borne significant financial responsibility. The minority view—supported by Hewlett-Packard (HP), as well as by the environmental NGOs—advocated for producers assuming responsibility for taking back and recycling their own obsolete products. After NEPSI disintegrated in disagreement over financing schemes in early 2004, the CTBC achieved a key victory by persuading Dell to join HP in endorsing a Statement of Principles in support of Producer Responsibility. By organizing around this Statement of Principles, the CTBC helped solidify the split within the industry by using its campaign against Dell to bring its position into alignment with its primary competitor—HP. For its part, HP had endorsed cost internalization because HP saw it could give the company a potential competitive advantage as an early investor in building a recycling infrastructure for its own products.

The CTBC's main policy campaign focused on passing local and state initiatives to build momentum for a national solution. State-level stakeholder dialogues involving CTBC representatives predated and paralleled NEPSI, offering forums for exchanging information and discussing policy options among local solid-waste officials, the industry, and activists. This created a groundswell of support for statewide solutions, resulting in a wave of e-waste bills proposed in 24 states by June 2003. Although many of the bills failed to incorporate full producer responsibility (Raymond Communications 2002), the momentum for legislation built swiftly.

By building public awareness, the CTBC forced e-waste issues toward the top of the public policy agenda. California was the first state to enact a full-fledged e-waste recycling bill in 2003, but due to last minute lobbying from the television industry and IBM, the bill dropped full, producer-responsibility mandates in favor of requiring only a small, front-end consumer fee to help finance recycling, similar to the existing "bottle bills" that do not provide incentives for design change. In 2004, Maine became the first state to enact a true producer-responsibility law. Minnesota and Massachusetts were close behind in similar efforts with the Minnesota bill coming very close to passage in the 2005 session. It is likely that the states will continue to be the focus of legislative action as long as the industry remains split and as long as the U.S. Congress remains uninvolved.

FRAMING MATTERS: E-WASTE AND EPR

The CTBC's progress at introducing EPR also depended on its ability to frame its position effectively. Scholars frequently have emphasized the power of framing in environmental politics (e.g., see Capek 1993; Hannigan 1995; Sandweiss 1998). Frames are ways of defining and understanding public issues and events. A frame identifies social *problems*, names their *causes*, implies a range of *solutions*, and attributes *moral responsibility* by iden-tifying victims, villains, heroes, and heroines (Entman 1993). For exam-ple, Americans became increasingly concerned about the environment in the 1960s in part because a number of recognized problems not previously thought of as connected—such as the destruction of wilderness and species, the human health effects of pesticides and industrial chemicals in the work-place and community, and declining air and water quality—were *reframed* as the larger issue of "the environment" (Schoenfeld, Meyer, and Griffin, 1979). This reframing of what had been treated as distinct problems in policy circles and public discourse drew attention to their larger, common causes: an industrialized economy based on unchecked growth and consumption, a view of nature as existing solely for human exploitation, and the lack of public accountability on the part of the state and corporate developers of technology. This new and overarching environmental frame also implied the need for more far-reaching policy solutions, such as limiting growth, phasing out toxic materials, and enforcing greater public transparency of industry and government. The new environmental frame of the 1960s included a sharpened moral vision more willing to attribute ecological destruction to corporate and government decision makers.

This approach helps us to see how the emergence of environmental policy, and struggles over it, are also contests over framing. It turns our attention to questions about which actors possess the power to define problems in the public arena, how they define them strategically, how they use rhetoric to persuade others to accept their frames, and why some frames are more successful than others. It shows how our definitions of problems often shape the range of reasonable responses to them.

Environmental sociologist John A. Hannigan (1995) identified five factors that help account for whether environmental claims succeed or fail at gaining acceptance among the media, policymakers, and the public. We use these factors to examine how the CTBC framed its claims about e-waste and the need for a European-style take-back system. Framing is especially important in the U.S. context, where the news media play a major role in the policy process. As Sigal (1973) noted, the U.S. government, from the municipal to the federal levels, is large, geographically dispersed, and highly decentralized, making it difficult for officials to communicate with each other.

Authority

Activists' claims typically must be articulated in part through established authorities to gain wide legitimacy. Local and state government representatives have been especially important bearers of the message that the costs of handling e-waste are prohibitive and that industry must internalize and reduce them. The movement of bills through state legislatures provided news pegs for ongoing coverage of the e-waste problem. The range of debate in the mainstream American news media is closely calibrated to the range of views voiced by political elites at any given time (Bennett 1990). When political leaders legitimize EPR as a solution, journalists are more likely to treat its advocates in NGOs as credible and relevant sources.

Cultural Consonance

Successful environmental frames are presented in ways that resonate with existing culture and beliefs. A full-frontal assault on the dominant political–economic paradigm of the United States, on its widespread faith in techno-logical progress, markets, and economic growth, would likely be dismissed in public discourse. Thus, the CTBC showed that producers taking back their products fit with widely shared American values. One tactic has been to discuss EPR as facilitating recycling, which is far more popular than reusing or reducing materials in America's high-consumption society. At the same time, it has been essential to distinguish real EPR from "bottle-bill type" recycling, which has no impact on greening product design, and to explain why EPR is a more effective and comprehensive approach. Another strategy has been to emphasize economic incentives, such as the promise of taxpayer relief and reduced disposal costs to high-volume institutional purchasers. After the EU directives passed, the CTBC appealed to national interests by noting that U.S. companies were demanding lower environmental standards at home than they would have to follow in Europe and thus were offering U.S. taxpayers and consumers second-class treatment.

The CTBC pointed to the health risks of improper handling of e-waste and was most successful when linking these risks with concerns about global-ization. Activists first put the problem on the public radar most emphatically with the milestone report and video, *Exporting Harm* (BAN et al. 2002), which exposed U.S. e-waste exports to Asia and the toll on its environment and people (see Puckett, this volume).

In addition, like a lighter judo opponent grappling with a heavier foe, the CTBC used the weight of dominant business rhetoric to take down the industry's own arguments. The campaign showed that producer responsibility, far from being the kind of "command and control" regulation lambasted by U.S. industry in the past, simply *internalizes previously externalized costs of pollution*, offers electronics companies *flexibility to innovate* in how they meet its targets for recycling and chemical phase-outs, and encourages them to *compete on grounds of design and recycling efficiency*.

One of the most challenging issues for the CTBC to frame has been some recyclers' use of cheap prison labor, which undercuts other recyclers' ability to pay employees a living wage and effectively evades workplace safety regulations, which are loosely enforced behind prison walls. The rise of a ferocious law-and-order mentality in the past decade—fed by the growing political power of prison-related industries and prison guards' unions, the news media's obsession with sensationalized crime coverage, and opportunistic "tough on crime" politicians—means there is little sympathy for inmates in America, which now imprisons a larger percentage of its population than any other democracy in the world. In 2003, activists began to take on the issue, carefully framing the problem in a report entitled *A Tale of Two Systems* that contrasted Dell's use of prison labor to recycle its computers with a HP recycling facility that did not use prisoners (SVTC and CTBC 2003; see Wood and Schneider, this volume).

Moral Drama

Successful environmental frames typically present problems as morally charged social dramas, as clashes of values embodied in clearly identifiable victims, villains, and heroes. Journalism prizes are not awarded for uncovering tales of moral ambiguity, and political leaders cannot advance legislation by ruminating on an issue's ethical complexity. To reach both targets, activists needed to clarify the values at stake in the EPR debate. This progress is evident in activists' use of images, which crystallized the CTBC's messages in particularly memorable ways. Early efforts, such as a 1999 SVTC report entitled *Just Say No to E-waste* featured mounds of junked computers in city dumps awaiting disposal (see Photo 22.2). These pictures symbolized the impending wave of electronics that would hit the waste stream in coming years, dramatizing the problem of producers' commitment to rapid obsolescence and the government's inability to handle the resulting surge of waste. But these images could not represent the sharp sting of injustice perpetrated by one entity against another. Three years later, the *Exporting Harm* report and video captured wide media attention in part because it added human figures to the stage. By revealing to Americans where much of their information-age garbage was going, the report brought home the painful truth that the industry's toxic products and U.S. policies that encouraged hazardous waste

PHOTO 22.2. Mounds of obsolete computers and electronics, an example of the growing problem of e-waste in Canada. Courtesy of the Recycling Council of Ontario.

dumping on the world's poor were destroying communities and lives (see Puckett, this volume).

Like investigative reporters, the CTBC relied on irony to command public attention and dramatize the need for producer responsibility. *Exporting Harm*, as many journalists noted, struck a chord because it revealed that much of the equipment delivered to U.S. recyclers was in fact exported overseas. Thus, responsible Americans who made the extra effort to bring their old computers to a recycling center were in fact the ironic victims of a sham perpetrated by some recyclers. Even the term "e-waste," popularized by U.S. activists and adopted widely in the media, reversed the public perception of Internet-age progress in all things by suggesting the environmental and health consequences of the throwaway tools of e-mail and e-commerce.

At the same time, the CTBC's framing of the issues needed to show that not all producers or recyclers were equally guilty. Allying with more responsible industry actors was crucial to gaining support for a strong take-back system. There had to be heroes, or at least models, to show that EPR was feasible. For example, the CTBC followed the *Exporting Harm* report by releasing an electronics recyclers' pledge of stewardship (Appendix E, this volume), in which numerous private recycling firms agreed to renounce exporting and dumping e-waste and the use of prison labor. The campaign's report on prison labor in recycling prompted Dell to stop its reliance on inefficient and unsafe facilities at federal penitentiaries by contrasting it with a state-of-the-art HP recycling operation:

> These recycling operations suggest two paths for the future of e-waste recycling in America. One path leads toward efficient, transparent, modern facilities staffed by free labor, possessed of their rights as contemporary employees, able to protect themselves and nearby communities from harm. The other path descends into a closed, Dickensian world of prisoners condemned to dangerous work for little pay under backward conditions. Depending on the path we choose, e-waste recycling can

contribute to community economic development and environmental protection, or can become the equivalent of breaking rocks on a high-tech chain gang. (SVTC and CTBC 2003, 5)

Urgency and Visibility

Environmental claims must demonstrate a threat's impact on the present or near future. Oil spills, where immediate effects are dramatized, command public attention more powerfully than the seepage of radon gas into homes, which is a long-term and invisible problem. Activists emphasized the problem's urgency by estimating the health and financial costs of handling e-waste over the coming five years. As states faced mounting budget deficits during the recession and stock market bust of 2000–02, the CTBC argued that states must pass take-back legislation because they could no longer afford to subsidize a wasteful industry.

Agenda for Action

Finally, environmental arguments must include a clear plan of action, including short-term measures that can provide tangible benefits, such as shutting down a polluting facility or cleaning up a fouled stream. The EU directives offered the CTBC a model long-term solution to the problem of e-waste and enabled the CTBC to pursue a proactive strategy rather than a reactive strategy. In the near term, the campaign developed clear steps for its major constituencies and tools for achieving them. It provided government with model local resolutions and state legislation, as well as with information on costs of e-waste and implementation of EPR policies, counterarguments to resistant industry actors, and public support. For activists, the CTBC produced CD-ROM and World Wide Web-based toolkits with numerous ideas for actions (see Wood and Schneider, this volume). For recyclers, the CTBC offered positive publicity from signing the pledge of stewardship and supporting EPR legislation. Soon the recyclers were rewarded when e-Bay agreed to launch a reuse and recycling initiative on its Web site that recommended these recyclers to e-Bay users. For the public, the campaign provided its annual environmental report card on electronics companies to help guide purchasing decisions, as well as information on how and where to recycle e-waste responsibly. For the health care industry's institutional purchasers, the CTBC worked with its affiliate, Health Care Without Harm, to define clear procurement guidelines for adoption by hospitals throughout the country. The CTBC also worked with government allies to incorporate its "green purchasing" criteria in a US$4 billion request for proposals for information technology purchasing on behalf of governments, issued by the Western States Contracting Alliance. Similar green procurement initiatives focused on college and university electronics purchasing.

THE FUTURE OF EPR IN THE UNITED STATES

Producer responsibility for electronics has made impressive inroads in the United States since the late 1990s. The industry has conceded, in the words of an invitation to a recent AEA forum on regulation, that "it is clear that European environmental policy is setting a pattern for the rest of the world" (AEA 2003b). Some of the leading producers have accepted that they will have to incorporate the cost of handling their products at the end of their useful lives into the prices they charge U.S. consumers.

Future advances in adopting EPR in the United States will depend on four factors. First, progress will continue to depend on the success of the EU directives on waste and toxics reduction as they are implemented, as well as more recently adopted take-back laws across Asia. Whether take-back provisions will result in safe recycling jobs at livable wages is an open question that may be answered differently in various parts of the world. We also will have to monitor whether EPR is reducing the furious and wasteful pace of electronics production and consumption, so that the volume of the new waste produced does not outweigh increased recycling. If, for unforeseen reasons, the EU directives cannot sufficiently slow the industry's merry-go-round business model of instant product obsolescence, legislation may need to create additional incentives for companies to transition to a new model. We need to think more about how reducing overall electronics consumption can become a way of evaluating EPR policies.

Second, the advancement of EPR may continue to face threats from international trade policy. The Central American Free Trade Agreement (CAFTA), adopted by the United States in 2005, prohibited the federal government from adopting a host of preferences that have sometimes been written into procurement policies, including preferences for environmentally sustainable products. Although only 19 states agreed to be bound by CAFTA's purchasing restrictions before it passed Congress, the trade agreement requires the federal government to try to persuade state and local governments to accept the treaty's terms. If the federal government pursues the matter aggressively, for example, by withholding federal money (such as highway funds) unless states comply with CAFTA, then state and local preferences for greener electronics will be vulnerable to challenge. Similar restrictions on government procurement policies were discussed in the Doha round of WTO negotiations until 2004, when members finally agreed to drop them, but the passage of CAFTA may keep the issue alive in the future. If environmental purchasing policies continue to be declared a restraint of trade, the movement for EPR will lose an important lever for change.

Third, EPR's success will depend on the quality of state and national laws on e-waste. Although legislation is mushrooming at the state level, future efforts to bring an *effective* version of producer responsibility to the United States will depend on whether regulators and legislators settle for a quick-fix waste-management solution—similar to the bottle-bill approach—or commit fully to an EPR system that forces the reinvention of electronics by internalizing the costs of toxic materials and inefficient design in producers' bottom lines.

Fourth, the success of the long-term EPR campaign in the United States depends on the CTBC's ability to attract more industry support through future efforts similar to the Dell campaign. By continuing to split the industry and then working with those companies that embrace EPR, the CTBC will be more likely to win over policy makers than if the industry presents a united front against EPR. By pointing out that some leading companies support the environmentally preferable solution to e-waste, the campaign must further isolate those who call for merely assessing a consumer fee on new equipment sold. EPR advocates will need to show that this approach confers an unfair competitive advantage on companies most responsible for historic e-waste (such as IBM and television producers) and will fail to relieve taxpayers by generating insufficient financing for recycling legacy waste.

More specifically, model legislation in the United States, at the state or national level, will need to incorporate the following elements (see CTBC 2003):

- A definition of "electronic equipment" broad enough to include historic waste (such as old televisions and computers and their peripherals) and any new gear that includes a circuit board, complex circuitry, signal processing, or electronics that contains one or more hazardous substances;
- Requirements that brand owners and producers take financial responsibility for developing and operating a system for taking back products;
- Performance goals and timetables that spur producer accountability and better product design;
- A comprehensive scope that covers all manufacturers and brand owners, regardless of their sales channels or end users;
- A system for collecting historic waste (equipment sold and discarded prior to passage of the law), financed according to producers' current market shares, or their share of products returned at end-of-life, or other fair methods of allocating costs across the industry;
- Release of taxpayers from all liability for costs of collection, handling, transporting, storing, recycling or disposing of e-waste;
- A ban on disposing of e-waste in landfills and incinerators, which risk severe environmental and health harms to the public;
- Phase-outs of the most hazardous materials used in production, including but not limited to lead, mercury, polyvinyl chloride, and brominated flame retardants;
- A requirement that all electronics containing hazardous materials carry labels disclosing the materials and safe disposal practices;
- Verifiable performance standards for electronics recyclers, including reporting and penalties for violations, worker health and safety regulations, no use of prison labor, and no export of hazardous waste;
- Procurement guidelines for public agencies' information technology purchasing that give preferences to more environmentally benign equipment, and rule out equipment not in full compliance with the legislation;
- Effective means of enforcement, including requirements for periodic reporting by producers, public availability of such reports, and a multistakeholder advisory board to review compliance; and
- A commitment to fostering local economic development and job creation through electronics recycling and increased re-use.

CONCLUSION

The arrival of EPR on U.S. shores as a policy solution to the e-waste crisis of the late 1990s was born of several developments. The EU provided model legislation and a way of thinking about producer responsibility as the larger solution to risks posed by electronics throughout their lifecycle. Because of the electronics industry's extension into global markets, the European laws have generated pressure on brand-name producers to raise environmental standards for their products worldwide. However, in contrast to Europe, in the United States, NGOs' advocacy has advanced EPR more than policy makers' efforts, and EPR has proceeded through different channels: a market-based campaign and a policy effort that bubbled up from local governments. Finally, in a nation of decentralized governance and a media-saturated political culture, NGOs' attention to framing EPR in the news and policy discourse has been especially important. The progress of EPR's adoption in the United States will continue to rely on staving off efforts to use international trade policy to trump state laws, on the success or failure of EPR in Europe and Asia, on the comprehensiveness of state and national legislation, and on NGOs' ability to attract industry support for EPR.

23 International Environmental Agreements and the Information Technology Industry

THE PRODUCTION OF PERSONAL and institutional computers and information-processing equipment requires a large array of materials, chemicals, and natural resources. Production materials include ceramics, heavy metals, and chemicals that are toxic to humans and other species (see Byster and Smith, "Electronics Life Cycle"; Hawes and Pellow, this volume; see also LaDou 1984; U.S. EPA 1995). During the early years of electronic product development, there was little awareness or concern about environmental or public health hazards. This positive image began to unravel during the early 1980s when serious groundwater contamination was discovered near large semiconductor manufacturing facilities in California (see Byster and Smith, "Grassroots to Global," this volume), Massachusetts, and Kyushu, Japan (see Yoshida, this volume), and when workers in semiconductor clean rooms began to complain of unexpectedly high rates of miscarriages. More recently, the environmental burdens generated by the disposal of millions of tons of discarded computers have become an increasingly large concern (Pellow and Park 2002; Siegel and Markoff 1985; Yoshida 2002).

However, just as globalization allowed the information technology (IT) industry to avoid some of the true social costs of its products and processes, global markets have led to tightened environmental regulations in some countries, and an increasing number of international environmental agreements are posing significant restrictions on the industry worldwide. The industry has responded in various ways. Some firms and sectors have met these new demands with cooperation and innovation, whereas other firms and most of the industry trade associations have opposed them.

This chapter focuses on the recent history of three pieces of international regulation, explores the potential role of international policy in regulating the global IT industry, identifies how the industry has addressed these policy developments, and acknowledges these policies' potential effects on environmental and occupational health protection.

THE GLOBALIZATION OF THE ELECTRONICS INDUSTRY

The IT industry experienced an explosive growth during the 1970s and 1980s. By the middle of the 1980s, the drive for more efficient and less costly production pushed manufacturers to transfer production processes from the United States, Northern Europe, and Japan to lower wage areas in Southern Europe, Ireland and Scotland, Central America, and Southeast Asia. Throughout the 1990s, firms began contracting out large parts of their processes to independent processing firms with facilities in low-wage and loosely regulated countries (see Lüthje, this volume).

As the production of computers and information-processing equipment increasingly has become a global process, the markets for IT firms also have become global. With falling tariffs, liberal trade agreements, and increasingly open markets, firms no longer depend on domestic markets but openly compete for sales and market share in countries throughout the world.

The globalization that has permitted the IT industry to organize into a global-supply chain and to market products throughout the world has created both social and environmental problems that are beyond the reach of national regulatory institutions. National environmental protection and workplace safety agencies are bound within their respective nations. As some national governments have recognized the limits of their regulatory controls on multinational corporations, global markets, the international flow of investment capital, and the planetary nature of environmental pollution, they are gradually ceding authority to multinational and international governing bodies to manage environmental conditions. This transition has not been steady or even. Many European and several industrializing countries have been at the forefront, whereas the United States has been quite reluctant.

The implications for the IT industry are substantial. Big equipment manufacturers can no longer afford to rely on the markets and comfortable government relations within their host countries. Large, brand-name companies can no longer afford to ignore the growing public concerns about working conditions, environmental protection, and community impacts in countries where their suppliers conduct their business. National electronics industry trade associations can no longer focus solely on domestic markets and local governments. The potential industry impacts that have relevance for environmental policy can be grouped into three areas.

First, global markets mean that the regulatory conditions of the most aggressive nations tend to shape the product design and management conditions for the entire industry. The mass production of common products for a global market generally requires firms to develop products that meet the specific conditions of the most stringent country. When a country with an important market share, such as Germany or Japan, raises its product standards, there is no economic advantage for industries to develop a specific product line for that country alone. So when the European Union (EU), ratchets up its environmental regulatory standards, global electronics firms generally find that they must improve their performance, even when large shares of their markets are unaffected.[1]

Second, international policies can be used to promote particular countries, firms, or industry sectors at others' expense. International policies, such as those of the United Nations (UN) and the World Trade Organization (WTO), are promoted to harmonize discordant national regulations and to create common platforms for conducting business. Such harmonization can offer a serious setback to firms that had been protected by unique national legislation, and it can benefit firms that had been held back by domestic trade or regulatory barriers. The EU designs its regulations in a manner that promotes European firms, even as it defends its policies as a means to protect the environment, public health, or cultural heritage. The EU's policies on genetically modified foods and hormone-laced beef offer recent examples (Mol 1993, 2001).

Third, new international fora are often beyond the conventional political reach of industry and trade association government relations offices. As electronics firms have grown in scale and employment, they have gained more political influence over local, state, and national governments. However, the extent of this political power at home does not extend into international fora. Multinational and international bodies usually include a wide range of countries, and many have few local investments from the electronics industry.

The development of a globalized IT industry also opens up opportunities for those who promote environmentally sound and socially responsible industries to develop and use national and international instruments to achieve their ends. Indeed, these advocates also have begun to link up and coordinate their activities globally. Since the late 1970s, the Silicon Valley Toxics Coalition (SVTC) has been the premier voice of criticism and advocacy for environmental accountability in the United States. National and community-based organizations in many countries that host electronics manufacturing facilities, such as California's Santa Clara Center for Occupational Safety and Health, Scotland's PHASE Two, India's Toxics Link, Pakistan's Society for Conservation and Protection of the Environment, Malaysia's Sahabat Wanita, Taiwan's Association for Victims of Occupational Injuries (TAVOI), the Asia Monitor Resource Centre (AMRC), Greenpeace, the European Environmental Bureau, and the Basel Action Network (BAN) have established relationships to strengthen their advocacy across national boundaries and within international fora (see Pellow and Matthews; McCourt; Agarwal and Wankhade; Ku; Leong and Pandita; Pandita; and Puckett, this volume).

THE EMERGENCE OF INTERNATIONAL ENVIRONMENTAL AGREEMENTS

International agreements and multinational compacts to protect the environment have a long history. In 1909, the United States and Canada established the International Joint Commission to protect water quality in the Great Lakes. Today, there are more than 300 international agreements and treaties covering issues ranging from the protection of atmospheric ozone to the regulation of commerce in endangered wildlife. The establishment of the United Nations Environment Programme (UNEP) in 1972 and the European Community by the Treaty of Rome in 1957 laid important foundations for multinational environmental protection policies and agreements (McCormick 1991; Porter and Brown 1991).

Under the UN, a broad array of agreements has been drafted, negotiated, and placed into force. UNEP grew out of the UN's first global environmental congress, the 1972 Stockholm Conference on the Human Environment, which was established to promote the protection of the global environment and was given specific authority to develop and promote international agreements.

One of UNEP's principle successes was its Regional Seas Program, which generated successful protection agreements for the Mediterranean and Baltic Seas and demonstrated the potential for using multinational treaties to co-ordinate policies to protect environmental resources. By the 1980s, UNEP was hosting multiple international agreement drafting sessions with success-ful conventions signed in areas ranging from wildlife protection to ocean dumping and atmospheric protection (Haas 1990).

Procedures for negotiating these conventions have developed over time. The agreements emerge from draft texts prepared in a series of negotiating sessions that are then signed by delegates at a formal diplomatic meeting. However, they do not become formal conventions open for implementation until a designated number of national governments votes to ratify them. The 1969 Vienna Convention on the Law of Treaties established procedures to as-sure some uniformity and consistency in treaty forms and protocols (Caldwell 1992; Jacobson and Weiss 1997).

Since the 1980s, the EU has become an increasingly important multina-tional governing body in pioneering industrial and social policy. The EU is a federation of 25 Western European countries (member states) bound together in a common market. Governance is conducted through an administrative body called the European Commission (EC) and two legislative bodies: the Council of Ministers and the European Parliament. The EU can adopt reg-ulations or directives to which member states must conform their national policies.

The EC has specialized departments, with the Environmental Directorate (DG Environment) focused on protecting the European environment. During the past decade, the DG Environment has promoted new environmental poli-cies and directives. These actions, in part, have occurred to due pressure from the more environmentally sensitive member states, through either lobbying or placing their experts in Commission positions.

To consider how these international agreements develop and how the IT industry is responding, it is useful to review the recent history of three international policies: the UN's Basel Convention, the EU's Directive on Waste from Electrical and Electronic Equipment (WEEE), and the proposed EU policy called Registration, Evaluation, and Authorization of Chemicals (REACH).

Electronic Waste Trade and the Basel Convention

As many industrialized nations tightened their regulatory requirements re-garding the management of hazardous industrial wastes, the disposal costs rose rapidly and made it increasingly attractive to transport the wastes to developing countries with lax regulations and weak enforcement. A largely unregulated and lucrative international industry emerged, which combined waste collection and shipment with indiscriminate disposal in unspecified locations. When activists exposed these practices in the nongovernment advocacy community, the resultant international outrage led Hungary and Switzerland in 1987 to call on the Governing Council of UNEP to begin negotiations for a multinational agreement regulating the international shipment of hazardous wastes. Later that year, UNEP convened an initial working group in Budapest to draft procedures for multinational negotiating sessions.[2]

The negotiations proved to be tense and nearly broke down due to several African nations' hostility and U.S. resistance concerning the inclusion of municipal wastes. In March 1989, the Basel Convention on the Control of Transboundary Movement of Hazardous Wastes and Their Disposal was adopted at a diplomatic meeting at Basel, Switzerland, and came into force in May 1992.

The Basel Convention has three guiding objectives:

- To minimize the generation of hazardous wastes;
- To encourage the disposal of wastes as close to the source of generation as possible; and
- To reduce the global transport of hazardous wastes (UNEP 1989).

Specifically, it requires that participating nations act to reduce the transboundary shipment of wastes by minimizing the generation of wastes and treating and disposing of them as close to the source of generation that is practical and conducive to environmentally sound management. Rather than ban the international trade in hazardous wastes, the Basel Convention creates a global management system for regulating such trade. Parties to the agreement must seek "prior informed consent" from importing nations before shipping wastes and are prohibited from exporting wastes to nations that have banned such imports.

Unhappiness with the provisions of the Basel Convention's "managed trade" provisions led to further initiatives. First, African countries convened a separate set of negotiations to draft a regional treaty. The Bamako Convention, adopted in 1991, prohibits importing into Africa the hazardous wastes exported by countries that are not party to the Basel Convention. It also adopts a broader definition of hazardous wastes and requires the application of the precautionary principle and clean production to reduce waste at the source. Beginning in 1992, activists from the nongovernmental environmental movement joined with government leaders from several industrializing nations to expand the Basel Convention to adopt an outright ban on exporting hazardous wastes from richer to poorer nations. Despite significant resistance from the waste exporting nations, in 1995 the Council of the Participating Parties voted to adopt an amendment to the Basel Convention banning toxic waste exports from the industrialized countries of the Organization for Economic Cooperation and Development (OECD) to the industrializing (non-OECD) countries. This amendment has not yet come into force because two-thirds of the participating countries must ratify it. Consequently, the proponents have launched a substantial campaign to win national ratifications (BAN 1999).

Although 118 countries signed the initial draft of the Basel Convention, by 2004, 155 countries had ratified it. Although representatives from the U.S. Department of State were actively involved in the Basel negotiations and signed the resulting agreement, the U.S. Senate has failed to ratify the treaty (see Puckett, this volume).

The U.S. IT industry has been quite outspoken about the need to maintain open global markets for product waste management. Electronic waste constitutes nearly 5 percent of the U.S. municipal solid-waste stream and is growing rapidly. The American Electronics Association (AEA), the largest American electronics trade association with over 6,000 corporate members, has distributed several position papers arguing for the need to maintain unhindered access between waste exporters and waste importers throughout the world. In a 1996 position paper, the AEA argued that open waste markets lead to efficiencies in waste handling and encourage electronic component recycling because recycling and reuse cannot be cost effective due to high wages in the United States.

The problem starts with defining hazardous wastes. Instead of the Basel Convention requirements that define wastes according to their "intrinsic hazard," U.S. industry and government officials prefer the OECD guidelines that created a three-tiered definition of wastes based more on the risks of shipping and disposal practices (OECD 1992). Under the OECD guidelines, nonhazardous wastes exported to recycling facilities do not need to be regulated. With the exception of the United States and Canada, most countries define discarded electronic products as hazardous waste. The United States treats discarded computers and other electronic consumer goods as "special wastes," and therefore, it exempts these wastes from the domestic hazardous waste regulations convention. This opens a loophole for the unregulated exporting of wasted electronic products when the exporter claims they are being transferred to an overseas recycling facility.

No such loophole exists in the Basel Convention, where all discards and residues are treated as wastes no matter how they are eventually treated, recycled, or disposed. By signing and ratifying the Basel Convention, EU member states have essentially precluded wastes from electronic product production and discarded electronic products, by definition hazardous wastes, from being shipped to poorer countries. Because the United States remains a nonsignatory, this limitation does not apply to electronic wastes originating there.

Electronic Product Take Back and the European WEEE Directive

Following several years of negotiations, the EU's Council of Ministers and Parliament passed two directives in February 2003 that specifically addressed electronic and electrical product wastes. One initiative, the Directive on Waste Electrical and Electronic Equipment (WEEE), focused on equipment manufacturer's responsibility to manage electronic wastes at the point of disposal. The other, the Restrictions on the Use of Certain Hazardous Substances in Electrical and Electronic Equipment (RoHS), focused on eliminating the use of substances that generate environmental hazards at the point of product disposal (EC 2003a, 2003b).

The EC first proposed the WEEE Directive in June 2000. At that point, the language included both manufacturer responsibility and chemical restrictions in one proposal. The Commission sought to stem the growing flood of waste from electrical and electronic equipment from entering waste disposal landfills or contributing to the residues being incinerated in centralized, waste-combustion facilities. Electrical and electronic equipment was growing at a rate three times that of the entire waste stream and contributed the waste stream's largest share of toxic heavy metals and organic pollutants (Arensman 2000; SVTC 2001). The mandate covered all electrical consumer products, from refrigerators to cell phones. Conceptually, the proposed directive followed earlier EU proposals focusing on manufacturers' responsibility for managing packaging wastes and for properly disposing of automobiles (see Davis, Witt, and Barkenbus 1997; and Lindhqvist 2000).[3] The idea was to place the "end-of-life" burden for product recycling and disposal on the original equipment producer and to reduce the use of toxic chemicals that made product recycling and disposal so hazardous and costly. Further, the proposed directive was created to encourage manufacturers to design more environmentally friendly products that are reusable and recyclable. The WEEE Directive requires companies that supply electronic equipment in the EU to establish programs that manage the collection and recycling of discarded products by August 2005. Although each producer may establish its own system, it was envisioned that producers would join together to financially and administratively support a separate electrical equipment collection and recycling system and that they would find innovative substitutes for the restricted chemicals. Four of those substances—lead, mercury, cadmium, and hexavalent chromium—were already targeted under the earlier directive on vehicles' end-of-life management, but this agreement also included three types of brominated flame retardants (INFORM 2003).

From the earliest initiatives, the European IT industry has played a cautious, but engaged role. Recognizing that some directive on electronic waste was sure to be enacted, the leading European trade associations met with government counterparts, offered technical input, provided constructive criticism, and closely followed the drafting process. Several European firms supported further harmonization of European waste laws and agreed that the use of dangerous chemicals should be minimized.

The American IT industry was far more hostile. Several American electronics industry trade associations, including the Telecommunications Industry Association, the Consumer Electronics Association, the Electronic Components, Assemblies and Materials Association, and the American Electronics Association, formed the Electronic Industry Alliance (EIA) to coordinate public and government relations. The EIA has taken a lead in promoting voluntary electronic equipment recycling programs and in defending the use of lead and mercury in electronic products.[4]

In addition, the AEA criticized the fact that the WEEE proposal assigned sole responsibility to manufacturers and argued that consumers and municipalities should share the costs for managing discarded electronic equipment with the industry. Further, the AEA resented the restrictions placed on production chemicals, arguing that the hazards associated with the heavy metals and organic substances were exaggerated and that investments in "sound science" would support a more balanced approach to managing the risks (Hunter and Lopez 1999).

The AEA sought assistance from the U.S. Trade Representative (USTR), a White House agency that promotes American business interests internationally. The USTR added the weight of the federal government in lobbying Commission staff members. In a January 1999 position paper, the U.S. Diplomatic Mission in Brussels asserted that the directive could become an "unnecessary barrier to trade" and threatened to seek redress before the WTO. Interestingly, the U.S. Environmental Protection Agency (EPA)—the agency with the technical expertise to understand chemical and waste management—played no formal role in this lobbying and was generally overshadowed by the more powerful Commerce and State Departments. The 2002 draft dropped the requirement that manufacturers use a percentage of recycled plastic in future electronic products, permitted incineration to be considered as a potential disposal option, and weakened the provisions concerning brominated flame retardants.

The environmental advocacy movement fought back by writing letters to the EU Commissioner; stressing the need for sole producer responsibility; decrying the weakening of sections dealing with chemical substances; meeting with the USTR to voice their concern over the U.S. lobbying in European internal matters; and writing a letter to the U.S. Vice President asking that the Trade Representative's efforts be curtailed (see Raphael and Smith, this volume).

The AEA countered with its own letter to the Vice President, claiming that the chemical restrictions and design requirements went "... far beyond the establishment of environmental standards applicable to 'waste' of electrical and electronic equipment and will hamper global trade of high-tech products, impede technological innovation and fail to benefit the environment" (AEA et al. 1999). The pressure from the U.S. trade associations, the State Department, and USTR was formidable. Several European firms and the European electronics trade association criticized the proposed directive. By the summer of 2002, the Commission staff split the proposed directive, allowing the product take-back part to proceed ahead with the planned schedule, but lengthening the schedule for the restrictions on hazardous substances. When the European Council and Parliament voted to approve the proposal, it appeared as two independent, but cooperative directives, with the product take-back provisions of the WEEE Directive effective 2005, and the RoHS Directive bans effective in several phases only after 2006.

Chemicals Policy and the European REACH Proposal

Following a three-year dialogue and research on current policies, in 2001, EC issued a *White Paper on Future Chemicals Strategy*, outlining a bold restructuring of European chemical management policy (EC 2001). The White Paper emphasized increased testing of all industrial chemicals and stricter management of particular high-hazard chemicals and put forward the following specific objectives:

- Making industry more responsible for generating knowledge about chemicals, evaluating their risks and maintaining their safety—establishing a new "duty of care";
- Extending responsibility for testing and management of substances along the entire manufacturing chain;
- Substituting substances of very high concern with chemicals of lesser concern and driving innovation in safer chemicals as substitutes; and
- Minimizing the use of animal testing in determining the potential risks of chemicals.

The centerpiece of the White Paper was the establishment of a new, integrated chemicals management scheme called REACH that would require government registration for most industrial chemicals, testing and evaluation for larger volume chemicals, and special government authorization for using the most dangerous ones. The White Paper and the REACH proposal were extensively reviewed and debated, and, in May 2003, the EC presented draft legislation for public comment. In October 2003, the EC adopted its final legislative proposal, which was sent to the European Parliament and Council of Ministers for review. The REACH process would require that:

- All chemicals in commerce marketed over one ton per year must be registered with a new central European chemicals management agency, with companies manufacturing chemicals over ten tons per year providing basic toxicity, exposure, and risk data;
- Chemicals produced or imported more than 100 tons per year or of high concern must undergo rigorous new evaluation procedures conducted by the member states; and
- Chemicals of greatest concern based on their inherent characteristics (carcinogens, mutagens, reproductive hazards, persistence, and bioaccumulative potential) must be specifically authorized for continued use....

The REACH proposal marked a broad reorientation of government policy on the use of toxic and hazardous chemicals. Under earlier government approaches, exemplified by the 1976 Toxic Substances Control Act in the United States and the EU's 1979 Sixth Amendment to the Dangerous Substances Directive, chemicals used in industrial production prior to 1980 were largely assumed to be safe unless some incident or scientific study proved otherwise. New chemicals coming to market after 1980 were subject to testing and government review. Although firms were supposed to understand the risks associated with their existing chemicals and report any outcomes of concern, governments did little to motivate firms to do the testing, and there was little enforcement of the responsibility to report the results of new testing. The lack of health and environmental information, the burden on government to prove chemicals dangerous on a case-by-case basis, and the increasing evidence of the harmful effects of some chemicals appeared to require new legislation.

The REACH proposal shifted the burden concerning the testing and safety of existing chemicals. The EC created a huge, new responsibility for European industry, as well as a law that would ensure harmony in the European common market and not disadvantage Europeans because of more lenient requirements for imported chemicals. Surprisingly, most of the chemical and manufacturing industry agreed, recognizing equally that the current system simply did not work and that the industry had a poor public image. Indeed, some European firms saw a benefit in harmonizing the disparate national government regulations and standards. Others saw new opportunities for chemical innovation and substitution in their production processes.

There has been less agreement on the proposal's actual impacts on the industry. One government study of the European industry estimated that the costs of implementing the REACH proposal provisions could range from €1.4 to €7 billion. Another study predicted substantial harm to the German chemical industry, and a study of the impacts on the British industry suggested that over a 20-year period, the industry might need to spend £620 million on testing. The study also suggested that there were substantial benefits with reduced costs of occupational injuries and disease that might add up to £1.3 billion over a ten-year period. A further analysis of the REACH legislation's final draft found that the occupational health benefits alone would exceed the implementation costs. Additional analyses, commissioned by government agencies, industry, and environmental organizations have reached substantially different conclusions (see Risk and Policy Analysis 2001, 2003; Risk and Policy Analysis and Statistics Sweden 2002).

The U.S. business community watched the REACH proposal's progress with significant alarm. The American Chemical Council (ACC), the largest trade association for the domestic chemical industry, has been openly critical of the European chemical industry trade association's reluctance to fully oppose the new proposal. In addition, the AEA prepared a lengthy position statement, arguing that the REACH proposal was too broad and unworkable; providing a series of recommendations to limit its registration, authorization, and data requirements; and calling for exemptions for polymers and chemical intermediates (AEA Europe 2003). The ACC, the AEA, the U.S. Chamber of Commerce, and other trade organizations sought the assistance of the U.S. Department of State, the Department of Commerce, and the USTR in trying to stop or delay the European initiative. These agencies lobbied the DG Enterprise and sent embassy staff to meet with business and environmental divisions of the member states.

During 2002, the State Department embassy staff circulated a U.S. government "nonpaper" directly based on the position papers of the ACC and other trade associations. This nonpaper critiqued the REACH proposal and included many of the arguments that the U.S. government had used with the WEEE Directive. The nonpaper argued that the economic burdens on industry would be excessively high, that the testing provisions would stifle innovations in new chemical development, that the program lacked "workability" and was not based on "sound science," and, finally, that there was little evidence that the risks from these chemicals were unacceptable. The official comments from the Departments of Commerce and the Trade Representative on the REACH proposal reflected these same concerns, whereas the comments from the U.S. EPA focused primarily on technical matters. Similar to the U.S. lobbying against the WEEE directive, the EPA was sidelined in the REACH discussions by the more industry-responsive Commerce and State Departments (Brown 2003).

Once the U.S. environmental advocacy community heard about the U.S. government's efforts to derail the European proposal, a broadly signed letter of protest was sent to the USTR's office demanding a meeting. That January 2003 meeting involved the staff of six national organizations. The government staff listened to the issues raised, but argued that they had a responsibility to present the U.S. industry's views to their European counterparts. A 2003 examination of internal agency documents found a concerted effort by U.S. agencies to derail the REACH process. A subsequent Congressional analysis and Congressional hearings have documented the U.S. industry's influence on the government's response to REACH (DiGangi 2003).

PROMOTING NEW DIRECTIONS FOR THE GLOBAL ELECTRONICS INDUSTRY

International agreements can and do have an effect on an industry as large and far-flung as the IT industry. The industry has successfully played a sophisticated game of geopolitics in locating its production operations, organizing its structural investments, and shaping its markets and market strategies.

This review has demonstrated opportunities to use international environmental policies to rectify many of the inequities and injustices that have arisen from geographic arrangements.

At least two of these are already having an effect on the industry. The Basel Convention restrained the shipment of electronic product wastes from European countries (and other Basel Convention parties) to industrializing countries. This kept the costs of disposing of electronic product wastes high in Europe, but it also opened opportunities for domestic recycling and reuse programs. Indeed, the high costs of disposal and the need to seriously promote the recycling and reuse of used electronic products in Europe laid the foundation for the WEEE and RoHS directives. The legal basis for the WEEE Directive is environmental protection. Because electronic product wastes can no longer be easily shipped offshore irresponsibly, the EC was well positioned to promote an aggressive product take-back program. If the directive drives a well-managed recycling and responsible disposal program financed by the producers and paid for within the product purchase price, this will be a serious improvement over current practices.

The RoHS directive is more blunt. The legal basis of the RoHS Directive is the elimination of trade barriers. Banning certain core substances from the manufacture of electronic products will drive innovation and substitution. Lead, mercury, cadmium, and hexavalent chromium have been used for a long time in industrial production, and knowledge of their inherent toxicity has been well recognized for an equally long time. The requirement to phase out these metals affects not only European firms but also U.S. firms and suppliers. Research and technical assistance on lead-free electronics have been rapidly developing and are well-acknowledged results of the European directive.[5]

International concern over brominated flame retardants also has been growing since the negotiations over the RoHS Directive. Although the directive only covers flame retardants used in European electronic products, new policy initiatives have arisen in Asia and the United States, where efforts have focused on the brominated compounds used in many polymer-based products. California and Maine passed laws to phase out the use of brominated flame retardants in electronic products, and the largest producer of brominated flame retardants in the United States has come under enough pressure to offer a voluntary phase-out.

If the European REACH proposal were to be adopted as now drafted, it would have a substantial impact on the international IT industry. Efforts to seriously restrict the use of carcinogens, mutagens, reproductive toxins, and persistent and bioaccumulative substances would affect the computer industry and provide a strong incentive to replace these chemicals in products. This could be a major driving force for chemical innovation and substitution. Importantly, the WEEE and RoHS directives, along with discussions about REACH, provide strong market signals to the industry about promoting more environmentally benign products and including life-cycle considerations in product designs. Numerous electronics firms, including Samsung, Fujitsu, Sony, and Electrolux, have initiated programs to encourage sustainable product design and hazardous chemical substitution.

The Basel Convention largely adopts a traditional approach to environmental protection, attempting to restrict the worst abuses. The WEEE Directive is different. Instead of attempting to stop product disposal, the directive attempts to establish a new management program that could have far-reaching implications for product design and materials management. It is too early to guess how the REACH proposal may develop, but given the amount of political capital that member states have invested in chemicals reform and the history of similar proposals, it is likely that the REACH proposal's basic principles will remain intact, and that it will be enacted by 2006.

CONCLUSION

Globalization offers a double-edged opportunity. The initial results in terms of environment and public health outcomes often appear to be negative. However, globalization also brings opportunities to develop new international accountability structures and to engage people and governments throughout the world in positive efforts toward managing industrial performance for social benefits. For instance, the EU demonstrated its increasing interest in developing strategic alliances with developing countries when it promoted two recent UN treaties and a new global chemicals initiative. The Stockholm Convention on Persistent Organic Pollutants (POPs) and the Rotterdam Convention on Prior Informed Consent established global structures for managing 12 global pollutants and for ensuring that developing countries have the right to know about incoming shipments of hazardous chemicals and the ability to regulate them. (The United States has failed to ratify both of these conventions.) In 2002, UNEP announced a new worldwide program called the Strategic Approach to International Chemicals Management (SAICM) to systematize and coordinate international chemicals management efforts.

Developing and implementing international agreements takes a concerted effort of many stakeholders. The process itself can have an educational and empowering effect on all those who participate. Whether the international IT industry is permitted to reap only the narrow economic benefits of globalization or whether it will be conditioned by international agreements to adopt a broader and more socially responsible mission remains to be seen.

NOTES

1. David Vogel (1995) refers to this as the "California effect."

2. For a short case study, see Tolba (1998, 97–124).

3. These directives have promoted the concept of "extended producer responsibility" (EPR), where manufacturing firms are encouraged to "take back" their products after the consumer has completed their useful life.

4. See the Electronics Industry Alliance's Internet site: www.eia.org.

5. For instance, the Massachusetts Toxics Use Reduction Institute has been working with several electronic industry firms to find alternatives to lead in electronic products largely driven by the anticipation of the RoHS Directive.

24   Design Change in Electrical and Electronic Equipment

Impacts of Extended Producer Responsibility Legislation in Sweden and Japan

ELECTRICAL AND ELECTRONIC EQUIPMENT (EEE) is regarded as a priority for diversion from landfills and incinerators because of its increasing overall volume[1] and the hazardous substances it contains. The rapid advancement of technology has increased the variety and complexity of EEE, making it difficult for conventional municipal collection and recycling infrastructures to handle the volume. The situation becomes even worse when adequate information (e.g., the location of hazardous substances or the means of disassembly) is not transferred from the manufacturers to the treatment facilities. These interrelated features make EEE waste problematic in terms of both quality and quantity.

A handful of studies (e.g., Lindhqvist 2000; OECD 1998; Raphael and Smith, this volume; Stevens 2004; Zoboli 2000) has suggested that extended producer responsibility (EPR) promotes changes in product design. However, empirical studies indicating the effectiveness of EPR programs in promoting upstream changes have been limited, especially for such complex products as EEE. Indeed, despite the recognition of regulation's role in stimulating innovation (Ashford, Heaton, and Priest 1979; Barde 1995; Norberg-Bohm 2000; Porter and van der Linde 1995), empirical research is rare, and no standard methods for evaluating environmental policy instruments have been established (Hildén et al. 2002). Evaluating an environmental policy becomes even more difficult when it contains many instruments addressing multiple goals, as is the case with many EPR programs.

This chapter reports on a study of the effectiveness of EPR legislation in promoting the environmentally conscious design of EEE manufacturers in Japan and Sweden.[2] Primary data, mainly qualitative in nature, were collected with in-depth, open-ended interviews with 24 representatives from 13 EEE manufacturers (9 in Japan and 4 in Sweden). Manufacturers were selected based on the contact possibility and availability of the interviewees during the study's timeframe.[3] Information gathered from manufacturers was complemented by interviews with experts on product policy and environmental product design, and with personnel in relevant governmental agencies. Information regarding the development of relevant regulations, government reports, and newsletters also were reviewed.

EPR LEGISLATION

The EPR legislation in Japan and Sweden differs in scope, in their allocation of responsibility for collection, and in their allocation of responsibility for recycling.[4] In its scope, for instance, the Japanese Specified Home Appliance Recycling Law, enforced in 2001, covers four large home appliances. By contrast, under the Swedish legislation enacted in July 2001, all EEE within the scope of the Waste Electrical and Electronic Equipment (WEEE) Directive (see Geiser and Tickner, this volume), except for refrigerators, freezers, and automatic dispensers, are covered.

In allocating responsibility for collection in Japan, retailers who had previously taken back approximately 80 percent of the four large home appliances (MoHW and MITI 1998) are required to take back old products when they sell similar new products (*old-for-new*). The collection of the rest is handled by local governments and designated legal entities. End users pay the cost of collection. In Sweden, legislation allocates physical and financial responsibility for collection to producers and retailers on old-for-new basis, whereas the rest remains on the shoulders of local governments. Producers and retailers must inform consumers of their duty to collect and consult with the local authorities regarding the location of aggregation stations. Neither country sets collection targets, although the adaptation of the WEEE Directive will require an annual, minimal collection of four kilograms WEEE per person from private households in Sweden.

TABLE 24.1. Characteristics of EPR Legislation for EEE in Japan and Sweden, 2001

Country	Coming into Force	Scope	Allocation of Responsibility for Collection	Allocation of Responsibility for Recycling
Japan: Specified Home Appliance Recycling (SHAR) Law	April 1, 2001	4 large home appliances[a]	Physical: Retailers: old-for-new, products that they themselves sold before Municipalities/designated legal entities: those not covered by retailers Financial: End users	Physical: Producers Financial: End users
Sweden: Ordinance on Producer Responsibility for Electrical and Electronic Products	July 1, 2001	All large and small EEE[b]	Physical and financial: Producers and retailers: old-for-new Municipalities: those not covered by retailers (physical and financial) (*Manner of implementation differs from what is stipulated by law: see Figure 24.1*)	

[a]TV sets with CRTs, refrigerators and freezers, air conditioners, and washing machines.
[b]Products included: (1) large and small home appliances except refrigerators and freezers, (2) information and communications technology and office equipment, (3) consumer equipment, (4) watches and clocks, (5) games and toys, (6) lighting equipment, (7) medical equipment, and (8) laboratory equipment.
Sources: Tojo (2000), Tojo (2001).

In allocating responsibility for recycling, Japanese producers of four large home appliances have a physical, individual responsibility for setting up regional aggregation stations, and for engaging in take-back, reuse, recycling, and the environmentally sound treatment of discarded products. Individual producers can charge end users a recycling fee when the products are discarded (*end-user-pays system*). They also must meet differentiated recycling rate requirements that are between 50 and 60 percent by weight, which should be fulfilled by product reuse, component reuse, and material recycling. The recovered products and components and recycled materials that do not have positive monetary value are not included in this percentage. Small producers may enter contracts with legally designated entities that fulfill the physical responsibility on their behalf.

The Swedish legislation assigns EEE producers and retailers the physical and financial responsibility for take-back, reuse, recycling, and environmentally sound treatment of discarded products, on an old-for-new basis regardless of the brand. The producers must provide recycling plants with information that facilitates safe and environmentally sound treatment. The Swedish legislation does not set any numerical recycling targets, which will be required upon its adoption of the European Union (EU) Directive. Table 24.1 summarizes some of the characteristics of the Japanese and Swedish EPR legislation for EEE as discussed previously.

EFFECTIVENESS IN PROMOTING ENVIRONMENTAL PRODUCT DESIGN

Both Japanese and Swedish manufacturers mentioned that environmental impacts differ from product to product, making it is difficult to generalize the relative importance of the end-of-life stage in the process of their product development. All company representatives interviewed conduct some forms of environmental product assessment that integrates life-cycle thinking, including energy efficiency, reduction of hazardous substances, and resource efficiency. The standards for the respective criteria often are drawn from relevant legislation, nonlegislative standards (e.g., eco-labels), and internal company goals (reflecting the content of anticipated legislation).

Research findings confirm that the changes envisioned in EPR programs have taken place. Three, interrelated elements can be identified among the measures with regard to end-of-life management associated with the WEEE: product design change; development of infrastructure, including financial mechanisms; and communication with recycling plants.

In both Japan and Sweden, product design for end of life, in terms of both material use and structure, has been taking place. Examples include reducing or avoiding the use of hazardous substances, reducing the number of components and screws, and achieving uniformity in the types of plastics and how they are made.

In Japan, manufacturers of four large home appliances discussed collaboration, leading to the establishment of two groups to meet the collection and recycling requirements.[5] Companies within these groups cooperated in establishing regional aggregation stations, take-back networks, and recovery and treatment facilities. However, each manufacturer manages at least one treatment plant and engages in compiling and communicating information from the downstream (recycling plant) to the upstream (product design department), accumulating knowledge on recovery technology, and grasping the actual cost for recovery and environmentally sound treatment of their discarded products.

With regard to financial mechanisms, some small manufacturers and importers of the four large appliances announced fees for take-back, recovery, and treatment. However, these fees are still far below the actual costs of recycling (Tanaka and Miyasaka 2000). Some producers were taking back computers from business users before the legislation was enforced, with the cost born by the users. When the interviews were conducted, a separate piece of EPR legislation for computers used in private households had not been finalized, but was anticipated. Most Japanese manufacturers of home appliances also produce personal computers. The companies that produce personal computers, but not electrical home appliances, started developing their own recycling plants relatively early.

In Sweden, one collective system was developed as a result of cooperation among various industry associations that are affected by the legislation. This organization, El-Kretsen (the El[ectronics] cycle) runs the system and is in charge of allocating responsibilities to producers and retailers in Sweden. As mentioned, the Swedish legislation stipulates that the industry is responsible for old-for-new forms of collection and recycling, whereas the rest remains in the hands of the local governments. Contrary to the legislation, the El-Kretsen system holds local governments responsible for collecting waste from private households and transferring it to regional aggregation stations, whereas producers take care of the transfer from the aggregation stations, recycling, and treatment. Business waste is either brought to the aggregation stations on an old-for-new basis or brought directly to the recyclers. Figure 24.1 presents simplified schematic maps of a system envisioned in legislation and the implementation mechanism developed by El-Kretsen.

The fee structure introduced by El-Kretsen combines (1) participation fees from producers delegating their responsibility to El-Kretsen and (2) fees collected based on the number and type of products currently on the market, regardless of the brand or degree of design for end of life. The fee finances the system for end-of-life management.

Establishing one collective system and the manner of its implementation was not without concerns. For example, the manufacturers of mobile phones that wanted to pay according to the product's features in relation to the recycling operation feared that this might not be easily achieved under the El-Kretsen system. Computer manufacturers that sell a substantial portion of their products to business customers explored the possibility of establishing an alternative system parallel to El-Kretsen's to meet their customers' needs better.

Japanese manufacturers that already had established recycling facilities also raised the issue of the benefits of the various types of information gained

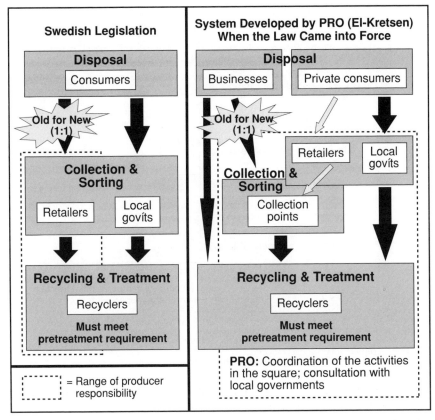

FIGURE 24.1. Extended Producer Responsibility Program for Electrical and Electronic Equipment in Sweden: Legislation and Implementation.
Source: Author, based on the legislation (SFS 2000:208) and Kollberg (2002).

from their recycling plants. Modes of communication between the upstream and the downstream include the Intranet, periodic meetings among the personnel in recycling plants and product design department, and seminars that allow designers to experience the dismantling of a discarded product.

In Sweden, producers generally did not establish their own recycling plants. However, some have established workshop/refurbishment plants, with the aim of gaining design improvements and the actual costs for recycling. In 1997, mobile phone manufacturers conducted a pilot project in collaboration with a major recycler in Sweden, a logistics company for transportation, and a number of retailers. During the project, extensive communication took place between the recycler and the producer, which contributed to designs for end of life, especially in terms of material use.

Figures 24.2 through 24.5 summarize factors affecting manufacturers' ability to measure managing their products end of life in Japan and Sweden.

A few manufacturers in Japan mentioned that enforcing the EPR legislation for large home appliances may encourage consumers to consider renting

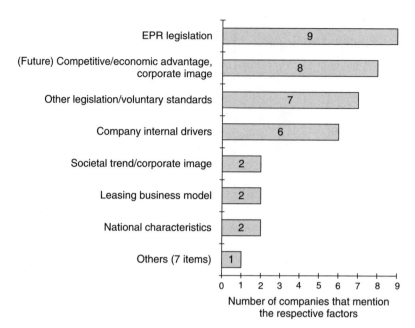

FIGURE 24.2. Factors *Promoting* the Undertaking of Measures Related to Design for End-of-Life for Electrical and Electronic Equipment Manufacturers in Japan. *Source:* Tojo (2004).

or leasing services, rather than purchasing certain products. In fact, taking advantage of the consumers' preference for convenience, and the existing distribution network, some convenience stores in Japan have started new businesses as secondhand products dealers (Tanaka 2001). The stores take back relatively new, large home appliances and pay a small sum to consumers (Tanaka 2001). Recognizing the business potential, some producers have started to run rental services, featuring their own products, as part of their business (Toshiba 2003).

DISCUSSION

The findings suggest that EPR legislation is a significant factor in promoting design change for end-of-life management in the two countries studied. All interviewees considered the EPR legislation's anticipated requirements as important to achieving design change in their product development strategies. Changes have been taking place, despite the factors that hinder them (e.g., costs, conflicts among design priorities, lack of demand from customers, infrastructure constraints, and lack of expertise).

Strength of the Anticipated Legislation

Both the Japanese and Swedish legislations were enacted, but neither had been implemented at the time of the interviews. Nevertheless, producers had started to take measures to reduce the environmental impacts at the design

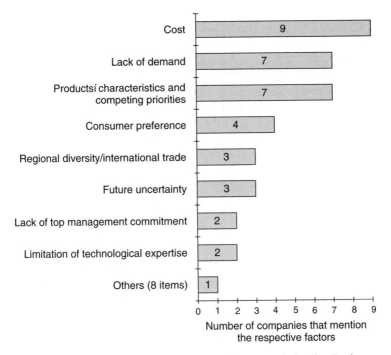

FIGURE 24.3. Factors *Hindering* the Undertaking of Measures Related to Design for End-of-Life for Electrical and Electronic Equipment Manufacturers in Japan. *Source:* Tojo (2004).

stage. Some manufacturers of four home appliances and computers in Japan and a mobile-phone manufacturer in Sweden suggested that the earlier an industry becomes engaged in recycling issues, the more benefit it will receive in the long run.

The Effect of Material Restrictions

The opinions regarding the RoHS Directive's effects were unanimous. Substance bans may be the most straightforward way of driving upstream design changes. One of the most visible actions taken by many manufacturers is the development of lead-free solders and halogen-free and bromine-free components. Some interviewees recognized that it is much easier to internally communicate the necessity of developing alternative substances through mandatory phase-outs, rather than through voluntary guidelines or commitments. However, uncertainty about the legislative requirements may encourage industries to be inactive, rather than active in their efforts toward design change.

The Effects on Component and Material Suppliers

EPR legislation has motivated material and component suppliers to develop preferred materials for end-of-life management. First, manufacturers' requests to develop materials for end-of-life management will directly influence

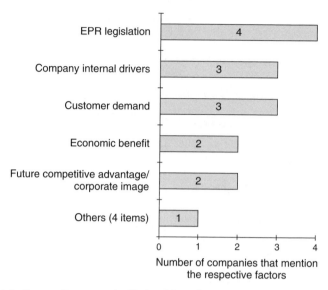

FIGURE 24.4. Factors *Promoting* the Undertaking of Measures Related to Design for End-of-Life for Electrical and Electronic Equipment Manufacturers in Sweden. *Source:* Tojo (2004).

them. As the manufacturers are pressured to achieve the increased recycling requirements, they look for material suppliers that can help them meet such requirements. If a material supplier does not change, it may experience difficulty continuing its business. Second, once the materials begin to be recycled, producers must find ways to reuse such materials, or sell them to a third party.

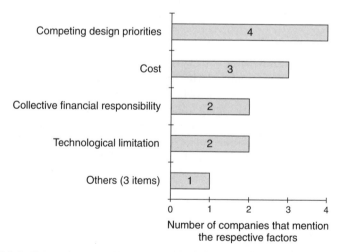

FIGURE 24.5. Factors *Hindering* the Undertaking of Measures Related to Design for End-of-Life for Electrical and Electronic Equipment Manufacturers in Sweden. *Source:* Tojo (2004).

If the third party handles a significant amount of the recycled materials, the material suppliers may put themselves at risk of decreasing business.

The Importance of Downstream Infrastructure in Promoting Design Change

The Specified Home Appliance Recycling (SHAR) Law in Japan has had a very positive influence on Japanese manufacturers' design changes. Most interviewees acknowledged that the enactment of the SHAR Law helped them establish a communication path between the upstream and the downstream parts of the product life cycle. The fact that all of the manufacturers have at least one recycling plant seems to be the key for establishing a strong feedback system.

Also, a Japanese manufacturer commented that without the proper infrastructure for end-of-life management, the efforts made upstream would be in vain. Indeed, without a collection system and proper separation of materials and parts, manufacturers have little incentive to improve the material and components selection and structure of products.

Collective Responsibility Lacks a Driver for Design Change

The Swedish respondents' views on legislation were divided. There were both very positive comments, such as, "The legislation is the strongest driving force"; and negative comments, such as, "Swedish legislation does not have any influence at all when it comes to promotion for design change." The latter comment points to the weakness of collective responsibility in terms of incentives to the producers to work on design change. The producers' responsibility, as stipulated in the Swedish law, as well as the practice of El-Kretsen, does not require the distinction of brands. Some prominent Swedish manufacturers strongly advocated individual responsibility during the development of the EU's WEEE Directive (ENDS 2001, 2002a).

The Scope of Legislation and Collection

In connection with the establishment of infrastructure, one difference between Europe and Japan is the scope of legislation. Differences in the existing distribution and collection infrastructure, especially those found between large and small appliances, pose challenges to many European programs with regard to the collection of smaller appliances. This may discourage the manufacturers of small appliances from striving for designing for their products' end of life. This was one reason why the Japanese EPR program for EEE started with a relatively narrow scope.

End-User-Pays Systems

When the SHAR Law was enacted, there was a concern that it may not provide producers with significant incentives for design change because of the end-user-pays system. Concerns became even greater when all the prominent manufacturers announced the same take-back/recycling fee for the same type of products. As recycling plants remain unprofitable, cost does matter for the manufacturers that run the plants, and incentives exist to reduce end-of-life costs by working with the upstream. The Japanese legislation does not allow recycled materials that do not have positive monetary value to be counted in the recycling percentage. This provides incentives for manufacturers to strive for design that enables reuse and recycling and to explore markets for recycled materials. Other concerns include the end-user-pays system and a potential increase in illegal dumping. In addition to the recycling fees that the individual producers charge, end users must pay collection fees. Municipalities have identified a subsequent increase in the amount of illegal dumping, though the government does not consider it to be significant (MoE 2002, 2003). However, an advantage of this system is the development of rental service by producers that may enhance products' design, which encourages the upgrading and reuse of components.

Individual versus Collective Responsibility

The study introduced earlier suggested that EPR legislation provides significant incentives for environmentally conscious designs. It also indicated the importance of individual versus collective responsibility. The experiences of the European countries (e.g., Switzerland, the Netherlands, Norway, and Sweden) that already have started to implement their national EPR legislation for EEE showed relatively good results in terms of collection and recycling, generally satisfying the collection rate mandated in the EU Directive.[6] Meanwhile, most producers' physical responsibility has been coordinated and fulfilled collectively by one or a few Producer Responsibility Organizations (PROs).

COLLECTIVE RESPONSIBILITY

As illustrated by the El-Kretsen system in Sweden, most of these PROs have handled all the administrative work, including communications with the recyclers, on behalf of producers. Apart from paying the bill, Swedish manufacturers have little contact with their products at end of life. When the fee structure is flat for the same type of products, regardless of the brand or design (collective financial responsibility), the companies producing more environmentally benign products end up subsidizing the companies that have not made such efforts. In addition, when one or a few PROs handle all the discarded products, this raises a concern that the PROs are an oligarchy with power over recyclers (Tojo 2004).

At the same time, the collective implementation of physical responsibility helps avoid the inefficiency of establishing multiple infrastructures and leads to an economy of scale. It also may help reduce the transaction costs for both individual producers and actors involved in collection and recycling (Tojo 2004). Having a collective body managing the infrastructure helps identify free riders, who have their products recycled without paying fees to the system (Veerman 2003; Vonkeman 2003). The stringent environmental requirements set by some PROs help secure the quality of recycling activities (Tojo 2004).

INDIVIDUAL RESPONSIBILITY

The implementation of individual financial responsibility (i.e., differentiating the fee depending on the actual recycling costs of the respective products) is certainly a better way to provide producers' incentives for design change. However, the EEE products' complexity in terms of structure and material use make it difficult to determine appropriate fees in accordance with their end-of-life environmental features. When a substantial proportion of the fee is used for logistics, rather than for recycling per se, it discourages PROs from differentiating the fee based on the degree of design for end of life (Huisinga 2003). The use of fees for future recycling of the products may make financial management complicated and require other mechanisms to handle historical and orphan products.[7] These factors are perceived to pose various administrative challenges when implementing individual responsibility.

OPERATIONAL MEANINGS OF INDIVIDUAL RESPONSIBILITY

The EPR legislation for EEE in Europe (e.g., the Netherlands and Switzerland) has revealed that in parallel with collective responsibility, individual implementations do exist (Tojo 2004). Based on a review of various implementation mechanisms, I propose that individual physical responsibility requires (1) distinction and (2) producers' control over the fate of the discarded products that they have manufactured/imported. The implementation of individual physical responsibility should enable producers to engage in individual financial responsibility so that producers pay the actual recycling costs of their own products (Tojo 2004). Although the final text of the EU WEEE Directive explicitly stated that each producer should bear individual financial responsibility for its own new products, it allows the producer to choose the actual implementation mechanism. In the process of transposing the EU WEEE Directive into national legislation, producers started to examine the feasibility of individual solutions (ENDS 2002a, 2002b; Tojo 2004). This allows recyclers to explore new business opportunities (Van Kalkeren 2003).

CONCLUSION

This study indicates that in Japan and Sweden, EPR legislation has been providing significant incentives for producers to work on designing products' end of life. The chapter has highlighted the importance of individual implementation in driving design changes and suggests individual responsibility. The existence of a few implementation mechanisms in which responsibility is fulfilled individually suggests the possibility of changing the existing EPR legislation in Europe, which mostly has been implemented collectively. Further studies of the implementation of EPR legislation and its impact on design change will be important in the coming years. Equally important will be efforts to ensure that the products collected are disposed of in environmentally sound ways. Serious concerns regarding the export of waste under the name of recycling have been highlighted (see Puckett, this volume). European recyclers share related concerns from the viewpoint of unfair competition (Tojo 2004), as do businesses in Japan, with its last-owner-pays system. Practical measures for addressing environmental and health standards for recycling activities also need further investigation.

Notes

The author is grateful to Thomas Lindhqvist, Gary Davis, and Lars Hansson, co-authors of key materials used in the preparation this document, and Philip Peck, for their invaluable input and sharing their experiences and thoughts.

1. The number of obsolete notebook computers in the United States, for instance, is projected to increase from 2 million units (1997) to 6.7 million units (2003), and in the case of cathode ray tube (CRT) monitors, from 13.7 million units (1997) to 26.1 million units (2003; National Safety Council 1999, 39–40).

2. The original study included automobile manufacturing, as well; only findings related to the EEE industry are reported here. For the full study, including further details regarding research methodology, see Tojo (2004).

3. Personnel were interviewed from the following manufacturers: Fujitsu Ltd., Hitachi Ltd., Matsushita Electric Industrial Corporation Ltd., Mitsubishi Electric Corporation, NEC Co., Ricoh Company Ltd., Sharp Corporation, Sony Corporation, Toshiba Corporation (Japan), AB Electrolux, Dell Computer AB, Ericsson, Siemens-Elema AB (Sweden).

4. A separate law for personal computers in Japan—Revised Law for Promotion of Effective Utilization of Resources—is not introduced in this section, as it was enacted after the study was conducted and its content was not discussed during the interviews. Likewise, because the EU WEEE and RoHS Directives (see Geiser and Tickner, this volume) were not in their final form during the interviews, many issues, such as whether the producers should be responsible individually or collectively, were yet to be determined.

5. One group has a large number of retailers specialized in selling their brand products and utilize them for takeback obligation. The other group consists of manufacturers who agree on establishing their own recycling plants and recycle their end-of-life products.

6. The collection rate per person per year was 5.1 kg in Switzerland (1999), 4.8 kg from private households in the Netherlands (2002), 7.2 kilograms in Norway (2001), and 10 kilograms in Sweden (July 200–June 2002), respectively. In Switzerland, about two thirds of the large and small electrical appliances collected and roughly 75 percent of ICT equipment collected, was materially recycled in 1999 (Elektronikkretur AS and Hvitevareretur AS 2002; NVMP Foundation 2002; Swedish EPA 2002; Türk 2001; Veerman 2003).

7. For example, use of recycling insurance has been suggested in Sweden as an alternative financial mechanism for durable, complex products. However, it would be challenging to set the size of premium that reflects the degree of design for end of life and an insurance company would require be required with additional efforts in establishing an effective downstream-upstream communication path.

25   ToxicDude.com

The Dell Campaign

SMALLER, FASTER, and cheaper—these are the defining qualities of today's computers and consumer electronics. Yet, despite the persistent pace of design advancements in consumer electronics, product designers often have largely ignored the public health threats and environmental consequences of the choices they make—from materials use to end-of-life management. The rapid proliferation of computers and consumer electronics has resulted in a global mountain of high-tech trash, a culture of obsolescence, and new products being designed for disposability rather than reuse and recycling (see Photo 25.1).[1]

IT'S TIME TO REBOOT THE SYSTEM

The Computer TakeBack Campaign (CTBC) was formed in early 2001 by a small group of environmental health and waste-reduction activists from the United States and Canada, in conjunction with organized labor and socially responsible investors, to hold corporations producing and marketing computers and consumer electronics accountable for the life-cycle effects of their products, particularly those sold in the United States (see Raphael and Smith, this volume). At issue were both the quantity and the toxicity of electronic waste ("e-waste"), because if electronics are less toxic and more recyclable at the waste end, the production process also will be less hazardous for the workers and surrounding communities.

The CTBC network of local, state, and national organizations works to establish and promote the principle of extended producer responsibility (EPR; see Appendix D, this volume). In two years, the CTBC defined the e-waste problem; organized broad support for a comprehensive, sustainable solution; and forced the U.S. computer industry's leading company—Dell Computer Corporation—to respond and begin reshaping its company policies.

A New Kind of Corporate Accountability

The CTBC's genesis emerged from the confluence of two important North American grassroots movements: environmental health and resource conservation. First are organizations like Silicon Valley Toxics Coalition (SVTC), whose two decades of victories for cleaner high-tech production has focused on the need for continuing product and process design changes and eliminating the use of toxic materials that injure workers, communities, and families. In the second group are such organizations as the GrassRoots Recycling Network (GRRN), with advanced strategies beyond recycling, which manage

PHOTO 25.1. Activists at the annual "MacWorld" trade show, protesting Apple Computer Inc.'s contributions to rapidly accumulating e-waste, San Francisco, January 2005. Courtesy of Silicon Valley Toxics Coalition.

waste at the end of the pipe. GRRN also critiques the reliance on taxpayer dollars to manage problems created by manufacturers' unsustainable design choices over which local governments and consumers have little control. For both movements, the answer was EPR, the emerging global framework that holds producers and brand owners financially responsible for their products' life-cycle effects and emphasizes product take-back and end-of-life management (see Raphael and Smith, this volume).

The power of EPR as a policy tool and organizing strategy attracted other organizations and constituencies to the CTBC,[2] and drew more activists and organizations into the campaign for sustainable production and consumption in the electronics industry. Ten U.S.-based organizations developed a platform in March 2001 that has been endorsed by hundreds of people in dozens of countries.[3] Product designers, corporate-accountability activists, nongovernmental organizations (NGOs) concerned with local economic development and job creation, organized labor, students, socially responsible investors, and environmentalists gave shape to the CTBC, developing and disseminating a comprehensive platform that animates the CTBC's goal statement: "Take it back, Make it clean, and Recycle responsibly."

The CTBC's EPR policy suggested two possible strategies, which were quickly recognized as providing complementary points of leverage:

- Build sustained consumer and market pressure on Dell Computer Corporation;[4] and
- Build public support for regulatory reforms embracing producer responsibility.

The CTBC member organizations recognized that the prospects of an EPR solution coming from the top down at the start of the George W. Bush years in 2000 were virtually nonexistent. However, state-level efforts to ban the disposal of e-waste in landfills were successful in a handful of states.

Why Dell?

In the personal computer (PC) industry sector, which is populated by nearly two dozen known name brands and scores of component suppliers throughout the computer equipment supply chain, the Dell Corporation stood out as the clear target for the CTBC's corporate campaign organizing for at least nine reasons:

1. The CTBC resisted the common market campaign strategy of targeting retailers as a means of influencing the company whose practices were the real objection. In a campaign pushing for EPR and end-of-life take-back, a focus on retailers would divert attention from the entities with the greatest control over the problem and the solution—the producers and brand owners.[5]

2. Dell *has no relationships with retailers*. Dell's business model is premised on direct, made-to-order sales executed over the Internet and toll-free phone numbers. Any producer-responsibility system must capture Dell's sales, including those that by-pass cash registers in traditional brick and mortar stores, which presumably would be a collection point for such fees.

3. But Dell's business model is more than a story about successfully cutting out independent retailers. It is fundamentally a *relationship with its customer base* that uniquely positions Dell to develop and successfully implement a comprehensive, national, take-back system. Dell is the only company in the computer industry that knows all of its customers by name, mailing address, e-mail address, phone number, date of purchase, product specification, and more—the very kind of information that a company would need to design a system to recover its obsolete products. Moreover, the CTBC realized that Dell could lock in customer loyalty by bundling take-back into the purchase of new Dell equipment as an added customer service.

4. In 2001, Dell was the clear *market-share leader* for PC sales, according to July 2001 data from Gartner-Dataquest, an electronics industry research company. The merger of Hewlett-Packard (HP) and Compaq created real competition for market-share leadership, a position that Dell and HP/Compaq regularly traded following HP's merger.

5. According to data from IDC, another electronics research firm, Dell was, and remains, the market-share leader for *sales of PCs to universities and educational institutions*, as well as to *government agencies.*

6. Dell is not so much a manufacturing company as it is a *marketing company*. Dell assembles made-to-order computers from parts supplied to it and attaches its logo. The CTBC believed that Dell was particularly susceptible to a strategy and associated tactics that attacked its brand name.

7. The company bears the name of its founder, Michael Dell, who is Chairman of the Board, a major stockholder, and the most visible personality of

the company. This also provides opportunities to *personalize the issue* to Michael Dell, who takes credit for the company's direction and success.

8. It was clear from industry analysts and journalists covering the PC industry that *if CTBC moved Dell to act, the rest of the industry sector would follow.* Dell does not strive for product innovation, but waits for innovation to take hold and then cuts the price. Because of its earlier market-share dominance and its ability to drive down costs, Dell defines, in other ways, how the sector as a whole acts.

9. Finally, after additional research, it became clear that Dell was an *environmental laggard* relative to the computer sector as a whole. Dell had low scores compared to its main rival, HP. On SVTC's 2001 "Computer Report Card," Dell ranked a poor fifteenth out of 28 companies surveyed and received a D-minus grade.

BUILDING THE COMPUTER TAKE-BACK CAMPAIGN

Comprehensive campaign and communications plans served as blueprints for building the CTBC.[6] Each of the two strategies identified key audiences, refined messages were to attract support and participation, and articulated tactics to increase market pressure on Dell and establish producer responsibility for e-waste. Some of the key audiences mentioned in the corporate campaign strategy included Dell, Inc. and Michael Dell, campus corporate accountability activists, the news media, institutional investors and PC buyers, and other PC makers. The campaign's key dimensions included: highlighting leaders and laggards, campus organizing, building a local campaign in Dell's home base of Austin Texas, and leveraging the global context.[7]

Leaders and Laggards

Identifying and publicizing levels of environmental performance by companies in the personal computer sector are at the core of the CTBC's market campaign strategy. This helps focus areas of praise and criticism for companies that are setting high and low performance standards and draws attention to where differences exist on a global scale, between domestic and foreign companies.

The two "Computer Report Cards," which were issued in November 2001 and January 2003 (see Table 25.1), drew considerable attention from the media, consumers, and the companies themselves. Dell Computer's Washington, DC-based public relations firm, Dittus Communications, contacted the CTBC's leaders in August 2002 to inquire when the Report Card would be released that year.

The release of the 2001 Computer Report Card, the CTBC's first nationally coordinated activity, included same-day media releases and events in 18 metropolitan areas. More than 20 companies were evaluated based on a standardized set of criteria relating to equipment take-back programs, hazardous materials use, worker health and safety, and ease of public access to information. Japanese and European firms ranked consistently higher than U.S. firms, and HP and IBM were the only U.S.-based firms in the top-ten

TABLE 25.1. Computer TakeBack Campaign (CTBC) Report Card, 2002

Rank 2002	Company Name	HQ	Percentage Total	Score	Rank 2001
1	Fujitsu	Japan	51.5	35	5
2	Canon	Japan	48.5	33	1
3	IBM	U.S.	47	32	3
4	NEC	Japan	45.6	31	6
4	Toshiba	Japan	45.6	31	2
6	Matsushita/Panasonic	Japan	44.1	30	13
7	Seiko Epson	Japan	44.1	30	12
7	Sony	Japan	44.1	30	5
9	Apple	United States	41.2	28	9
10	Hitachi	Japan	38.2	26	10
11	HP/Compaq	United States	33.8	23	8/13
12	Oki	Japan	32.4	22	10
13	Brother	Japan	27.9	19	8
13	Dell	United States	27.9	19	15
15	Sharp	Japan	26.5	18	17
16	Samsung	Korea	25	17	16
17	Micron	United States	20.6	14	18
17	Lexmark	United States	20.6	14	21
19	Philips	Europe	17.6	12	20
20	Viewsonic	United States	10.3	7	22
21	Lucky Goldstar	Korea	5.9	4	28
22	e-Machines	United States	4.4	3	28
23	Acer	Taiwan	2.9	2	24
23	Gateway	United States	2.9	2	20
25	AST	Taiwan	1.5	1	28
26	Daewoo	Korea	0	0	28
26	NEC International	Europe	0	0	28
26	Wyse Technologies	Taiwan	0	0	28

rankings. Both Report Cards were instrumental in demonstrating that Dell, a market-share leader, lagged far behind its largest competitor, HP, on broad measures of environmental performance. The company-by-company grades in the 2002 Report Card are shown in Table 25.1.

Dell's lower ranking but ascending market share and public profile underscored the CTBC's decision to choose this company as its target. Dell's initial response to becoming the CTBC's national corporate target was to select UNICOR (trade name of Federal Prison Industries, Inc.) as its primary recycling partner and required customers to pay US$30–$60 to ship their computers. For Dell, selecting UNICOR was a matter of driving down costs. The CTBC was concerned that reliance on prison labor undercut the development of the free market infrastructure necessary to operate a robust, national e-waste collection and recycling system. Moreover, because prisoners are not covered by the same worker health and safety protections as regular employees, they are more endangered by the toxic materials contained in discarded computers and electronics.

Dell's partnership with prisons provided an opportunity for the CTBC to highlight the "Recycle responsibly" element of its platform, which until then Dell had understood as just "Take it back." The CTBC's ability to draw considerable attention to Dell's prison–labor partnership and contrast it with HP's higher recycling standards led Dell to end its prison-labor relationship a few days after the CTBC's most widely distributed critique was published.[8]

The CTBC extended its leader/laggard approach beyond brand owners and original equipment manufacturers. The "Electronics Recyclers' Pledge of True Stewardship" (Appendix E, this volume) developed and circulated by SVTC and the Basel Action Network (BAN), articulated environmentally superior performance criteria for electronics recycling companies by providing specific content for the CTBC's "Recycle Responsibly" goal. Recognizing that standards for the downstream processing of collected e-waste are just as important as effective take-back programs, the Pledge of True Stewardship identified a very small number of e-waste recycling firms that had pledged to meet the performance criteria, including: banning the export of hazardous e-waste, landfilling, and incineration; documenting the disposition of materials; protecting worker health and safety; and not using prison labor.

Developing and applying standardized criteria to actors throughout the e-waste value chain is crucial to defining expectations and framing essential elements of the system to protect the public's health from the threats posed by e-waste and high-tech production.

On Campus

Research showed that Dell was a leading seller of computer equipment to colleges and universities. Although recycling is a daily practice rather than a political issue for many of today's college students, corporate accountability is an important theme for young activists. The CTBC's campaign for producer responsibility combined the recycling "habit" and anticorporate sentiment to attract people from the first generation of Americans that had grown up using personal computers and who internalized the values of recycling and conservation.

Campus computer take-back activism originally had been stewarded by Ecopledge.com, a national, student, corporate accountability organization, through a network of campus chapters. By late spring 2003, the CTBC's organizers were coordinating actions at college campuses in 20 different states. These students provided an activist base that helped challenge Dell's brand identity.

Focusing on Dell's long-standing, now-defunct advertising campaign featuring Steven, "the Dell Dude," the CTBC and Ecopledge.com went on the offensive, releasing "Dude, why won't they take back my old Dell?"—a report outlining Dell's poor record on take-back and its overall poor environmental performance—and calling on the company and CEO Michael Dell to lead the industry to an e-waste solution (Ecopledge.com et al. 2002). This report, coupled with postcards, petitions, posters, and stickers bearing Michael Dell's picture and corporate logo, was used on numerous campuses across the country and at community venues in Dell's hometown of Austin, Texas.

Campus organizing continues to be a strategic focal point, with fresh tactics and activities evolving each semester. The CTBC distributed hundreds of its Campus Campaign Kit CDs, providing a plug-and-play opportunity for students with few resources to participate in the campaign and remain fully informed of the e-waste problem and the producer-responsibility solution. Campus activists continue developing new tactics—using hazmat suits as their petitions for students to sign, and tearing Dell ads from national newspapers demanding take-back and mailing them to Michael Dell. A handful of campuses began working with faculty, student government, and administrators to influence campus IT procurement and equipment disposal policies. Given the size of Dell's market share among educational institutions, CTBC's strategy to change campus computer purchasing contracts to require take-back, hazardous materials phase-outs, and environmentally superior downstream processing is having a substantial impact on Dell's policy.[9]

The campus campaign attracted media attention when campus newspapers and student online magazines ("zines") picked up on the issue. The widely respected *Chronicle of Higher Education* wrote a long feature on the e-waste topic and potential costs to campuses, delving into the CTBC's concerns with Dell (Carlson 2003).

By late 2003, more than 150 student groups, representing all 50 states, co-signed an ad directed at Michael Dell, asking him to support the essential elements of the CTBC platform. In an April 2004 open letter to students on its website, Michael Dell responded to the platform's three planks and pledged to test a "free with purchase" recycling offer. Later that month, Michael Dell and GRRN activists held a nationwide Web and phone conference for student activists.

In Dell's Backyard

Dell is the largest private employer in the Austin area, where Dell and its top executives have established a high philanthropic profile. The CTBC leadership realized that the Dell corporate campaign would be bolstered by a partnership with a strong grassroots organization in Austin, Texas. In March 2002, the Texas Campaign for the Environment (TCE) was recruited to join CTBC. Soon TCE's staff of door-to-door organizers was generating hundreds of personal letters to Dell and state legislators every week.

TCE is a constant reminder to Dell that the CTBC is serious about Dell committing to a comprehensive, sustainable solution to the e-waste problem. TCE staff and volunteers were a potent force at Dell's 2002 annual shareholder meeting, at numerous civic events, at Michael Dell's public appearances, in the media, and in the community, talking with people about the need for Dell to lead its industry to a solution. Creative tactics, such as an e-waste fashion show outside the designer dress shop owned by Michael Dell's wife, moved coverage off the business pages of the daily newspapers and onto the fashion pages. TCE provided an important local bridge between the national campaign and Dell—with direct contact with Dell management and indirect contact through prominent community members who support TCE's objectives.

Austin provided an important tactical opportunity for the CTBC to launch the first of its activist Web sites, www.toxicdude.com. The 2002

National Recycling Coalition conference held in Austin brought together hundreds of people. Many joined a press conference launching the Web site and spoke with the media about the e-waste problem in their states and communities.

The CTBC decided to make Dell's 2003 annual shareholder meeting in Austin a defining moment. An eight-day truck tour dubbed, "Hard Drive Across the West" traveled to cities, collecting obsolete Dell computers, monitors, and other e-waste and holding press conferences. The e-waste was delivered to Dell outside the annual meeting. Michael Dell was questioned inside the meeting about his commitment to take back obsolete Dells. The week of activities included a town-hall meeting on e-waste opened by populist agitator Jim Hightower (see his "Foreword: Technology Happens," this volume), a full-page ad from concerned Austin area religious leaders, and more than four dozen volunteer demonstrators greeting shareholders upon their arrival. Although the original plan was to focus on Dell's use of prison labor, two weeks before the annual meeting, Dell announced it had ended its relationship with UNICOR, so the CTBC developed a broader message about the need to make recycling a computer as easy as buying one.

Leveraging the Global Context

The high-tech industry operates through extremely efficient global supply chains. However closely knit those supply chains are, there are significant differences among countries in the regulation of e-waste, and significant global double standards within the operations of single companies. For example, Dell's take-back efforts in Europe are significantly more advanced than its actions in the United States.[10]

The CTBC asked a very simple question—why were U.S. consumers getting second-class treatment from global corporations? Dell and all of its competitors operate producer-responsibility take-back programs in Japan, South Korea, and Taiwan, as well as in European countries (see Geiser and Tickner, this volume), but it was actively resisting such programs in the United States.

The global impact of the e-waste problem was most acutely and dramatically illustrated in the documentary video, *Exporting Harm* and its accompanying report, released in early 2002 by the BAN and SVTC. *Exporting Harm* documented the export of e-waste from the United States to Guiyu, China, where literal mountains of e-waste were dismantled under horrific, primitive conditions that contaminated the air, land, water, and people of that area (see Puckett; Raphael and Smith, this volume). The global media attention, and the presence of equipment asset tags from prominent cities, institutions, and agencies, thrust the e-waste issue onto the world's screen and led to the first major public recognition of the e-waste issue, as well as the need for producer responsibility and environmentally superior recycling standards.

Recognizing the outreach and communications opportunities from global media exposure, the CTBC planned and staged its largest one-day demonstration at the entrance to the International Consumer Electronics Show in Las Vegas, Nevada, on its opening day in January 2003. Activists from TCE formed a high-tech chain gang, dressed in prison uniforms and chained to

PHOTO 25.2. Activists with Texas Campaign for the Environment protesting Dell Inc.'s use of prison labor for computer recycling by bringing e-waste to the 2003 Consumer Electronics Show in Las Vegas, hours before CEO Michael Dell's keynote speech. Courtesy of Michael Picker.

obsolete computer equipment, in front of the Las Vegas Convention Center hours before Michael Dell's keynote speech about trends in the industry (see Photo 25.2).[11] The global media coverage was extensive, and the CTBC proved it could become a serious challenge to Dell and its place in the industry.

The Consumer Electronics Show visibility events were synchronized with the simultaneous, multicity releases of the "Computer Report Card" and the unveiling of the CTBC's main Web site, www.computertakeback.com. Combined, these actions shined the bright light of public scrutiny on Dell Computer and offered an opportunity for companies to promote plans and practices that surpassed Dell's efforts. Dell did not sit idly by, however, and over the next several months, it responded with a series of announcements and events orchestrated by two public relations firms, whose relationships with Dell commenced immediately following the Consumer Electronics Show. Clearly, the CTBC had forced Dell to take notice and craft a response.

THE CAMPAIGN'S IMPACT: FORCING DELL TO ACT

The CTBC forced Dell to respond and act, even though the company initially contended that each new announcement and initiative was purely a business decision. When the campaign started, Dell had very limited product-recovery programs that were geared to its very high-end customers, but then it began a shift toward greater responsibility for its e-waste. Dell held one-day obsolete computer collection events around the country 14 months after the CTBC's first report focused on Dell. Moreover, Dell now actively markets asset recovery services to large customers. In March 2003, when Dell began selling its own branded printers, it offered to take back any printer with a printer purchase. Dell dropped its partnership with prison labor for its consumer-recycling program, and it is working with socially responsible investors to develop benchmarks and metrics for future performance.

Interestingly, Dell's series of one-day computer collection events during the spring and summer of 2003 were largely located in cities where the CTBC had no established grassroots presence.[12] Despite the absence of an organized presence in these cities, by recruiting and engaging volunteers, the CTBC distributed thousands of fliers and talked directly with hundreds of people about the importance of *responsible computer recycling*, which does not include the use of prison labor.

In October 2003, at the first annual E-Scrap Conference, high-level Dell and HP executives publicly voiced support for producer responsibility. Dell spokesperson Pat Nathan acknowledged the CTBC's key role in bringing the company to this position. She even encouraged large buyers to include producer take-back in their requests for bids. This also marked the beginning of frank, constructive dialogue between Dell's management and the CTBC about key elements of the CTBC's platform and bottom line. In February 2004, both Dell and HP went on record in favor of producer take-back legislation proposed in Minnesota.

When the CTBC released another Computer Report Card in May 2004, Dell received high marks and recognition as the most improved computer company. Also at that time, the CTBC released a "Statement of Principles on Producer Responsibility for Electronic Waste," which Dell and HP endorsed. In July 2004, Dell and HP became the first companies to offer temporary, free, nationwide, voluntary take-back programs in the United States. With Dell and HP—the two market leaders in PCs—supporting key elements of CTBC's program, the CTBC had much more leverage in state and national policy discussions. At Dell's 2004 shareholder meeting, Michael Dell stated that the company was looking at e-waste solutions on a global level and touted a pilot e-waste collection program in Malaysia.

We might never fully know which constituencies, actions, and messages were key in bringing about the shifts in Dell's position and actions. Each of a wide range of constituencies—students, procurement officers, community activists, Dell shareholders and religious leaders—using a variety of messages and tactics, may have played a role. Table 25.2 contains a rough chronology of the campaign's key activities and Dell's actions.

CONCLUSION

Although this discussion has focused on the Dell campaign, the CTBC also has devoted substantial effort to moving state-level policy to embrace producer responsibility for e-waste. Outreach to and collaboration with

TABLE 25.2. Chronology of CBTC's Dell Campaign

November 2001	"Computer Report Card"; multi-city media releases, extensive media coverage
February 2002	"Exporting Harm" released with significant global media coverage
March 2002	GRRN/ Ecopledge.com "Dude, Why Won't They Take Back My Old Dell" report; TCE joins campaign
May 2002	Dell announces program for consumers to mail back, at their own cost, equipment to Dell, but recycling goes to UNICOR
June 2002	Dell requests and meets CTBC representatives
July 2002	Dell's Annual Shareholder Meeting, questions about take-back programs; TCE meets Michael Dell
September 2002	National Recycling Coalition conference; ToxicDude Web site launched, www.toxicdude.com; Dell requests, meets CTBC leadership
September–October 2002	SRI dialogue process commences, Dell begins mail-back program and drops "Steven the Dude" advertising campaign
January 2003	CTBC actions at International Consumer Electronics Show in Las Vegas; Computer Report Card Web site launched, www.computertakeback.com; launched; Dell requests, meets CTBC leadership; Dell and others join EPA in voluntary "Plug into E-Cycling" program
February 2003	CTBC launches state policy strategies in ten states; "Recycler's Pledge of True Stewardship"; Dell introduces new VP of Sustainable Business to coordinate e-waste and sustainable business practices
March 2003	Dell expands PR team, Dell announces one-day collection events in five cities and offers to take back printers for free
April 2003	Dell's initial one-day collection events
May 2003	Dell extends one-day collection events to 10 more cities
June 2003	SVTC, CTBC release "Tale of Two Systems" report
July 2003	CTBC "Hard Drive Across the West" e-waste collection tour events in five cities; CTBC questions Michael Dell at Shareholder's Meeting; Dell ends UNICOR relationship; announces new equipment recovery
September–November 2003	CTBC communicates essential elements of its bottom line to Dell, commencing discussion of EPR principles and measuring the company's progress
July 2004	Dell endorses "Computer TakeBack Campaign Statement of Principles"

health-care institutions, government agencies, universities, and group-purchasing organizations to establish "green" procurement guidelines for computer equipment are as likely to shape the future computer industry as is targeted market campaigning.

The pace of change created by—and experienced by—the CTBC mirrors the industry we are working to reform. Although the United States still lags far behind Europe in establishing EPR for e-waste, the push for reform is bottom-up in nature, with pressure coming largely from activist efforts, rather than top-down, as is found among environmental regulators within national and EU governments. At each turn, however, corporate influences in public policy, in agency rule making and programming, and in the public posture of such groups as the National Recycling Coalition (a nonprofit group that frequently gives political cover to companies targeted by activists), can hinder the gains made through citizen organizing. EPR is a compelling demand because it protects public health and the environment without taxpayer dollars; gives industry the opportunity to make good on its 30-year-old "don't regulate us because we know how to do it ourselves" mantra; and aligns corporate practices with the values embraced by America's 75 million citizen recyclers and the growing knowledge of pollution's human-health effects.

The CTBC has advanced more rapidly than anticipated and prompted more responsive action by Dell and the electronics industries than expected for a variety of reasons. First, the shocking images from the U.S. e-waste poisoning Chinese workers, children, and the environment, as documented in *Exporting Harm* (see Puckett, this volume), presented a compelling case for change. Second, many North Americans personally faced the dilemma of what to do with the ubiquitous, obsolete electronics in their homes and offices, so the issue resonated widely. In addition, the electronics industry prides itself on innovation and responsiveness to consumers. Michael Dell's early claims of a lack of consumer demand for computer recycling were undercut quickly by thousands of letters and e-mails and overwhelming response at some of the company's free collection events. In contrast to those of other major industry sectors, IT and computer industry leaders, and the companies themselves, are relatively young and ready to adapt. Dell's decision to embrace key elements of the CTBC's demands less than three years after it was designated as the national corporate target was in part due to the successes of high-level environmental advocates in Europe and Japan in establishing EPR policies. This gave the CTBC a strong message regarding U.S. consumers' second-class treatment and took away an industry response that the CTBC's demands were impractical or impossible to achieve. Finally, the CTBC seized new opportunities for "just-in-time organizing" and used various new technologies to effectively confront the technology sector.

NOTES

1. "ToxicDude.com" in this chapter's title refers to the campus-oriented Web site of the Computer TakeBack Campaign's Dell corporate campaign. Due to the campaign's success, the Web site is no longer in service. Read on...

2. CTBC's founding organizations include: As You Sow Foundation, Californians Against Waste, Clean Water Action, Clean Production Network, Communications Workers of America, GrassRoots Recycling Network, INFORM, Institute for Local Self-Reliance, Materials for the Future, Mercury Policy Project, Silicon Valley Toxics Coalition, and Texas Campaign for the Environment. For a complete overview of the Computer TakeBack Campaign, see www.computertakeback.com.

3. The Computer TakeBack Campaign Platform is available online at www.computer takeback.com. (See also the Computer TakeBack Campaign Statement of Principles, Appendix D, this volume.)

4. In July 2003, Dell Computer Corporation was formally renamed Dell Inc.

5. Because many so-called computer manufacturers may only assemble products and contract out the construction of their products, the only product the company sells is their brand and support services, therefore we call them "brand owners."

6. Although the CTBC decided to focus first on personal computers, because many consumers can understand the problem of computer obsolescence, CTBC's platform, advocacy

and model policy apply producer responsibility to all consumer electronics that have a circuit board.

7. The Computer Report Card does not just target Dell, but through public policy campaigns and exposes attempts to move the entire computer and consumer electronics industry. See www.computertakeback.com.

8. See Markoff (2003) about Dell's use of prison labor, and Flynn (2003) about Dell terminating its prison labor partnership.

9. Students in a Santa Clara University class interviewed campus IT procurement officials at several in the Silicon Valley area universities to give better shape to the campus procurement strategy.

10. In the first meeting with Dell representatives CTBC learned that the European Union (EU) mandates on hazardous material phase-outs in electronics, Restriction on Hazardous Substances, would affect all Dell computers. Company officials explained that Dell would phase out these toxins from all their equipment, not just those machines destined for the EU market, a good example of public policy in one jurisdiction raising the bar globally.

11. See www.computertakeback.com for media coverage and photos.

12. The notable exception was Austin, Texas, where discussions between TCE and Dell resulted in the Company agreeing not to use prison labor recycling for materials collected in Austin.

Appendix A

Principles of Environmental Justice

WE THE PEOPLE OF COLOR, gathered together at this multinational People of Color Leadership Summit to begin to build a national and international movement of all peoples of color to fight the destruction and taking of our lands and communities, do hereby re-establish our spiritual interdependence to the sacredness of our Mother Earth; to respect and celebrate each of our cultures, languages and beliefs about the natural world and our roles, in healing ourselves; to ensure environmental justice; to promote economic alternatives which would contribute to the development of environmentally safe livelihoods; and, to secure our political, economic, and cultural liberation that has been denied for over 500 years of colonization and oppression, resulting in the poisoning of our communities and land and the genocide of our peoples, do affirm and adopt these Principles of Environmental Justice[1]:

1. Environmental justice affirms the sacredness of Mother Earth, ecological unity and the interdependence of all species, and the Earth to be free from ecological destruction.
2. Environmental justice demands the public policy be based on mutual respect and justice for all peoples, free from any form of discrimination or bias.
3. Environmental justice mandates that right to ethical, balanced and responsible uses of land and renewable resources in the interests of a sustainable planet for humans and other living things.
4. Environmental justice calls for the universal protection from extraction, production, and disposal of toxic/hazardous wastes and poisons and nuclear testing that threaten the fundamental right to clean air, land, water, and food.
5. Environmental justice affirms the fundamental right to political, economic, cultural and environmental self-determination of all peoples.
6. Environmental justice demands the cessation of the production of all toxins, hazardous wastes, and radioactive materials, and that all past and current producers be held strictly accountable to the people for detoxification and the containment at the point of production.
7. Environmental justice demands the right to participate as equal partners at every level of decision-making including needs assessment, planning, implementation, enforcement and evaluation.
8. Environmental justice affirms the right of workers to a safe and healthy work environment, without being forced to choose between an unsafe

livelihood and unemployment. It also affirms the right to those who work at home to be free from environmental hazards.

9. Environmental justice protects the rights of victims of environmental justice to receive full compensation and reparations for damages as well as quality health care.

10. Environmental justice considers governmental acts of environmental injustice a violation of international law, the Universal Declaration on Human Rights, and the United Nations Convention on Genocide.

11. Environmental justice must recognize a special legal and natural relationship of Native Peoples to the U.S. Government through treaties, agreements, compacts, and covenants affirming sovereignty and self-determination.

12. Environmental justice affirms the need for urban and rural ecological policies to clean up and rebuild our cities and rural areas in balance with nature, honoring the cultural integrity of all our communities, and providing fair access for all to the full range of resources.

13. Environmental justice calls for the strict enforcement of principles of informed consent, and a halt to the testing of experimental reproductive and medical procedures and vaccinations on people of color.

14. Environmental justice opposes the destructive operations of multinational corporations.

15. Environmental justice opposes military occupation, repression and exploitation of lands, peoples and cultures, and other life forms.

16. Environmental justice calls for education of present and future generations which emphasizes social and environmental issues, based on our experience and an appreciation for our diverse cultural perspectives.

17. Environmental justice requires that we, as individuals, make personal and consumer choices to consume as little of Mother Earth's resources and to produce as little waste as possible; and make the conscious decision to challenge and reprioritize our lifestyles to insure the health of the natural world for present and future generations.

Adopted today, October 27, 1991, in Washington, D.C.

NOTE

1. First National People of Color Leadership Summit, Washington, D.C., October 24–27, 1991. *Source:* Environmental Justice Resource Center, Clark Atlanta University [online] www.ejrc.cau.edu/princej.html. Accessed January 2006.

Appendix B

The Silicon Principles of Socially and Environmentally Responsible Electronics Manufacturing

1. *Establish a comprehensive toxics use reduction program*[1]

   - Phase out the use of chlorofluorocarbons and other chlorinated solvents
   - Phase out all carcinogens, reproductive toxins and neurotoxins
   - Phase out the use of acutely toxic gases
   - Implement in-process acid recycling
   - Develop toxics use reduction plans, materials and waste audits, and mass balance materials accounting

2. *Develop health and safety education programs and health monitoring*

   - Health and safety training must be sensitive to the diversity of workforce
   - Health monitoring must be comprehensive and available for public inspection
   - Establish non-discriminatory transfers for pregnant production workers
   - Earmark at least 5 percent of all R & D money for environmental, health and safety programs

3. *Work with local communities to establish "good neighbor agreements"*

   - Include emergency planning and worst-case scenario planning, including transportation planning
   - Provide full disclosure to local communities, with regular monitoring, including inspections
   - Establish a corporate commitment to hire, train, and promote local residents

4. *Implement a worker improvement program and economic impact statements*

   - Assure that workers are involved in process design and workplace governance
   - Assess environmental, social, and economic impacts of new technologies and new facilities

5. *Support national R & D policy directed by civilian (not military) needs*

   - Support a change in federal R & D funding from Department of Defense to Department of Commerce

6. *Establish corporate policies requiring equal standards for sub-contractors and suppliers*

   - Establish technical assistance and technology transfer to encourage pollution prevention at all stages of production, rather than shift the pollution down the production chain to smaller contractors
   - Hire contractors who adhere to good labor and environmental policies, and in particular, hire union contractors where they exist.

7. *Establish corporate standards that are enforced equally, both domestically and internationally*

   - Establish corporate policies that assure worldwide full compliance with the strictest standards
   - Require all facilities worldwide to make full disclosure of toxics used, stored, and released on and off site

8. *Establish a life-cycle approach to all manufacturing, from R & D to final disposal*

   - Design new products using a life-cycle perspective
   - Internalize costs of disposal; guarantee return and safe disposal of all used products

9. *Work closely with local communities and workers to ensure full oversight and participation*

   - Commit to open partnership with workers and community to assure comprehensive participation

NOTE

1. Silicon Valley Toxics Coalition, and Campaign for Responsible Technology, June 1996.

Appendix C

Sample Shareholder Resolutions

1. INTERNATIONAL ENVIRONMENTAL STANDARDS
   FOR ELECTRONICS INDUSTRY SUBCONTRACTORS
   AND SUPPLIERS[1]

Whereas the electronics industry, the world's fastest growing manufacturing industry plans to build more than 100 new plants costing $1–3 billion each in the next few years; often in countries, we believe, with environmental and occupational health standards less stringent than those in the U.S.;

Whereas the manufacture of semiconductor chips requires toxic chemicals in large enough quantities to have resulted in groundwater contamination at some plants so severe that many high-tech companies are listed on the EPA's National Priorities (Superfund) List. Manufacturing semiconductor chips requires using and discharging millions of gallons of water each day, and new plants are being built in arid areas where water is limited;

Whereas electronics companies contract out much of their production work to hundreds of suppliers, contractors and vendors throughout the world. We believe that the rapid growth rate of the industry encourages subcontracting with companies that have less stringent environmental and occupational health standards. We believe that (insert company's name) policies should include clear definitions of environmental responsibility and occupational health standards, for themselves and suppliers;

Therefore be it resolved that Shareholders request the Board of Directors to report, at reasonable cost and omitting proprietary information, on the company's contract supplier standards and compliance mechanisms for all manufacturing and waste management vendors, subcontractors, suppliers with contracts in excess of $1,000,000 annually. This report should be made available to shareholders by (insert date) and to other interested parties upon request.

Supporting Statement

We request that the report referred to above:

1. Summarize and attach copies of current company policies regarding supplier, vendor, and subcontractor standards related to environmental and occupational health responsibilities;
2. Summarize and attach copies of company environmental assessment and compliance policies designed to ensure comprehensive environmental protection at suppliers, vendors, and subcontractors for manufacturing and assembling facilities in other countries, including any corporate policies that require adherence to strict international environmental standards;

3. Describe policies to assure full disclosure of toxic chemical reporting to workers and the community for each manufacturing and waste management vendor, supplier and subcontractor with a contract in excess of $1,000,000 annually;

4. Describe provisions for supplier standards to be translated into the languages of the country, posted prominently at all sites where the company has contracts and available to local communities;

5. Describe procedures or plans to encourage and support suppliers, vendors and subcontractors to raise their standards consistent with points 1–4, (rather than terminate contracts where conduct has been inadequate), including technical assistance, technology transfer, and mentoring to encourage pollution prevention at all stages—from design to disposal—in the life-cycle of production; and

6. Describe procedures or plans for external monitoring, with a timeline for implementation, in conjunction with local non-governmental organizations to oversee and ensure environmental and occupational health accountability consistent with points 1–5 above.

2. Producer Responsibility for Product Take-back and Recycling[2]

Whereas Compaq emphasizes its commitment to environmental leadership. Yet the technical innovation responsible for leadership in designing and marketing computers has not yet extended to full responsibility for minimizing the environmental impacts of products during their manufacture, use and end-of-life.

The manufacture of one computer workstation can require more than 700 chemical compounds, about half of which are hazardous, including arsenic, brominated flame-retardants, cadmium, hexavalent chromium, lead, and mercury. Cathode ray tubes in monitors can contain several pounds of lead, and have been identified as hazardous waste and banned from landfills in California. For these reasons it is important to consider the management of discarded products.

Currently, most computers are not recycled. A study by the National Safety Council concluded that 20 million computers became obsolete in 1998 and estimated that only 11 percent were recycled. More than 40 million computers are expected to become obsolete in 2001.

Companies committed to environmental leadership should help to find solutions for the growing problems created by electronic waste.

As a global company, Compaq must prepare to comply with the European Union's new law mandating extended producer responsibility. This law requires manufacturers of electronic equipment marketed in Europe to reduce use of hazardous components and pay for recycling of their products.

Some companies take products back if individual customers pay a fee for it. While take-back is laudable, we believe the fees provide a significant disincentive for consumers to recycle.

Producer responsibility creates a powerful incentive to design products that are environmentally preferable, easier to upgrade, disassemble and recycle. Innovation and competitiveness are key to solving the challenges posed by toxic components and end-of-life management of our products.

We believe Compaq can avoid financial, legal and reputational risk, gain competitive advantage, and build brand name in the marketplace by assuming responsibility for its products.

Be it resolved that Shareowners of Compaq request that the Board of Directors prepare a report, at reasonable cost, on the feasibility of adopting a policy, implementing programs, and auditing progress of producer responsibility for their products. The company agrees to release a report within six months of the annual meeting of shareholders.

Supporting Statement

The report should study the feasibility of taking financial and/or physical responsibility for products throughout their life cycle. It should include a commitment to setting goals for reduced use of hazardous materials in manufacturing; and for collection, detoxification, disassembly and recycling of discarded equipment to the highest degree practicable. The report should discuss measures being taken to ensure that recycling is accomplished in a manner that minimizes risks to workers; assess our company's liability if our products are discovered to have leached toxic contaminants into groundwater in a manner that harms human health; and assess the impact on our company's reputation if we do not establish comprehensive producer responsibility for our products.

NOTES

1. Drafted by religious shareholders with the Interfaith Center on Corporate Responsibility (ICCR), c. 1998.

2. Filed by Calvert Asset Management Company with Compaq Computer Corporation in 2002.

Appendix D

Computer TakeBack Campaign Statement of Principles

WE SUPPORT THE POLICY of producer responsibility in the United States for electronic products at the end of their useful lives, wherein brand-name manufacturers/producers work with consumers and state and local governments to properly collect and manage electronic products in an environmentally responsible fashion.[1] Manufacturers and producers accept responsibility for continually improving the environmental aspects of the design of their products and for the end-of-life management of their products. This policy will have many benefits for consumers, electronics producers, local governments, the public health and the environment.

This statement refers to the responsibility for the environmentally responsible management of the electronic waste from products sold to all customers in the future. As for products sold in the past ("legacy" electronic waste, including "orphan" products for which the relevant producer/brand owner is no longer in business), we advocate that all due measures should be taken to allocate primary responsibility to those who manufactured and sold these products in the first instance. For that orphan waste which cannot be allocated to past producers, we support the principle that current electronics producers as well as those entering the market in the future should share in the responsibility of managing this electronic waste based on an equitable cost allocation related to historic market share (see Point 3 of alternative policy section, below).

We support the objective of producer responsibility to create incentives for producers to improve the design of their products to minimize their life-cycle impacts on the environment. In particular, we support activities designed to:

- Phase out the use of potentially hazardous substances consistent with the recent European Reduction of Hazardous Substances (RoHS) Directive and other worldwide standards as they become law;
- Improve options to upgrade equipment over the course of the equipment's life; and
- Increase the integration of non-hazardous recovered materials into new products.

We believe that producer responsibility can operate most effectively through the competitive marketplace, but that all stakeholders—consumers, producers, governments, and the general public—play an important role. All stakeholders need assurances that all producers are held to the same high environmental standards. Therefore, we support a public policy framework in the United States that provides for individual producer responsibility, through mechanisms that assure proper end of life management of producers' own products sold in the future. It is expected that individual producers may choose to cooperate with others in carrying out this responsibility in order to achieve efficiencies of scale. We do not advocate an "advanced recovery fee" approach to financing the management of electronic waste, such as was adopted through SB20 in California, and was considered as well in the National Electronic Product Stewardship Initiative process. We support an alternative financing model which allows for responsible companies to avoid an Advanced Recovery Fee and provides for cost internalization of end of life management costs by producers for new products entering the marketplace, combined with industry sponsored programs designed to offset the incremental costs borne by local governments and others to collect discarded electronic products. We recognize that to be viable and effective, this preferred alternative policy approach includes:

1. Ambitious, workable and progressive goals and timetables to assure that both legacy and future electronic waste will be properly recovered and managed;
2. Effective and enforceable environmental standards to assure that hazardous electronic waste will be properly managed in strict compliance with international and domestic laws that govern export of hazardous electronic waste, worker safety, public health and environmental protection, and the use of market labor rather than incarcerated labor;
3. A convenient, fair and equitable system of collection that does not create economic disincentives for consumers to participate and is premised upon financial participation by producers so that taxpayers, local governments, or others do not shoulder all the financial burdens of recycling and disposing of electronic products (large institutions whose electronic waste is regulated by federal law may be subject to fees to cover the costs of proper recycling and disposal of their historic waste);
4. Consumer awareness designed to optimize performance of the system; and
5. Flexibility for producers to design and implement recovery and recycling systems that best suit their particular business model while complying with all applicable laws.

NOTE

1. Computer TakeBack Campaign, May 2004. *Source:* www.computertakeback.com/the_solutions/principles.cfm. Endorsed by the Hewlett-Packard Corporation and Dell Computer in 2004. For further information, see: www.computertakeback.com.

Appendix E

Electronics Recycler's Pledge of True Stewardship

WE, THE SIGNING and registered recycling company, agree to uphold the following:[1]

I. We will not allow any hazardous E-waste[2] we handle to be sent to solid waste (nonhazardous waste) landfills or incinerators for disposal or energy recovery, either directly or through intermediaries.

II. Consistent with decisions of the international Basel Convention on the Control of Transboundary Movements of Hazardous Wastes and their Disposal, we will not allow the export of hazardous E-waste we handle to be exported from developed to developing countries[3] either directly or through intermediaries.

III. We will not allow any E-waste we handle to be sent to prisons for recycling either directly or through intermediaries.

IV. We assure that we have a certified, or otherwise comprehensive and comparable "environmental management system" in place and our operation meets best practices.

V. We commit to ensuring that the entire recycling chain, including downstream intermediaries and recovery operations such as smelters, are meeting all applicable environmental and health regulations. Every effort will be made to only make use of those facilities (e.g., smelters), which provide the most efficient and least polluting recovery services available globally.

VI. We agree to provide visible tracking of hazardous E-Waste throughout the product recycling chain. The tracking information should show the final disposition of all hazardous waste materials. If there is a concern about trade secrets, an independent auditor acceptable to parties concerned can be used to verify compliance with this pledge.

VII. We agree to provide adequate assurance (e.g., bonds) to cover environmental and other costs of the closure of our facility, and additionally to provide liability insurance for accidents and incidents involving wastes under our control and ownership. Additionally we will ensure due diligence throughout the product chain.

VIII. We agree to support Extended Producer Responsibility (EPR) programs and/or legislation in order to develop viable financing mechanisms for end-of-life that provides that all legitimate electronic recycling companies have a stake in the process.

IX. We further agree to support design for environment and toxics use reduction programs and/or legislation for electronic products.

NOTES

1. Basel Action Network, Silicon Valley Toxics Coalition, and Computer Take-Back Campaign, August 22, 2002 (revised and officially launched, February 25, 2003). *Source:* www.ban.org/pledge/Electronics_Recycler_Pledge.pdf. For a list of signatories, see www.ban.org/pledge/Locations.html; for information about signing the pledge, see www.ban.org/pledge1.html.

2. Following best interpretation of the definitions of the Basel Convention, "hazardous electronic waste" will for the purposes of this pledge include circuit boards, cathode ray tubes (CRTs), as well as computers, monitors, peripherals, and other electronics containing circuit boards and/or CRTs. It will also include mercury and poly-chlorinated bi-phenyl (PCB) containing components, lamps, and devices. The definition of "hazardous electronic waste" will not include nonhazardous wastes such as copper unless it is contaminated with a Basel hazardous waste such as lead, cadmium, PCB, mercury, etc. The definition of "hazardous electronic waste" includes non-working materials exported for repair unless assurances exist that hazardous components (such as CRTs or circuit boards) will not be disposed of in the importing country as a result. The definition of "hazardous electronic waste" does not include working equipment and parts that are certified as working, that are not intended for disposal or recycling, but for re-use and resale. The term "hazardous e-waste" as used in this Pledge does not pertain to, nor is synonymous with any current legal U. S. definitions of "hazardous waste," but is meant for the purposes of this Pledge only.

3. Following the definitions of the Basel Convention and its Basel Ban Amendment, developing countries are any country not belonging to either the European Union, the Organization of Economic Cooperation and Development (OECD), or Liechtenstein. For a complete list of OECD and EU countries see www.ban.org/country_status/country_status.html, and find countries shaded in gray.

Acronyms Used

ABS	acrylonitrile-butadiene styrene
ACC	American Chemical Council
ACFTU	All-China Federation of Trade Unions
AEA	American Electronics Association
AFL	American Federation of Labor
AIDS	Acquired Immunodeficiency Syndrome
AIWA	Asian Immigrant Women's Advocates
AMD	Advanced Micro Devices, Inc.
AMRC	Asia Monitor Resource Centre
AoP	Assembly of the Poor (Thailand)
AP	*Arom Pongpa-ngan* Foundation (Thailand)
ASIC	application-specific integrated circuits
BAN	Basel Action Network
BEJC	Border Environmental Justice Campaign
BFR	brominated flame retardant
BIR	Bureau of International Recycling
BLS	Bureau of Labor Statistics
BOI	Board of Investment (Thailand)
BS	British Standard (UK)
CAFOD	Catholic Agency for Overseas Development
CDN	Canada
CEC	Commission for Environmental Cooperation
CEE	central and eastern Europe
CEREAL	(Center for Labor Education and Action) (Mexico)
CFC	chlorofluorocarbon
CGIL	(General Confederation of Italian Labor)
CI	confidence interval
CIO	Congress of Industrial Organizations
CITU	Centre of Indian Trade Unions
CM	contract manufacturing, contract manufacturers
CMF	Corporate Mortality File (IBM)
COSH	committees on occupational safety and health
COSHH	control of substances hazardous to health
CPU	central processing unit
CRT	Campaign for Responsible Technology
CRT	cathode ray tube
CSIA	China Semiconductor Industry Association
CTBC	Computer TakeBack Campaign
CWA	Communications Workers of America
DADDPS	diaminodiphenylsulfone
DCE	dichloroethylene
DDS	dapsone
DEC	Digital Equipment Corporation

DFI	direct foreign investment (see also FDI)
DIW	Department of Industrial Works (Thailand)
DPP	Democratic Progressive Party (Taiwan)
DVD	digital video disc
ECOSH	Electronics Committee on Safety and Health
EDF	Environmental Defense Fund
EEE	electrical and electronic equipment
EGE	ethylene glycol ether
EHC	Environmental Health Coalition
EIA	Electronics Industries Alliance
EIA	environmental impact assessment
EIGNC	Electronic Industry Good Neighbor Campaign
EMF	electromagnetic fields
EMG	Environmental Monitoring Group
EMS	electronics manufacturing services
EPA	Environmental Protection Agency
EPR	extended producer responsibility
EPZ	export processing zone
ERC	employee representative committee
ESI	Employees' State Insurance (India)
EU	European Union
FDI	foreign direct investment (see also DFI)
FIE	federal invested enterprise
FOW	Friends of Women Foundation (Thailand)
FTZ	free trade zone
GATT	General Agreement on Tariffs and Trade
GDP	gross domestic product
GE	General Electric Corporation
GFTU	Guangdong Federation of Trade Unions (China)
GMB	General, Municipal, Boilermakers and Allied Trade Union (UK)
GMEEA	ethylene glycol monoethyl ether acetate
GMME	ethylene glycol monomethyl ether
GMMEA	ethylene glycol monomethyl ether acetate
GRRN	GrassRoots Recycling Network
GUF	Global Union Federation
HDD	hard disk drive
HIV	Human Immunodeficiency Virus
HK	Hong Kong
HP	Hewlett-Packard Corporation
HSCE	Health and Safety Consultation with Employees (UK)
HSE	Health and Safety Executive (UK)
HSIP	Hsinchu Science-based Industrial Park (Taiwan)
IAER	International Association of Electronics Recyclers
IBM	International Business Machines Corporation
IC	integrated circuit
ICFTU	International Confederation of Free Trade Unions
ICRT	International Campaign for Responsible Technology
IDM	integrated device manufacturer
IEAT	Industrial Estate Authority of Thailand
IFA	International Framework Agreement
ILO	International Labour Organization

IMF	International Metalworkers' Federation
IOHP	Inverclyde Occupational Health Project (Scotland)
iSEZ	Integrated Special Economic Zone (India)
ISO	International Organization for Standardization
ISRI	Institute for Scrap Recycling Industries
ISTC	Iron and Steel Trades Confederation (Scotland)
IT	information technology
ITA	Information Technology Agreement
MDA	methylenedianiline
MNC	multinational corporation
MOCA	methylenebis-*o*-chloroaniline
MOEA	Ministry of Economic Affairs (Taiwan)
MPDA	m-phenylenediamine
MSDS	Material Safety Data Sheet
MTUC	Malaysian Trade Union Congress
NAFTA	North American Free Trade Agreement
NAICS	North American Industrial Classification System
NEPSI	National Electronic Products Stewardship Initiative
NEPZ	Noida Export Processing Zone (India)
NGO	non-governmental organization
NIOSH	National Institute for Occupational Safety and Health
NLRB	National Labor Relations Board
NPIID	Network of People Impacted By Industrial Development (Thailand)
NPRI	National Pollution Release Inventory (Canada)
NRIE	Northern Region Industrial Estate (Thailand)
NSUK	National Semiconductor (UK) Ltd.
NTD	new Taiwan dollars
ODM	original design manufacturer
OECD	Organisation for Economic Co-operation and Development
OEM	original equipment manufacturer
OEPP	Office of Environmental Policy and Planning (Thailand)
OHS	occupational health and safety
OSH	occupational safety and health
OSHA	Occupational Safety and Health Administration
OT	overtime
PC	personal computer
PCB	poly-chlorinated bi-phenyl
PCB	printed circuit board
PCD	Pollution Control Department (Thailand)
PCE	perchloroethylene, also known as tetrachloroethylene
PHASE	Project on Health and Safety in Electronics
PHASE Two	People for Health and Safety in Electronics (Scotland)
PMR	proportional mortality ratio
PODER	People Organized in Defense of Earth and her Resources
PR	public relations
PRO	producer responsibility organization
PVC	polyvinyl chloride
R & D	research and development
RCA	Radio Corporation of America
RCA-WSHG	RCA Workers' Self-help Group (Taiwan)
REACH	Registration, Evaluation, and Authorization of Chemicals

RETC	Registry of Toxic Waste Emissions and Shipments (Mexico)
RMB	Yuan Renminbi (currency China)
RoHS	Restrictions of Hazardous Substances
RR	risk ratio
SCCOSH	Santa Clara Center for Occupational Safety and Health
SEEPZ	Santa Cruz Electronics Export Processing Zone (India)
SEIJAL	State of Jalisco Electronic Information System (Mexico)
SEMATECH	Semiconductor Manufacturing Technology, Inc.
SEPROE	Secretariat of Economic Development (Jalisco, Mexico)
SEZ	special economic zone
SHAR	Specified Home Appliance Recycling (Japan)
SIA	Semiconductor Industry Association
SIC	standard industrial classification
SIPA	Science-based Industrial Park Administration (Taiwan)
SMT	surface mount technology
SNEEJ	Southwest Network for Environmental and Economic Justice
SS	support supplier
STUC	Scottish Trades Union Congress
SVTC	Silicon Valley Toxics Coalition
SWOP	SouthWest Organizing Project
TAVOI	Taiwan Association for Victims of Occupational Injuries
TCA	1,1,1 trichloroethane
TCE	Texas Campaign for the Environment
TCE	trichloroethylene
TEAN	Taiwan Environmental Action Network
TISI	Thai Industrial Standards Institute
TNC	transnational corporation
TRI	Toxic Release Inventory
TSMC	Taiwan Semiconductor Manufacturing Company, Ltd.
TV	television
TW	Taiwan
UAB	University of Alabama at Birmingham
UC	University of California
UE	United Electrical Workers Union
UK	United Kingdom
UMC	United Microelectronics Corporation (Taiwan)
UN	United Nations
UNEP	United Nations Environment Programme
UNI	Union Network International
UNICOR	Federal Prison Industries, Inc. (USA), trade name of
UNIDO	United Nations Industrial Development Organization
US	United States
USA	United States of America
USTR	United States Trade Representative
WEEE	waste electrical and electronic equipment
WeLeaP!	Women's Leadership Project
WEPT	Work and Environment Related Patients' Network of Thailand
WHO	World Health Organization
WTO	World Trade Organization

References

Adams, G. 1996. Letter to Stan R. Ciraulo, General Manager, IBM Corporation, September 29.

AEA. 2003a. "Defining the High-Tech Industry: AEA's New NAICS-based Industry Definition." Santa Clara, CA: American Electronics Association. Available: www.aeanet.org/Publications/idmk_naics_pdf.asp.

AEA. 2003b. "European Environmental Regulations: A Precedent for the U.S.?" Santa Clara, CA: American Electronics Association. Available: www.aeanet.org/bayarea/ewaste.

AEA Europe. 2003. "REACH Regulation Public Internet Consultation," July 9. Brussels. Available: www.aeanet.org.

AEA [American Electronics Association], EIA [Electronics Industry Alliance], et al. 1999. Letter to Vice President Albert Gore, Jr. May 7.

Aglietta, M. 1979. *A Theory of Capitalist Regulation: The U.S. Experience.* London and New York: Verso.

Ailamazian, E. K. 1990. "Effect of Ecological Factors on the Course of Pregnancy," *Vestn Akad Med Nauk SSR* 7:23–25.

Alexandrova, A. B. 2001. "The Extent of Poverty among Women in the Republic of Belarus: The Results of the Sociological Research," *Report Minsk.* Available: www.owl.ru/content/library/books/p1775.shtml.

Alston, D., ed. 1990. *We Speak for Ourselves: Social Justice and Environment.* Washington, DC: The Panos Institute.

Amnesty International. 2004. "Belarus: Stop the Silencing of Trade Union Activists." March 29. Available: web.amnesty.org/pages/blr-290304-action-eng.

AMRC. 1998. *We in the Zone: Women Workers in Asia's Export Processing Zones.* Hong Kong: Asia Monitor Resource Center.

AMRC. 2003. *China: Developments and Tensions in a Changing World.* Hong Kong: Asia Monitor Resource Center.

Angel, D. P. 1994. *Restructuring for Innovation: The Remaking of the U.S. Semiconductor Industry.* New York: Guilford Press.

Anonymous. 1998. "National Semiconductor's Communications Plan." January 19.

Anthony, D. 1928. "Labor Conditions in the Canning Industry in the Santa Clara Valley of the State of California." Ph.D. diss., Stanford University, California.

Arensman, R. 2000. "Ready for Recycling?," *Electronic Business*, November.

Asahi S. 2002. "New Law Is Prepared for Soil Contamination Countermeasures." January 25.

Ashford, Nicholas A., G. R. Heaton, Jr., and W. C. Priest. 1979. "Environmental, Health, and Safety Regulation and Technological Innovation." In *Technological Innovation for a Dynamic Economy,* ed. C. T. Hill and J. M. Utterback, 161–221. New York: Pergamon Press.

Ashwin, S., and S. Clarke. 2002. *Russian Trade Unions and Industrial Relations in Transition.* Basingstoke: Palgrave Macmillan.

Aymerich, I. 2001. *Sociología de los Derechos Humanos. Un Modelo Weberiano Contrastado con las Investigaciones Empíricas.* Valencia: Universidad de Valencia.

Bacon, D. 1993. "Silicon Valley on Strike! Immigrants in Electronics Protest Growing Sweatshop Conditions." Available: dbacon.igc.org/Strikes/15SilValSweatshops.htm.

Bailar J. C. III, M. Bobak, B. Fowler, A. Hay, J. LaDou, C. Maltoni, D. T. Teitelbaum, A. Watterson, and C. Woolfson. 2000. "Open Letter to the Health and Safety Executive," *International Journal of Occupational and Environmental Health* 6(1):71–72.

Bailar, J. C. III, M. Greenberg, R. Harrison, J. LaDou, E. Richter, and A. Watterson. 2002. "Cancer Risk in the Semiconductor Industry: A Call for Action," *International Journal of Occupational and Environmental Health* 8(2):171–79.

Balakrishnan, R., ed. 2002. *The Hidden Assembly Line: Gender Dynamics of Subcontracted Work in a Global Economy*. Bloomfield: Kumarian Press.

BAN. 1999. "The Basel Ban: A Triumph for Global Environmental Justice." Briefing Paper No. 1. May. Seattle: Basel Action Network.

BAN. 2005. "The Digital Dump: Exporting Re-use and Abuse to Africa." Seattle: Basel Action Network, October 24. Available: http://www.ban.org/BANreports/10-24-05/.

BAN [Basel Action Network], SVTC [Silicon Valley Toxics Coalition], Toxics Link India, SCOPE (Pakistan), Greenpeace China. 2002. *Exporting Harm: The High-Tech Trashing of Asia*. Available: www.svtc.org/cleancc/pubs/technotrash.htm.

Barde, J.-P. 1995. "Environmental policy and policy instruments." In *Principles of Environmental and Resource Economics*, ed. H. Folmer, H. L. Gabel, and H. Opschoor. Aldershot, UK: Elgar.

Barlow, M., and T. Clarke. 2003. "Making the Links: A Citizen's Guide to the World Trade Organization and the Free Trade Area of the Americas." International Edition. Ottawa: The Council of Canadians. Available: www.canadians.org/documents/making_the_links_int.pdf.

Barrett, L. 1997. "Factors Point to Bright Sales Future for Chips," *Silicon Valley/San Jose Business Journal*, May 16. Available: www.bizjournals.com/sanjose/stories/1997/05/19/newscolumn3.html.

Bauer, S., I. Wolff, N. Werner, and P. Hoffman. 1992. "Health Hazards in the Semiconductor Industry. A Review," *Polish Journal of Occupational Medicine and Environmental Health* 5(4):299–314.

Beall, C., E. Delzell, P. Cole, and I. Brill. 1996. "Brain Tumors among Electronics Industry Workers," *Epidemiology* 2:129.

Beall, C., T. J. Bender, H. Cheng, et al. 2005. "Mortality Among Semiconductor and Storage Device-Manufacturing Workers," *Journal of Occupational and Environmental Medicine* 47(10):996–1014.

Beck, U. 1992. *Risk Society: Towards a New Modernity*. London: Sage.

Beckman, D. 2003. "The Great Tech Job Exodus . . ." *Tech Worker News*, January 24. Available: www.techsunite.org/news/techind/offshoring1.cfm.

Beech, H. 2003. "The Sky is Falling," *Time*, July 28.

Bello, W., S. Cunningham, and L. K. Poh. 1998. *A Siamese Tragedy: Development and Disintegration in Modern Thailand*. London: Zed Books.

Benner, C. 1998. "Win the Lottery or Organize: Traditional and Non-Traditional Labor Organizing in Silicon Valley," *Berkeley Planning Journal* 12:50–71.

Bennett, W. L. 1990. "Towards a Theory of Press-State Relations," *Journal of Communication* 40:103–25.

Bhavani, T. A. 2002. "Small-scale Units in the Era of Globalization: Problems and Prospects," *Economic and Political Weekly* [Mumbai, India], July 20.

Bluestone, B., and B. Harrison. 1982. *The Deindustrialization of America: Plant Closings, Community Abandonment, and the Dismantling of Basic Industry*. New York: Basic Books.

Borrus, M., E. Dieter, and S. Haggard, eds. 2000. *International Production Networks in Asia: Rivalry or Riches?* London: Routledge.

Borrus, M., and J. Zysman. 1997. "Wintelism and the Changing Terms of Global Competition. Prototype of the Future?" BRIE Working Paper No. 96B. Berkeley, CA: Berkeley Roundtable on the International Economy.

Bound, J. P., P. W. Harvey, B. J. Francis, F. Awwad, and A. C. Gatrell. 1997. "Involvement of Deprivation and Environmental Lead in Neural Tube Defects," *Archives of Disease in Childhood* 76(2):107–112.

Brenner, R. 2002. *The Boom and the Bubble: The US in the World Economy.* London and New York: Verso.

Brown, Garrett D. 2002. "The Global Threats to Workers' Health and Safety on the Job," *Social Justice* 29(3).

Brown, V. J. 2003. "REACHing for Chemical Safety," *Environmental Health Perspectives* 111(14):A766–69.

Bulkeley, W. M. 2004. "IBM Settles Workers' Cancer Claims," *Wall Street Journal*, June 24, p. B4. Available online: www.wsj.com.

Bundit, T., ed. 1999. "Thai Labor Law Enforcement Problems." Bangkok: *Arom Pongpangan* Foundation. [In Thai.]

Bundit, T. 2000. "Analysis of Workplace Health and Safety Law Enforcement Problems." Paper presented at the ILO Trade Union Workshop on Occupational Safety and Health, Thailand. June 25–27. Bangkok: *Arom Pongpangan* Foundation. [In Thai.]

Bundit, T. 2004. Personal communication to Tira Foran, September 5. Bangkok, Thailand.

Business Week. 2002. "The Decline of the Maquiladora," April 29.

Business Week. 2003. "The Information Technology 100," June 23, pp. 90–98. Available: www.businessweek.com/pdfs/2003/0325_it100score.pdf.

Byster, L. A., and T. Smith. 1999. "High-Tech and Toxic: Global Labor Pains in the Electronics Industry," *Forum for Applied Research and Public Policy* 14(1):69–76.

CAFOD. 2004. "Clean Up Your Computer: Working Conditions in the Electronics Sector." London: Catholic Agency for Overseas Development. Available: cafod.org.uk/policy_and_analyses/policy_papers/private_sector/clean_up_ your_computer_report.

Caldwell, L. 1992. *International Environmental Policy: From the Twentieth to the Twenty-First Century.* 3rd ed. Durham, NC: Duke University Press.

California Regional Water Quality Control Board. 1995. "Site Management System, Annual Report." San Francisco Bay Region, May.

Canfield, R. L., C. Henderson, Jr., D. Cory-Slechta, et al. 2003. "Intellectual Impairment in Children with Blood Lead Concentrations Below 10μ g per Deciliter," *New England Journal of Medicine* 348 (16, April 17):1517–26.

Cantlupe, J. 2003. "Tracking of Toxic Wastes Is Found Outdated," *San Diego Union Tribune*, 30 March, pp. B1, 7.

Capek, Stella M. 1993. "The 'Environmental Justice' Frame: A Conceptual Discussion and an Application," *Social Problems* 40(1):5–24.

Carlson, S. 2003. "Old Computers Never Die—They Just Cost Colleges Money in New Ways," *Chronicle of Higher Education.* February 14.

Castells, M. 1996, 2000. *The Information Age: Economy, Society and Culture.* 3 vols. Oxford, UK, and Malden, MA: Blackwell.

Castells, M. 1998. *End of Millennium.* Oxford, UK, and Malden, MA: Blackwell.

Cecilia. 1992. "We Thought the Right to Form Unions Was a Fundamental Right?" In *Struggling for Space: Stories of Indian Women's Struggles*, ed. Sujatha Gothoskar. Kowloon, Hong Kong: Committee for Asian Women.

Chalermchai C. and V. Pruktaratikul. n.d. "Measurement of Lead Concentration in Work Areas and Ducts, Seagate Technology (Thailand)." [Report]. Department of Occupational Health and Safety, Faculty of Public Health, Mahidol University. [In Thai.]

Chang, S., Wen-ling Tu, Wen-chun Yang, and Li-fang Yang. 2001. "A Study of the Environmental and Social Aspects of Taiwanese and U.S. Companies in the Hsinchu Science-based Industrial Park." [Report]. Corporate Accountability Project. Berkeley, CA: Nautilus Institute.

Chee H. L., and K. G. Rampal. 2004. "Work-related Musculoskeletal Problems among Women Workers in the Semiconductor Industry in Peninsular Malaysia," *International Journal of Occupational and Environmental Health* 10:63–71.

Chee, H. L., K. G. Rampal, and A. Chandrasakaran. 2004. "Ergonomic Risk Factors of Work Processes in the Semiconductor Industry in Peninsular Malaysia," *Industrial Health* 42:373–81.

Chen, H.-M. 2002. "De-construction of Environmental Myth on HSIP and High-tech Industries." Master's thesis, Graduate School of Journalism, Chengchi University, Taipei, Taiwan.

Chhachhi, A. 1997a. "Dormant Volcanoes or Fresh Green Vegetables? Women Electronic Workers in Delhi." Unpublished monograph. ISS/FREA Research Project. The Hague, Netherlands: Institute of Social Studies.

Chhachhi, A. 1997b. "The Experience of Job Loss in the Electronics Industry," Paper presented at the seminar on "Policies and Strategies for Working Women in the Context of Industrial Restructuring," Jamia Humdard University, New Delhi, September 22–25.

Chhachhi, A. 1999. "Gender Flexibility, Skills and Industrial Restructuring: The Electronic Industry in India." Working Paper 296. The Hague, Netherlands: Institute of Social Studies.

China Labor Bulletin. 2002. "Guangdong Federation of Trade Unions Declared Migrant Workers' Organization in Zhejiang Illegal," August 8. Hong Kong.

China Labor Bulletin. 2004. "'Dagongmei'—Female Migrant Laborers," March 8, Hong Kong.

Chiu, H.-M. 2001. "The Environmental Movement against High-Tech Dangers in Taiwan." Unpublished Working paper. Red Green Study Group, UK.

Chiu, H.-M. 2003. "Standing Against Chemical Poison to Workers in Northern Thailand: the Story of Mayuree Taeviya and Friend for Friend Club." E-mail communication to the International Campaign for Responsible Technology, November.

Chiu, Y.-T. and S.-L. Ko. 2002. "Shortage of Rainfall Leaves Fields Fallow," *Taipei Times*, December 12, p. 1.

Chow, Chung-yang. 2004. "Workers Protest at Low Wages, Long Hours," *South China Morning Post*, October 7.

Chowdhury, N. 2002. "The Tide Turns for Seagate Technology," *Far Eastern Economic Review*, May 2. Available: www.feer.com/articles/2002/0205_02/p036money.html.

Clapp, R. W. 2003a. Declaration of Richard Clapp, D.Sc., in Support of Plaintiffs' Opposition to IBM's Motion for Summary Judgment. In re: San Jose Workers litigation, Master Case No. CV 772093; Superior Court of the State of California, in and for the County of Santa Clara. Endorsed and filed September 12.

Clapp, R. W. 2003b. Declaration of Richard Clapp in Support of Motion for Reconsideration re Exclusion of Richard Clapp's Corporate Mortality File analyses. In re: San Jose Workers litigation, Master Case No. CV 772093; Superior Court of the State of California, in and for the County of Santa Clara. Endorsed and filed October 20.

Clean Computer Campaign. 1999. "Analysis of the AEA Claims that the Proposed European Directive on Waste from Electrical and Electronic Equipment (WEEE Directive)

Will Conflict with the WTO Trade Rules." Available: www.svtc.org/cleancc/pubs/ sayno.htm.

CLIST. 2003. "MMI Women Workers Need International Solidarity Support." E-mail communication to the International Campaign for Responsible Technology, December. Bangkok: Center for Labour Information Service and Training.

Corn, M., and R. Cohen. 1993. "Prospective Exposure Assessment. Supplement to the Final Report." School of Hygiene and Public Health, Baltimore, MD: The Johns Hopkins University.

Correa, A., R. H. Gray, R. Cohen, N. Rothman, F. Shah, H. Seacat, and M. Corn. 1996. "Ethylene Glycol Ethers and Risks of Spontaneous Abortion and Subfertility," *American Journal of Epidemiology* 143(7):707–17.

Cowie, J. 1999. *Capital Moves: RCA's Seventy-year Quest for Cheap Labor.* New York: Norton.

CTBC. 2003. "Essential Elements of Legislation." San Jose, CA: Computer TakeBack Campaign. Available: www.computertakeback.com/legislation_and_policy/essentials.cfm.

Dangler, J. F. 1989. "Electronics Sub-Assemblers in Central New York: Non-Traditional Homeworkers in a Non-Traditional Homework Industry." In *Homework: Historical and Contemporary Perspective on Paid Labour at Home*, ed. Eileen Boris and Cynthia R. Daniels. Chicago: University of Illinois Press.

Datsenko, I. I., G. G. Semenova, and O. P. Novak. 1984. "Hygienic Features of the Work of Electronics Industry Workers and Ways of Improving Them," *Vrach Delo* 12:91–4.

David, N. 1996. *Worlds Apart: Women and the Global Economy*. Geneva: International Confederation of Free Trade Unions.

Davis, G., C. Witt, and J. Barkenbus. 1997. "Extended Product Responsibility: A Tool for a Sustainable Economy," *Environment* 39(7):10–15 ff.

DEC. 1986. "Study of Miscarriage Rates." Hudson, MA: Digital Equipment Corporation.

DeJule, R. 1998. "New Fab Construction: Flexible Facility Architecture, Safety and Energy Usage Concerns Become Paramount as Costs Soar," *Semiconductor International* (January): 81–85.

Delgado, Y. 2001. "El Empleo Femenino, en la Industria Electrónica de la Zona Metropolitana de Guadalajara 1986–1994." Master's thesis, Universidad de Guadalajara, Mexico.

Denisov, L. A. 2000a. "Organisation of Social-Hygienic Monitoring in Zelenograd," *Gig Sanit* 4:3–8.

Denisov, L. A. 2000b. "Significance of Social-Hygienic Monitoring in the Control of Environmental Quality and Population's Health," *Gig Sanit*: 3–8.

Department of Civil Works and Planning. 2004. "*Wang pang anakot prathet thai nai pawa sing waet lom wikrit.*" [Planning the Future of Thailand in the Context of Environmental Crisis] *Matichon Daily*, September 2, p. 2.

DGFT [Directorate General of Foreign Trade], Ministry of Commerce and Industry, Government of India. 2003. "Re-2003/2002-07." Policy Circular No. 19. November 11.

DIEESE. 2001. "Diagnóstico: Indústria Metal Mecânica na Zona Franca de Manaus." São Paulo, Brazil: DIEESE—Subseção Confederação Nacional des Metalúrgicos da CUT.

DiGangi, J. 2003. "US Intervention in EU Chemical Policy." September. Unpublished manuscript. Boston, MA: Environmental Health Fund.

DoE [Department of Electronics], Government of India. 1999. *Guide to Electronics Industry in India 1999*. New Delhi.

DoE [Department of Electronics, Ministry of Information Technology, Government of India]. 2002. Annual Report.

Doner, R. F., and P. Brimble. 1998. "Thailand's Hard Disk Drive Industry." Working Paper 98-02. Information Storage Industry Center, University of California, San Diego, October. Available: isic.ucsd.edu/papers/thailandhdd.shtml.

EC. 2001. "White Paper on A Strategy for a Future Chemicals Policy." A5-0356/2001. Brussels: European Commission, April.

EC. 2003a. "Directive 200/95/EC of the European Parliament and of the Council on the Restriction on the Use of Certain Hazardous Substances in Electrical and Electronic Equipment, January 27, 2003," *Official Journal of the European Union.* Brussels: European Commission, February 13.

EC. 2003b. "Directive 200/96/EC of the European Parliament and of the Council on Waste Electrical and Electronic Equipment." Brussels: European Commission, January 27.

Eckhouse, J. 1991. "Trade Pact Called Good for Environment," *San Francisco Chronicle,* December 7.

Ecopledge.com, GrassRoots Recycling Network, Promoting Corporate Responsibility About Waste, and Computer TakeBack Campaign. 2002. "Dude, Why Won't They Take Back My Old Dell?" March. Available: www.grrn.org/e-scrap/Dell_TakeBack_Report. pdf.

EIA. 2002. "Statement of the Electronic Industries Alliance Regarding Report on E-Waste Recycling in China." [Press release.] Arlington, VA: Electronic Industries Alliance, February 25. Available: www.eia.org/news/pressreleases/2002-02-25.43.phtml.

EIROnline. 2003. "Problems Facing the Trade Union Movement Analysed." European Industrial Relations Observatory Online. Available: www.eiro.eurofound.eu.int/2003/08/feature/pl0308106f.html.

Eisenscher, M. 1993. "Silicon Fist in a Velvet Glove." Unpublished paper. November. San Jose, CA.

Elektronikkretur AS and Hvitevareretur AS. 2002. "Environmental Report 2001." Oslo.

Elliott, R. C., J. R. Jones, D. M. McElvenny, et al. 1999. "Spontaneous Abortion in the British Semiconductor Industry: An HSE Investigation," *American Journal of Industrial Medicine* 36:557–72; Comment in *American Journal of Industrial Medicine* 36:584–586.

Elson, D., and R. Pearson. 1980. "Nimble Fingers Make Cheap Workers: An Analysis of Women's Employment in Third World Export Manufacturing," *Feminist Review* (Spring):87–107.

Elson, D., and R. Pearson. 1989. "Introduction: Nimble Fingers and Foreign Investments." In *Women's Employment and Multinationals in Europe,* ed. D. Elson and R. Pearson, 1–11 London: Macmillan Press.

EMG. 2002. "HSIP Environmental Monitoring Group Annual Report." Hsinchu, Taiwan: Environmental Monitoring Group.

ENDS. 2001. "Electroscrap Financing 'Must Be Individual,'" *ENDS Environment Daily,* May 11. London: Environmental Data Services.

ENDS. 2002a. "Firms, NGOs and Consumers in WEEE Plea," *ENDS Environment Daily,* February 15. London: Environmental Data Services.

ENDS. 2002b. "Firms Team Up to Tackle Electroscrap Recycling," *ENDS Environment Daily,* December 16. London: Environmental Data Services.

Entman, R. M. 1993. "Framing: Toward Clarification of a Fractured Paradigm," *Journal of Communication* 43:51–58.

Environment Ministry. Government of Japan. 2002. *The Draft for the Soil Environment Protection Law.* [In Japanese.]

EPR Working Group. 2003. "A Prescription for Clean Production, Pollution Prevention and Zero Waste." Available: www.grrn.org/epr/epr_principles.html.

Ernst and Young. 2002. "India: The Hardware Opportunity." In association with the Manufacturers Association of Information Technology (MAIT). New Delhi, India.

Ernst, D. 1983. *The Global Race in Microelectronics.* Frankfurt and New York: Campus.

Ernst, D. 2002. "The Economics of Electronics Industry: Competitive Dynamics and Industrial Organization." In *The International Encyclopedia of Business and Management*

(IEBM), Handbook of Economics, ed. William Lazonick. London: International Thomson Business Press.

Ernst, D., and D. O'Connor. 1992. *Competing in the Electronics Industry: The Experience of Newly Industrializing Economies.* Paris: OECD.

Esser, J., B. Lüthje, and R. Noppe. 1997. *Europäische Telekommunikation im Zeitalter der Deregulierung. Infrastruktur im Umbruch.* Münster: Westfälisches Dampfboot.

Ettema, J. S., and T. L. Glasser. 1998. *Custodians of Conscience: Investigative Journalism and Public Virtue.* New York: Columbia University Press.

Ewell, M., and K. O. Ha. 1999a. "Why Piecework Won't Go Away: The Practice Helped Fuel Growth at Solectron, and Others Imitated It," *San Jose Mercury News*, June 28.

Ewell, M., and K. O. Ha. 1999b. "Piecework Practices Curtailed," *San Jose Mercury News*, October 17.

Falk, R. 1999. *Predatory Globalization: A Critique.* Malden, MA: Polity Press.

Fan, M.-H. 1997. "Color Change of Beautiful Kuan-Si Village: Document of Anti-Kuan-Si Industrial Park," *Chuchien Magazine* [Hsinchu, Taiwan] 3:34–44.

Feenberg, A. 1991. *Critical Theory of Technology.* New York: Oxford University Press.

Feenberg, A. 1999. *Questioning Technology.* New York: Routledge.

Ferber, D. 2004a. "Beset by Lawsuits, IBM Blocks a Study that Used Its Data," *Science (Occupational Medicine)* 304:937–39.

Ferber, D. 2004b. "Authors Turn Up Heat over Disputed Paper," *Science (Occupational Medicine)* 304:1891.

Ferguson, C. H., and C. R. Morris. 1993. *Computer Wars: How the West Can Win in A Post-IBM World.* New York: Times Books.

Fernández-Kelly, M. Patricia. 1983. *For We Are Sold, I and My People: Women and Industry in Mexico's Frontier.* Albany, NY: State University of New York Press.

Ferriss, S. 2003. "Paying the Price of Free Trade: Shattered Dreams," Cox News Service, August 31.

Ferus-Comelo, A. 2005. "Globalisation and Labour Organisation in the Electronics Industry." Ph.D. diss., Economic Geography. University of London.

Fishbein, B. 1996. "'Extended Producer Responsibility': A New Concept Spreads Around the World," *Demanufacturing Partnership Program Newsletter* 1(2). Rutgers University, New Jersey. Available: accounting.rutgers.edu/raw/gsm/dpp/win96.htm.

Fisher, J. 2002. "Cancer in the Semiconductor Industry" [editorial], *Archives Environmental Health* 57(2):95–97.

Florini, A. M. 2000. "The Third Force: the Rise of Transnational Civil Society." Washington DC: Carnegie Endowment for International Peace.

Flynn, L. J. 2003. "Dell Stops Hiring Prisoners for Its Recycling Program," *New York Times*, July 4, p. C3.

Forsyth, T. 1994. "Shut-Up or Shut-Down: How a Thai Medical Agency Was Closed After It Questioned Worker Safety at a Factory Owned by Thailand's Largest Employer," *Asia, Inc.* (April):30–37.

Fox, S. 1991. *Toxic Work: Women Workers at GTE Lenkurt.* Philadelphia: Temple University Press.

Fröbel, F., J. Heinrichs, and O. Kreye. 1977. *Die Neue Internationale Arbeitsteilung.* Reinbek: Rowohlt.

Frolova, N. M. 2001. "Risk of Health Disorders Among Women Working with Precise Sterile Technologies," *Med Tr Prom Ekol* 10:13–17.

Frontera Norte-Sur. 2001. "Tijuana Maquiladora Workers Sickened by Alleged Gas Leak," June 14.

Fuentes, A., and B. Ehrenreich. 1983. *Women in the Global Factory.* Boston: South End Press.

Gabayet O., Luisa E. 1990. "Women in Transnational Industry: The Case of the Electronic Industry in Guadalajara, Mexico." Texas Papers on Mexico, No. 90-04. Austin: University of Texas.

Gabayet O., Luisa E. 1994. "Las Mujeres en la Industria Electrónica de Guadalajara: Lo Público y Lo Privado." In *La Condición de la Mujer en Jalisco*, ed. Rosa Rojas and María Rodríguez Batista. Jalisco: Universidad de Guadalajara.

GAO. 2003. "International Trade: Mexico's Maquiladora Decline Affects US-Mexico Border Communities and Trade." Report No. GAO–03–891, July. Washington, DC: General Accounting Office, United States Government.

Garabrant, D. H., and R. Olin. 1986. "Carcinogens and Cancer Risks in the Microelectronics industry," *State of the Art Reviews: Occupational Medicine* 1:119–34.

Gassert, T. H. 1985. *Health Hazards in Electronics: A Handbook*. Hong Kong: Asia Monitor Resource Center.

Gerber, J. 2000a. "Minimum Wages in San Diego and Tijuana," *Cross Border Economic Bulletin*, January.

Gerber, J. 2000b. "Wage and Salary Trends in the Maquiladora Industry," *Cross Border Economic Bulletin*, May.

Gilder, G. 1989. *Microcosm: The Quantum Revolution in Economics and Technology*. New York: Simon and Schuster.

Globalisation Monitor. 2004. Special issue on cadmium poisoning at GP battery factory, China. [Hong Kong.] August. [In Chinese.]

GoI [Government of India]. 2003. *Economic survey of India, 2002–2003*. New Delhi.

Goldsberry, C. 2002. "Market Snapshot: Consumer Electronics," *Injection Molding Magazine*, August.

Goldstein, N. 1989. "Silicon Glen: Women and Semiconductor Multinationals." In *Women's Employment in Multinationals in Europe*, ed. D. Elson and R. Pearson, 111–28. London: Macmillan Press.

Gottlieb, R. 2001. *Environmentalism Unbound: Exploring New Pathways for Change*. Cambridge, MA: MIT University Press.

Gray, R. 1993. "Final Report Retrospective and Prospective Studies of Reproductive Health Among IBM Employees in Semiconductor Manufacturing." School of Hygiene and Public Health, The Johns Hopkins University, Baltimore, Maryland.

Greider, W. 1997. *One World, Ready or Not: The Manic Logic of Global Capitalism*. New York: Simon and Schuster.

Grove, A. S. 1996. *Only the Paranoid Survive: How To Exploit the Crisis Points That Challenge Every Company and Career.* New York: Doubleday.

Guía de la Industria Maquiladora. 2001. 2(3). Tijuana, Mexico.

Haas, P. 1990. *Saving the Mediterranean: The Politics of International Environmental Cooperation*. New York: Columbia University Press.

Habermas, J. 1974. *Theory and Practice*. London: Heineman.

Habermas, J. 1976. *Towards a Rational Society: Student Protest, Science, and Politics*. Boston: Beacon Press.

Hadano City. Japan. 1993. "General View of Environment Countermeasures." [In Japanese.]

Hadano City. Japan. 1996. "Clean up of Geo-Pollution by Simple Clean-up System." [In Japanese.]

Hamilton, F. 1991. "Our First Union." In *Common Interests: Women organizing in Global Electronics*, ed. Women Working Worldwide, 27–32. London.

Hannigan, John A. 1995. *Environmental Sociology: A Social Constructionist Perspective*. New York and London: Routledge.

Harrison, M. 1992. "Semiconductor Manufacturing Hazards." In *Hazardous Materials Toxicology: Clinical Principles of Environmental Health*, ed. John B. Sullivan and Gary Krieger, 472–504. Baltimore, MD: Williams and Wilkins.

Harttranft, M. 1996. "Locals Seek Fed Help in Sparton Cleanup," *Albuquerque Journal*, February 2, p. C-2.

Hawes, A. 1998. "Reflections of SCCOSH Founders." In *Silicon Dreams: Workers' Memorial Day Book*. San Jose, CA: Santa Clara Center for Occupational Safety and Health, May 3.

Hawes, A. 2003. Personal correspondence with David N. Pellow via the Internet. October 12.

Held, D., A. McGrew, D. Goldblatt, and J. Perraton. 1999. *Global Transformations: Politics, Economics, Culture*. Stanford, CA: Stanford University Press.

Henderson, J. 1989. *The Globalisation of High Technology Production: Space and Semiconductors in the Restructuring of the Modern World*. London: Routledge.

Herbert, B. 2003a. "Sick and Suspicious" [Op-ed.], *New York Times*, September 4.

Herbert, B. 2003b. "Clouds in Silicon Valley" [Op-ed.], *New York Times*, September 8.

Herbert, B. 2003c. "Early Warnings" [Op-ed.], *New York Times*, September 12.

Herbert, B. 2003d. "I.B.M. Families Ask, 'Why?'" [Op-ed.], *New York Times*, September 15.

Herrick, R. F., J. H. Stewart, D. Blicharz, et al. 2005. "Exposure Assessment for Retrospective Follow-up Studies of Semiconductor- and Storage Device-Manufacturing Workers," *Journal of Occupational and Environmental Medicine* 47(10):983–995.

Hildén, M., J. Lepola, P. Mickwitz, et al. 2002. "Evaluation of Environmental Policy Instruments: A Case Study of the Finnish Pulp & Paper and Chemical Industries." Boreal Environmental Research Monograph, No. 21. Helsinki: Finnish Environment Institute.

Hillman, G. 1982. "ECHOES: IBM's Environmental, Chemical and Occupational Evaluation System," *Journal of Occupational Medicine* 24(10):827–35.

Hoffer, F. 1997. "Traditional Trade Unions during Transition and Economic Reform in Russia." Interdepartmental Action Programme on Privatization, Restructuring and Economic Democracy (IPPRED) Paper No 8. Geneva, ILO.

Holdcroft, J. 2003. "EPZs–Globalisation's Great Deceit," *Metal World* 3:22–26.

Hong Kong Trade Development Council. 2005. "Market Profile on Chinese Mainland." Available: www.tdctrade.com/main/china.htm.

Hossfeld, K. J. 1988. "Division of Labor, Division of Lives: Immigrant Women Workers in Silicon Valley." Ph.D. diss., Sociology, University of California, Santa Cruz.

Hossfeld, K. J. 1990. "Their Logic Against Them: Contradictions in Sex, Race, and Class in Silicon Valley." In *Women Workers and Global Restructuring*, ed. K. Ward. Ithaca: ILR Press.

Hossfeld, K. J. 1991a. "Introduction." In *Common Interests: Women Organizing in Global Electronics*, ed. Women Working Worldwide, 13–18. London.

Hossfeld, Karen J. 1991b. "Why Aren't High-Tech Workers Organized?" In *Common Interests: Women Organizing in Global Electronics*, ed. Women Working Worldwide, 37–51. London.

HRW. 1996. "No Guarantees: Sex Discrimination in Mexico's Maquiladora Sector," *Human Rights Watch* 8(6).

HSE. 2001. "Cancer Among Current and Former Workers at National Semiconductor (UK) Ltd, Greenock: Results of an Investigation." London: Health and Safety Executive.

HSE. 2003. "Inspections by the Health and Safety Executive in 2002 of Manufacturers of Semiconductors in Great Britain." London: Health and Safety Executive. Available: www.hse.gov.uk/fod/eng-util/semicon.pdf.

HSE. 2005. "HSE Proposes Further Research at NSUK, Greenock." [Press release.] London: Government News Network. 14 June. Available: www.gnn.gov.uk/imagelibrary/detail.asp?MediaDetailsID=116070.

Huisinga, A. 2003. "ICT Milieu." Personal Communication to Naoko Tojo, April 11. Woeden, Netherlands.

Hunter, R., and M. Lopez. 1999. "Position of the American Electronics Association (AEA) on the European Commission's Draft Directive on Waste from Electrical and Electronic Equipment (WEEE)." Available: www.svtc.org/cleancc/pubs.

Hyogo Prefecture. Japan. 1995. "White Paper of Environment." [In Japanese.]

Ianin, E. P. 2000. "Chemical Content of Dust Released by Electrical Enterprises," *Med Tr Prom Ekol* 8:24–27.

ICFTU. 2001. "Report for the WTO General Council Review of Trade Policies of Malaysia." Geneva: International Confederation of Free Trade Unions, December 3–5.

Ichihashi, K., et al. 1992. "Situation of Well Pollution by Trichloroethylene in Hyogo Prefecture," *Proceedings of 2nd Workshop on Groundwater Pollution and Its Prevention.* [In Japanese.]

ICRT. 1999. Letter to Vice-President Albert Gore, Jr. San Jose, CA: International Campaign for Responsible Technology. Available: www.svtc.org/cleancc/weee/euweee/ustrgore/gorelet.htm.

Ilic, M. 1999. *Women Workers in the Soviet Interwar Economy: From Protection to Equality.* Basingstoke, Macmillan.

ILO. 1996. *Safe Work in Clean Environment.* [Newsletter]. Sub-Regional Office for Central and Eastern Europe, International Labour Organization, Budapest.

ILO. 1998. "Impact of Flexible Labour Market Arrangements in the Machinery, Electrical and Electronic Industries." Geneva: International Labour Organization.

ILO. 2001. "Health Care in Central and Eastern Europe." SES Papers 22. InFocus Programme on Socio-Economic Security, International Labour Organization, Geneva.

ILO. 2002. "Lifelong Learning in the Mechanical and Electrical Engineering Industries." Geneva: International Labour Organization.

ILO. 2004. "Towards a Fair Deal for Migrant workers in the Global Economy." Report VI for the International Labor Conference, 92nd Session. Geneva: International Labor Organization.

INEGI. 2000. "Twelfth General Census of Population and Housing." Mexico City: National Institute for Statistics, Geography and Information Systems. Available: www.ini.gob.mx/indica2000/mpo/bc4.htm. [In Spanish.]

INFORM. 2003. "European Union (EU) Electrical and Electronic Products Directives." July. New York.

Intel. 2005a. "Innovation More Important Than Ever In Platform Era." [Press release.] Intel Developer Forum, San Francisco, March 1. Available: ftp://download.intel.com/museum/Moores_Law/Articles-Press_Releases/Press_Release_Mar2005.pdf.

Intel. 2005b. "Moore's Law: Made Real by Intel Innovation." Available: www.intel.com/technology/silicon/mooreslaw.

Iritani, E., and R. Boudreaux. 2003. "Mexico's Factories Shift Gears to Survive," *Los Angeles Times*, January 5.

IRPTC [International Register of Potentially Toxic Chemicals]. 1984. "Maximum Allowable Concentrations and Tentative Safe Exposure Levels of Harmful Substances in the Environmental Media." Moscow, Russia: United Nations Environment Programme (UNEP) and Centre of International Projects, State Committee for Science and Technology (GKNT).

Ishenalieva, Ch. A. 1994. "Reproductive Health of the Women Working in Semiconductor Manufacturing." Reproduktivnoe zdorov'e zhenshin, zanyatykh na proizvodstve poluprovodnikov (abstract). Moscow: Russian State Library.

ISO. 2000. "ISO Gives Thumbs Up to Standards for Personal Financial Planning Advisers, Thumbs Down to OH&S Work." Press release, no. 776, June 22. Geneva, Switzerland: International Organization for Standardization. Available: www.iso.org/iso/en/commcentre/pressreleases/2000/Ref776.html.

Jacobson, H. K., and E. B. Weiss, eds. 1997. *Engaging Countries: Strengthening Compliance with International Environmental Accords.* Cambridge, MA: MIT Press.

Japan Times. 2001. "Owners Must Test for Pollution Before Development Land," September 29.

Jefferson, LaShawn R., and P. McKinney. 1998. "A Job or Your Rights: Continued Sex Discrimination in Mexico's Maquiladora Sector," *Human Rights Watch* 10(1, December):B. Available: hrw.org/reports98/women2.

Jordan, M., and K. Sullivan. 2003. "Trade Brings Riches, but not to Mexico's Poor: NAFTA's Critics Say Pact Has Failed to Improve Lives of Impoverished Majority," *Washington Post*, March 22, p. A10.

Kabeer, N. 2000. *The Power to Choose: Bangladeshi Women and Labor Market Decisions in London and Dhaka.* London: Verso.

Kedrick, S. 1994. "Dying to Work: Toxic Tragedy or Misdiagnosis?" *Business in Thailand* 24:16–23.

Kelly, P. 2002. "Spaces of Labor Control: Comparative Perspectives from Southeast Asia," *Transactions of the Institute of British Geographers* 27:395–411.

Kennedy, D. 2004. "Science, Law, and the IBM Case" [Editorial.], *Science* 305(5682, July 16):309. Available: www.sciencemag.org/cgi/content/summary/305/5682/309.

Kenney, M. 1999. "Transplantation? A Comparison of Japanese Television Assembly Plants in Japan and the US." In *Remade in America*, eds. Paul Adler, W. Mark Fruin, and Jeffrey Liker. New York: Oxford University Press.

Kimitsu City, Department of Environment. 1993. "The First Report of Clean-up Measures of Geo-Pollution." [In Japanese.]

Kobayashi, T. 1993. "Restoration of Groundwater Contamination by Trichloroethylene." In *Situation and Clean-up Measures of Groundwater and Soil Contamination*, 402–05. Kogyo Gijutsukai. [In Japanese.]

Kollberg, M. 2003. "Exploring the Environmental Effectiveness of Extended Producer Responsibility Programmes. An Analysis of Approaches to Collective and Individual Responsibility for WEEE Management in Sweden and the UK." Master's thesis, International Institute for Industrial Environmental Economics, Lund University, Sweden.

Kraul, C. 1996. "Flood of Workers Flows North to Booming Tijuana," *Los Angeles Times*, September 24.

Ku, Y.-L. 1996. "The Power of Tears," *China Daily Times*, May 1, p. 32.

Kuehr, R., and E. Williams, eds. 2003. *Computers and the Environment: Understanding and Managing Their Impacts.* Dordrecht, NL: Kluwer.

Kumar, R. 1986. *Export Processing Zones in India.* New Delhi: Oxford University Press.

La Jornada. 1997. "Contaminacion, el Precio del Desarrollo en Mesa de Otay." July 19.

LaDou, J. 1983. "Potential Occupational Health Hazards in the Microelectronics Industry," *Scandinavian Journal of Work, Environment and Health* 9(1):42–46.

LaDou, J. 1984. "The Not-So-Clean Business of Making Chips," *Technology Review* 87:4, May–June.

LaDou, J. 1994. "Health Issues in the Global Semiconductor Industry," *Annals of the Academy of Medicine* [Singapore] 23(5, September).

LaDou, J. 1996. "In Many Areas of the World, the Migration of Reproductive Hazards Precedes the Development and Implementation of Reproductive Policy," *International Journal of Occupational and Environmental Health* 2(1):73–75.

LaDou, J. 1998. Letter to Linda Rosenstock, Director, National Institute of Occupational Safety and Health, January 27.

LaDou, J. 2000. Letter to David H. Wegman, Consultant, Silicon Industry Association, December 15.

LaDou, J., ed. 1986. Special Issue on "The Microelectronics Industry," *State of the Art Reviews: Occupational Medicine* 1(1, January–March). Philadelphia: Hanley and Belfus.

LaDou, J., and T. Rohm. 1998. "The International Electronics Industry," *International Journal of Occupational Medicine* 4:1–18.

Larrabee, G. B. 1993. "Environmentally Responsible Manufacturing." Paper presented at the International Symposium on Semiconductor Manufacturing, September 20–21. Available: ieeexplore.ieee.org/iel4/5477/14749/00670303.pdf.

Lee, C.-W. 2002. "Drought: HSIP Is Really Scared This Time," *China Times*, February 28, p. 5.

Lee, C.-L. 2000. "Treatment Price for Waste Solvent Is Going High; SIPA Plans To Build Incinerator To Turn the Waste Solvent into Fuel," *United Daily*, July 21, p. 4.

Lim, L. 1978. "Multinational Firms and Manufacturing for Export in Less-Developed Countries: The Case of the Electronics Industry in Malaysia and Singapore." Ph.D. diss., University of Michigan, Ann Arbor.

Lin, Chieh-yu and K. Chen. 2001. "Chen 'on His Knees' for Less Red Tape," *Taipei Times*, August 17, p. 1.

Lin, Z.-H., and H.-C. Suen. 2001. "An Epidemiological Study on Health Outcomes among Former RCA Employees (III)." [Report.] Institute of Occupational Safety and Health, Council of Labor Affairs, Taipei, Taiwan. [In Chinese.]

Linden, G. 1998. "Building Production Networks in Central Europe: The Case of the Electronics Industry." Working Paper 126. Berkeley Roundtable on International Economics, University of California, Berkeley.

Lindhqvist, T. 2000. "Extended Producer Responsibility in Cleaner Production." Ph.D. diss., Environmental Economics, University of Lund, Sweden.

Lindquist, D. 2002. "A Boost for Baja: Aircraft Parts Plant Will Help Slumping Maquiladoras," *San Diego Union Tribune*, February 22, p. C-1.

Lineback, J. R. 1998. "Silicon Strategies: Motorola Looks for Partner to Build Fab in Poland," *Semiconductor Business News*, March 30.

Loh, C. H., Shih, T. S., Hsieh, A. T., Chen, Y. H., Liao, G. D., and Liou, S. H. 2004. "Hepatic Effects in Workers Exposed to 2-methoxy Ethanol," *Journal of Occupational and Environmental Medicine* 46(7):707–13.

Lou, Q. J., ed. 2003. "China's Electronics and Information Industry–Study on Development Model." Beijing: Economics Publishing House. [In Chinese.]

Los Angeles Times. 2003. "Mexican Official Urges Unemployed to Be Creative," July 27, p. A19.

Lu, Se-Hui and Shu-Chen Tan. 2002. "Lin, Hsin-Yi Announce Fallow Plan To Solve the Problem of Water Shortage in HSIP," *Industry and Business*, February 28, p. 3.

Lüthje, B. 2001a. "Silicon Valley: Vernetzte Produktion, Industriearbeit und Soziale Bewegungen im Detroit der 'New Economy,'" *Prokla* 31(1):79–102.

Lüthje, B. 2001b. *Standort Silicon Valley: Ökonomie und Politik der vernetzten Massenproduktion.* Frankfurt and New York: Campus-Verlag.

Lüthje, B. 2002a. "Electronics Contract Manufacturing: Global Production and the International Division of Labor in the Age of the Internet," *Industry and Innovation* 9(3):227–47.

Lüthje, B. 2002b. "The Detroit of the New Economy: The Changing Workplace, Manufacturing Workers and the Labor Movement in Silicon Valley." Paper presented to the American Historical Association, San Francisco, January 6.

Lüthje, B. 2003a. "The IT Industry: Labor Flexibility, Production Networks, and the Global Downturn," *Asian Labor Update*. Hong Kong: Asia Monitor Resource Center.

Lüthje, B. 2003b. "Manufactura Electrónica por Contrato: de Producción Global y la División Internacional del Trabajo en la Era del Internet." In *La Industria Electrónica en*

México: Problemática, Perspectivas y Propuestas, ed. Enrique Dussel Peters, Juan José Palacios, and Guillermo Woo. Jalisco, Mexico: University of Guadalajara.

Lüthje, B. 2004a. "Global Production, Industrial Development and New Labor Regimes in China: The Case of Contract Manufacturing" (unpublished).

Lüthje, B. 2004b. "High-Tech Industrie." In *Historisch-Kritisches Wörterbuch des Marxismus*, Vol. 5, ed. Wolfgang Fritz Haug. Berlin and Hamburg: Argument-Verlag.

Lüthje, B., W. Schumm, and M. Sproll. 2002. *Contract Manufacturing: Transnationale Produktion und Industriearbeit im IT-Sektor.* Frankfurt and New York: Campus-Verlag.

Maizlish N., L. Rudolf, K. Dervin, and M. Sankaranarayan. 1995. "Surveillance and Prevention of Work-related Carpal Tunnel Syndrome: An Application of the Sentinel Events Notification System for Occupational Risks," *American Journal of Industrial Medicine* 27(5):715–29.

Malik, F. 1999. "The Electrical Engineering Industry of the Czech Republic. Part 2," *Czech Business and Trade.*

Markoff, J. 2003. "2 PC Makers Given Credit and Blame in Recycling," *New York Times*, June 27, p. C3.

Materials for the Future Foundation. 1999. "Bay Area Electronic Recycling: From the Corporate Office to the Curbside." Available: www.materials4future.org/PUBS/curbside.pdf.

Matthews, G. 2002. *Silicon Valley, Women, and the California Dream: Gender, Class, and Opportunity in the Twentieth Century.* Stanford, CA: Stanford University Press.

Matveev, N. V. 2003. *Medical Informatics in Occupational and Environmental Health of Russia: Need for Reforms.* Nizhny Novgorod, Russia: NNRIHOP.

Maugh, T. H. II. 2003. "'Safe' Lead Levels Lower IQ in Children, Study Finds," *Los Angeles Times*, April 17.

May, R. 1999. "Joining the Union: The Role of the Union Recruitment Campaign." Master's thesis, London School of Economics and Political Science.

Mazurek, J. 1999. *Making Microchips: Policy, Globalization and Economic Restructuring in the Semiconductor Industry.* Cambridge, MA: MIT Press.

McBride, E. 2002. "A New Order: Thailand's 16th Constitution..." [special supplement], *The Economist*, February 28. Available: www.economist.com/surveys/PrinterFriendly.cfm?Story_ID=998338.

McCook, A. 2004. "Researchers Boycott Journal: Contributors Cry Foul Play after the Publisher Refuses to Include a Controversial Article," *The Scientist*, June 23. Available: www.biomedcentral.com/news/20040623/04.

McCormick, J. 1991. *Reclaiming Paradise: The Global Environmental Movement*, Bloomington: Indiana University Press.

McCurdy, S. A., M. B. Schenker, and S. J. Samuels. 1991. "Reporting of Occupational Injury and Illness in the Semiconductor Manufacturing Industry," *American Journal of Public Health* 81(1):85.

McElvenny, D. M., A. J. Darnton, J. T. Hodgson, S. D. Clarke, R. C. Elliott, and J. Osman. 2001. "Cancer among Current and Former Workers at National Semiconductor UK, Ltd., Greenock: Results of an Investigation by the Health and Safety Executive." Suffolk, UK: HSE Books. Available: www.hse.gov.uk/statistics/nsukrept.pdf.

McKie, R. 2004. "IBM Fights To Suppress Cancer Probe. Computer Giant Accused of Persuading Scientific Journal To Block Academic Investigation of Illness in Employees," *The Observer* [London], June 20. Available: www.guardian.co.uk.

Meng, Wei-The. 2000. "Empirical Research on Causal Factors and Control Policy of Corporate Crime." Ph.D. diss., Central Police University, Taoyuan, Taiwan.

MII [Ministry of Information Industry. Government of China]. 2002. *Situation and Trends in Electronics and IT Industry, 2001*. Beijing: People's Publishing House. [In Chinese.]

MII [Ministry of Information Industry. Government of China]. 2003. *Situation and Trends in Electronics and IT Industry, 2002*. Beijing: People's Publishing House. [In Chinese.]

Missingham, B. D. 2003. *The Assembly of the Poor in Thailand: From Local Struggles to National Social Movement*. Chiang Mai: Silkworm Books.

Mitter, S. 1986. *Common Fate, Common Bond: Women in the Global Economy*. London: Pluto Press.

MoCIT [Data Bank and Information Division. Ministry of Communication and Information Technology. Government of India]. 2000. "Electronics Industry Information System." New Delhi.

MoCIT [Department of Electronics, Ministry of Communication and Information Technology], Government of India. 2002. "Annual Report." New Delhi.

MoCIT [Department of Information Technology, Ministry of Communication and Information Technology, Government of India]. 2003a. "National Electronic/ IT Hardware Manufacturing Policy." Draft paper. New Delhi. Available: www.mit.gov.in/hwpolicy.asp.

MoCIT [Department of Information Technology, Ministry of Communications and Information Technology, Government of India]. 2003b. "Annual Report."

MoE [Ministry of Environment. Japan]. 2002. "About the Illegal Dumping of Waste Home Appliances" [Press Release.] June 12. Available: www.env.go.jp/press/press.php3?serial=3405.

MoE [Ministry of Environment. Japan]. 2003. "About the Illegal Dumping of Waste Home Appliances" [Press Release.] March 24. Available: www.env.go.jp/press/press.php3?serial=4002.

MoHW [Ministry of Health and Welfare] and MITI [Ministry of International Trade and Industry. Japan]. 1998. "About the Proposal for the Specified Home Appliance Recycling Law." Available: www.nippo.co.jp/kaden.htm. [In Japanese.]

Mokhoff, N. 2005. "Vanderbilt University to Conduct SIA-Sponsored Cancer Study," *EE Times*, August 8. Available: www.eet.com/news/latest/showArticle.jhtml? articleID=167100069.

Mol, Arthur, P. J. 2001. *Globalization and Environmental Reform: the Ecological Modernization of the Global Economy*. Cambridge, MA: MIT Press.

Mol, A. P. J., ed. 1993. *European Integration and Environmental Policy*. London: Belhaven Press.

Montague, P. 1997. "The Toxic Substances Control Act," *Rachel's Environmental and Health News*, No. 564, September 18. Available: www.rachel.org/bulletin/index.cfm?issue_ID=557.

Montague, P. 2005. "The Precautionary Principle in a Nutshell," Environmental Research Foundation, August 27. Available: www.precaution.org/lib/pp_def.htm.

Moody, K. 1997. *Workers in a Lean World*. London: Verso.

Müller, W. 2003. "Am Ganges und am Jangtse sprießen die IT-Jobs," *Frankfurter Rundschau*, September 3.

Myant, M., and S. Smith. 1999. "Czech Trade Unions in Comparative Perspective," *European Journal of Industrial Relations* 5(3):265–85.

NACEC. 2002. "Action Plan to Enhance the Comparability of Pollutant Release and Transfer Registers in North America." Montréal, Canada: North American Commission for Environmental Cooperation, June. Available: www.cec.org/files/pdf/POLLUTANTS/PRTR_action_plan_June02-e.pdf.

Nash, J., and M. Patricia Fernández-Kelly, eds. 1983. *Women, Men, and the International Division of Labor*. Albany, NY: State University of New York Press.

National Safety Council. 1999. "Electronic Product Recovery and Recycling Baseline Report. Recycling of Selected Electronic Products in the United States." Washington DC.

Nautilus Institute. 2002. "Beyond Good Deeds: Case Studies and a New Policy Agenda for

Corporate Accountability." Corporate Accountability Project. Berkeley, CA: Nautilus Institute for Security and Sustainability.

Negri, A., and M. Hardt. 2000. *Empire.* Cambridge, MA: Harvard University Press.

Nelson, R. 1988. *Workers on the Waterfront: Seaman, Longshoreman, and Unionism in the 1930s.* Urbana: University of Illinois Press.

NEPSI. 2001. [Home Page.] National Electronic Products Stewardship Initiative. Available: eerc.ra.utk.edu/clean/nepsi/index.htm.

NEPSI. 2003. "National Electronics Product Stewardship Dialogue Achieves Milestone: Stakeholders Agree on Financing Approach for Management of Used Electronics." National Electronic Products Stewardship Initiative. Available: eerc.ra.utk.edu/clean/nepsi/pdfs/nepsipress3-19.pdf.

NIOSH. 1980. U.S. Department of Health, Education and Welfare, Center for Disease Control, National Institute of Occupational Safety and Health Interim Report #2. Health Hazard Evaluation Project No. HHE 79-66. Signetics Corporation. Sunnyvale, CA, January 31.

NIOSH. 2005. *NIOSH Pocket Guide to Chemical Hazards.* Pub. No. 2005-151. U.S. Department of Health and Human Services, Center for Disease Control, National Institute of Occupational Safety and Health, Cincinnati, OH.

Nippon K. S. 2002. "Landowner Is Responsible for Taking Action for Soil Contamination," January 26. [In Japanese.]

Nirei, H., et al. 1994. "Geo Pollution Unit," *Journal of the Geological Society of Japan* 100(6):425–435. [In Japanese.]

Norberg-Bohm, V. 2000. "Beyond the Double Dividend: Public and Private Roles in the Supply of and Demand for Environmentally Enhancing Technologies." In *Innovation and the Environment*, 123–35. Paris: OECD.

Nudelstejer, A. 2000. "Conquista California a México," *La Frontera*, June 16.

NVMP Foundation. 2002. *Monitoring Report for 2001.* Dutch Association for the Disposal of Metal and Electrical Products [NVMP], Zoetermeer, Netherlands. Available: www.nvmp.nl.

OECD. 1992. "Council Decision C(92)39." Paris: Organization for Economic Cooperation and Development.

OECD. 1998. "Extended and Shared Responsibility. Phase 2. Framework Report." Paris: Organisation for Economic Co-operation and Development.

Office of the President. 1994. "Federal Actions to Address Environmental Justice in Minority Populations and Low-Income Populations." Executive Order 12898. 59 FR 7629, 1994 WL 43891 (Pres.). Washington, DC, February 11.

Ohtsuka, T. 1994. "Allocating Cleanup Costs of Soil Contamination in Metropolitan Area," *Jurist* 1040:97. [In Japanese.]

Olmedo, C. Y., and M. Murria. 2002. "The Formalization of Informal/ Precarious Labor in Contemporary Argentina," *Revista International Sociology* 17(3).

ON Semiconductor. 2005. [Corporate Web site.] Available: www.onsemi.com.

O'Neill, R. 1997. "One Million Dying Today . . . and Counting." In *Workplace Roulette: Gambling with Cancer*, ed. Matthew Firth, James Brophy, and Margaret Keith, x–xii. Toronto: Between the Lines.

Ong, A. 1987. *Spirits of Resistance and Capitalist Discipline: Factory Women in Malaysia.* Albany, NY: State University of New York Press.

Pandita, S., and V. Kanhere. 1998. "The Plight of Workers in Export Processing Zone in India." [Study report.] Available: www.pria.org/cgi-bin/projectsdesc.htm? r_reportid= 15. New Delhi: Society for Participatory Research in Asia.

Papachan, S. n.d. "Dignity in Labour—Malaysian County Report." [Conference presentation.] Available: www.itcilo.it/english/actrav/telearn/global/ilo/frame/epzmal.htm.

Park, Edward Jang-Woo. 1992. "Asian Americans in Silicon Valley: Race and Ethnicity in the Postindustrial Economy." Ph.D. diss., Ethnic Studies, University of California at Berkeley.

Pastides, H., E. J. Calabrese, D. W. Hosmer, and D. R. Harris. 1988. "Spontaneous Abortion and General Illness Symptoms among Semiconductor Manufacturers," *Journal of Occupational Medicine* 30:543–51.

Pellow, D. N., and L. S.-H. Park. 2002. *The Silicon Valley of Dreams: Environmental Injustice, Immigrant Workers, and the High-Tech Global Economy.* New York: New York University Press.

Plazola, C., ed. 1997. *Sacred Waters: Life Blood of Mother Earth.* Albuquerque, NM, and San Jose, CA: Southwest Network for Environmental and Economic Justice and Campaign for Responsible Technology.

Pocekay, D., S. A. McCurdy, S. J. Samuels, S. K. Hammond, and M. B. Schenker. 1995. "A Cross-sectional Study of Musculoskeletal Symptoms and Risk Factors in Semiconductor Workers," *American Journal of Industrial Medicine* 28(6):861–71.

Polish Ecological Club. 2003. [Web site.] Available: www.most.org.pl/pke-zg/int.

Popov, A. 1997. "Russia: a New Source of Semiconductors for Hong Kong," *Business and Technology Information Quarterly.* Hong Kong Industrial Technology Centre Corporation. June.

Porter, G., and J. Brown. 1991. *Global Environmental Politics.* Boulder, CO: Westview Press.

Porter, M. E., and C. van der Linde. 1995. "Towards a New Conception of the Environment-Competitiveness Relationship," *Journal of Economic Perspectives* 9(4):97–118.

Portes, A., M. Castells, and L. Benton, eds. 1989. *The Informal Economy: Studies in Advanced and Less Developed Countries.* Baltimore: Johns Hopkins University Press.

President's Council on Sustainable Development. 1997. *Sustainable America: A New Consensus for Prosperity, Opportunity, and a Healthy Environment for the Future.* Washington, DC: U.S. Government Printing Office.

Putnam, R. 2000. *Bowling Alone: The Collapse and Revival of American Community.* New York: Simon and Schuster.

Quintero, C. 2001. "Sindicatos en Maquiladoras. De la Concertación a la Colusión." In *Memoria de la Conferencia Internacional: Libre Comercio, Integración y el Futuro de la Industria Maquiladora. Producción Global y Trabajadores Locales.* Mexico City: CEPAL-STPS-el Colegio de la Frontera Norte.

Radosevic, S. 2002. "The Electronics Industry in Central and Eastern Europe: an Emerging Production Location in the Alignment of Network Perspectives." Working Paper No. 21. London: CSESC, University College.

Rajalakshmi, T. K. 1999. "Sita and Her Daughters: Women Workers at an Indian EPZ," *Third World Resurgence,* No. 107, July.

Ramstad, E. 1994. "Intel Will Introduce New Chip in 1995," *Albuquerque Journal,* January 29, p. B-6.

Raymond Communications. 2002. "Electronics Recycling: What to Expect from Global Mandates." College Park, MD.

Regalado, A., and William M. Bulkeley. 2004. "IBM Cancer Data Fuel Debate Over Publication," *Wall Street Journal,* June 24, p. B1. Available online: www.wsj.com.

Reinhart, A. 1997. "Intel" [cover story], *Business Week,* December 22. Available: www.businessweek.com/1997/51/b3558001.htm.

Richards, B. 1998. "Semiconductor Plants Aren't Safe and Clean as Billed, Some Say," *Wall Street Journal,* October 5.

Rigby, M. 1999. "Electronics." In *European Trade Unions: Change and Response,* ed. M. Rigby, R. Smith, and T. Lawlor. London: Routledge.

Risk and Policy Analysis, Ltd. 2001. "Regulatory Impact Assessment of the EU White Paper: A Strategy for a Future Chemicals Policy. Final Report for the UK Department of Environment, Transport, and the Regions." London. May.

Risk and Policy Analysis, Ltd. 2003. "Assessment of the Impact of the New Chemicals Policy on Occupational Health. Final Report Prepared for European Commission Environment Directorate General." London. March.

Risk and Policy Analysis, Ltd., and Statistics Sweden. 2002. "Assessment of the Impact of New Regulations in the Chemicals Sector. Final Report Prepared for the European Commission, Director-General Enterprise." London. June.

Robinson, J. G., and J. McIlwee. 1989. "Obstacles to Unionization in High-Tech Industries," *Work and Occupations* 16:115–36.

Rosa, K. 1994. "The Conditions and Organizational Activities of Women in Free Trade Zones—Malaysia, Philippines and Sri Lanka, 1970–1990." In *Dignity and Daily Bread*, ed. S. Rowbotham and S. Mitter. London: Routledge.

Rosenbaum, R. 2000. "Making the Invisible Visible: A Study of the Purchasing Power of Maquila Workers in Mexico." Center for Reflection, Education, and Action.

Rothman, J. D. 2003. "Environmental Enforcement Across Borders: Is the US/Mexico Border an Extreme Case?" Report presented at the Commission for Environmental Cooperation "Transboundary Law Enforcement Workshop," January 9–10, Washington, DC.

Roy, D. 1980. "Fear Stuff, Sweet Stuff and Evil Stuff: Management's Defences against Unionization in the South." In *Capital and Labour: Studies in the Capitalist Labour Process,* ed. Theo Nichols, 395–415. Glasgow, Scotland: Athlone Press.

Rudolph, L., and S. H. Swan. 1986. "Reproductive Hazards in the Microelectronics Industry," *State of the Art Reviews: Occupational Medicine* 1:135–43.

Ruiz, V. 1987. *Cannery Women/Cannery Lives: Mexican Women, Unionization, and the Food Processing Industry, 1930–1950.* Albuquerque: University of New Mexico Press.

Salangina, L. I., L. S. Dubeikovskaia, Iu. N. Sladovka, O. L. Markova. 2001. "Hygienic Evaluation of Work Conditions and Health State of Women Engaged into Soldering," *Med Tr Prom Ekol* 10:8–13.

Sanchez, R. A. 2002. "Governance, Trade, and the Environment in the Context of NAFTA," *American Behavioral Scientist* 45(9):1369–93.

Sandford, R. 2000a. "Outlook Brightens for Eastern Europe Semiconductor Industry," *Semiconductor Magazine* 1(6):5.

Sandford, R. 2000b. "The Russian Bear Begins to Roar," *Semiconductor Magazine* 1(11):5.

Sandweiss, S. 1998. "The Social Construction of Environmental Justice." In *Environmental Industries, Political Struggles: Race, Class and the Environment*, ed. D. E. Camacho, 31–57. Durham, NC: Duke University Press.

Sargeson, S. 2001. "Assembling Class in a Chinese Joint Venture Factory." In *Organising Labour in Globalising Asia*, ed. J. Hutchison and A. Brown, 48–70. London: Routledge.

Sassen, S. 1996. *Losing Control? Sovereignty in an Age of Globalization*. New York: Columbia University Press.

Sayer, A., and R. Walker. 1992. *The New Social Economy: Reworking the Division of Labor.* Cambridge, MA: Blackwell.

SCCOSH. 1998. *Silicon Dreams: Workers' Memorial Day Book.* San Jose, CA: Santa Clara Center for Occupational Safety and Health, May 3.

Schenker, M. B. 1992. "Epidemiologic Study of Reproductive and Other Health Effects among Workers Employed in the Manufacture of Semiconductors." Final Report. Semiconductor Industry Association, December.

Schenker, M. B., E. B. Gold, J. J. Beaumont, B. Eskenazi, S. K. Hammond, B. L. Lasley, et al. 1995. "Association of Spontaneous Abortion and Other Reproductive Effects with Work in the Semiconductor Industry," *American Journal of Industrial Medicine* 28:639–59.

Schoenberger, K. 2002. "Daring To Complain," *San Jose Mercury News*, November 24.

Schoenfeld, A. C., R. F. Meier, and R. J. Griffin. 1979. "Constructing a Social Problem: The Press and the Environment," *Social Problems* 27(1):38–61.

Scottish Enterprise. 1989. "Locate in Scotland: Scotland Europe's Centre of Excellence in Electronics."

SIPA. 2004. "Quarterly Report: Employee Profile." Hsinchu, Taiwan: Science Industrial Park Administration, December. Available: eweb.sipa.gov.tw/en/statistics/statistics/quarterly/2004/Dec/hsi20000_12_06.htm.

SEMATECH. 1992. Employee meeting video. October 8. Austin, TX: Semiconductor Manufacturing Technology, Inc.

Semenova, G. S., G. N. Semakina, M. A. Fil'ts, O. P. Novak, and N. N. Abashina. 1986. Assessment of Visual Fatigue and Work Capacity Evaluation Electronics Industry Workers, *Oftalmol Zh* 8:460–63.

Shameen, A. 2003. "Outsourcing: You Want It, We Make It," *Far Eastern Economic Review*, March 20.

SIA. n.d. "Economy." SIA Issues. Available: www.sia-online.org/iss_economy.cfm.

SIA. 2004. "SIA to Conduct Worker Health Study." Semiconductor Industry Association, March. Available: www.sia-online.org/pre_release.cfm?ID=307.

Siegel, L., and J. Markoff. 1985. *The High Cost of High Tech: The Dark Side of the Chip*. New York: Harper and Row.

Sigal, L. V. 1973. *Reporters and Officials*. Lexington, MA: D.C. Heath.

Simonov, V. V. 1997. "Will the Russian Electronic Industry Survive? *Channel Articles* 10(1):4.

Smith, R. 1992. "Chip Makers Promise Action on Toxics," *San Jose Mercury News*, December 4.

Smith, T. 1984a. "IBM Spill Spreading Toward Public Wells," *Silicon Valley Toxics News* 2(1).

Smith, T. 1984b. "300 in Health Suit," *Silicon Valley Toxics News* 2(1).

Smith, T., and C. Raphael. 2003. "High-Tech Goes Green," *YES! A Journal of Positive Futures*, Spring:28–30.

SO. 2002. "Social and Labor Conduct: Nokia do Brasil Tecnologia Ltda." Brazil: Social Observatory.

Soldatenkova, N. A., and L. L. Prilutskaia. 1987. "Determining the Levels of Cadmium, Lead and Nickel in the Urine of Workers," *Gig Tr Prof Zabol* 2:53–55.

Sonnenfeld, D. A. 2002. "The Politics of Production and Production of Nature in Silicon Valley's Electronics Industry," *International Journal of Business and Society* 3(2): 1–24.

Sotelo, A. 1999. *Globalización y Precariedad del Trabajo en México*. Mexico City: Ediciones El Caballito.

Sproll, M. 2003. "Las Redes Transnacionales de Producción: America Latina, Asia, y Europa des Este en la Manufactura por Contrato en la Industria Electrónica," *Memoria: Revista Mensual De Politica y Cultura* (177) November.

Srishti. 2002. "Recycling Responsibility: Traditional Systems and New Challenges of Urban Solid Waste in India." A Srishti Report, June. New Delhi: Srishti School of Art, Design and Technology.

St. Sure, J. Paul. 1957. "Some Comments on Employer Organization and Collective Bargaining Since 1934." Interview by Corinne Gilb, Institute of Industrial Relations, University of California, Berkeley.

Standing, G. 1999. "Global Feminization through Flexible Labor: A Theme Revisited," *World Development* 27(3):583–602.

Stein, N. 2003. "No Way Out," *Fortune*, 147(1), January 20.

Steinbeck, J. 1966 [1939]. *The Grapes of Wrath*. New York: Viking.

Steinbeck, J. 1992 [1936]. *In Dubious Battle*. New York: Penguin.

Stevens, C. 2004. "Extended Producer Responsibility and Innovation." In *Economic Aspects of Extended Producer Responsibility*, 199–217. Paris: Organisation for Economic Cooperation and Development.

Storper, M., and R. Walker. 1989. *The Capitalist Imperative: Territory, Technology, and Industrial Growth*. New York: Blackwell.

Sturgeon, T. J. 1997. "Turn-Key Production Networks: a New American Model of Industrial Organization?" Working Paper No. 92A. Berkeley: Berkeley Roundtable on the International Economy, University of California at Berkeley.

Sturgeon, T. J. 1999. "Turn-Key Production Networks: Industry Organization, Economic Development, and the Globalization of Electronics Contract Manufacturing." Ph.D. diss., University of California at Berkeley.

Sukran R., ed. 1999. *State of the Thai Environment 1997–1998*. Bangkok: Green World Foundation.

Sullivan, K. 2003. "A Toxic Legacy on the Mexican Border," *The Washington Post*, February 16, pp. A17, 33.

Summers, L., 1991. Office Memorandum, December 12. Available: www.ban.org/whistle/summers.html.

Suzuki, Y. 1993. "Investigations and Remediations at Geo-Pollution Site," *Abstracts from the Symposium on Geo-Pollution*. Tokyo: Geological Society of Japan, p. 58. [In Japanese.]

SVTC. 1999. "Just Say No to E-Waste: Background Document on Hazards and Waste From Computers." San Jose, CA: Silicon Valley Toxics Coalition. Available: www.svtc.org/cleancc/pubs/sayno.htm.

SVTC. 2001. "Poison PCs and Toxic TVs: California's Biggest Environmental Crisis That You've Never Heard Of." Unpublished manuscript. San Jose, CA: Silicon Valley Toxics Coalition. June. Available: www.svtc.org/cleancc/pubs/poisonpc.htm.

SVTC and CTBC. 2003. "Corporate Strategies for Electronics Recycling: A Tale of Two Systems." San Jose, CA: Silicon Valley Toxics Coalition and Computer TakeBack Campaign. Available: www.svtc.org/cleancc/pubs/prison_sum.htm.

Sweden, Government of. 2000. "Producer Responsibility for Electrical and Electronic Products Ordinance, April 6, 2000." Ordinance No. SFS 2000:208. Stockholm, April 27. Available: www.internat.environ.se/documents/issues/technic/pdfdok/sfs.pdf.

Swedish EPA [Environmental Protection Agency]. 2002. Summary. [The situation for extended producer responsibility in packaging, newspaper, tyres, cars, WEEE and batteries.] Available: www.environmentdaily.com/docs/swedeepa2.doc.

SWOP. 1995. *Intel Inside New Mexico: A Case Study of Environmental and Economic Injustice*. Albuquerque, NM: SouthWest Organizing Project.

Taipei Times. 2003. "China the World's Processing Plant," November 18.

Tanaka, T. 2001. "Report on the Recycling of Electrical Home Appliances," *Nikkei Ecology* 24:44–46. [In Japanese.]

Tanaka, T. and K. Miyasaka. 2000. "Specified Home Appliance Recycling Law. 5 Questions," *Nikkei Ecology* 17:45–50. [In Japanese].

Tara B. 1996. "Spatial Mobility and Health Risks Among Factory Workers in the Northern Regional Industrial Estate." Master's thesis, Geography, Chiang Mai University, Thailand.

Tara B. 1998. "The North at Risk: Environmental Pollution and Health in Lumphun, Thailand." Paper given at the "Skillshare Symposium on Persistent Organic Pollutants (POPs)." Local Development Institute, Bangkok, Thailand, November 1.

Telford, M. 1998. "SEMI's Fifth Executive Mission to the CIS. Plans Shift to the Domestic Market," *Semiconductor International* 11(6, August 1):2.

Terosil. 2002. "Environmental Health and Safety Policy." Available: www.terosil.com/company.html.

Terry, J. 1934. "The Terror in San Jose," *The Nation*, August 8.

Theobald, S. 1996. "Employment and Environmental Hazard: Women Workers and Strategies of Resistance in Northern Thailand," *Gender and Development*, 4(3):16–21.

Theobald, S. 1998. "Occupational Hazards in the Electronics Industry: Gendered Repercussions," *Gender, Technology and Development* 2(1):81–96.

Theobald, S. 2002. "Gendered Bodies: Recruitment, Management and Occupational Health in Northern Thailand's Electronics Factories," *Journal of Women's Health* 35(4):7–26.

Thomas, T. L., P. D. Stolley, A. Stemhagen, E. T. Fontham, M. L. Bleecker, P. A. Stewart, et al. 1987. "Brain Tumor Mortality Risk Among Men with Electrical and Electronics Jobs," *Journal of the National Cancer Institute* 79(2):233–38.

Tiwari, G. 2003. "Transport and Land-Use Policies in Delhi," *Bulletin of World Health Organization* 81(6):444–50.

Tocqueville, A. de. 1835. *Democracy in America*. London: Saunders and Otley.

Tojo, N. 2000. "Analysis of EPR Policies and Legislation through Comparative Study of Selected EPR Programmes for EEE—Based on the In-Depth Study of a Japanese EPR Regulation," *IIIEE Communications* (10). International Institute of Industrial Environmental Economics, Lund University, Sweden.

Tojo, N. 2001. "Effectiveness of EPR Programme in Design Change. Study of the Factors that Affect the Swedish and Japanese EEE and Automobile Manufacturers." Report No. 2001:19. International Institute of Industrial Environmental Economics, Lund University, Sweden.

Tojo, N. 2004. *Extended Producer Responsibility as a Driver for Design Change—Utopia or Reality?* Ph.D. diss., Environmental Economics, Lund University, Sweden.

Tolba, M. K., with Iwona Rummel-Bulska. 1998. *Global Environmental Diplomacy: Negotiating Environmental Agreements for the World, 1973–1992.* Cambridge, MA: MIT Press.

Toshiba. 2003. "Rental Package Service. Electrical Home Appliances." Toshiba Service & Engineering Co., Ltd. Available: www.toshiba.co.jp/tcn/pack/index_j.htm. [In Japanese.]

Toxics L. 2003. "Scrapping the Hi-Tech Myth: Computer Waste in India." New Delhi, February. Available: www.toxicslink.org/docs/06037_Hi_Tech_Myth.pdf.

Toxics L. 2004. "E-waste in Chennai." [Report.] New Delhi, January.

Tu, Wen-ling. 2004. "Challenges of Environmental Planning and Grassroots Activism in the Face of IT Industrial Dominance: A Study of Science-based Industrial Parks in Taiwan." Ph.D. diss., Landscape Architecture and Environmental Planning, University of California at Berkeley.

Turati, M. 1999. "Revelan Hay 163 Tiraderos Tóxicos," *El Norte* (Monterrey), April 27.

Türk, V. 2001. "An Evaluation of the Swiss Ordinance on the Return, the Taking Back and the Disposal of Electrical and Electronic Appliances (ORDEA)." Unpublished manuscript. International Institute of Industrial Environmental Economics, Lund University, Sweden.

UNCTAD. 2001. *World Investment Report: Promoting Linkages.* New York and Geneva: United Nations Conference on Trade and Development.

UNEP. 1989. "Basel Convention on the Control of Transboundary Movements of Hazardous Wastes and their Disposal," 28 I.L.M. 657. United Nations Environment Programme, March 22.

UNIDO. 2003. Industrial Statistics Databases. ESDS International, University of Manchester.

UNU. 2004. "UN Study Shows Environmental Consequences from Ongoing Boom in Personal Computer Sales." [Press release.] Tokyo: United Nations University, March 7. Available: www.eurekalert.org/pub_releases/2004-03/tca-uss030204.php.

US EPA. 1995. "Profile of the Electronics and Computer Industry." Office of Compliance, Environmental Protection Agency, Washington, DC.

US EPA. 2001. "Desktop Computer Displays: A Life Cycle Assessment." EPA/744-R-01-004a and EPA/744-R-01-004b. Washington, DC: Environmental Protection Agency, December. Available: www.epa.gov/oppt/dfe/pubs/comp-dic/lca/index.htm.

US EPA. 2002. "Life-Cycle Assessment of Desktop Computer Displays: Summary of Results." EPA/744-R-01-005. Washington, DC: Environmental Protection Agency, March. Available: www.epa.gov/oppt/dfe/pubs/comp-dic/lca-sum/.

Vågerö, D., and R. Olin. 1983. "Incidence of Cancer in the Electronics Industry, Using a new Swedish Cancer Environment Registry as a Screening Instrument," *British Journal of Industrial Medicine* 40:188–92.

Valiya N. 2000. Interview by David A. Sonnenfeld and Tira Foran, June 14. Industrial Estate Manager, Northern Region Industrial Estate, Lamphun, Thailand.

Van Kalkeren, B. 2003. Interview by Naoko Tojo via telephone, May 28. Recydur BV, Apeldoorn, Netherlands.

Veerman, K. 2003. E-mail communication to Naoko Tojo, June 5. Minister, Ministry of Housing, Spatial Planning and the Environment [VROM], The Hague, Netherlands.

Virtual Guide to Belarus. 2003. "Belarus Semiconductor Industry." Available: www.belarusguide.com/industry1/semiconductor.htm.

Vogel, D. 1995. *Trading Up: Consumer and Environmental Regulation in a Global Economy.* Cambridge, MA: Harvard University Press.

Vonkeman, B. 2003. Personal communication to Naoko Tojo, April 8. Managing director, Dutch Association for the Disposal of Metal and Electrical Products [NVMP], Zoetermeer, Netherlands.

Voravidh C. 2000. "Women Workers and the Development of Social Movement Trade Union." Paper presented for Seminar on "Dynamics in Thai Political Economy," Faculty of Economics, Chulalongkorn University, Bangkok, Thailand.

Voravidh C. 2004. Interview by Tira Foran, May 18. Faculty of Economics, Chulalongkorn University, Bangkok, Thailand.

Wade, R., M. Williams, T. Mitchell, J. Wong, and B. Tuse. 1981. "Semiconductor Industry Study." State of California, Division of Industrial Relations, Division of Occupational Safety and Health, Task Force on the Electronics Industry.

Wang, J. D. 1999. "Epidemiological Study and Health Risk Assessment for Residents Living near a Contaminated Site Polluted by Volatile Chlorinated Compounds." [Report commissioned by the Taiwan Environmental Protection Administration.] Institute of Environmental Health, Taiwan University, Taipei. [In Chinese.]

Wangel, A. 2001 "Manufacturing Growth with Social Deficits: Environmental and Labor Issues in the High Tech Industry of Penang, Malaysia." [Report.] Corporate Accountability Project. Berkeley, CA: Nautilus Institute for Security and Sustainability, October.

Watterson, A., ed. 2003. *Public Health in Practice.* Basingstoke: Palgrave/Macmillan.

Watterson, A., and C. Constantinoaia. 2004. "Analysis of National Occupational Health and Safety Policies in Joint OSH Strategy for the Enlarged Europe," *TUTB Newsletter*, April 22–23, pp. 54–56. Trade Union Technical Bureau, European Trade Union Confederation, Brussels.

Watterson, A, J LaDou, and PHASE Two. 2003. "Health and Safety Executive Inspection of UK Semiconductor Manufacturers," *International Journal of Occupational and Environmental Health* 9(4):392–95.

Watterson, A., M. Silberschmidt, and M. Robson. 2001. "Occupational Health in Central and Eastern Europe in the 1990s: Resources and Suggested Research Agenda," *International Journal of Occupational and Environmental Health* 7(3):233–45.

Weiss, J., J. Kaluzny, and H. Lesiewwska-Junk. 1992. "Analysis of the Place of Regulation of C-11 Transmitters at the Tele-electronic Works 'Telkom-Telfa' in Bydgoszcz from the Point of View of Visual Hygiene," *Klin Ocnza* 94(4):99–100.

Williams, E. D., R. U. Ayres, and M. Heller. 2002. "The 1.7 Kilogram Microchip: Energy and Material Use in the Production of Semiconductor Devices," *Environmental Science and Technology* 36(24):5504–10.

Wilson, R. 1986. "'Workers' Rights in High Tech: A Global Perspective." Report prepared for Integrated Circuit, the national network for a New High Tech Agenda. Oakland, California: Integrated Circuit.

Wise, T. A. 2003. "NAFTA's Untold Stories," *Americas Program Policy Report*, Interhemispheric Resource Center, June.

Wong, M. 2002. "Flexible Employment in Thailand," *Asian Labour Update,* Issue 45, October-December. Available: www.amrc.org.hk/4505.htm.

Wrensch, M., S. H. Swan, J. Lipscomb, et al. 1990. "Pregnancy Outcomes in Women Potentially Exposed to Solvent-Contaminated Drinking Water in San Jose, California," *American Journal of Epidemiology* 131:283–300.

WWW. 1991. *Common Interests: Women Organizing in Global Electronics.* London: Working Women Worldwide.

Yoachum, S. and M. Malone. 1980. "The Chemical Handlers," *San Jose Mercury News*, April 6–8.

Yoachum, S., J. A. Izumi, and R. Wisdom. 1983. "Clean Industry, Dirty Water," *San Jose Mercury News*, July 10–12.

Yoshida, F. 2001. *IT Pollution.* Tokyo: Iwanami Shoten.

Yoshida, F. 2002. *The Economics of Waste and Pollution Management in Japan.* Tokyo: Springer-Verlag.

Zoboli, R. 2000. "Environmental Regulation and Innovation in the End-of-Life Vehicle Sector." In *Innovation-oriented Environmental Regulation. Theoretical Approaches and Empirical Analysis*, ed. J. Hemmelskamp, K. Rennings, and F. Leone, 235–66. Heidelberg: Physica-Verlag.

Resources

Asia Monitor Resource Centre (AMRC)
Unit 4, 18 Floor, Hollywood Centre
233 Hollywood Rd. Sheung Wan,
Hong Kong CHINA
Tel: +85 2 2332 1346, Fax: 2385 5319
URL: www.amrc.org.hk
E-mail: admin@amrc.org.hk

Basel Action Network (BAN)
c/o Earth Economics
122 S Jackson, Suite 320
Seattle, WA 98104 USA
Tel: +1 206 652 5555, Fax 652 5750
URL: www.ban.org
E-mail: inform@ban.org

**Catholic Agency for Overseas
    Development (CAFOD)**
Romero Close
Stockwell Rd.
London SW9 9TY UK
Tel: +44 20 7733 7900, Fax: 7274 9630
URL: www.cafod.org.uk
Email: cafod@cafod.org.uk

**Centre for Research on Multinational
    Corporations (SOMO)**
Keizersgracht 132
1015 CW Amsterdam
The NETHERLANDS
Tel: +31 20 639 12 91, Fax: 639 13 21
URL: www.somo.nl/index_eng.php
Email: info@somo.nl

**Computer TakeBack Campaign
    (CTBC)**
760 N 1st St.
San Jose, CA 95112-6302 USA
Tel: +1 408 287 6707, x321, Fax: 287 6771
URL: www.computertakeback.com
E-mail: info@etakeback.org

Environmental Health Coalition
401 Mile of Cars Way, Suite 310
National City, CA 91950 USA
Tel: +1 619 474 0220, Fax: 474 1210
URL: www.environmentalhealth.org
E-mail: ehc@environmentalhealth.org

Greenpeace International
Ottho Heldringstraat 5
1066 AZ Amsterdam
The NETHERLANDS
Tel: +31 20 718 20 00, Fax: 514 81 51
URL: www.greenpeace.org/international/
    campaigns/toxics/electronics
Email: supporter.services
    @int.greenpeace.org

**International Campaign for Responsible
    Technology (ICRT)**
760 N 1st St.
San Jose, CA 95112-6302 USA
Tel: +1 408 287 6707, Fax: 287 6771
URL: www.svtc.org/icrt
E-mail: svtc@svtc.org

***International Journal of Occupational
    and Environmental Health***
URL: www.ijoeh.com

International Metalworkers' Federation
Case Postale 1516
CH-1227 Geneva SWITZERLAND
Tel: +41 22 308 5015, Fax: 308 5055
URL: www.imfmetal.org
E-mail: info@imfmetal.org

Lowell Center for Sustainable Production
University of Massachusetts Lowell
One University Ave.
Lowell, MA 01854 USA
Tel: +1 978 934 2980, Fax: 934 2025
URL: www.sustainableproduction.org
E-mail: lcsp@uml.edu

People Organized in Defense of Earth and Her Resources (PODER)
PO Box 6237
Austin, TX 78762-6237 USA
Tel: +1 512 472 9921, Fax: 472 9922
URL: www.poder-texas.org
E-mail: poder@austin.rr.com

PHASE Two
c/o Inverclyde Employment Rights Centre
16 Nicolson St. Greenock
Inverclyde PA15 1JX SCOTLAND
Tel: +44 1475 888039, Fax: 888415
E-mail: iaerc@gconnect.com

Silicon Valley Toxics Coalition (SVTC)
760 N 1st St.
San Jose, CA 95112-6302 USA
Tel: +1 408 287 6707, Fax: 287 6771
URL: www.svtc.org
E-mail: svtc@svtc.org

SouthWest Organizing Project (SWOP)
211 10th St. SW
Albuquerque, NM 87102-2919 USA
Tel: +1 505 247 8832, Fax: 247 9972
URL: www.swop.net

Southwest Network for Environmental and Economic Justice (SNEEJ)
PO Box 7399
Albuquerque, NM 87194 USA
Tel: +1 505 242 0416, Fax: 242 5609
URL: www.sneej.org
E-mail: info@sneej.org

Taiwan Association for Victims of Occupational Injuries (TAVOI)
104/10F-2, No. 32, Jin-Jou St.
Taipei, Taiwan

Tel: +88 62 2571 5591, 8687 1260
Fax: 2581 1787
URL: www.hurt.org.tw
E-mail: occupaku@ms15.hinet.net

Taiwan Environmental Action Network
2F, No. 148, Sec. 3, Musin Rd.
Wunshan District, Taipei City
11660 Taiwan
Tel: +88 62 2938 1423, Fax: 2938 3402
URL: www.iepanet.org/index2.php
E-mail: tean@iepanet.org

Texas Campaign for the Environment
611 S. Congress Ave., Suite 200
Austin, TX 78704 USA
Tel:. +1 512 326 5655, Fax: 326 5922
URL: www.texasenvironment.org
E-mail: robin@texasenvironment.org

Thai Labour Campaign
PO Box 219
Ladprao Bangkok 10310 THAILAND
Tel: +66 2 933 0585, Fax: 933 1951
URL: www.thailabour.org
E-mail: campaign@thailabour.org

Toxics Link
H-2 (Ground Fl.)
Jungpura Extension
New Delhi 110 014 INDIA
Tel: +91 11 243 28006, 243 20711
Fax: 243 21747
URL: www.toxicslink.org
E-mail: tldelhi@toxicslink.org

Worksafe! A California Coalition
1188 Franklin St.
San Francisco, CA 94109 USA
Tel: +1 510 302 1071, Fax: 835 4913
URL: www.worksafe.org

Contributors

RAVI AGARWAL is founding Director of Toxics Link, an environmental NGO based in India, working on issues of waste, waste trade, and toxics for over a decade; he is a Communications Engineer by training.

LESLIE BYSTER is a consultant with the International Campaign for Responsible Technology (ICRT); she was Communications and Program Director, Silicon Valley Toxics Coalition (SVTC), San Jose, California, for over ten years.

SHENGLIN CHANG is Associate Professor, Plant Sciences and Landscape Architecture Department, University of Maryland, College Park; and Member of the Advisory Committee, Taiwan Environmental Action Network (TEAN).

HUA-MEI CHIU is a professional journalist and environmental activist from Taiwan, and a Ph.D. Candidate in the Department of Sociology, University of Essex, England.

ANIBEL FERUS-COMELO has a Ph.D. in economic geography from the University of London and is currently involved in research and education in India.

TIRA FORAN has conducted research with the Conservation Science Institute and Environmental Defense Fund, Oakland, California; he is a Ph.D. Candidate in the Department of Geosciences, University of Sydney, Australia.

CONNIE GARCÍA is former Policy Advocate, Border Environmental Justice Campaign, Environmental Health Coalition, San Diego, California.

KEN GEISER is Professor of Work Environment; and Co-Director, Lowell Center for Sustainable Production, University of Massachusetts Lowell.

AMANDA HAWES is Partner, Alexander, Hawes and Audet; and founder and former Executive Director of the Santa Clara Committee on Occupational Safety and Health (SCCOSH), San Jose, California.

JIM HIGHTOWER produces daily radio and online commentaries; he was editor of *The Texas Observer*, a biweekly magazine of news and opinion, and served two terms as Texas Agriculture Commissioner; his website is www.jimhightower.com.

YU-LING KU is Secretary-General, Taiwan International Workers' Association (TIWA); and Consultant, Taiwan Association for Victims of Occupational Injuries (TAVOI), Taipei.

JOSEPH LADOU, M.D., is Director, International Center for Occupational Medicine, University of California, San Francisco; and Editor, *International Journal of Occupational and Environmental Health*.

APO LEONG is Executive Director, Asia Monitor Resource Centre (AMRC), Hong Kong, China. He founded the Hong Kong Trade Union Education Center in 1984, and was Senior Researcher with the Hong Kong Confederation of Trade Unions.

BOY LÜTHJE is Research Fellow, Institute of Social Research; and Adjunct Professor, Department of Social Sciences, Johann Wolfgang Goethe University, Frankfurt am Main, Germany.

GLENNA MATTHEWS is Visiting Scholar, Institute of Urban and Regional Development, University of California at Berkeley; and author of *Silicon Valley, Women, and the California Dream*.

JAMES MCCOURT is Coordinator, People for Health and Safety in Electronics (PHASE Two); and Manager, Inverclyde Advice and Employment Rights Centre, Scotland.

SANJIV PANDITA is Occupational Safety and Health Officer, Asia Monitor Resource Centre (AMRC), Hong Kong, China.

RAQUEL PARTIDA ROCHA is a Researcher with the Department of Urban Studies, University of Guadalajara, Mexico.

DAVID PELLOW is Director, California Cultures in Comparative Perspective; and Associate Professor, Department of Ethnic Studies, University of California, San Diego.

JIM PUCKETT is Coordinator of the Basel Action Network (BAN), Seattle, Washington.

CHAD RAPHAEL is Associate Professor of Communications, Santa Clara University, California; and President, Board of Directors, Silicon Valley Toxics Coalition, San Jose, California.

ROBIN SCHNEIDER is Executive Director, Texas Campaign for the Environment, a statewide grassroots organization mobilizing citizens to protect public health and the environment.

AMELIA SIMPSON is Director of the Environmental Health Coalition's Border Environmental Justice Campaign, and is based in San Diego, California.

TED SMITH is founder, former Executive Director, and now Senior Strategist, Silicon Valley Toxics Coalition (SVTC), San Jose, California; and Coordinator, International Campaign for Responsible Technology (ICRT).

DAVID SONNENFELD is Associate Professor, Department of Community and Rural Sociology, Washington State University, Richland, Washington; and Research Associate, Environmental Policy Group, Wageningen University, the Netherlands.

ROBERT STEIERT is Director, Information and Communication Technology Industries, for the International Metalworkers' Federation (IMF), Geneva, Switzerland.

JOEL TICKNER is Assistant Professor, Department of Community Health and Sustainability, and Project Director, Lowell Center for Sustainable Production, University of Massachusetts, Lowell.

NAOKO TOJO recently completed her Ph.D., and continues as Assistant Professor at the International Institute for Industrial Environmental Economics (IIIEE), Lund University, Sweden.

WEN-LING TU is Assistant Professor, Department of Public Policy and Management, Shih Hsin University, Taiwan; and a founding member and Co-Chair of the Taiwan Environmental Action Network (TEAN).

KISHORE WANKHADE is Program Coordinator, Toxics Link, Mumbai, India.

ANDREW WATTERSON is Professor and Chair, Occupational and Environmental Health Research Group, University of Stirling, Scotland.

DAVID WOOD is former Executive Director, GrassRoots Recycling Network (GRRN), Madison, Wisconsin; and was organizing director of the US nationwide Computer TakeBack Campaign (CTBC).

FUMIKAZU YOSHIDA is Professor, Graduate School of Economics, Hokkaido University, Japan.

Index